ANALYSIS OF FINANCIAL STATEMENTS

ANALYSIS OF FINANCIAL STATEMENTS

FIFTH EDITION

LEOPOLD A. BERNSTEIN

JOHN J. WILD

McGraw-Hill

New York   San Francisco   Washington, D.C.   Auckland   Bogotá
Caracas   Lisbon   London   Madrid   Mexico City   Milan
Montreal   New Delhi   San Juan   Singapore
Sydney   Tokyo   Toronto

Library of Congress Cataloging-in-Publication Data

Bernstein, Leopold A.
    Analysis of financial statements / by Leopold A. Bernstein and
John J. Wild. — 5th ed.
      p.   cm.
    An expanded version of this text was published under the title:
Financial statement analysis.
    Includes bibliographical references and index.
    ISBN 0-07-094504-7
    1. Financial statements.   I. Wild, John J.   II. Bernstein,
Leopold A.   Financial statement analysis.   III. Title.
HF5681. B2B462 1999
657'.3—dc21   98-56045
                                                     CIP

McGraw-Hill

A Division of The McGraw-Hill Companies

    5 6 7 8 9 0 AGM/AGM   0 9 8 7 6 5 4 3

ISBN 0-07-094504-7

*The sponsoring editor for this book was Kelli Christiansen, the editing supervisor was John M.
Morriss, and the production supervisor was Elizabeth J. Strange. It was set in Times Roman by
Graphic Arts Center.*

Printed and bound by Arcata Graphics.

McGraw-Hill books are available at special quality discounts to use as premiums and sales promotions, or for use in corporate training programs. For
more information, please write to the Director of Special Sales, McGraw-
Hill, Professional Publishing, Two Penn Plaza, New York, NY 10121-2298.
Or contact your local bookstore.

This publication is designed to provide accurate and authoritative information in regard to the
subject matter covered. It is sold with the understanding that neither the author nor the publisher is
engaged in rendering legal, accounting, or other professional service. If legal advice or other expert
assistance is required, the services of a competent professional person should be sought.
—From a Declaration of Principles jointly adopted by a Committee of the American Bar Association
and a Committee of Publishers.

 This book is printed on recycled, acid-free paper containing a minimum of 50% recycled,
de-inked fiber.

To my wife Cynthia, children Debbie and Jeffrey,
and Distinguished Professor Emanuel Saxe—
Teacher, Colleague, and Friend

—L. A. B.

To my wife Gail and children Kimberly, Jonathan,
Stephanie, and Trevor

—J. J. W.

PREFACE

We are all aware of the exciting and dynamic practice of financial statement analysis, as well as its enormous implications for economic development, allocation of financial resources, and the economic well-being of a wide range of individuals. Because of these implications, financial statement analysis plays a very prominent role for both information users and providers. This book's goal is to give readers a distinct competitive advantage in an increasingly competitive marketplace as it continues to set the standard in showing the keys to effective financial statement analysis. Our challenge is to equip the reader with the analysis skills necessary to compete in the business world.

We know financial statements are relevant to many individuals, including investors, creditors, consultants, managers, auditors, directors, analysts, regulators, employees, and politicians. Yet our experience in teaching this material tells us we must engage readers by showing the relevance of material and conveying its excitement. This book meets this need as it is aimed at readers with broad career interests as well as those specializing in business fields. This broadens the book's appeal and the perspectives of those readers not accustomed to thinking in the larger decision-making context. The book fulfills another important need: It is written to meet the needs of today's readers of financial statements. It presents a new pedagogy that includes the impact of technology, all within our global economy.

Three key considerations guided our efforts in writing the book: (1) to make the material *relevant* to readers; (2) to encourage readers to think in an *evaluative* or inferential manner; and (3) to make the material *accessible* and interesting to readers. We next describe how we accomplish these important objectives.

Relevance

To engage readers we must make the material relevant to them. We recognize that "users" include more than creditors and equity investors. While these two user groups and their decisions are an important focus of this book, they are *not* the only focus. We have chosen to adopt a broader notion of the financial statement user by linking analysis to many other direct and indirect users of financial statements. This requires readers to think about the relevance of financial statements from different and unique perspectives, including political and community activists, environmentalists, school board members, lawyers, and entrepreneurs. We design and frame the book to support this broader perspective, and several distinctive features help us in this regard:

- *Analysis Viewpoints.* Analysis Viewpoints are a unique feature that asks readers to assume the role of a financial statement user. We confront readers with a situation requiring consideration of one or more aspects of financial statements. Traditional examples include a banker deciding loan eligibility and an investor analyzing a company's stock. Less traditional examples include a community activist evaluating corporate social responsibility and an environmentalist fighting for tougher pollution controls. An example follows:

ANALYSIS VIEWPOINT

YOU ARE THE DIRECTOR
You are a new member of the board of directors of a toy merchandiser. You are preparing for your first meeting with the company's independent auditor. A stockholder has written you a letter raising concerns about earnings quality. What are some questions or issues that you can raise with the auditor to address these concerns and fulfill your fiduciary responsibilities to shareholders?

- *Excerpts from practice.* Numerous excerpts from practice illustrate key points throughout this book. They continually reinforce the relevance of financial statement analysis. Excerpts include accounting and market data, annual report disclosures, newspaper clippings, and financial press cut-outs. An interesting revenue recognition policy is reproduced on the top of the next page.
- *Annual Reports.* Financial statements from two companies are reproduced in this book and used for illustration purposes. The innovative annual report of Adaptec is referenced often. Experi-

The company sells certain whiskey in barrels in bond under agreements which provide for future bottling. In prior years, profits on such transactions were reflected as of the date of sale. The present company policy is to treat such profits as deferred income until the whiskey is bottled and shipped.

—Schenley Industries, Inc.

ence shows us that frequent use of annual reports heightens interest and learning. An annual report also exposes readers to information beyond financial statements. A Comprehensive Case drawing on the financial statements of the Campbell Soup Company serves as a capstone portrayal of our analysis techniques.

Evaluative

We believe readers must learn to effectively evaluate evidence from financial statement analysis for sound business decisions. While computations and analysis results are important, the evaluative task is crucial to reaping the benefits of analysis. After extensive feedback from financial statement users, we designed this book to support an important objective: increased emphasis of the evaluative aspect of analysis. Part One, which covers Chapters 1 and 2, sets the tone for increased evaluative emphasis. Financial statements are introduced immediately in the book to begin our focus on evaluating a company's performance in planning, financing, investing, and operating activities. Our early analysis of Adaptec's financial statements allows us to focus directly and often on evaluation. Alternative views from different users are also introduced early and reinforced often. This book's unique introduction to financial statement analysis provides a natural springboard that leads to the financial analysis in Part Two. We focus throughout on introducing analysis tools and techniques in an evaluative manner. Features helping us accomplish this include the following:

- *Chapter Linkages.* Linkages launch every chapter and establish bridges between topics and concepts in prior, current, and upcoming chapters. We have found these linkages to greatly assist readers in developing a broader perspective on financial statement analysis. Linkages also show the applicability and relevance of analysis tools and techniques across topics.

- *Research Insights.* Research Insights describe research relevant to analysis of financial statements. These insights summarize and communicate important research that bears on our application and interpretation of financial statements. Examples include recent evidence on fundamental analysis, the relation between accounting numbers and stock prices, and the impact of company size for informativeness of prices. An example is reproduced below:

ANALYSIS RESEARCH INSIGHT 1.1

ACCOUNTING NUMBERS AND STOCK PRICES

Do accounting numbers such as net income "explain" changes in a company's stock prices? The answer is yes. Evidence from research shows a definite link between the "news" conveyed in net income and the price changes in a company's stock (returns). "Good news" net income is accompanied by positive stock price changes, whereas "bad news" net income is associated with negative price changes. The more good or bad the net income, the greater the accompanying stock price reaction. Similar evidence is obtained for other summary financial statement numbers, such as book value.

Research also shows us that the relation between accounting numbers and stock prices is influenced by many factors. These include factors such as risk, size, leverage, and variability, which decrease the influence of numbers like net income on prices, and factors such as growth and persistence, which increase its impact. Our analysis must recognize those influences that impact the relevance of accounting numbers for security analysis.

Fundamental analysis research offers guidance in our use of financial statement information for predicting *future* stock price changes. Evidence indicates that financial statements help to reveal the permanent and transitory portions of net income. Permanent portions are much more long-lasting in their impact on stock prices and are commensurately of greater magnitude in their influence on prices.

Accessible and Interesting

Learning financial statement analysis is easier and more satisfying if the material is accessible and interesting. We have spent considerable time and effort designing a book that is user-friendly and engaging. Several features are visibly apparent, others are more subtle. For example, we describe theoretical concepts and specialized analysis techniques in uncomplicated terms. We present data and illustrations in readable and understandable frameworks. We streamline chapters to move quickly to important points and emphasize concise writing. We introduce industry and economic data throughout the book, often in graphical form. Other special features help us in making the material more accessible and interesting, including the following:

- *Visual Appeal.* Extensive use of graphs, charts, and tables show how topics relate to business practices of actual companies. These graphics draw on annual reports, surveys of business practices, and specialized reports of investor and creditor agencies.

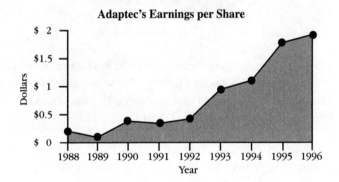

- *Objectives.* Chapters open with a list of key objectives that highlight important chapter goals. They help focus readers' attention on the most important issues in a chapter.
- *Clarity.* We took great care in writing this book in a clear, readable, and lively style. Extensive reviews and feedback from financial statement analysis users helped us achieve this clarity.
- *Streamlining.* This book's streamlined presentation emphasizes succinct writing, a flexible design, and tightened organization. This book especially appeals to analysis courses augmented with

additional readings, cases, projects, research, and writing assignments.

- *Contemporary.* We carefully crafted this book to ensure that we include the most contemporary material and up-to-date techniques. Moreover, we convey current financial practices of companies through both graphical and textual presentations. For example, see the pie chart for methods in accounting for leases.

Lease Types for Companies

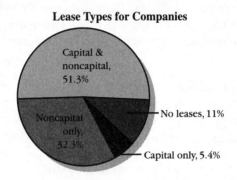

- *Previews.* Previews are included at the beginning of the two major parts of this book. These previews assist readers in integrating the material and understanding linkages between sometimes difficult financial statement analysis topics.

Reader feedback gives us confidence that we have achieved our goal of making financial statement analysis accessible and interesting.

ORGANIZATION AND CONTENT

This book's design encourages flexible learning styles. While the book is comprehensive in covering all topics of relevance for financial analysis, its organization encourages readers to choose topics and depth of coverage as desired.

Many books lack a tight, integrated flow of topics from chapter to chapter. In this book, readers are told in Chapter 1 how the book's topics are related to each other. One way we achieve integration is by organizing material into two parts:

1. Overview
2. Financial Analysis

Overview

Part One is an overview of financial statement analysis. We emphasize understanding business activities—planning, financing, investing, and operating. We describe strategies underlying business activities and their effects on financial statements, and we discuss the objectives of analysis. We demonstrate popular tools and techniques in analyzing and interpreting financial statements. Our attention is directed at users of financial statements whose well-being depends on reliable and relevant analysis. An important and unique feature is our use of Adaptec's annual report as a means to instill both the relevant and interesting nature of analysis. Two chapters comprise Part One.

- *Chapter 1.* We begin our analysis of financial statements by considering their relevance in business decisions. This leads us to focus on users, their needs, and how analysis addresses these needs. We describe business activities and how they are captured in financial statements.
- *Chapter 2.* This chapter begins by describing the analysis objectives of users. We discuss both stock and debt valuation. The importance and limitations of accounting data for our analysis are described and assessed.

Financial Analysis

Part Two examines the processes and methods of financial statement analysis. We stress the objectives of users and describe analytical tools and techniques for meeting those objectives. The means of analysis range from computation of ratio and cash flow measures to earnings prediction and valuation. We apply analysis tools that enable us to reconstruct the economic reality embedded in financial statements. We demonstrate how analysis tools and techniques enhance users' decisions—including company valuation and lending decisions. We show how financial statement analysis reduces our uncertainty and strengthens our confidence in making timely business decisions. Throughout the book we illustrate how an understanding of accounting supplemented by knowledge of the analysis tools and techniques improves business decisions, and this reinforces the integrated presentation of financial statement analysis in this book. Six chapters and a Comprehensive Case comprise Part Two:

- *Chapter 3.* Chapter 3 begins our study of the application and interpretation of analysis tools. We present analysis tools as a means to reveal insights into company operations and future performance. Attention in this chapter is directed at accounting-based ratios, turnover, and operating activity measures, with special emphasis on assessing liquidity.

- *Chapter 4.* We study forecasting and pro forma analysis of financial statements in this chapter. We explain the flow of cash through a company's business activities and its implications for liquidity. Both short-and long-term forecasting of cash flows is described, and attention is directed at applying these analysis tools in practice.

- *Chapter 5.* This chapter focuses on capital structure and its implications for solvency. We analyze the importance of financial leverage and its effects on risk and return. Analytical adjustments to accounting book values are evaluated for solvency assessments. We also describe earnings coverage measures and their interpretation.

- *Chapter 6.* Chapter 6 emphasizes return on invested capital and explains variations in its measurement. Special attention is directed at return on assets and return on common equity. We explore disaggregations of both these return measures and describe their relevance. Financial leverage is explained and analyzed.

- *Chapter 7.* This chapter expands our returns analysis to focus on profitability. We emphasize the components of income and their evaluation. Special attention is directed at sales, cost of sales, taxes, selling, and financing expenses. We explain profitability analysis tools, including their interpretation and adjustment.

- *Chapter 8.* Chapter 8 concludes returns analysis with earnings-based analysis and valuation. Our earnings-based analysis focuses on assessing earnings quality, earnings persistence, and earning power. Attention is directed at techniques to aid us in measuring and applying these analysis concepts. Our discussion of earnings-based valuation focuses on issues in estimating company value and forecasting earnings.

- *Comprehensive Case.* This case is a comprehensive analysis of financial statements and related notes. We describe steps in analyzing statements and the essential attributes of an analysis report. Our analysis is organized around the building blocks of financial statement analysis: liquidity, cash analysis, capital structure, solvency, return on invested capital, asset utilization, operating performance, and profitability.

TARGET AUDIENCE

This best-selling book is targeted to professionals and nonprofessionals of all fields. Both professionals and nonprofessionals find the book beneficial in their lives as they are rewarded with an understanding of both the techniques of analysis and the expertise to apply them. They also acquire the skills to successfully recognize business opportunities and the knowledge to capitalize on them. The book's contemporary content and practice orientation make it the book of choice in financial statement analysis.

Financial statement analysis is an exciting and dynamic field. The winds of change are upon us, and this book reflects these innovations and advances. We urge you to study this book and join us in our collective challenge to effectively analyze financial statements.

ACKNOWLEDGMENTS

We are thankful for the encouragement, suggestions, and counsel provided by many instructors, professionals, and students in writing this book. It has been a team effort and we recognize the contributions of all of these individuals. They include the many professionals who read portions of this book in various forms:

Kenneth Alterman
(*Standard & Poor's*)

Clyde Bartter
(*Portfolio Advisory Co.*)

Hyman C. Grossman
(*Standard & Poor's*)

Richard Huff
(*Standard & Poor's*)

Michael A. Hyland
(*First Boston Corp.*)

Robert J. Mebus
(*Standard & Poor's*)

Robert Mednick
(*Arthur Andersen*)

William C. Norby
(*Financial Analyst*)

David Norr
(*First Manhattan Corp.*)

Thornton L. O'Glove
(*Quality of Earnings Report*)

Paul Rosenfield
(*AICPA*)

George B. Sharp
(*CITIBANK*)

Fred Spindel
(*Coopers & Lybrand*)

Frances Stone
(*Merrill Lynch & Co.*)

Jon A. Stroble
(*Jon A. Stroble & Associates, Ltd.*)

Jack L. Treynor
(*Treynor-Arbit Associates*)

Neil Weiss
(*Jon A. Stroble & Associates, Ltd.*)

Gerald White
(*Grace & White, Inc.*)

We also want to recognize the many instructors and colleagues who provided valuable comments and suggestions to further improve the book:

Rashad Abdel-Khalik
(*University of Florida*)

Robert N. Anthony
(*Harvard University*)

Hector R. Anton
(*New York University*)

Terry Arndt
(*Central Michigan University*)

Mark Bauman
(*University of Illinois–Chicago*)

William T. Baxter
(*CUNY–Baruch*)

Martin Benis
(*CUNY–Baruch*)

Shyam Bhandari
(*Bradley University*)

xvi

Fred Bien
(*Louisiana State University*)

John S. Bildersee
(*New York University*)

Vince Brenner
(*Louisiana State University*)

Abraham J. Briloff
(*CUNY–Baruch*)

Gary Bulmash
(*American University*)

Joseph Bylinski
(*University of North Carolina*)

Douglas Carmichael
(*CUNY–Baruch*)

Philip Chuey
(*Youngstown State University*)

Benny R. Copeland
(*North Texas State University*)

Maurice P. Corrigan
(*Teikyo Post University*)

Wallace N. Davidson III
(*University of North Texas*)

Harry Davis
(*CUNY–Baruch*)

Peter Lloyd Davis
(*CUNY–Baruch*)

Peter Easton
(*Ohio State University*)

Eric S. Emory
(*Sacred Heart University*)

William P. Enderlein
(*Golden Gate University*)

Calvin Engler
(*Iona College*)

Thomas J. Frecka
(*University of Notre Dame*)

John Gentis
(*Ball State University*)

Philip Gerdin
(*University of New Haven*)

Edwin Grossnickle
(*Western Michigan University*)

Peter M. Gutman
(*CUNY–Baruch*)

J. Larry Hagler
(*East Carolina University*)

Jerry Han
(*SUNY–Buffalo*)

Frank Heflin
(*Yale University*)

Yong-Ha Hyon
(*Temple University*)

Henry Jaenicke
(*Drexel University*)

Kenneth H. Johnson
(*Georgia Southern University*)

Jo Koehn
(*Central Missouri State University*)

Homer Kripke
(*New York University*)

Russ Langer
(*San Francisco State University*)

Burton T. Lefkowitz
(*C. W. Post College*)

Steven Lillien
(*CUNY–Baruch*)

Thomas Lopez
(*Pace University*)

Mostafa Maksy
(*Northeastern Illinois University*)

Brenda Mallouk
(*University of Toronto*)

Ann Martin
(*University of Colorado at Denver*)

Martin Mellman
(*Hofstra University*)

Belinda Mucklow
(*University of Wisconsin*)

Hugo Nurnberg
(*CUNY–Baruch*)

Stephen Penman
(*University of California at Berkeley*)

Tom Porter
(*Boston College*)

Larry Prober
(*Rider University*)

William Ruland
(*CUNY–Baruch*)

Stanley C. W. Salvary
(*Canisius College*)

Emanuel Saxe
(*CUNY–Baruch*)

Lenny Soffer
(*Northwestern University*)

Reed Storey
(*Financial Accounting Standards Board*)

K. R. Subramanyam
(*University of Southern California*)

Rebecca Todd
(*Boston University*)

Jerrold Weiss
(*Lehman College*)

Kenneth L. Wild
(*University of London*)

Richard F. Williams
(*Wright State University*)

Philip Wolitzer
(*Marymount Manhattan College*)

Christine V. Zavgren
(*Clarkson University*)

Stephen Zeff
(*Rice University*)

Mark Bauman, University of Illinois–Chicago, provided valuable advice and help in this edition. His contribution was exceptional and much appreciated.

Special thanks go to our families for their patience, understanding, and inspiration in completing this book, and we dedicate the book to them. We also thank Leonard and Mary Wild, Thomas and Darlene Kieliszewski, and Thomas, Rosemary, Karen, Robert, Shirley, and Kenneth. To you and to all who contributed to the book, we extend our sincere appreciation.

Leopold A. Bernstein
John J. Wild

 **Leopold A. Bernstein** is Professor of Business at Bernard M. Baruch College, City University of New York. He received his MBA from Harvard University and his PhD from New York University. Professor Bernstein is a consultant to many financial institutions and accounting firms, and is a Certified Public Accountant.

Professor Bernstein has taught numerous courses and professional training programs in financial statement analysis and accounting. He is a recognized teacher, known for his expertise in financial statement analysis and his commitment to professional instruction and education. He is a recipient of several prestigious honors, including the Graham and Dodd Award from the Financial Analysts Federation for outstanding contribution, the Best Article Award from the *Journal of Accountancy,* and the Gold Medal Award from the Massachusetts Society of CPAs. He is sought after for expert witness testimony in financial statement analysis and company valuation, and he conducts professional training programs for major domestic and international financial institutions.

Professor Bernstein is active in several important organizations. He is also the author of several notable books including *Financial Statement Analysis, Cases in Financial Statement Reporting and Analysis, Advanced Accounting,* and *Understanding Corporate Reports: A Guide to Financial Statement Analysis.* His more than 30 research publications appear in the *Financial Analysts Journal, Harvard Business Review, The Accounting Review, The Journal of Commercial Bank Lending, The Journal of Accountancy, The Financial Review, The CPA Journal,* and many other business and professional periodicals.

Professor Bernstein and his wife Cynthia enjoy biking, travel, and music. They make their home in Haworth, New Jersey.

 **John J. Wild** is Professor of Business and Vilas Research Scholar at The University of Wisconsin at Madison. He has previously held appointments at Michigan State University and The University of Manchester in England. He received his BBA, MS, and PhD from The University of Wisconsin.

Professor Wild teaches courses in accounting and analysis at both the undergraduate and graduate levels. He has received the Mabel W. Chipman Excellence-in-Teaching Award and the Departmental Excellence-in-Teaching Award at The University of Wisconsin. He also received the Beta Alpha Psi and Roland F. Salmonson Excellence-in-Teaching Award from Michigan State University. Professor Wild is a past KPMG Peat Marwick National Fellow and is a prior recipient of Fellowships from The American Accounting Associations and The Ernst and Young Foundation. He is a frequent speaker at universities and at national and international conferences.

Professor Wild is an active member of both The American Accounting Association and its sections, including Financial Reporting, Managerial, International Accounting, and Auditing. He has served on several committees of these organizations, including the Outstanding Accounting Educator Award, National Program Advisory, Publications, and Research Committees. His research on financial accounting and analysis appears in *The Accounting Review, Journal of Accounting Research, Journal of Accounting and Economics, Contemporary Accounting Research, Journal of Accounting, Auditing & Finance, Journal of Accounting and Public Policy, Auditing: A Journal of Theory and Practice,* and other accounting and business periodicals. He is Associate Editor of *Contemporary Accounting Research,* and has served on editorial boards of several respected journals, including *The Accounting Review, Accounting and Business Research, The British Accounting Review,* and the *Journal of Accounting and Public Policy.* Also, Professor Wild is author of *Financial Statement Analysis, Financial Accounting,* and *Fundamental Accounting Principles*—all published by McGraw-Hill.

Professor Wild, his wife, and four children enjoy travel, music, sports, and community activities. They make their home in Madison, Wisconsin.

CONTENTS IN BRIEF

PART ONE

FINANCIAL STATEMENT ANALYSIS AND REPORTING   1

Chapter 1   Overview of Financial Statement Analysis   3
Chapter 2   Analysis Objectives and Financial Reporting   57

PART TWO

FINANCIAL ANALYSIS APPLICATION AND INTERPRETATION   109

Chapter 3   Short-Term Liquidity   111
Chapter 4   Forecasting and Pro Forma Analysis   151
Chapter 5   Capital Structure and Solvency   176
Chapter 6   Return on Invested Capital   234
Chapter 7   Profitability Analysis   270
Chapter 8   Earnings-Based Analysis and Valuation   322

COMPREHENSIVE CASE APPLYING FINANCIAL STATEMENT ANALYSIS   CC1
SUPPLEMENT A FINANCIAL STATEMENTS: ADAPTEC   A2
                                    CAMPBELL SOUP   A32
INDEX   IN1

C O N T E N T S

PART ONE

FINANCIAL STATEMENT ANALYSIS AND REPORTING   1

Chapter One

Overview of Financial Statement Analysis   3

Focus on Analysis: Adaptec   6
Users of Financial Statements   8
Business Activities in a Market Economy   9
    Planning Activities   9
    Financing Activities   11
    Investing Activities   14
    Operating Activities   15
Financial Statements Capture Business Activities   16
    Balance Sheet   18
    Income Statement   19
    Statement of Shareholders' Equity   20
    Statement of Cash Flows   21
    Links between Financial Statements   22
Information Accompanying Financial Statements   26
    Management's Discussion and Analysis (MD&A)   26
    Management Report   26
    Auditor Report   27
    Explanatory Notes 27
    Supplementary Information   28
    Social Responsibility Reports   29
    Proxy Statements   29
Preview of Financial Statement Analysis   30
    Building Blocks of Analysis   31
    Comparative Financial Statement Analysis   32
    Common-Size Financial Statement Analysis   37
    Ratio Analysis of Financial Statements   40
    Specialized Analysis Tools   45

Financial Statement Analysis in an Efficient Capital Market   45
   Capital Market Efficiency   45
   Market Efficiency Implications for Financial Statement Analysis   45
Preview of This Book's Organization   48
Appendix 1A Investment Theory and Financial Statement Analysis   52

Chapter Two

Analysis Objectives and Financial Reporting   57

Objectives of Financial Statement Analysis   59
   Creditors   59
   Equity Investors   62
   Management   66
   Auditors   67
   Directors   68
   Mergers and Acquisition Analysts   68
   Regulators   69
   Other Important Users   69
Accounting Information: Basis of Analysis   69
   Accounting Measurement and Reporting of Business Activity   70
   Relevance of Accounting Information   71
   Information Environment for Financial Statement Analysis   73
Accounting Principles and Limitations   74
   Monetary Expression   74
   Simplification and Summarization   74
   Judgment and Incentives   74
   Interim Disclosures and Estimates   76
   Historical Cost Measurement   77
   Unstable Monetary Unit   77
   Need to Understand Accounting Measurements and Disclosures   77
   Implications of Accounting Risk   79
Additional Analysis Techniques   80
   Reconstruction of Business Activities and Transactions   80
   Indirect Evidence and Evaluation   82
   Industry Comparability Analysis of Financial Statements   85
   Analytical Use of Accounting Standards and Assumptions   85
   Traditional Market Measures   88
Appendix 2A Accounting Principles Underlying Financial Statements   90
Appendix 2B Additional Tools and Sources for Financial
            Statement Analysis   102

[PART TWO

FINANCIAL ANALYSIS APPLICATION AND INTERPRETATION 109

Chapter Three

Short-Term Liquidity 111

Importance of Short-Term Liquidity 113

Analyzing Working Capital 114

Current Assets 115

Current Liabilities 117

Working Capital Measure of Liquidity 118

Current Ratio Measure of Liquidity 118

Using the Current Ratio for Analysis 122

Cash-Based Ratio Measures of Liquidity 129

Operating Activity Analysis of Liquidity 130

Accounts Receivable Liquidity Measures 130

Inventory Turnover Measures 135

Liquidity of Current Liabilities 140

Additional Short-Term Liquidity Measures 142

Current Assets Composition 142

Liquidity Index 143

Acid-Test (Quick) Ratio 144

Cash Flow Measures 145

Financial Flexibility 145

Management's Discussion and Analysis 146

What-If Analysis 146

Chapter Four

Forecasting and Pro Forma Analysis 151

Cash Flow Patterns 153

Short-Term Cash Forecasting 154

Importance of Forecasting Sales 155

Cash Flow Forecasting with Pro Forma Analysis 155

Long-Term Cash Forecasting 162

Analysis of Prior Cash Flows for Forecasting 163

Forecasting Sources and Uses of Cash Flows 167

Specialized Cash Flow Ratios 172

Cash Flow Adequacy Ratio   172
Cash Reinvestment Ratio   173

Chapter Five

Capital Structure and Solvency   176

Keys to Solvency Analysis   178
Importance of Capital Structure   179
    Characteristics of Debt and Equity   181
    Motivation for Debt Capital   182
    Measuring Effects of Financial Leverage   186
Accounting Implications for Capital Structure Analysis   188
    Adjustments to Book Values of Liabilities   189
    Adjustments to Book Values of Assets   193
Capital Structure Composition and Solvency   195
    Long-Term Projections in Analyzing Solvency   196
    Common-Size Statements in Solvency Analysis   197
    Capital Structure Measures for Solvency Analysis   198
    Interpretation of Capital Structure Measures   202
Asset-Based Measures of Solvency   203
    Asset Composition in Solvency Analysis   203
    Asset Coverage in Solvency Analysis   204
Importance of Earnings Coverage   205
    Relation of Earnings to Fixed Charges   205
    Times Interest Earned Analysis   214
    Relation of Cash Flow to Fixed Charges   214
    Earnings Coverage of Preferred Dividends   218
    Interpreting Earnings Coverage Measures   219
Capital Structure Risk and Return   221
Appendix 5A Rating Debt Obligations   223
Appendix 5B Predicting Financial Distress   229
Appendix 5C Analytical Adjustments to the Long-Term Debt
       to Equity Ratio   231

Chapter Six

Return on Invested Capital   234

Importance of Return on Invested Capital   236
    Measuring Managerial Effectiveness   237
    Measuring Profitability   237

Measure of Forecasted Earnings   237
Measuring for Planning and Control   237
Components of Return on Invested Capital   238
Defining Invested Capital   238
Defining Income   243
Adjustments of Invested Capital and Income   244
Computing Return on Invested Capital   244
Analyzing Return on Assets   247
Disaggregating Return on Assets   248
Relation between Profit Margin and Asset Turnover   249
Asset Turnover Analysis   253
Analyzing Return on Common Equity   256
Disaggregating Return on Common Equity   257
Computing Return on Invested Capital   260
Assessing Growth in Common Equity   263
Financial Leverage and Return on Common Equity   263
Return on Common Shareholders' Equity versus Investment   266

Chapter Seven

Profitability Analysis   270

Analyzing Company Profitability   272
Factors in Measuring Company Income   273
Two-Phase Analysis of Income   275
Analyzing Company Revenues   276
Major Sources of Revenues   276
Persistence of Revenues   283
Relations between Revenues, Receivables, and Inventories   285
Revenue Recognition and Measurement   286
Analyzing Company Cost of Sales   287
Measuring Gross Profit (Margin)   288
Analyzing Changes in Gross Profit   288
Interpreting Changes in Gross Profit   290
Analyzing Company Expenses   291
Selling Expenses   292
Depreciation Expense   295
Maintenance and Repairs Expenses   295
Amortization of Special Costs   296
General and Administrative Expenses   296
Financing and Other Expenses   296

Income Tax Expenses 298
Variation Analysis of Income and Its Components 305
Break-Even Analysis 305
Break-Even Analysis Case 307
Limitations in Break-Even Analysis 312
Uses and Implications of Break-Even Analysis 313

Chapter Eight

Earnings-Based Analysis and Valuation   322

Earnings Quality 324
Measuring Earnings Quality 325
Balance Sheet Analysis and Earnings Quality 331
External Factors and Earnings Quality 334
Earnings Persistence 334
Recasting and Adjusting Earnings for Analysis 335
Determinants of Earnings Persistence 341
Persistence of Extraordinary Items in Earnings 344
Earnings-Based Valuation 350
Relation between Stock Prices and Accounting Data 352
Fundamental Valuation Multiples 353
Earning Power and Forecasting for Valuation 356
Illustration of Earnings-Based Valuation 358
Earning Power 358
Earnings Forecasting 360
Interim Reports for Monitoring and Revising Earnings Estimates 364

Comprehensive Case: Applying Financial Statement Analysis   CC1

Steps in Analyzing Financial Statements CC3
Building Blocks of Financial Statement Analysis CC5
Reporting on Financial Statement Analysis CC6
Specialization in Financial Statement Analysis CC8
Comprehensive Case: Campbell Soup Company CC8
Preliminary Financial Analysis CC8
Short-Term Liquidity CC19
Cash Flow Analysis and Forecasting CC23
Capital Structure and Solvency CC35
Return on Invested Capital CC38
Analysis of Asset Utilization CC42

Analysis of Operating Performance and Profitability CC43
Summary Evaluation and Inferences CC46

Supplement A Financial Statements A1

Adaptec, Inc. A2
Campbell Soup Company A32

Interest Tables I1

Index IN1

Financial Statement Analysis and Reporting

CHAPTER 1: OVERVIEW OF FINANCIAL STATEMENT ANALYSIS

Chapter 1 introduces us to financial statement analysis and its importance in making business decisions. We see how financial statements capture and report on business activities. Financial reports of Adaptec are analyzed as an opening illustration of financial statement analysis. You'll learn about important financial features of several companies, including The Limited, McDonald's, Nike, PepsiCo, and Wal-Mart. We'll see how financial statement analysis fits with theories of market efficiency, and we'll also learn about financial statement analysis research and how financial numbers affect stock prices.

CHAPTER 2: ANALYSIS OBJECTIVES AND FINANCIAL REPORTING

This chapter describes the primary users of financial statements, including creditors, investors, managers, auditors, directors, analysts, regulators, employees, and customers, and explains how this information affects their business decisions. We discuss the accounting dual-entry system and its measurement of business activities. Accounting requires estimates and assumptions, and we discuss how these limit the reliability and relevance of our analysis. We introduce specialized analysis techniques and discuss the usefulness of comparability analysis. We'll learn about fundamental analysis research and the value of financial statements in predicting companies' values.

Overview of Financial
Statement Analysis

A LOOK AT THIS CHAPTER

We begin our analysis of financial statements by considering their relevance in analyzing an actual company. This leads us to focus on financial statement users, their information needs, and how financial statement analysis helps address these needs. We describe the major types of business activities and how they are revealed in financial statements. We conduct a preliminary financial statement analysis of a company to illustrate these important concepts. We learn that financial statement analysis has several purposes and benefits.

A LOOK AHEAD

Chapter 2 reviews objectives of financial statement analysis from the perspective of specific users. We consider the relevance and limitations of accounting information and describe specialized financial statement analysis techniques. Chapters 3 through 8 focus on mastering the tools of financial statement analysis. A comprehensive financial statement analysis of a company completes the book.

THIS CHAPTER WILL:

- Explain why financial statement analysis is important.
- Identify financial statement users and information relevant for their decisions.
- Describe major types of business activities and their impact on financial statements.
- Explain the purpose of each financial statement and the linkages between them.
- Identify additional information in a financial reporting system and its relevance.
- Analyze and interpret the financial statements of an actual company as a preview to more fundamental analysis.
- Describe several financial statement analysis techniques and their relevance.
- Explain the purpose of financial statement analysis in an efficient market.
- Describe important investment theories and their implications for financial analysis (Appendix 1A).

PREVIEW OF CHAPTER 1

Financial statement analysis applies analytical tools and techniques to general-purpose financial statements and related data to derive estimates and inferences useful in business decisions. It is a screening tool in selecting investment or merger candidates, and is a forecasting tool of future financial conditions and consequences. It is a diagnostic tool in assessing financing, investing, and operating activities, and is an evaluation tool for managerial and other business decisions. Financial statement analysis reduces our reliance on hunches, guesses, and intuition, and in turn it diminishes our uncertainty in decision making. It does not lessen the need for expert judgment but rather establishes an effective and systematic basis for making business decisions. This chapter describes users of financial statements and explains business activities underlying financial statements. We introduce several fundamental tools and techniques of financial statement analysis. Special attention is devoted to a preliminary financial statement analysis of an actual company, Adaptec. The content and organization of this chapter are as follows:

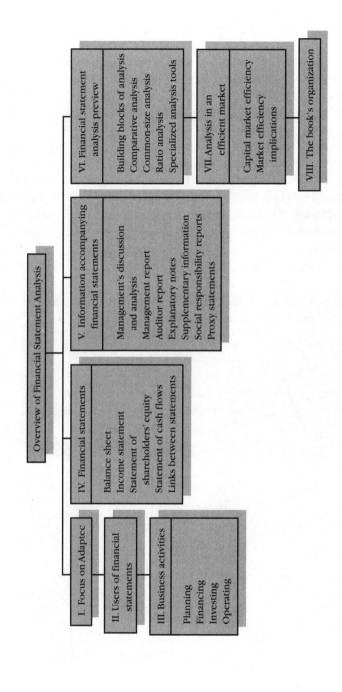

Overview of Financial Statement Analysis

I. Focus on Adaptec

II. Users of financial statements

III. Business activities

Planning
Financing
Investing
Operating

IV. Financial statements

Balance sheet
Income statement
Statement of shareholders' equity
Statement of cash flows
Links between statements

V. Information accompanying financial statements

Management's discussion and analysis
Management report
Auditor report
Explanatory notes
Supplementary information
Social responsibility reports
Proxy statements

VI. Financial statement analysis preview

Building blocks of analysis
Comparative analysis
Common-size analysis
Ratio analysis
Specialized analysis tools

VII. Analysis in an efficient market

Capital market efficiency
Market efficiency implications

VIII. The book's organization

FOCUS ON ANALYSIS: ADAPTEC

Financial statements report a company's past financial performance and current financial position. They are designed to provide information on four primary business activities: planning, financing, investing, and operating activities. This book emphasizes financial statement analysis by helping us read, understand, and use financial statements for making better decisions. Today's advanced technology increases the importance of expert financial statement analysis. We are required to sort through a vast maze of information to gain insight into a company's current and future prospects. Analyzing financial statements helps us sort through and evaluate information, focusing attention on reliable information most relevant to our business decisions.

    Adaptec, Inc., is a company in advanced communications and technology. Adaptec supplies computer hardware and software to facilitate interaction between computer systems and peripheral devices like printers, disk drives, CD-ROMs, and scanners. Its 1996 annual report is reproduced in Supplement A near the end of the book.

Adaptec requires considerable resources to finance its operations. The company's 1996 balance sheet reveals contributions from shareholders of more than $182 million and more than $134 million from creditors. Are we willing to contribute to the financing of Adaptec—either through an investment in stock or through a loan? Financial statement analysis helps us make this decision. A review of Adaptec's financial performance reveals considerable growth since 1992—net revenues (339%), net income (607%), and total assets (366%) show striking increases. Financial markets recognize this growth and, as noted in its annual report, Adaptec's common stock, valued between $14 and $19½ a share in the first quarter of 1995, traded between $35⅛ and $56⅜ by the fourth quarter of 1996 (see Selected Financial Data section in Supplement A). But what are its future prospects? Are you willing to buy Adaptec's shares at $15, or $35, or $55, or some other value? Financial statement analysis helps us answer these questions.

We use and rely on financial statements in making important decisions. Shareholders and creditors assess future company prospects for investing and lending decisions. Boards of directors, as shareholders' representatives, use financial statement information in monitoring management's decisions. Employees and unions use financial statements in labor negotiations. Suppliers use financial statements in establishing credit terms. Customers use financial statements in deciding whether to establish supplier relationships. Public utilities set customer rates by referring to financial statements. Information intermediaries, like Dunn & Bradstreet, Moody's, and Standard & Poor's, use financial statements in making buy-sell recommendations and setting credit ratings. Auditors use financial statements in assessing the "fair presentation" of their clients' financial statement numbers.

More specifically, when analyzing Adaptec, creditors perform financial statement analysis to answer the following types of questions:

- What are reasons for Adaptec's need for additional financing?
- What are Adaptec's likely sources for payment of interest and principal?
- How has Adaptec handled its prior short- and long-term financing?
- What are Adaptec's likely needs for future financing?

Shareholders and potential shareholders also require information in analyzing Adaptec. Financial statement analysis helps shareholders answer the following questions:

- What are Adaptec's current and long-term operating prospects?
- What is Adaptec's future earnings potential?
- Are Adaptec's earnings vulnerable to significant variability?
- What is Adaptec's current financial condition?
- What factors most likely determine Adaptec's financial position?
- What is Adaptec's capital (financing) structure?
- What risks and rewards do Adaptec's capital structure present?
- How does Adaptec compare with its competitors?

Sound decision making begins with identifying the most pertinent questions for the objectives at hand. While financial statement analysis does not provide all the answers, every decision is aided by such analysis. This book helps develop skills needed by financial statement users when making business decisions.

USERS OF FINANCIAL STATEMENTS

Financial statement users are broadly classified into two groups. **Internal users,** primarily the mangers of a company, are involved in making operating and strategic decisions for the business. As employees, they typically have complete access to a company's information system. Internally generated financial reports are, therefore, specifically tailored to the unique information needs of an internal decision maker, such as a CEO, CFO, or internal auditor. **External users** are individuals not directly involved in the company's operations. These users must rely on information provided by management as part of the financial reporting process. This book stresses the analysis needs of external users of general-purpose financial statements. Nevertheless, many analysis techniques described here are usefully applied by internal users.

There are many classes of external users of financial statements. **Creditors** are bankers, bondholders, and other individuals who lend money to business enterprises. Creditors look to financial statements for evidence concerning the ability of the borrower to pay periodic interest payments and repay the principal amount when the loan matures. **Equity investors** include existing and potential shareholders of a company. Existing shareholders need financial information in deciding whether to continue holding the stock or sell it. Potential shareholders need financial information to help in choosing among competing alternative investments. Equity investors are generally interested in assessing the future profitability and/or riskiness of a company. **Merger and acquisition analysts** are interested in determining the economic value and assessing the financial and operating compatibility of potential merger candidates. **Auditors** use financial analysis techniques in determining areas warranting special attention during their examination of a client's financial statements. A company's **board of directors,** in their role as appointees of shareholders, monitors management's actions. **Regulatory agencies** utilize financial statements in the exercise of their supervisory functions, including the Securities and Exchange Commission, which vigilantly oversees published financial statements for compliance with federal securities laws. Certain price-regulated industries, such as public utilities, submit financial reports to regulators for rate-determination purposes. Other users include **employees** (in evaluating the fairness of their wages and working conditions), **intermediaries** (in offering investment advice), **suppliers** (in determining the creditworthiness of customers), and **customers** (in evaluating the staying power of their suppliers). All of these users rely on the analysis of financial statements.

BUSINESS ACTIVITIES IN A MARKET ECONOMY

A business pursues a number of activities in a desire to provide a saleable product and to yield a satisfactory return on investment. Adaptec supplies hardware and software products that enhance performance of computer-related tasks. Financial statements and related disclosures are designed to inform us about four major activities of a company: planning, financing, investing, and operating. It is important to understand each of these major business activities before we can effectively analyze a company's financial statements.

Planning Activities

A company exists to implement specific goals and objectives. Adaptec aspires to deliver high-quality technology-based computer products. A company's goals and objectives are captured in a **business plan** or strategy that describes the company's purpose, strategy, and tactics for activities. A business plan assists managers in focusing their efforts and identifying expected opportunities and obstacles. Knowledge or insight into a business plan considerably aids our analysis of a company's current and future prospects. We look for information on company objectives and tactics, market demands, competitive analysis, sales strategies (pricing, promotion, distribution), management performance, and financial projections. Information of this type, in varying forms, is often revealed in financial reports to outsiders. It is also available through less formal means, such as press releases, industry publications, analysts' newsletters, and popular magazines.

Two important sources for information on a company's business plan are the Shareholders' Letter and Management's Discussion and Analysis. Adaptec, in its Shareholders' Letter from its 1996 annual report, discusses various business opportunities and plans: "a growing market for the expandability and speed offered by Adaptec's products . . . We have achieved strategic supplier status with several important customers . . . Our leadership position in this market was further underscored . . . We anticipate further growth with the market acceptance of new peripherals . . . acquiring complementary companies and technologies . . . prepare for new market opportunities in the longer term through ongoing development of products based on serial interfaces." Additional discussion appears in the Management's Discussion and Analysis section of Adaptec's financial report. These two sources are excellent starting points in constructing a company's

JOHN G. ADLER
Chairman of the Board

F. GRANT SAVIERS
President and Chief Executive Officer

business plan. Much more information on a company's business plan and strategy is found in its annual report and other direct and indirect sources.

It is important to stress business planning is not cast in stone and is fraught with expectations. Can Adaptec be certain of the future of high-performance connectivity or the delivery of digital data? Can Adaptec be certain silicon, semiconductors, or other raw material costs will not increase? Can Adaptec be sure how competitors will react? These and other questions add *risk* to our analysis. While all actions involve risk, some actions involve more than others. Financial statement analysis helps us estimate the degree of risk, or uncertainty, and yields more informed and better decisions. While information taken from financial reports does not provide irrefutable answers, it does help us gauge the soundness of a company's business opportunities and strategies, and better understand its financing, investing, and operating needs.

Financing Activities

A company requires financing to carry out its business plan. Adaptec needs financing in purchasing raw materials for production, in acquiring complementary companies and technologies, and in pursuing research and development. **Financing activities** are the means companies use to pay for these ventures. Because of their magnitude, and their potential in determining the success or failure of a venture, companies take care in acquiring and managing their financial resources.

There are two main sources of business financing: equity investors (also referred to as *owners* or *shareholders*) and creditors (also called *lenders*). Decisions concerning the composition of financing activities are not separate from conditions existing in financial markets. Financial markets are potential sources of business financing. In looking to financial markets, a company considers several issues including: the amount of financing necessary, source(s) of financing (owners or creditors), timing of repayment, and structure of the financing agreement(s). Decisions on these issues determine a company's organizational structure, affect its growth, influence its riskiness, and determine the power of outsiders in business decisions.

Equity investors are a major supplier of financing. Adaptec's balance sheet shows it raised more than $182 million by issuing stock to equity investors. Investors provide financing in a desire for a fair return on their investment, weighing both the return and risk of financing. **Return** is the equity investors' share of company earnings, and takes one of two forms: earnings distribution or earnings reinvestment. **Earnings distribution** involves a company paying cash or other assets to investors. **Dividend payout** refers to the amount of earnings distributed, and often is described as a percent: Dividend paid ÷ Earnings. Adaptec is a "growth company," which is evidenced by a zero dividend payout. **Earnings reinvestment** refers to increasing company value through earnings financing. **Equity growth** is the amount of earnings reinvested, and is often described as a percent: Equity growth ÷ Equity investors' value in the company. Adaptec's equity growth is 27.8 percent ($103,375/$371,644).

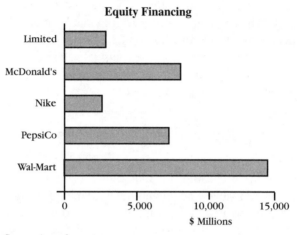

Equity Financing

$ Millions

Source: Annual reports.

Equity financing can be in cash or any asset or service contributed to a company in exchange for shares. Private offerings of shares usually involve selling shares to one or more individuals or organizations. Public offerings involve selling shares to the public. There are significant costs with public offerings of shares, including government regulatory filings, stock exchange listing requirements, and brokerage fees to selling agents. Public offerings of shares provide substantial funds for business activities. Many corporations offer their shares for trading on organized exchanges like the New York, Tokyo, Singapore, and London stock markets. Adaptec's common stock trades in the over-the-counter market under the NASDAQ symbol ADPT.

Companies also obtain financing from creditors. Creditor financing of business activities often occurs through loans. Creditors include organizations like banks, savings and loans, and other financial or nonfinancial institutions. Creditors also include individuals, for example, a manager, an employee, or a financier. Adaptec's balance sheet shows that creditor financing is 20.8 percent ($134,541/$646,486) of total financing.

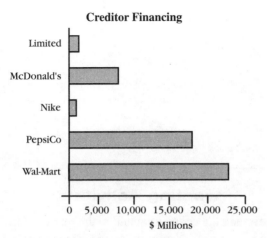

Creditor Financing

0   5,000 10,000 15,000 20,000 25,000
$ Millions

Source: Annual reports.

Creditor financing is different than equity financing in that an agreement, or **contract,** is usually established requiring repayment of the loan with interest at a specific date(s). While interest is not always expressly stated in these contracts, it is always implicit. Loan periods are variable and depend on the desires of both creditors and companies. Loans can be as long as 50 years or more or as short as a week or less. Even employees who are paid periodically, say weekly or monthly, are providing a form of credit financing. When employees provide services to the business but do not receive pay for a week, they are providing a source of short-term financing. Nearly 40 percent ($22,440/$56,717) of Adaptec's accrued liabilities relate to compensation and related taxes. There are numerous instances of this implicit creditor financing—utility, supplier, and tax payments.

Like equity investors, creditors are concerned with return and risk. Unlike equity investors, creditors' returns are usually specified in loan contracts. For example, a 20-year 10 percent fixed-rate loan is straightforward—that is, creditors receive a 10 percent annual return on their investment for 20 years. Adaptec's long-term loan is due in June 1998, requiring interest payments of 7.65 percent (see note 4 to statements). Equity investors' returns are not guaranteed and depend on the level of future earnings. Risk for creditors is the likelihood a business is unsuccessful and defaults in repaying its loans and interest. In this situation, creditors might not receive their money due, and bankruptcy or other legal remedies ensue. Such remedies always impose costs on creditors.

ANALYSIS VIEWPOINT

YOU ARE THE BANKER

Adaptec requests a $50 million loan from your bank. How does the composition of Adaptec's financing sources (creditor and/or owner) affect your loan decision? Do you have any reluctance making the loan to Adaptec given its current financing composition? (*Note: Solutions to analysis viewpoints appear at the end of each chapter.*)

Investing Activities

Investing activities are the acquisition and maintenance of investments by companies to sell products or provide services. Financing provides the funds necessary to acquire the investments needed to carry out business plans. Investments include land, buildings, equipment, legal rights (patents, licenses, copyrights), inventories, human capital (managers, employees), information systems, and all components necessary for operating a company. Adaptec's balance sheet shows its 1996 investment, or asset, base is $646 million.

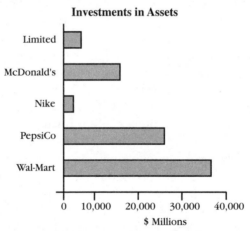

Source: Annual reports.

Information on both financing and investing activities assists us in putting some of the puzzle together revealing business performance. Notice also that the value of investments always equals the value of financing obtained. Any excess financing not invested is simply reported as cash (or some other noncash asset). Companies differ in the amount and

composition of their investments. Many companies demand huge investments in acquiring, developing, and selling their products, while others
require little investment. Size of investment does not necessarily determine company success. It is the efficiency and effectiveness with which a
company carries out its operations that determine earnings and returns to
owners.

Investing decisions involve several factors including type of investment necessary (including technological and labor intensity), amount
required, acquisition timing, asset location, and contractual agreement
(purchase, rent, lease). Adaptec's assets are 72 percent current ($465,280/
$646,486) and 28 percent noncurrent ($181,206/$646,486). Like financing
activities, decisions on investing activities determine a company's organizational structure (centralized or decentralized operations), affect growth,
and influence riskiness of operations. Nearly 40 percent of Adaptec's identifiable assets are in Asia ($259,179/$646,486) (see note 9 in its 1996
report). This affects our assessment of the riskiness of its assets.

Investment total and composition are of value to both insiders and
outsiders of a company as a measure to assess earnings. Adaptec's income
statement shows its 1996 net income is $103,375, and its return on
beginning-of-year investment is 23.7 percent ($103,375 ÷ $435,708)—
a seemingly adequate return. In comparison, if the same $103,375 income
is obtained with investments of $10,000,000, we might question Adaptec's
long-term viability in light of its low 1 percent return on investment. Such
analysis, while revealing, is not a complete picture. We still need to consider costs of financing. For example, while a 16 percent return looks
appealing, we might think otherwise if financing costs equal 17 percent.

Operating Activities

One of the more important pieces in analyzing a company is operating
activities. **Operating activities** represent the "carrying out" of the business plan given necessary financing and investing. These activities involve
at least five basic components: research, purchasing, producing, marketing, and labor. A proper mix of key components of operating activities
depends on the type of business, its plans, and "input" markets. Input markets for operating activities include raw materials for production. Examples are supplier markets, labor markets, technology markets, and
consumer markets. Management decides on the most efficient and effective mix for their company's competitive advantage.

Operating activities are a company's primary source of income.
Income measures a company's success in buying from input markets and

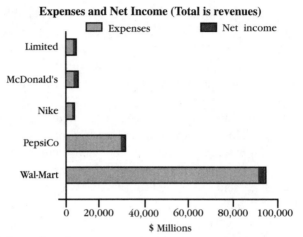

Source: Annual reports.

selling in output markets. How well a company does in devising business plans and strategies, and deciding on materials comprising the mix of operating activities, determines business success or failure. Our analysis of income numbers, and their component parts, measures a company's success in efficiently and effectively managing these business activities.

FINANCIAL STATEMENTS CAPTURE BUSINESS ACTIVITIES

Business activities—planning, financing, investing, and operating—are synthesized into a cohesive picture of how businesses function in a market economy. Exhibit 1.1 portrays these business activities from the beginning to the end of one period; in practice, this process continues indefinitely. Step one for the company is formulating plans and strategies. Next, a company pursues financing from equity investors and creditors. Financing is used to acquire investments in land, buildings, equipment, merchandise, labor, and other resources to produce goods or services (the operating activities).

The top level of Exhibit 1.1 shows investing and financing activities at the business's inception (termed *beginning of period*). Actual amounts needed for investing and financing activities are specified in the business plan. Investing and financing are intentionally displayed opposite each other to emphasize their equality or balance. That is, financing is always in the form of investments, and investments cannot exceed their financing.

Exhibit 1.1   **Dynamics of Business Activities**

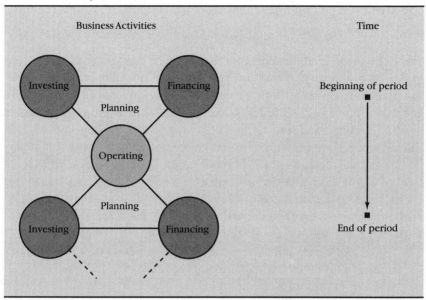

Provided with financing and investments, a company commences its operating activities to carry out business plans. A "merge" layout (∇) is used to stress that operating activities (lower apex) derive from a combination of planning (cohesive center), financing (right apex), and investing (left apex) activities. A company raises additional financing for further investments or repays suppliers of financing if investment requirements shrink. However, investing always equals financing (referred to as the accounting equation).

At the end of the period—typically quarterly or annually in practice—**financial statements** are prepared. An "extract" layout (Δ) is used to indicate preparation of these statements. These statements update listings of financing and investing activities, and summarize operating activities for the most recent period(s). This is the role of financial statements and our object of analysis. Financial statement reporting of financing and investing activities occurs at a point in time, whereas operating activities are reported for a period of time. In Exhibit 1.1, there are two disclosure points: beginning of period and end of period. Four primary financial statements are prepared: the balance sheet, the income statement, the statement of shareholders' (owners') equity, and the statement of cash flows.

Balance Sheet

The **accounting equation** is the basis of the financial reporting system:

$$\text{Assets} = \text{Liabilities} + \text{Shareholders' equity}$$

The left-hand side of this equation relates to the economic resources controlled by a company, or **assets.** These resources are valuable in representing potential sources of future revenues through operating activities. To engage in operating activities, a company obtains funding to invest in assets. The right-hand side of this equation identifies funding sources. **Liabilities** are funding from creditors and represent obligations of a company or, alternatively, claims of creditors on assets. **Shareholders' equity** is a total of (1) funding invested or contributed by shareholders (contributed capital) and (2) accumulated earnings since inception in excess of distributions to shareholders (retained earnings). From the shareholders' point of view, these amounts represent their claim on company assets.

A balance sheet summarizes the financial position of a company at a given point in time. Most companies are required under accepted accounting practices to present a classified balance sheet. In a classified balance sheet, assets and liabilities are separated into current and noncurrent accounts. **Current assets** are expected to be converted to cash or used in operations within one year or the operating cycle, whichever is longer. **Current liabilities** are obligations that the company must settle in the same time period. The difference between current assets and current liabilities is **working capital.**

It is revealing to rewrite the accounting equation in terms of underlying business activities:

$$\text{Investing activities} = \text{Financing activities}$$

Recognizing the two financing sources, this is rewritten as:

$$\text{Investments} = \text{Creditor financing} + \text{Shareholder financing}$$

Exhibit 1.2 shows balance sheets of Adaptec, dated March 31, 1996, and 1995 (all of its financial statements are shown in Supplement A). Adaptec's 1996 investments equal $646,486 million. Of this amount, creditors' claims total $134,541 million, while the remaining $511,945 million represent claims of shareholders. Adaptec's financial statements are also available at its web site [http://www.adaptec.com].

EXHIBIT 1.2   Adaptec Balance Sheet

Consolidated Balance Sheets

IN THOUSANDS

As of March 31	1996	1995
Assets		
Current assets		
Cash and cash equivalents	$ 91,211	$ 66,835
Marketable securities	204,283	179,911
Accounts receivable, net of allowance for doubtful accounts of $4,220 in 1996 and $4,431 in 1995	89,487	56,495
Inventories	55,028	31,712
Prepaid expenses and other	25,271	15,519
Total current assets	465,280	350,472
Property and equipment, net	92,778	67,863
Other assets	88,428	17,373
	$646,486	$435,708
Liabilities and Shareholders' Equity		
Current liabilities		
Current portion of long-term debt	$ 3,400	$ 3,400
Note payable	46,200	—
Accounts payable	23,974	22,008
Accrued liabilities	56,717	31,006
Total current liabilities	130,291	56,414
Long-term debt, net of current portion	4,250	7,650
Commitments (Note 7)		
Shareholders' equity		
Preferred stock		
Authorized shares, 1,000		
Outstanding shares, none	—	—
Common stock		
Authorized shares, 200,000		
Outstanding shares, 53,020 in 1996 and 51,677 in 1995	182,932	140,191
Retained earnings	329,013	231,453
Total shareholders' equity	511,945	371,644
	$646,486	$435,708

See accompanying notes.

Income Statement

An income statement measures a company's financial performance between balance sheet dates and, hence, reflects a period of time. It lists revenues, expenses, gains, and losses of a company over a time period. The bottom line, or **net income,** shows the increase (or decrease) in net worth of a company (assets less liabilities), before considering distributions to and contributions from shareholders. In practice, net income is determined using the **accrual basis of accounting.** Under this method, revenues are recognized when a company sells goods and/or renders services, independent of receiving cash. Expenses, in turn, are recognized when related revenue is recorded, independent of paying cash. Income statements of Adaptec for fiscal years ended March 31, 1996, 1995, and 1994 appear in Exhibit 1.3. In 1996, Adaptec earned net revenues of $659,347 million. Of this amount, $555,972 million is offset with a variety of expenses, yielding net income of $103,375 million.

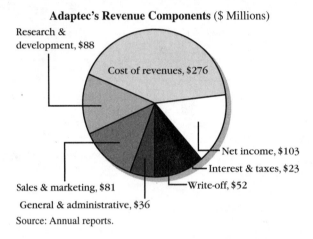

Adaptec's Revenue Components ($ Millions)

Research & development, $88

Cost of revenues, $276

Net income, $103

Interest & taxes, $23

Write-off, $52

Sales & marketing, $81

General & administrative, $36

Source: Annual reports.

Statement of Shareholders' Equity

The statement of shareholders' equity reports changes in component accounts comprising equity. This statement is useful in identifying reasons for changes in shareholders' claims on the assets of a company. As we discuss in subsequent chapters, accepted practice excludes certain gains and losses from net income that, instead, are directly reported in the statement of shareholders' equity. Adaptec's statement of shareholders' equity for fiscal years ended March 31, 1996, 1995, and 1994, is shown in Exhibit 1.4. During the 1994–1996 period, individual equity account balances changed due to several reasons: selling stock under employee purchase and option plans, repurchasing of stock, issuing stock for an acquisition, and reinvesting of net income. Particularly important is the change in Adaptec's Retained Earnings balance. Through this account, income statements link consecutive balance sheets. Specifically, Adaptec had retained earnings of $100,349 million in 1993 and reports net income of $58,950 million in 1994, resulting in $159,299 million ($100,349 + $58,950) of retained earnings in 1994. Since dividends represent distributions from retained earnings, the Retained Earnings balance generally represents an upper

EXHIBIT 1.3   **Adaptec Income Statement**

Consolidated Statements of Operations

IN THOUSANDS, EXCEPT PER SHARE AMOUNTS

Year Ended March 31	1996	1995	1994
Net revenues	$659,347	$466,194	$372,245
Cost of revenues	275,939	205,596	189,526
Gross profit	383,408	260,598	182,719
Operating expenses			
Research and development	87,628	60,848	39,993
Sales and marketing	81,548	58,737	46,192
General and administrative	35,784	23,229	19,399
Write-off of acquired in-process technology	52,313	—	—
	257,273	142,814	105,584
Income from operations	126,135	117,784	77,135
Shareholder settlement	—	—	(2,409)
Interest income	12,694	7,932	5,183
Interest expense	(840)	(1,179)	(1,306)
	11,854	6,753	1,468
Income before income taxes	137,989	124,537	78,603
Provision for income taxes	34,614	31,135	19,653
Net income	$103,375	$ 93,402	$ 58,950
Net income per share	$ 1.89	$ 1.75	$ 1.10
Weighted average number of common and			
common equivalent shares outstanding	54,569	53,357	53,602

See accompanying notes.

limit on the amount of potential dividend distributions. This is not yet an issue for Adaptec since, as indicated at the bottom of the Selected Financial Data in its 1996 annual report, Adaptec "does not currently plan to pay cash dividends to its shareholders in the near future."

Statement of Cash Flows

Under accrual accounting, net income does not typically equal net cash flow except over the life of a company. Since accrual accounting yields numbers different from cash flow accounting, and cash flows are important, there is a need for periodic reporting of cash inflows and outflows. For

EXHIBIT 1.4   Adaptec Statement of Shareholders' Equity

Consolidated Statements of Shareholders' Equity

IN THOUSANDS

| | Common Stock | | Retained | |
	Shares	Amount	Earnings	Total
Balance, March 31, 1993..........................	50,714	$124,806	$100,349	$225,155
Sale of common stock under employee				
purchase and option plans........................	1,577	7,728	—	7,728
Income tax benefit of employees' stock				
transactions	—	5,783	—	5,783
Net income	—	—	58,950	58,950
Balance, March 31, 1994..........................	52,291	138,317	159,299	297,616
Sale of common stock under employee				
purchase and option plans........................	1,426	11,245	—	11,245
Income tax benefit of employees' stock				
transactions	—	5,929	—	5,929
Repurchases of common stock....................	(2,040)	(15,300)	(21,248)	(36,548)
Net income	—	—	93,402	93,402
Balance, March 31, 1995..........................	51,677	140,191	231,453	371,644
Sale of common stock under employee				
purchase and option plans........................	1,218	16,512	—	16,512
Issuance of common stock in connection				
with acquisition	385	17,232	—	17,232
Income tax benefit of employees' stock				
transactions	—	10,947	—	10,947
Repurchases of common stock....................	(260)	(1,950)	(5,815)	(7,765)
Net income	—	—	103,375	103,375
Balance, March 31, 1996..........................	53,020	$182,932	$329,013	$511,945

See accompanying notes.

example, analyses involving reconstruction and interpretation of business transactions often require the statement of cash flows. The statement of cash flows details cash inflows and outflows related to a company's operating, investing, and financing activities over a period of time. Adaptec's statement of cash flows for 1996, 1995, and 1994 appears in Exhibit 1.5. Adaptec's 1996 cash balance increased by $24,376 million, from $66,835 million to $91,211 million. Of this net cash change, Adaptec's operating activities provided $103,379 million, its investing activities used $95,297 million, and its financing activities provided $16,294 million.

Links between Financial Statements

Financial statements are linked at points in time and across time. These links are portrayed in Exhibit 1.6 using Adaptec's financial statements for 1995–1996. Notice Adaptec's statement of retained earnings is included in

EXHIBIT 1.5   Adaptec Statement of Cash Flows

Consolidated Statements of Cash Flows

IN THOUSANDS

Year Ended March 31	1996	1995	1994
Cash Flows From Operating Activities:			
Net income	$103,375	$ 93,402	$ 58,950
Adjustments to reconcile net income to net cash provided by operating activities:			
Write-off of acquired in-process technology, net of taxes	39,686	—	—
Depreciation and amortization	17,593	15,662	11,489
Provision for doubtful accounts	250	150	2,069
Changes in assets and liabilities:			
Accounts receivable	(30,727)	(1,311)	(13,020)
Inventories	(20,516)	7,228	(5,563)
Prepaid expenses	(8,973)	460	(5,470)
Other assets	(19,111)	(4,107)	(11,478)
Accounts payable	(167)	2,354	(2,781)
Accrued liabilities	21,969	4,251	8,867
Net Cash Provided by Operating Activities	103,379	118,089	43,063
Cash Flows From Investing Activities:			
Purchase of Trillium, Future Domain and Power I/O, net of cash acquired	(31,177)	—	—
Investments in property and equipment	(39,748)	(31,576)	(17,314)
Investments in marketable securities, net	(24,372)	(32,291)	(20,250)
Net Cash Used for Investing Activities	(95,297)	(63,867)	(37,564)
Cash Flows From Financing Activities:			
Proceeds from issuance of common stock	27,459	17,174	13,511
Repurchase of common stock	(7,765)	(36,548)	—
Principal payments on debt	(3,400)	(3,400)	(2,968)
Net Cash Provided by (Used for) Financing Activities	16,294	(22,774)	10,543
Net Increase in Cash and Cash Equivalents	24,376	31,448	16,042
Cash and Cash Equivalents at Beginning of Year	66,835	35,387	19,345
Cash and Cash Equivalents at End of Year	$ 91,211	$ 66,835	$ 35,387

See accompanying notes.

its statement of shareholders' equity. Adaptec began 1996 with the investing and financing amounts reported in the balance sheet on the far left side of Exhibit 1.6. Its investments, comprising both cash ($66,835) and noncash assets ($368,873), totaled $435,708. These investments are financed from both creditors ($64,064) and equity investors, the latter comprising receipts from both stock issuances ($140,191) and retained earnings ($231,453). Adaptec's 1996 operating activities are reported in the middle "column" of Exhibit 1.6. The statement of cash flows reports how operating, investing, and financing activities impact cash. Adaptec's $66,835 cash balance at the beginning of 1996 grew to $91,211 at year-end. This end-of-year cash figure is reported in the year-end balance sheet on the far right side of Exhibit 1.6. Adaptec's net income ($103,375) computed from revenues less expenses is reported in the income statement. The income figure helps explain the change in retained earnings reported in the

ANALYSIS   RESEARCH   INSIGHT   1.1

ACCOUNTING NUMBERS AND STOCK PRICES

Do accounting numbers such as net income explain changes in a company's stock prices? The answer is yes. Evidence from research shows a definite link between the "news" conveyed in net income and the price changes in a company's stock (returns). "Good news" net income is accompanied by positive stock price changes, whereas "bad news" net income is associated with negative price changes. Also, the more good or bad is net income, the greater is the accompanying stock price reaction. Similar evidence exists for other summary financial statement numbers such as book value.

Research also shows us that many factors influence the relation between accounting numbers and stock prices. These include company factors, such as risk, size, leverage, and variability, which decrease the influence of numbers like net income on prices, and factors, such as earnings growth and persistence, which increase their impact. Our analysis must recognize those influences impacting the relevance of accounting numbers for security analysis.

Fundamental analysis research offers guidance in our use of financial statement information for predicting future stock price changes. Evidence indicates financial statements help reveal the permanent and transitory portions of net income. Permanent portions are much more long-lasting in their impact on stock prices and are commensurately of greater magnitude in their influence on prices.

---

statement of retained earnings. Adaptec chooses not to pay cash dividends and, thus, dividends do not affect its Retained Earnings balance. Adaptec's Retained Earnings balance is carried to the shareholders' equity section of its year-end balance sheet.

In sum, Adaptec's balance sheet is a listing of its investing and financing activities at a *point in time*. The three statements of (1) cash flows, (2) income, and (3) shareholders' equity explain changes (typically from operating activities) over a *period of time* in Adaptec's investing and financing activities. Every transaction captured in these three latter statements impacts the balance sheet. Examples are revenues and expenses affecting net income and subsequently carried to retained earnings, or cash transactions in the statement of cash flows and summarized by the cash balance on the balance sheet, or all revenue and expense accounts affecting one or more balance sheet accounts. Consequently, financial statements are inherently linked: point-in-time balance sheets are explained by the period-of-time income statement, statement of cash flows, and statement of shareholders' equity.

EXHIBIT 1.6   Financial Statement Links for Adaptec

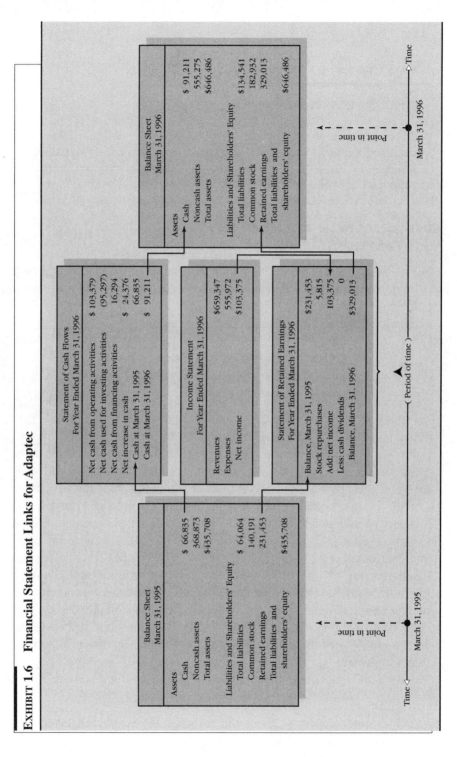

Balance Sheet
March 31, 1995

Assets
Cash $ 66,835
Noncash assets   368,873
Total assets $435,708

Liabilities and shareholders' Equity
Total liabilities $ 64,064
Common stock   140,191
Retained earnings   231,453
Total liabilities and
    shareholders' equity $435,708

Statement of Cash Flows
For Year Ended March 31, 1996

Net cash from operating activities $ 103,379
Net cash used for investing activities   (95,297)
Net cash from financing activities   16,294
Net increase in cash $ 24,376
Cash at March 31, 1995   66,835
Cash at March 31, 1996 $ 91,211

Income Statement
For Year Ended March 31, 1996

Revenues $659,347
Expenses   555,972
Net income $103,375

Statement of Retained Earnings
For Year Ended March 31, 1996

Balance, March 31, 1995 $231,453
Stock repurchases   5,815
Add: net income   103,375
Less: cash dividends   0
Balance, March 31, 1996 $329,013

Balance Sheet
March 31, 1996

Assets
Cash $ 91,211
Noncash assets   555,275
Total assets $646,486

Liabilities and Shareholders' Equity
Total liabilities $134,541
Common stock   182,932
Retained earnings   329,013
Total liabilities and
    shareholders' equity $646,486

Time

March 31, 1995   Point in time

(Period of time)

Point in time   March 31, 1996   Time

25

ANALYSIS VIEWPOINT

YOU ARE THE INVESTOR

You are interested in buying Adaptec stock. Your review of Adaptec's financial statements reveals a near 25 percent decline in net cash flow for 1996, while net income increased by 10 percent. Based on your review of these statements, are you interested in buying Adaptec stock?

INFORMATION ACCOMPANYING FINANCIAL STATEMENTS

Formal financial statements are not the sole output of a financial reporting system. Additional information is communicated by companies through a number of resources. A thorough financial statement analysis involves examining these additional sources of information.

Management's Discussion and Analysis (MD&A)

Companies with publicly traded debt and equity securities are required by the Securities and Exchange Commission to provide a Management's Discussion and Analysis (MD&A) in their financial reports. The MD&A section reviews a company's financial condition and results of operations. Management must highlight any favorable or unfavorable trends and identify significant events and uncertainties affecting the company's liquidity, capital resources, and results of operations. They must also disclose prospective information involving material events and uncertainties known to cause reported financial information to not be indicative of future operating activities or of future financial condition. The MD&A also reports qualitative information regarding the effects of inflation and changing prices if material to financial statement trends. Companies are encouraged, but not required, to provide forward-looking information. The MD&A for Adaptec's 1996 financial statements includes a year-by-year analysis along with an analysis of its liquidity and capital resources by business activity (see Supplement A).

Management Report

A management report sets out the responsibilities of management in preparing a company's financial statements. The purposes of this report are (1) to reinforce senior management's responsibilities for the company's financial and internal control system, and (2) to reinforce the shared roles of management, directors, and auditor in preparing financial statements. Adaptec's Report of Management highlights the role of its Audit Committee of the Board of Directors in providing assurance on the integrity of its financial statements.

Auditor Report

An external auditor is an independent certified public accountant hired by management to assess whether the company's financial statements are prepared in conformity with generally accepted accounting principles. Auditors provide an important check on financial statements prior to their public release. There are four types of auditor opinions:

- **Unqualified (clean) opinion.** Financial statements "present fairly" (according to accepted accounting practices) a company's financial performance and position.
- **Qualified opinion.** This is an unqualified opinion except for the item(s) relating to the qualification.
- **Adverse opinion.** Financial statements do not "present fairly" a company's financial performance and position.
- **Disclaimer of opinion.** Audit is insufficient in scope to render an opinion.

Sound financial statement analysis requires a review of the auditor's report to ascertain whether the company received an unqualified opinion before conducting any analysis. Adaptec's Report of Independent Accountants, prepare by Price Waterhouse LLP, is shown in Exhibit 1.7. Adaptec received an unqualified opinion. The auditor's report (as is typical) stresses that with "reasonable," but not complete, assurance the financial statements are free of material misstatement, and in the auditor's opinion these statements "present fairly" the financial position of Adaptec.

Explanatory Notes

Explanatory notes accompanying financial reports play an integral role in financial statement analysis. Notes are a means of communicating additional information regarding items included and excluded from the body of the statements. It is the often technical nature of notes that creates a need for a certain level of accounting sophistication on the part of financial

EXHIBIT 1.7   Adaptec's Auditor Report

Report of Independent Accountants

To the Board of Directors and
Shareholders of Adaptec, Inc.:

In our opinion, the accompanying consolidated balance sheets and the related consolidated statements of operations, of cash flows and of shareholders' equity present fairly, in all material respects, the financial position of Adaptec, Inc. and its subsidiaries at March 31, 1996 and 1995, and the results of their operations and their cash flows for the years then ended in conformity with generally accepted accounting principles. These financial statements are the responsibility of the Company's management; our responsibility is to express an opinion on these financial statements based on our audits. We conducted our audits of these statements in accordance with generally accepted auditing standards which require that we plan and perform the audit to obtain reasonable assurance about whether the financial statements are free of material misstatement. An audit includes examining, on a test basis, evidence supporting the amounts and disclosures in the financial statements, assessing the accounting principles used and significant estimates made by management, and evaluating the overall financial statement presentation. We believe that our audits provide a reasonable basis for the opinion expressed above. The financial statements of Adaptec, Inc. as of and for the year ended March 31, 1994 were audited by other independent accountants whose report dated April 25, 1994 expressed an unqualified opinion on those statements.

San Jose, California
April 22, 1996

statement users. Explanatory notes include information on (1) accounting principles and methods employed, (2) detailed disclosures regarding individual financial statement elements, (3) commitments and contingencies, (4) business combinations, (5) transactions with related parties, (6) stock option plans, (7) legal proceedings, and (8) significant customers.

Supplementary Information

Certain supplemental schedules required by accounting regulatory agencies appear in either the notes to financial statements or, in the case of companies with publicly traded securities, in exhibits to Form 10-K filed with the Securities and Exchange Commission (SEC). Supplemental schedules include information on (1) business segment data, (2) export sales, (3) marketable securities, (4) valuation accounts, (5) short-term borrowings, and (6) quarterly financial data. Several supplemental schedules appear in the 1996 annual report of Adaptec. An example is the information on segment operations included as note 9 to Adaptec's financial statements. The SEC is responsible for overseeing financial reporting to external users for companies with publicly traded securities. It requires annual financial reports to be audited by independent auditors. Companies must file annual and quarterly reports with the SEC. Annual reports are referred to as **Form 10-K reports,** and much of this information overlaps with annual reports to shareholders. Quarterly reports are known as **10-Q reports.** Additional SEC filings are required if certain events occur. Examples include a **Form 8-K report** if a company changes auditors and a *registration statement* if a company issues new shares. Much of this information is available at the SEC's [http://www.sec.gov/edgarhp.htm] web site.

Social Responsibility Reports

Companies increasingly recognize their need for social responsibility. This recognition is not simply altruistic but, rather, translates often into meaningful financial benefits. In our analysis of financial statements, we scrutinize companies on their social responsibility. Our findings are based on management's commitment to employees, its integrity, its devotion to human resource development, and many nonquantifiable (yet relevant) analysis factors. Adaptec's social responsibility report is shown in Exhibit 1.8. This report declares Adaptec's commitment to "the importance of giving back to the communities where Wally and Molly are growing and learning . . . Adaptec in fiscal 1997 is making a special $150,000 donation to support literacy and reading programs to help children get a head start on their futures." While social responsibility reports like Adaptec's are increasing, there is as yet no standard format or accepted practice in this area.

Proxy Statements

Shareholder votes are solicited for electing directors and for votes on corporate actions such as mergers, acquisitions, and authorization of securities. A **proxy** is a means whereby a shareholder authorizes another person(s) to act for him/her at a meeting of shareholders. A **proxy statement** contains information necessary for shareholders in voting on matters

EXHIBIT 1.8   Adaptec's Social Responsibility Report

Adaptec in the Community

PROVIDING OPPORTUNITIES

Wally and Molly are the information users of tomorrow. But they are the children of today, and often children need our help. Adaptec believes in the importance of giving back to the communities where Wally and Molly are growing and learning. In fiscal 1996 we helped the groups and agencies below in their efforts to make our world more livable for children.

Through our commitment to children, Adaptec in fiscal 1997 is making a special $150,000 donation to support literacy and reading programs to help children get a head start on their futures.

The Children's Health Council
Make-A-Wish Foundation
United Way
The Tech Museum of Innovation
Leavey School of Business, Santa Clara University
Reading Research Center, Mission San Jose Elementary School
Junior Achievement
Second Harvest Food Bank
Ronald McDonald House
Leukemia Society of America
Adaptec Scholarship
Indian Peaks Elementary School
Milpitas High School
San Jose State University
Bellarmine College Preparatory
Girl Scouts of Santa Clara County
Los Altos Educational Foundation
Keys School

for which the proxy is solicited. Proxy statements contain a wealth of information regarding a company including: identity of shareholders owning 5 or more percent of outstanding shares, biographical information on the board of directors, compensation arrangements with officers and directors, employee benefit plans, and certain transactions with officers and directors.

PREVIEW OF FINANCIAL STATEMENT ANALYSIS

In analyzing financial statements, users have a variety of tools available from which to select those best suited to their specific needs. In this sec-

ANALYSIS VIEWPOINT

YOU ARE THE COMMUNITY ACTIVIST

You are an activist scrutinizing a company's commitment to its community. What can you learn about a company's community commitment from an analysis of financial statements?

tion, we introduce certain tools of analysis and apply them to Adaptec's 1996 annual report including: comparative financial statement analysis, common-size financial statement analysis, and ratio analysis. We briefly discuss other, more specialized, analyses (described more fully in latter parts of the book).

Building Blocks of Analysis

Whatever approach to financial statement analysis taken and whatever methods used, we always examine one or more important aspects of a company's financial condition and results of operations. Our financial analysis, motivated by various objectives, falls within any or all of the six areas of inquiry below—in any sequence and with the degree of relative emphasis required under the circumstances. These six areas of inquiry and investigation are the building blocks of financial statement analysis.

- **Short-term liquidity.** A company's ability to meet short-term obligations.
- **Funds flow.** Future availability and disposition of cash.
- **Capital structure and long-term solvency.** A company's ability to generate future revenues and meet long-term obligations.
- **Return on investment.** A company's ability to provide financial rewards sufficient to attract and retain suppliers of financing.
- **Asset utilization.** Asset intensity in generating revenues to reach a sufficient level of profitability.
- **Operating performance.** A company's success at maximizing revenues and minimizing expenses from long-run operating activities.

Each of these six areas of inquiry, and the tools used in analyzing them, receive emphasis throughout the book.

Comparative Financial Statement Analysis

Financial statement users conduct comparative financial statement analysis by setting consecutive balance sheets, income statements, or statements of cash flows side by side, and reviewing changes in individual categories on a year-to-year or multiyear basis. The most important item revealed by comparative financial statement analysis is *trend*. A comparison of statements over several years reveals direction, speed, and extent of a trend(s). Analysis also compares trends in related items. For example, a year-to-year 10 percent sales increase accompanied with a 20 percent increase in freight-out costs requires investigation and explanation. Similarly, a 15 percent increase in accounts receivable and a sales increase of only 10 percent warrants investigation into the reasons for this difference in the rate of increase. Comparative financial statement analysis is also referred to as *horizontal* analysis given the left-right (or right-left) movement of our eyes as they review comparative statements. Two techniques of comparative analysis are especially popular: year-to-year change analysis and index-number trend series analysis.

Year-to-Year Change Analysis

Comparing financial statements over relatively short time periods—two to three years—is performed with analysis of year-to-year changes in line items. A year-to-year change analysis for short time periods is manageable and understandable. It has the advantage of presenting changes in absolute dollar amounts as well as in percentages. Both change analyses are relevant since different dollar sizes of bases in computing percent changes can yield large percent changes inconsistent with their actual importance. For example, a 50 percent change from a base figure of $1,000 is generally less significant than the same percent change from a base of $100,000. Thus, reference to dollar amounts is necessary to retain a proper perspective and to make valid inferences on the relative importance of changes.

    Computation of year-to-year changes is straightforward. However, a few clarifying rules should be borne in mind. When a negative amount appears in the base and a positive amount in the next period (or vice versa), we cannot compute a meaningful percent change. Also, when there is no figure for the base year, no percent change is computable. And, when an item has a value in the base year and none in the next period, the decrease is 100 percent. Each of these points is underscored in Illustration 1.1.

Illustration 1.1

Complications and how we confront them in an analysis of changes are depicted under four scenarios:

			Change Analysis	
Scenario Item	*Year 1*	*Year 2*	*Amount*	*Percent*
Net income (loss)	$(4,500)	$1,500	$ 6,000	—
Tax expense	2,000	(1,000)	(3,000)	—
Notes payable	—	8,000	8,000	—
Notes receivable	10,000	—	(10,000)	(100%)

Comparative financial statement analysis typically reports both the cumulative total for the period under investigation and the average (or median) for the period. Comparing yearly amounts with an average computed over a number of years highlights unusual happenings for a particular period, as average values smooth out erratic or unusual fluctuations.

Exhibit 1.9 reports a year-to-year comparative analysis using Adaptec's 1995 and 1996 income statements. While net revenues increase by 41.4 percent, the cost of revenues increases by only 34.2 percent, resulting in a 47.1 percent boost in gross profit. Despite this boost in gross profit, income from operations increases by only 7.1 percent. A major reason for this relatively small income increase is Adaptec's write-off of in-process technology associated with its acquisition of several businesses.

Index-Number Trend Series Analysis

Comparing financial statements covering more than two or three periods using year-to-year change analysis is often cumbersome. An excellent procedure to effect longer-term trend comparisons is index-number trend series analysis. Analyzing data using index-number trend analysis requires choosing a base year, for all items, with a preselected index number usually set to 100. Since a base year represents a frame of reference for all comparisons, it is best to choose a "normal" year with regard to business conditions. One of the earliest years in the series often usefully serves this purpose, yet, if it is atypical, choose another year. As in computing year-to-year percentage changes, certain changes, like those from negative to positive amounts, cannot be expressed by means of index numbers. Also, all index numbers are computed by reference to the base year. See Illustration 1.2 for an example.

EXHIBIT 1.9   Adaptec's Comparative Income Statements

	1996	1995	Change ($)	Change (%)
Net revenues	$659,347	$466,194	$193,153	41.4%
Cost of revenues	275,939	205,596	70,343	34.2
Gross profit	$383,408	$260,598	$122,810	47.1
Operating expenses:				
Research and development	87,628	60,848	26,780	44.0
Sales and marketing	81,548	58,737	22,811	38.8
General and administrative	35,784	23,229	12,555	54.0
Write-off of technology	52,313	0	52,313	—
Income from operations	$126,135	$117,784	$ 8,351	7.1
Interest income	12,694	7,932	4,762	60.0
Interest expense	(840)	(1,179)	(339)	(28.0)
Income before income taxes	$137,989	$124,537	$ 13,452	10.8
Provision for income taxes	34,614	31,135	3,479	11.2
Net income	$103,375	$ 93,402	$ 9,973	10.7%

Illustration 1.2

Century Technology's cash balance (in $ thousands) at December 31, Year 1 (the base year), is $12,000. The cash balance at December 31, Year 2, is $18,000. Using 100 as the index number for Year 1, the index number for Year 2 equals 150 and is computed as:

$$\frac{\text{Current year balance}}{\text{Base year balance}} \times 100 = \frac{\$18,000}{\$12,000} \times 100 = 150$$

The cash balance of Century Technology at December 31, Year 3, is $9,000. The index for Year 3 is 75 and is computed as:

$$\frac{\$9,000}{\$12,000} \times 100 = 75$$

When using index numbers, we compute percent changes by reference to the base year. The change in cash balance between Year 1 and Year 2 is 50 percent (index 150 − index 100), and is easily inferred from the index numbers. However, the change from Year 2 to Year 3 is not 75 percent (150 − 75), as a direct comparison might suggest, but rather is 50 percent (i.e., $9,000/$18,000). This latter computation involves computing the Year 2 to Year 3 change by reference to the Year 2 balance. The percent change is, however, computable using index numbers only, for example, 75/150 = 0.50, or a change of 50 percent.

In conducting index-number trend analysis, we need not analyze every item in financial statements. Rather, we should attempt to eliminate insignificant items. We should also exercise care in using index-number trend comparisons because of certain weaknesses attributed to changes in company and industry factors. In assessing changes in *current* financial condition, comparative statements of cash flows are often useful. An index-number trend comparison is also useful in comparing changes in the *composition* of working capital items over years.

Interpretation of percent changes, including those using index-number trend series, must be made with an awareness of potentially inconsistent applications of accounting principles over time. Where possible, we adjust for these inconsistencies. Also, the longer the time period for comparison, the more distortive are effects of price-level changes (Supplement C considers these effects). An important outcome of trend analysis is its power in conveying insight into management's philosophies, policies, and motivations (conscious or otherwise) underlying the changes revealed. The more diverse the economic environments comprising the periods of analysis, the better our picture of how a company deals with adversity and takes advantage of opportunities.

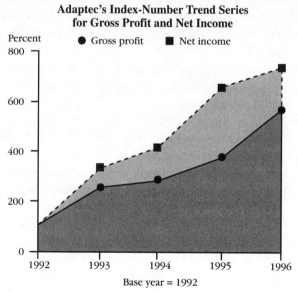

**Adaptec's Index-Number Trend Series
for Gross Profit and Net Income**

Percent   ● Gross profit   ■ Net income

Base year = 1992

Source: Annual reports.

EXHIBIT 1.10   Adaptec's Index-Number Trend Series (base year 1992)

	1996	1995	1994	1993	1992
Net revenues	439	310	248	207	100
Cost of revenues	326	243	224	206	100
Gross profit	583	396	278	209	100
Operating expenses:					
Research and development	500	347	228	150	100
Sales and marketing	382	275	216	152	100
General and administrative	340	221	184	148	100
Income from operations	769	718	470	383	100
Net income	707	639	403	338	100
Total assets	466	314	259	204	100
Shareholders' equity	439	319	255	193	100

Index-number trend analysis for selected financial statement items of Adaptec are reported in Exhibit 1.10. Data used in preparing this analysis are taken from the Selected Financial Data in Adaptec's 1996 annual report. We see that net revenues are 439 percent compared to the period of analysis, while gross profit is an even greater 583 percent. The largest increase among operating expenses is the 500 percent for research and development (R&D). While this rate of increase exceeds that of net revenues, this is not necessarily cause for concern. The advanced computer technology business requires R&D for continual innovation and improvement. A slower rate of increase in R&D, while providing higher short-term earnings, is likely at the expense of long-term earnings. Total assets are 466 percent at the end of this period, and the 439 percent value for shareholders' equity indicates Adaptec has achieved asset growth without reliance on excessive borrowing.

Data in Exhibit 1.10 use 1992 as the base year. To illustrate the sensitivity of inferences to the choice of base year, Exhibit 1.11 reports similar indices using 1993 as the base year. Notice growth rates for net revenues and gross profit are less than one-half those reported in Exhibit 1.10, implying 1992 might be a less than representative starting point. In this regard, consider growth rates in selling and administrative expenses. In Exhibit 1.10, growth rates in sales and marketing expenses (382%) and general and administrative expenses (340%) are lower than the growth in net revenues. Yet in Exhibit 1.11, growth rates in sales and marketing expenses (251%) and general and administrative expenses (230%) exceed

Exhibit 1.11   Adaptec's Index-Number Trend Series (base year 1993)

	1996	1995	1994	1993
Net revenues	212	150	120	100
Cost of revenues	158	118	109	100
Gross profit	280	190	133	100
Operating expenses:				
Research and development	333	231	152	100
Sales and marketing	251	181	142	100
General and administrative	230	149	125	100
Income from operations	201	188	123	100
Net income	209	189	119	100
Total assets	229	154	127	100
Shareholders' equity	227	165	132	100

the 212 percent value for net revenues. This simple exercise emphasizes the importance of proper base year selection.

Common-Size Financial Statement Analysis

Financial statement analysis benefits from knowing the proportion of a total group or subgroup an item represents. In analyzing a balance sheet, it is common to express total assets, liabilities, and capital each as 100 percent, and individual items within these categories as a percent of their respective total. In analyzing an income statement, net revenues is commonly set at 100 percent with other income statement items expressed as a percent of net revenues. Since the sum of these individual items totals 100 percent, this analysis technique is said to yield **common-size financial statements.** This technique is also referred to as **vertical analysis** given the up-down (or down-up) movement of our eyes as they review the statements. Common-size financial statement analysis is an inquiry into the internal structure of financial statements. In analyzing a balance sheet, a structural analysis focuses on two elements:

- Sources of financing, including the distribution of financing among current liabilities, noncurrent liabilities, and equity capital.
- Composition of investments, including current and noncurrent assets.

Common-size balance sheet analysis is often extended to examine the proportions comprising particular subgroups. For example, in assessing liquidity of current assets, it is often important to know what proportion of current assets is comprised of inventories, and not simply what proportion inventories are of total assets. Common-size income statement analysis is often of even greater importance. An income statement readily lends itself to a common-size analysis, where each item is related to a key quantity (e.g., sales). To varying degrees, sales level affects each expense, and it is instructive for our analysis to know what proportion of sales is absorbed by various expense items. An exception is income tax expense, which is related to pre-tax income, and not sales.

Temporal (time) comparisons of common-size statements of a company are valuable in showing changing proportions of components within groups of assets, liabilities, expenses, and other financial statement categories. Illustration 1.3 supports this point. Nevertheless, we must exercise care in interpreting changes and trends.

Illustration 1.3

Account balances for patents and total assets of MicroDisc, Inc., for the most recent three years are:

	Year 3	Year 2	Year 1
Patents	$ 50,000	$ 50,000	$ 50,000
Total assets	$1,000,000	$750,000	$500,000
Patents/Total assets	5%	6.67%	10%

While the dollar amounts of patents remain unchanged during this period, increases in total assets progressively reduce patents as a percent of total assets. Since this percent varies with either the change in the absolute dollar amount of an item or the change in the total balance for its category, interpretation of common-size analysis requires examination of both actual figures and the basis for their computation.

Common-size statements are especially useful for intercompany comparisons because financial statements of different companies are recast in common-size format. Comparison of a company's common-size statements with competitors' or industry common-size statistics alerts our attention to differences in account structure or distribution; the reasons for these should be explored and understood. Yet common-size statements fail to reflect the relative sizes of companies under analysis. A comparison of selected common-size statement items of Campbell Soup Company to industry statistics is part of the Comprehensive Case at the end of the book.

Adaptec reports a common-size income statement in its 1996 annual report under the heading Results of Operations. At least two items are noteworthy. First, cost of revenues is decreasing as a percent of sales. Second, the write-off of acquired technology amounts to 8 percent of 1996 sales. Common-size balance sheets of Adaptec appear in Exhibit 1.12. A major change is the increase in other assets from 4.0 percent to 13.7 percent of total assets. Absent this increase, total current assets as a percent of total assets is similar to prior years. The financing side of the balance sheet reveals an increase in current liabilities, primarily due to notes payable. This, in turn, caused total liabilities to increase from 14.7 percent to 20.8 percent of total assets.

EXHIBIT 1.12   Adaptec's Common-Size Balance Sheets

	1996	1995
Current assets:		
Cash and cash equivalents	14.1%	15.3%
Marketable securities	31.6	41.3
Accounts receivable, net of allowance	13.8	13.0
Inventories	8.5	7.3
Prepaid expenses and other	3.9	3.6
Total current assets	71.9%	80.5%
Property and equipment, net	14.4	15.5
Other assets	13.7	4.0
Total assets	100.0%	100.0%
Current liabilities:		
Current portion of long-term debt	0.5%	0.8%
Note payable	7.1	0.0
Accounts payable	3.7	5.0
Accrued liabilities	8.8	7.1
Total current liabilities	20.1%	12.9%
Long-term debt	0.7	1.8
Common stock	28.3	32.2
Retained earnings	50.9	53.1
Total shareholders' equity	79.2%	85.3%
Total liabilities and equity	100.0%	100.0%

Ratio Analysis of Financial Statements

Ratios are among the most popular and widely used tools of financial analysis. Yet their function is often misunderstood and, consequently, their significance often overrated. A ratio expresses a mathematical relation between two quantities. A ratio of 200 to 100 is expressed as 2:1, or simply 2. While computation of a ratio is a simple arithmetic operation, its interpretation is far more complex. To be meaningful, a ratio must refer to an economically important relation. For example, there is a direct and crucial relation between an item's sales price and its cost. Accordingly, the ratio of cost of goods sold to sales is a significant one. In contrast, there is no obvious relation between freight costs and the balance of marketable securities.

Ratios are tools providing us with clues and symptoms of underlying conditions. Ratios, properly interpreted, identify areas requiring further investigation. Analysis of a ratio reveals important relations and bases of comparison in uncovering conditions and trends difficult to detect by inspecting individual components comprising the ratio. Ratios, like other analysis tools, are future oriented, and we must adjust the factors affecting a ratio for their probable future trend and magnitude. We must also assess factors potentially influencing future ratios. Consequently, the usefulness of ratios depends on our skillful interpretation of them, and is the most challenging aspect of ratio analysis. See, for instance, Illustration 1.4.

Illustration 1.4

Consider interpreting the ratio of gasoline consumption to mileage driven, referred to as miles per gallon (mpg). In comparing the ratio of gas consumption to mileage driven, person X claims to have the superior performing vehicle, that is, 28 mpg compared to person Y's 20 mpg. Is person X's vehicle superior?

Assuming they drive identical cars, there are several factors affecting gas consumption requiring analysis before we can properly interpret these ratios and judge whose performance is better: (1) weight of load driven, (2) type of terrain, (3) city or country driving, (4) grade of fuel used, and (5) travel speed of cars. Numerous as these factors influencing gas consumption are, evaluating a gas consumption ratio is, nevertheless, a more simple analysis than evaluating most financial statement ratios. This is because of the interrelations in business variables and the complexity of factors affecting them.

Factors Affecting Ratios

Beyond the internal operating conditions affecting a company's ratios, we must be aware of the effects of economic events, industry factors, management policies, and accounting methods. Our discussion of accounting methods later in the book highlights their influence on the measurements comprising ratios. Any weaknesses in accounting measurements impact the effectiveness of ratios. For instance, historical cost values are sometimes less relevant to a decision than current market values.

Prior to computing ratios, or similar measures like trend indices or percent relations, we must confirm that the numbers underlying their computation are valid and consistent. For example, when inventories are valued using LIFO and prices are increasing, the current ratio is understated because LIFO inventories (the numerator) are understated. Similarly, certain pension liabilities are often unrecorded and disclosed in notes only. We normally want to recognize these liabilities when computing ratios like debt to equity. We must also want to recognize that when we make adjustments for one ratio, consistency often requires they be made for other ratios. For example, the omission of a pension liability implies understated pension expenses. Accordingly, net income numbers often require adjustment in ratio computation. We need also remember the usefulness of ratios depends on the quality of the numbers in their computation. When a company's internal accounting controls or other governance and monitoring mechanisms are unreliable in producing credible figures, the resulting ratios are equally unreliable.

Ratio Interpretation

Ratios must be interpreted with care since factors affecting the numerator can correlate with those affecting the denominator. For instance, companies can improve the ratio of operating expenses to sales by reducing costs that stimulate sales (e.g., research and development). If this cost reduction ultimately yields long-term declines in sales or market share, a seemingly short-term improvement in profitability can significantly damage a company's future prospects and must be interpreted accordingly. We should remember many ratios have important variables in common with other ratios. Consequently, it is not necessary for us to compute all possible ratios to analyze a situation. Ratios, like most techniques in financial analysis, are not significant in themselves and are interpretable only in comparison with (1) prior ratios, (2) predetermined standards, or (3) ratios of competitors. The variability of a ratio over time is often as important as its trend.

Illustration of Ratio Analysis

We often compute numerous ratios using a company's financial statements. Some ratios have general application in financial analysis, while others are unique to specific circumstances or industries. Exhibit 1.13 lists selected ratios having general applicability for most businesses; the ratios are grouped by major financial analysis objectives. Data used in this illustration are from Adaptec's 1996 annual report.

Several ratios are applicable in assessing **short-term liquidity.** Most common is the *current ratio*—reflecting current assets available to satisfy current liabilities. Adaptec's current ratio of 3.57 implies there are $3.57 of current assets available to meet each $1 of currently maturing obligations. A more stringent test of short-term liquidity, the *acid test ratio,* uses only the most liquid current assets (cash, short-term investments, accounts receivable). Adaptec has $2.95 of liquid assets to cover each $1 of current liabilities. We also assess short-term liquidity by estimating the length of time needed for conversion of receivables and inventories to cash. Adaptec's *collection period* for receivables is approximately 40 days, and there are approximately 57 days between production and sale of inventories. These ratios together indicate an operating (or cash-to-cash) cycle of 97 (40 + 57) days.

To assess Adaptec's financing, we examine its **capital structure** and **long-term solvency.** The *debt-to-capital ratio* shows 20.8 percent of assets are financed by creditors, or 79.2 percent from equity investors. The *long-term debt to equity ratio* is 0.8 percent, highlighting Adaptec's greater reliance on short-term debt. The *times interest earned ratio* indicates over $165 of earnings is available to cover each $1 of interest. These ratios are especially reassuring for a credit analysis.

There are two popular ratios for assessing different aspects of **return on investment.** Adaptec's *return on total assets* of 19.21 percent implies a $1 asset investment generates 19.21¢ of earnings before after-tax interest. But shareholders are especially interested in management's performance using equity capital. Adaptec's *return on equity capital* of 23.4 percent is impressive. **Operating performance** ratios often link income statement line items to sales, and are not unlike results from common-size income statement analysis. Several operating ratios for Adaptec are reported in Exhibit 1.13. **Asset utilization** ratios, relating sales to different asset categories, are important determinants of return on investment. Adaptec's large working capital (i.e., the excess of current assets over current liabilities) is a potential hindrance to larger returns.

EXHIBIT 1.13   Financial Statement Ratio Computations for Adaptec

---

Short-Term Liquidity Ratios

$$\text{Current ratio} = \frac{\text{Current assets}}{\text{Current liabilities}} = \frac{\$465,280}{\$130,291} = 3.57$$

$$\text{Acid test ratio} = \frac{\begin{array}{c}\text{Cash} + \text{Cash equivalents} + \\ \text{Marketable securities} + \text{Accounts receivable}\end{array}}{\text{Current liabilities}}$$

$$= \frac{\$91,211 + \$204,283 + \$89,487}{\$130,291} = 2.95$$

$$\text{Collection period} = \frac{\text{Average accounts receivable}}{\text{Credit sales} \div 360} = \frac{(\$56,495 + \$89,487) \div 2}{\$659,347 \div 360} = 40 \text{ days}$$

$$\text{Days to sell inventory} = \frac{\text{Average inventory}}{\text{Cost of revenues} \div 360} = \frac{(\$31,712 + \$55,028) \div 2}{\$275,939 \div 360} = 57 \text{ days}$$

Capital Structure and Solvency Ratios

$$\text{Total debt to total capital} = \frac{\text{Current liabilities} + \text{Long-term liabilities}}{\text{Equity capital} + \text{Total liabilities}}$$

$$= \frac{\$130,291 + \$4,250}{\$511,945 + \$130,291 + \$4,250} = 20.81\%$$

$$\text{Long-term debt to equity} = \frac{\text{Long-term liabilities}}{\text{Equity capital}} = \frac{\$4,250}{\$511,945} = 0.83\%$$

$$\text{Times interest earned} = \frac{\text{Income before income taxes} + \text{Interest expense}}{\text{Interest expense}}$$

$$= \frac{\$137,989 + \$840}{\$840} = 165.27$$

Return on Investment Ratios

$$\text{Return on total assets} = \frac{\text{Net income} + \text{Interest expense} (1 - \text{Tax rate})}{\text{Average total assets}}$$

$$= \frac{\$103,375 + \$840(1 - 0.34)}{(\$435,708 + \$646,486) \div 2} = 19.21\%$$

$$\text{Return on common equity} = \frac{\text{Net income}}{\text{Average equity capital}}$$

$$= \frac{\$103,375}{(\$371,644 + \$511,945) \div 2} = 23.4\%$$

continued

Ratio analysis yields valuable insights, as is apparent from our preliminary analysis of Adaptec. We must, however, keep in mind these calculations are based on the numbers reported in Adaptec's annual report. As

EXHIBIT 1.13   *concluded*

Operating Performance Ratios

$$\text{Gross profit ratio} = \frac{\text{Gross profit}}{\text{Net revenues}} = \frac{\$383,408}{\$659,347} = 58.15\%$$

$$\text{Operating profit to sales} = \frac{\text{Income from operations}}{\text{Net revenues}} = \frac{\$126,135}{\$659,347} = 19.13\%$$

$$\text{Pretax profit to sales} = \frac{\text{Income before income taxes}}{\text{Net revenues}} = \frac{\$137,989}{\$659,347} = 20.93\%$$

$$\text{Net income to sales} = \frac{\text{Net income}}{\text{Net revenues}} = \frac{\$103,375}{\$659,347} = 15.68\%$$

Asset Utilization Ratios

$$\text{Sales to cash} = \frac{\text{Net revenues}}{\text{Average cash}} = \frac{\$659,347}{(\$66,835 + \$91,211) \div 2} = 8.34$$

$$\text{Sales to accounts receivable} = \frac{\text{Net revenues}}{\text{Average accounts receivable}}$$
$$= \frac{\$659,347}{(\$56,495 + \$89,487) \div 2} = 9.03$$

$$\text{Sales to inventories} = \frac{\text{Net revenues}}{\text{Average inventories}} = \frac{\$659,347}{(\$31,712 + \$55,028) \div 2} = 15.20$$

$$\text{Sales to working capital} = \frac{\text{Net revenues}}{\text{Average working capital}}$$
$$= \frac{\$659,347}{[(\$350,472 - \$56,414) + (\$465,280 - \$130,291)] \div 2} = 2.10$$

$$\text{Sales to fixed assets} = \frac{\text{Net revenues}}{\text{Average fixed assets}} = \frac{\$659,347}{(\$67,863 + \$92,778) \div 2} = 8.21$$

$$\text{Sales to total assets} = \frac{\text{Net revenues}}{\text{Average assets}} = \frac{\$659,347}{(\$435,708 + \$646,486) \div 2} = 1.22$$

Market Measures

$$\text{Price to earnings ratio} = \frac{\text{Market price per share}}{\text{Earnings per share}} = \frac{\$48.25 \div 2}{\$1.89} = 25.53$$

$$\text{Earnings yield} = \frac{\text{Earnings per share}}{\text{Market price per share}} = \frac{\$1.89}{\$48.25 \div 2} = 3.92\%$$

$$\text{Dividend yield} = \frac{\text{Dividends per share}}{\text{Market price per share}} = \frac{0}{\$48.25 \div 2} = 0\%$$

$$\text{Dividend payout ratio} = \frac{\text{Dividends per share}}{\text{Earnings per share}} = \frac{0}{\$1.89} = 0\%$$

$$\text{Price to book ratio} = \frac{\text{Market price per share}}{\text{Book value per share}} = \frac{\$48.25}{\$511,945 \div 53,020} = 5.00$$

we stress throughout this book, our ability to draw useful insights and make valid intercompany comparisons is greatly enhanced by our skill in *adjusting* reported numbers *prior to* inclusion in these analyses.

Specialized Analysis Tools

Beyond the multipurpose tools of financial statement analysis already discussed, we have available a variety of special-purpose tools. Special-purpose tools focus on specific financial statements or segments of statements, or they concentrate on a particular industry (e.g., occupancy-capacity analysis for hotels, hospitals, or airlines). They include cash forecasts, analysis of cash flows, statements of variation in gross profit, and break-even analysis. We describe each of these tools later in the book.

ANALYSIS IN AN EFFICIENT CAPITAL MARKET

Capital Market Efficiency

The **efficient market hypothesis,** or EMH for short, deals with the reaction of market prices to financial and other data. The EMH has its origins in the **random walk hypothesis.** This hypothesis asserts that the size and direction of the next stock price change, at any point in time, is random. There are three common forms of this hypothesis. The *weak form* EMH asserts that prices reflect fully the information contained in historical price movements. The *semistrong form* EMH asserts that prices reflect fully all publicly available information. The *strong form* EMH asserts that prices reflect *all* information including "inside" information. There is considerable research on EMH. Early evidence so strongly supported both weak and semistrong form EMH that efficiency of capital markets became a maintained or generally accepted hypothesis. More recent research, however, questions the generality of EMH. A number of stock price anomalies have been uncovered suggesting investors can earn excess returns using "simple trading strategies." Nevertheless, as a first approximation, current stock price is a reasonable estimate of company value.

Market Efficiency Implications
for Financial Statement Analysis

EMH assumes there exist competent and well-informed analysts using tools of analysis like those described in this book. It also assumes analysts are continually evaluating and acting on the regular stream of information entering the marketplace. Yet extreme proponents of EMH claim that if all information is instantly reflected in market prices, attempting to reap consistent advantages through financial statement analysis is futile. This position presents a paradox. On one hand, financial statement analysts are assumed capable in keeping our security markets efficient, yet these same analysts arguably fail to recognize their efforts to yield excess returns are futile. Moreover, should analysts suddenly realize their efforts are futile, the efficiency of our market ceases.

Several factors might explain this apparent paradox. Foremost among them is that EMH is built on aggregate, rather than individual, investor behavior. Focusing on macro- (or aggregate) behavior highlights average performance but ignores or masks individual performance based on ability, determination, and ingenuity, as well as superior individual timing in acting on information. Few doubt that important information travels fast, encouraged by the magnitude of financial stakes involved. Nor do we doubt securities markets are rapid processors of information. Indeed, we contend the speed and efficiency of our market are evidence of analysts at work, motivated by personal rewards.

EMH's alleged implication for the futility of financial statement analysis fails to recognize an essential difference between information and its proper interpretation. That is, even if all information available at a given point in time is impounded in security price, price does not necessarily reflect value. A security can be under- or overvalued, depending on the extent of an incorrect interpretation or evaluation of available information by the aggregate market. Market efficiency depends not only on availability of information but also on its correct interpretation. Financial statement analysis is complex and demanding. The spectrum of financial statement users varies from an institutional analyst who concentrates on but a few companies in one industry to an unsophisticated chaser of rumors. All act on information, but surely not with the same insights and competence. A competent analysis of information entering the marketplace requires a sound analytical knowledge base and an **information mosaic**— to fit new information links in the chain of analytical information for evaluation and interpretation. Not all of us possess the ability and preparation to expend efforts and resources needed in producing an information mosaic. The timing aspect also cannot be underestimated in the marketplace. Movement of new information, and its proper interpretation, flows from the well-informed and proficient segment of users to less-informed and inefficient users. This is consistent with a gradual pattern in processing new information.

ANALYSIS RESEARCH INSIGHT 1.2

INFORMATIVENESS OF STOCK PRICES

Are stock prices equally informative across companies? The answer is no. Research shows small companies' stock prices are less informative than those of large companies. This is implied from evidence showing earnings reports of small companies yield larger and more prolonged stock price reactions. This implies earnings are more important in determining stock prices of small firms. This evidence also suggests *all* financial statement information relevant in setting prices is potentially more informative for small companies.

Analysis research indicates financial markets are less able to anticipate information conveyed in financial statements of small companies. This timing difference is likely tied to the lower quality and/or more sporadic disclosure of information about small companies. Research also reveals less accurate and more variable forecasts of financial numbers for small companies. Consequently, analysis and interpretation of small companies' financial statements are likely to demand more time and effort because of limited availability of alternative information.

Resources necessary for competent analysis of equity securities are considerable and imply that certain market segments are more efficient than others. Securities markets for our largest companies are more efficient (informed) because of a following by a greater number of analysts due to potential rewards from information search and analysis compared with smaller, less prominent companies. Extreme proponents of EMH must take care in sweeping generalizations. In the annual report to shareholders of Berkshire Hathaway, chairman and famed investor Warren Buffet expresses amazement that EMH is embraced by many scholars and analysts. This, Buffet maintains, is because by observing correctly that the market is frequently efficient, they conclude incorrectly it is *always* efficient. Buffet declares, "the difference between these propositions is night and day."

We must also remember that the function and purpose of financial statement analysis of equity securities are often construed too narrowly by those who judge usefulness in an efficient market. While the search for over- and undervalued securities is an important function of financial analysis, the importance of assessing risk and avoiding losses in the total framework of business decision making cannot be overemphasized. Examples include credit and lending decisions, forming an audit opinion by the auditor, and valuing companies whose shares are not publicly traded. Prevention of serious losses or risk exposures is at least as important an objective of financial statement analysis as the discovery of misvalued securities. We must also recognize the value of fundamental financial analysis not only as a means of maintaining market efficiency and preserving the integrity of our capital markets, but also as a means by which we as users—having obtained, analyzed, and interpreted information—reap personal rewards. For us, rewards of financial statement analysis, long before its conversion to a "public good," are tangible and potentially large. Our rewards might not be discernible, however, in the performance of investor behavior aggregated to comprise major market segments, such as mutual funds. Instead, they remain as individual, but real, as the efforts expended to produce them. Financial statement analysis does not provide answers to all problems of security analysis or risk assessment. Yet it consistently directs us to the relevant underlying economics of the case at hand. It imposes the discipline of assessing future potentialities against past and present performance, and it is a safeguard against grievous errors of judgment recurringly made by individuals in times of speculative euphoria.

PREVIEW OF THIS BOOK'S ORGANIZATION

This book is organized into eight chapters within two parts. It begins by looking at the environment of financial statement analysis, then at a company's business activities, and, finally, it looks at applying and interpreting financial statement analysis techniques (see Exhibit 1.14). Chapters 1 and 2, or Part One, describe the environmental context within which financial statement analysis occurs. These chapters preview financial statement analysis, describe its accounting and economic environment, and articulate the analysis objectives.

Part Two of this book (Chapters 3 through 8) investigates in great depth the primary areas of emphasis in financial statement analysis, the analytical adjustments to accounting reports, and the contemporary tools and techniques in practice. That is, the books begins by discussing the business and accounting environment of financial statement analysis before describing very specific ratios, tools, techniques, adjustments,

EXHIBIT 1.14   **Organization of the Book**

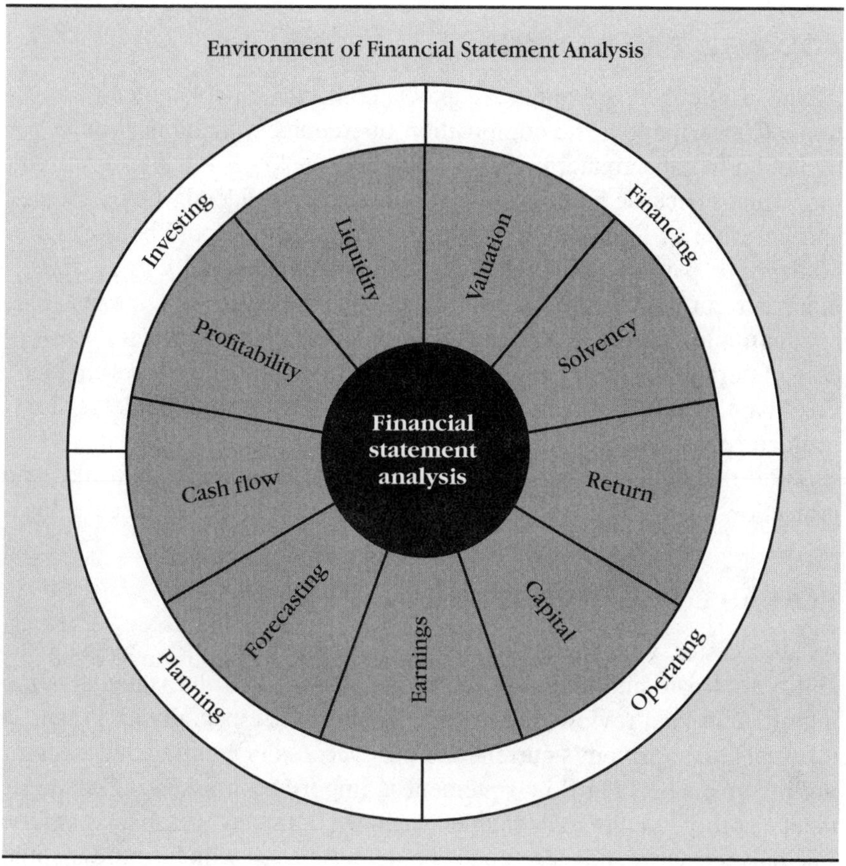

Environment of Financial Statement Analysis

Investing · Liquidity · Valuation · Financing · Profitability · Solvency · **Financial statement analysis** · Cash flow · Return · Forecasting · Earnings · Capital · Planning · Operating

computations, and strategies that users apply to survive and prosper in business.

The book concludes with a Comprehensive Case analysis of the financial statements of Campbell Soup Company. We apply and interpret many of the analysis techniques described in the book. Supplement A reproduces annual report excerpts from two companies that are often referred to in the book: Adaptec and Campbell Soup. Throughout this book, the relation of new material to topics covered in earlier chapters is described to reinforce how all the material comprises an integrated structure for financial statement analysis.

GUIDANCE ANSWERS TO ANALYSIS VIEWPOINTS

YOU ARE THE BANKER

A banker is concerned about Adaptec's ability to satisfy its loan obligations. Concern about the composition of Adaptec's financing sources is twofold. First, the greater is owner financing, the lower is a banker's credit risk. This is because interest must be paid before dividends are distributed and, in event of liquidation, credit financing must be paid before shareholders are paid. Second, creditors are also concerned with Adaptec's other current and future creditor financing. Creditors often write **debt covenants** to restrict a company's future lending, or require collateral in case of default, or limit the amount of dividends payable to shareholders. For Adaptec, nearly 80 percent of financing is from shareholders. Moreover, current assets are more than three times current liabilities, suggesting short-term obligations are adequately covered. Accordingly, with adequate protection from debt covenants, your bank can confidently make the loan.

YOU ARE THE INVESTOR

As an investor, your review of financial statements focuses on Adaptec's ability to create and maintain future net income. All the statements are important in your review. The income statement is especially important as it reveals management's current and past success in creating and sustaining income. The cash flow statement is important in assessing management's ability to meet cash payments and the company's cash availability. The balance sheet shows Adaptec's asset base from which future income is generated, and reports on liabilities and their due dates to creditors. Adaptec's 10 percent increase in earnings is strong, especially considering earnings would be 30 percent larger without the "one-time" write-off of in-process technology. Moreover, Adaptec's 25 percent decline in net cash flow is deceptive since (1) if we exclude the write-off then its operating cash flows increase significantly, and (2) its substantial decrease in cash due to investing activities involves the purchase of various assets having greater future returns possibilities.

YOU ARE THE COMMUNITY ACTIVIST

Analysis of financial statements can reveal important information on a company's commitment to its community. Major contributions to the community are periodically disclosed in notes to the statements. Increasingly, companies are including a social responsibility statement. This statement reports, albeit in summary form, important contributions to the community. Adaptec includes a statement, Adaptec in the Community, at the end of its 1996 annual report highlighting some of its contributions. This information is not taken lightly by investors, creditors, and others with a financial stake. Social responsibility often translates into additional company value attributed to employee morale and dedication, perceived integrity of management, and other subjective factors.

Investment Theory and Financial Statement Analysis

The practice of financial statement analysis is dynamic and challenging. Scholars actively scrutinize this practice and sometimes challenge conventional techniques and analyses. Various theories exist and are designed to provide insight into financial statement analysis processes. We briefly review some of the major theories.

PORTFOLIO THEORY

Considerable work is directed at the problem of portfolio construction. **Portfolio theory** maintains that both *risk and return* must be considered—provided a formal framework for quantifying both exists—and shows how the relation between security risks and returns is accounted for in portfolio construction. In its basic form, portfolio theory begins with the assumption that future security returns are estimable, and then equates risk with the variance of the returns distribution. Under certain assumptions, portfolio theory evidences a linear relation between risk and return. In this framework, it suggests how much of each security to hold in constructing a portfolio. The two-dimensional risk-return approach reinforces to an investor the trade-off between risk and return. Portfolio theory assumes **rational investors** resist increases in risk without commensurate increases in expected returns. Yet, by proper diversification, we lower risk while preserving expected returns. The relation between the risk accepted and the return expected is fundamental to all modern investing and lending decisions. While this may be obvious, it is worth emphasizing the greater the perceived degree of risk of an investment or of a loan, the greater is the required rate of return to compensate for this risk.

CATEGORIES OF RISK

Risk is commonly linked with uncertainty surrounding outcomes of future events. While many investors and creditors make subjective evaluations of risk, scholars boast of statistical measures of risk arising from beta coefficient theory. **Beta coefficient theory** maintains that the total risk associated with an investment is comprised of two elements: **systematic risk,** the risk attributed to prevailing market movements, and **unsystematic risk,** the risk unique to a specific security. This theory offers a quantitative expression of systematic risk (referred to as **beta**). A beta of 1 implies security price moves with the volatility of the market. The higher (lower) a security's beta, the greater (lower) is its expected return. Treasury bills have a beta of zero because they are essentially riskless; that is, they do not fluctuate with the market. A stock with a beta of 1.20 is expected to rise or fall 20 percent faster than (but in the same direction as) the market. A stock with a beta of 0.90 is expected to yield market value changes 10 percent less in amplitude than those of the market. Thus, we expect higher returns from higher beta stocks in a *bull market* but larger than average declines in a *bear market.*

Unsystematic risk is the residual risk unexplained by market movements and, by definition, no unsystematic risk exists for the market. By that same reasoning, there is almost no unsystematic risk in a highly diversified portfolio of stocks. As portfolios become larger and more diversified, their unsystematic risk approaches zero. Proponents of portfolio theory maintain the market does not reward exposure to unsystematic risk when it is removable by proper diversification. They believe the implication of this theory for stock investors is to diversify, and if investors expect the market to rise, to increase the beta of their portfolios, and vice versa. Experimental studies indicate as much as 30 percent or more of a specific stock's price movements are due to market (systematic) risk and this influence is as high as 85 percent or more in a well-diversified portfolio of 30 or more stocks.

A portfolio manager who does not wish to rely only on market movements for returns, or who does not wish to forecast market movements, should seek **nondiversification**—that is, exposure to the amount of unsystematic risk required for achieving the desired rate of return. This strategy emphasizes analysis of individual securities, as emphasized in this book, as opposed to overall portfolio risk balancing. Thus, reaping the rewards of exposure to unsystematic risk depends on our ability to identify misvalued securities and to properly assess their risk.

COMPONENTS OF UNSYSTEMATIC RISK

Those of us wishing to obtain our rewards from exposure to unsystematic or nonmarket risk through rigorous analysis of individual securities must focus on the various components of this risk. While these components are undoubtedly interrelated and subject to the influence of such elements of systematic risk as overall political, economic, and social factors, we can nevertheless usefully classify them as follows:

- **Economic risk.** Economic risks are inherent in a company's operating environment, including general economic risk (fluctuations in business activity), capital market risk (including changes in interest rates), and purchasing power risk.
- **Business risk.** Business risk is the uncertainty regarding a company's ability to earn a satisfactory return on its investments in light of the cost and revenue factors affecting this return, including factors of competition, product mix, and management ability.
- **Financial risk.** This refers to risks of capital structure and a company's ability to meet fixed and senior charges and claims.
- **Accounting risk.** Accounting risk is inherent in the selection and application of accounting methods, including management latitude in influencing the output of the accounting process.

Beta theorists assume investors are averse to risk and seek to diversify away a security's unsystematic risk, exposing investors only to market risk. Yet these theorists must recognize that historical betas for individual securities are quite unstable over time and, consequently, historical betas are seemingly imperfect predictors (at best) of a security's future betas. While theories are easier to apply to stock aggregates than to the evaluation of individual stocks, they are less reliable and inaccurate instruments for investment purposes.

Another, and perhaps more troublesome, issue is the assumption by beta theorists that past volatility is a sufficient measure of risk without reference to a security's current price. Is a security trading significantly above its true value, as determined by some method of fundamental analysis, no more risky than a security of equal volatility (beta) trading significantly below its true value? We know paying an excessive price for a stable, high-quality security is potentially as risky as investing in an unseasoned speculative security. While theorists have yet to effectively address this issue, they have braved the question of how the market values securities.

RELATION BETWEEN ACCOUNTING AND MARKET MEASURES OF RISK

Research shows accounting measures of risk, such as dividend payout ratios, capitalization ratios, coverage, and asset growth, are reflected in market risk measures like beta. Hence, selecting and ranking portfolios according to accounting risk measures is similar to portfolio formation using market-determined risk measures. Research also evidences a relation between systematic risk and a company's leverage (and other accounting risk measures). Research also considers the use of *fundamental betas,* where beta is a function of a company's changing fundamentals like earnings, asset structure, financial structure, and growth rates. An important implication is that the same economic (accounting-expressed) determinants that cause a stock to be more risky also cause it to have high systematic risk (beta).

CAPITAL ASSET PRICING MODEL

The capital asset pricing model (CAPM) extends portfolio theory in a manner intended to explain how prices of assets are determined—in short, in providing greater return for greater risk. This model assumes investors desire to hold securities in efficient portfolios providing maximum return for a given risk level. Several simplifying assumptions underlie the model, including:

- Existence of a riskless security.
- Investors able to borrow or lend unlimited amounts at the riskless rate.

- Investors possess identical investment horizons and act on the basis of identical expectations and predictions.

Using these assumptions, the expected return on an individual security, $E(R_i)$, relates to its systematic risk, β_i, in the following linear form:

$$E(R_i) = E(R_0) + [E(R_M) - E(R_0)]\beta_i$$

This return formulation suggests, under conditions of equilibrium, a security's (or any asset's) expected return equals the expected return of a riskless security, $E(R_0)$, plus a premium for risk taking. The risk premium consists of a constant, $[E(R_M) - E(R_0)]$, defined as the difference between the market expected return and the riskless security return (i.e., short-term government bond return) multiplied by a security's systematic risk (beta). CAPM implies each security's expected return is related to its risk. Risk is measured as the security's systematic movements with the market, and it cannot be eliminated by portfolio diversification. A major implication is only systematic (i.e., beta) risk is rewarded by the market, whereas holding unsystematic risk (potentially removable through diversification) earns no additional return.

Analysis Objectives and Financial Reporting

A LOOK BACK

We began our study of financial statement analysis with a preliminary analysis of Adaptec. We saw how financial statements report on important business activities, and the role of analysis in an efficient market.

A LOOK AT THIS CHAPTER

We begin in this chapter by describing the financial statement analysis objectives of the primary users. We discuss stock valuation and contrast it with debt valuation. We describe and assess the importance and limitations of accounting data for financial statement analysis. We also identify specialized financial statement analysis techniques and their relevance to business decisions.

A LOOK AHEAD

Chapter 3 begins Part Two, where our focus is on more strategic application and analysis of financial statements. We explore various analytical tools in assessing current and anticipated liquidity in Chapter 3.

THIS CHAPTER WILL:

- Identify the primary users of financial statements and discuss their objectives and information needs.
- Describe common stock valuation and compare it with the valuation of debt.
- Explain double-entry accounting and how it aids in measuring business activities.
- Describe the relevance of accounting information in financial statement analysis.
- Identify limitations of accounting data and their consequences for financial statement analysis.
- Discuss specialized financial statement analysis techniques.
- Explain how accounting rules are determined (Appendix 2A).
- Describe the role of technology in financial statement analysis (Appendix 2B).
- Identify sources of information for financial statement analysis (Appendix 2B).

PREVIEW OF CHAPTER 2

Financial statement analysis depends on the objectives of its users. While similarities exist, there are unique circumstances and objectives facing every user. To master financial statement analysis, we must understand users and their objectives. Financial statement analysis depends also on the accounting numbers comprising the statements. The recording function, the double-entry system, and classification are an integral part of accounting, and we must understand them to fully exploit our analysis of financial statements. Accounting information is also subject to certain limitations impairing our analysis. We must recognize and adapt our analysis for these limitations. This chapter describes the objectives and applications of primary users of financial statements. We introduce several important accounting functions and discuss their implications for analysis. We also discuss techniques of analysis that exploit our accounting knowledge. The content and organization of this chapter are as follows:

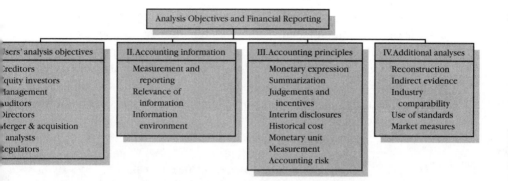

OBJECTIVES OF FINANCIAL STATEMENT ANALYSIS

Learning financial statement analysis involves knowing and understanding the process of analysis with emphasis on its major objectives. The objectives of financial statement analysis depend on our perspective and the tasks confronting us. To understand this analysis and its objectives, we review information needs and analytical goals of some important users of financial statements: credit grantors, equity investors, management, auditors, directors, merger and acquisition analysts, and regulators.

Creditors

Credit grantors are lenders of funds to a company with a promise of repayment. This type of business financing is temporary since credit grantors expect repayment of their funds along with interest. Credit grantors lend funds in many forms and for a variety of purposes.

Trade creditors provide goods or services to a company and expect payment within a reasonable period, often determined by the industry norm. Most trade credit is short term, ranging from 30 to 60 days, with cash discounts occasionally given for early payment. Trade creditors do not usually receive (explicit) interest for an extension of credit. Instead, trade creditors' profits derive directly from profit margins on the business transacted.

Nontrade creditors provide financing to a company in return for a promise, usually in writing, of payment with interest (explicit or implicit) on specific future dates. This type of financing can be either short or long term, and can originate from a variety of sources.

Companies often obtain short-term credit through banks or through the sale of commercial paper. They often obtain long-term credit through financial institutions like banks in the form of term loans or through insurance companies in the form of bonds or notes in private placements. Companies can also obtain long-term financing through public sale of notes or bonds in securities markets. Leasing and conditional sales are additional forms of financing.

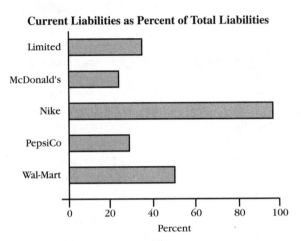

Current Liabilities as Percent of Total Liabilities

Source: Annual reports

Credit financing is also available through "hybrid" securities. Sales of **convertible bonds,** often subordinated, combine the borrowing of money with an added feature of an option to the lender. This option allows lenders to exchange their claims for equity interests should they consider it profitable. Issuance of **preferred stock,** stock senior to common equity but junior to debt, combines the "fixed" interest features of a loan with "unguaranteed" principal repayment of equity.

An important characteristic of all pure credit financing transactions is the fixed nature of rewards accruing to credit grantors. Should the company prosper, credit grantors' rewards are limited to a contractually fixed rate of interest or to the profit on goods or services provided. However, should the company incur losses or encounter adversities, a credit grantor's principal can be jeopardized. This "asymmetric" nature of a creditor's risk-return relation has a major effect on the creditor's perspective and the manner and objectives of credit analysis undertaken.

Credit grantors focus on the **security provisions** for their loans. These provisions are usually of two types: security in the form of the fair market value of assets pledged or other promises to limit business activities reducing company value (e.g., dividend payment restrictions) or security in repayment of principal and interest. For this purpose, credit grantors look to existing resources, and the reliability, timing, and stability of future cash flows. Creditors require definite links between management's projections and existing resources, along with demonstrated ability to achieve projections. Creditors are especially concerned with the sensitivity of earnings to recessionary periods. They generally are more conservative and heavily rely on financial statement analysis. Their analysis focuses on assessing a borrower's demonstrated ability to control cash flows and to maintain a sound financial base under varying economic and operating circumstances.

Techniques of financial statement analysis and the criteria of evaluation for credit grantors vary with the term, security, and purpose of a loan. With short-term credit, the grantor's primary concerns are current financial condition, the liquidity of current assets, and their rate of turnover. We fully describe these considerations in Chapter 3.

Evaluation of long-term credit, including valuation of bonds, requires more detailed and forward-looking inquiry and analysis. Long-term credit analysis includes projections of cash flows and evaluation of the extended earning power of the company. A company's extended earning power is a determining source of assurance of its ability to meet interest and principal payments arising from debt along with its other commitments under varying conditions. Thus, profit analysis is very important to long-term creditors. We examine these issues more completely in Chapters 6–8.

Credit analysis, whether long or short term, also looks at capital structure because it bears on risk and on the creditor's margin of safety. The relation of equity capital to creditor financing is an indicator of the risk exposure to credit grantors. This relation also reflects management's attitude toward risk and influences income coverage of fixed charges.

Creditors generally view asset values in the context of financial statement assumptions—namely, whether a company is a going concern. When a company's going-concern status is in doubt, liquidation values are more applicable. For this reason, creditors tend to conservatively adjust asset values, and make allowance for future contingencies, especially when a company is a doubtful going concern.

Equity Investors

Equity investors are providers of funds to a company in return for the risks, uncertainties, and rewards of ownership (there is no promise of repayment). Equity investors are the major providers of most business financing. Equity capital offers a cushion or safeguard for both preferred stock and credit financing that is senior to it. Equity investors are entitled to distributions only after the claims of senior securities are met—equity investors have a **residual interest.** With a going-concern entity, residual interest implies equity investors can receive distributions after satisfying obligations of senior claimants for debt interest and preferred dividends. In liquidation, equity investors have claims to the residual only after the claims of creditors and preferred stockholders. Thus, when a company prospers, equity investors reap gains above the amounts due senior claimants. But conversely, equity investors are the first to absorb losses when a company collapses, and their losses are generally limited to the amount invested.

Because of the risks confronting equity investors, their information needs are among the most demanding and comprehensive of all users of financial data. This is because equity investors' interests are affected by all aspects and phases of operations, financial condition, and capital structure. We briefly examine the kinds of difficulties equity investors confront.

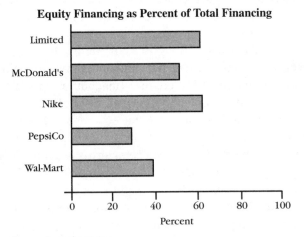

Equity Financing as Percent of Total Financing

Source: Annual reports

Common Stock Valuation

Valuation of common stock is a major objective of equity investors. It is a task involving financial statement analysis *plus* assessing factors like economic and industry conditions, competitive pressures, strategic advantages, and management and employee quality.

The equity investor, having no legal claim to a definite dividend or capital distribution, looks to three principal rewards: (1) current dividends, (2) special distributions such as rights, and (3) future capital gains from increasing market value. Ultimately, the most important determinant of both dividends and market value is earnings. Earnings, the source of dividends and retained earnings, along with earnings expectations, are major elements in determining the price of stock.

The theoretical basis of stock valuation is **present value theory.** This approach maintains the value of a stock at time t (V_t) equals the sum of all dividends expected, discounted to the present at any appropriate rate of interest:

$$V_t = \frac{D_{t+1}}{(1 + k)} + \frac{D_{t+2}}{(1 + k)^2} + \ldots + \frac{D_{t+n}}{(1 + k)^n} + \ldots$$

where D_{t+n} is the dividend in the $(t + n)$th year, and k is the discount rate or investors' required rate of return. Dividend distributions are the appropriate valuation attribute because only payouts to owners can increase their level of consumption.

Common Stock versus Debt Valuation

The present value model of stock valuation is similar to the conventional means of debt valuation. We calculate the value of debt (or purchase price) by discounting coupon payments and the principal repayment to the present using a discount rate equal to the desired yield. In stock valuation, the expected dividends correspond to the debt's coupons. The stock valuation model does not include a residual stock price because it assumes infinite dividend projection (consistent with the going-concern assumption). Because the discounting factor (the denominator) increases over time, the valuation impact of residual price is increasingly negligible. The logic and mathematical elegance of the stock valuation model is readily apparent, but we must recognize important differences between the inputs required of the stock and debt models. These differences are important since our purpose is to relate the scope and the techniques of financial statement analysis to valuation of equity securities.

In debt valuation, we typically know both the coupon payments and principal. Thus, as we described under the objectives of credit grantors, the major questions involve availability of funds for payment of interest and principal. While our assessment of the likelihood of funds availability involves the entire company's prospects, estimation is less difficult than obtaining inputs for the stock valuation model. The basic and important difference in an analysis of debt versus equity is with the *certainty of evidence*. No matter how "right" we are in making assumptions and forecasts, a major part of our reward from common stock analysis—future capital values—depends on other market participants (i.e., on ultimate market confirmation of our assessments). No such dependence on validation by the marketplace exists in our analysis of debt.

Stock Valuation Data Requirements

We require certain data to quantify the inputs for the stock valuation model. A fundamental problem with any dividend-based valuation model is the estimation of future distributions to owners. This task is all the more difficult due to the discretionary nature of dividend payments. However, we know dividend policies are slow to change. Companies are hesitant to increase dividend payouts unless they can indefinitely maintain higher levels with little likelihood of forced cuts in future payouts. Thus, observed dividend payouts are less indicative of company value except in the very long run. It is clear, however, that expected payouts are based largely on earnings and the earning power of assets. This reasoning underlies recent advances in developing an accounting-based equity valuation model. The model uses the accounting *clean surplus relation:*

$$BV_t = BV_{t-1} + NI_t - D_t$$

where
BV_t = Book value of common equity at end of period t
BV_{t-1} = Book value of common equity at end of period $t-1$
(or beginning of period t)
NI_t = Net income for period t
D_t = Dividends declared during period t

Under clean surplus accounting, net income includes all changes to common equity other than those due to transactions with owners (capital contributions are treated as negative dividends). While income determination in practice does not always adhere to clean surplus accounting, it is a very reasonable approximation.

If we restate the clean surplus relation in terms of D, and substitute this relation for D in the stock valuation model, we obtain the following (equivalent) stock valuation formula expressed in terms of accounting data:

$$V_t = BV_t + \frac{NI_{t+1} - (k \times BV_t)}{(1 + k)} + \frac{NI_{t+2} - (k \times BV_{t+1})}{(1 + k)^2} + \ldots + \frac{NI_{t+n} - (k \times BV_{t+n-1})}{(1 + k)^n} + \ldots$$

The focus of discounting in this model is the stream of future **abnormal earnings,** or *residual income,* of the company $[(NI - (k \times BV)]$. Abnormal earnings are the excess of reported earnings over the level of earnings expected from multiplying the required rate of return by the company's beginning-of-period book value. The logic underlying calculation of abnormal earnings is intuitive. If a company achieves a rate of profitability in excess of its required rate of return, value is created (i.e., abnormal earnings are positive). If a company achieves a rate of profitability less than its required rate of return, abnormal earnings will be negative (i.e., value declines).

This accounting-based stock valuation model shows equity investors need not focus their analysis on estimation of future dividends—a focus on future earnings is sufficient. The projection of future earnings (see Chapter 8) is, of course, a demanding task subject to its own uncertainty. For example, financial statement users evaluate reported earnings and often adjust them to yield a valid basis for projection. The more distant the projections of earnings, the more uncertain the estimates. Another factor, for both models, is the appropriate level for the **discount factor,** k. This level depends to a large extent on the risk involved. *Risk* reflects factors such as industry stability, prior earnings variability, and a company's leverage.

No one stock valuation model has proved an accurate forecaster of stock prices under all conditions. Perhaps the factors bearing on determination of stock prices are too numerous or too complex for inclusion in a workable formula, or perhaps not all factors are adequately measured (maybe due to simplifying assumptions). But whatever method of stock valuation we use, be it a simple short-term projection of earnings capitalized at a predetermined rate or a more sophisticated model, the results are only as accurate or reliable as the inputs used in calculations. The reliability and validity of these inputs—be they earnings projections, expected payout ratios, risk factors, or capital structure assumptions—depend on the quality of our financial statement analysis.

Management

Management consists of those individuals hired by the company's owners (or their representatives) to effectively and efficiently manage assets and liabilities. They are interested in the company's financial condition, profitability, and future possibilities. Management has a number of means available to monitor and stay abreast of the ever-changing circumstances of the company. Financial analysis is one important means of facilitating these objectives. Financial analysis by management is continual and comprehensive due to their constant and unlimited access to accounting information and other data. Their analysis of ratios, trends, economic relations, and other significant factors is often systematic and alert to changing business conditions. Timely detection and reaction to these changes are major objectives. Exhibit 2.1 lists benefits to management from analysis of financial statements.

Since management has superior access to inside information, what is their interest in analysis of financial statements? One important reason for management utilizing the tools of analysis is that such data compel them to view the company in the way important outsiders, like creditors and equity investors, must view it. This gives management an insight into valuation

---

Exhibit 2.1   **Benefits to Management from Monitoring**
                    Financial Statements

- Recognition that no business event occurs in isolation. Management aims to discern whether an event is the cause or consequence of additional, potentially underlying, conditions.
- Recognition that management must not blindly act on isolated events. There is a need for careful examination of related economic consequences. Management should ascertain the cause(s) of an event; positive or negative assessments should be withheld until a full analysis is undertaken.
- Organization of relevant data and analysis of patterns relative to prior experience or external conditions. This permits management to "see the forest through the trees"—minimizing the possibility of being lost among a maze of financial facts and figures.
- Encourages prompt and effective actions as conditions unfold—rather than "post mortem" analysis of causes and effects.

ANALYSIS   RESEARCH   INSIGHT 2.1

COMMON STOCK VALUATION

Are accounting numbers useful in stock valuation? For many years, proponents of the efficient markets hypothesis followed an *informational perspective* of accounting—accounting numbers, and earnings in particular, were viewed as "signals" serving to alter investors' beliefs about future cash flows and dividends.

Recent analysis research encourages a *measurement perspective* on accounting. This approach asserts that the accounting system has properties useful in capturing the wealth-generating process of a company. Specifically, book value represents the worth of a company at a point in time, while earnings measure the change in company value over a period of time.

Research reveals the following findings:

- As the reporting period decreases, accounting earnings are more closely correlated with stock price change than is cash flow.

- The correlation between accounting earnings and stock price changes increases dramatically for longer reporting periods, especially for periods exceeding two or three years.

- Earnings less sensitive to accounting recognition criteria and assumptions are more highly correlated with stock price changes.

- Expected abnormal earnings are more highly correlated with stock prices than are expected dividends.

and other uses of financial data they might not otherwise gain. Analysis of financial statements can sometimes provide management with valuable clues to important changes in underlying operating, investing, and financing activities. Recognition of these changes and timely action to check adverse trends are the essence of managerial control. Management derives important advantages from systematic monitoring of financial data.

Auditors

Auditors are outsiders who examine and provide assurance that financial statements are prepared in accordance with accepted practices. The product of an audit is an expression of opinion on the fairness of financial statements. The basic objective of an audit is to provide some assurance about the absence of material errors and irregularities, intentional or otherwise, in financial statements. Financial statement analysis, and its tools and techniques, represent an important set of audit procedures. Because errors and irregularities can significantly affect various financial, operating, and investing relations, analysis of these relations can sometimes reveal their potentiality. Application of financial statement analysis as part of the audit program is often most effective in the early stages of an audit because it often reveals areas of greatest change and vulnerability— areas to which an auditor will want to direct attention. At the completion of an audit, these tools represent a final check on the reasonableness of financial statements as a whole.

Directors

Directors are elected representatives of shareholders who oversee their interests in the company. This representation typically involves oversight of dividend policy, establishing management compensation or incentive programs, hiring and firing of management and the external auditor, and setting company goals. Because of directors' responsibilities to shareholders, they should be vigilant overseers of the company's business activities. This demands an understanding and appreciation of financing, investing, and operating activities. Financial statement analysis aids directors in ful-filling their oversight responsibilities to shareholders.

Merger and Acquisition Analysts

Merger and acquisition analysts are individuals interested in valuing a company for purchase or for merger with one or more other entities. This task represents an attempt to determine economic value, the relative worth of merging entities, and/or the relative bargaining positions of interested parties. Financial statement analysis is a valuable technique in determining economic value and in assessing the financial and operational compatibility of merger candidates. Objectives of the merger and acquisition analyst are similar to an equity investor's except the analysis must often be extended and stress the valuation of assets, including intangible assets such as goodwill, and any off-balance-sheet liabilities in an acquisition or merger plan.

Regulators

Regulators are those with authority or significant influence over rules guiding the preparation of financial statements. Government agencies and politicians have both the authority over and demand for financial statement information. The Internal Revenue Service, a government agency, applies tools and techniques of financial statement analysis to both audit tax returns and check the reasonableness of reported amounts. Other regulatory agencies use analysis techniques in the exercise of their supervisory and rate-determination functions. Politicians often use financial statements to support the perceived need, or lack thereof, for legislation affecting companies. For example, excessive earnings in an industry can invite additional income tax levies.

Other Important Users

Financial statement analysis serves the needs of many other important users. *Financial intermediaries,* such as stockbrokers, use financial data in making investment recommendations. *Employees* of a company are interested in assessing the fairness of their wages and their future employment prospects. *Labor unions* use techniques of financial statement analysis in attempting to gain the upper hand in collective bargaining discussions. *Suppliers* must investigate a company's financial soundness prior to making sales on credit. *Customers* use analysis techniques to determine profitability (or staying power) of their suppliers, the suppliers' returns, and other relevant factors. *Lawyers* use analysis techniques to advance their investigative and legal work, and *economists* use them in research and policy debates.

ANALYSIS VIEWPOINT

YOU ARE THE DIRECTOR

You are named a director of a major company. Your lawyer warns you about litigation risk and the need to constantly monitor management and the financial health of the company. How can financial statement analysis assist you in performing your director duties?

ACCOUNTING INFORMATION: BASIS OF ANALYSIS

The analytical processes underlying the inferences of financial statement users make use of a vast array of information, including economic, industry, social, and political data. Yet, the most important quantitative data are financial accounting data. Since financial accounting data are the product of conventions, measurements, and judgments, their apparent precision is sometimes misleading. Skillful use of accounting data for financial analysis requires a thorough understanding of the accounting framework underlying their computation, including the practices governing measurement of assets, liabilities, equities, and operating results for a company.

Accounting Measurement and Reporting of Business Activity

Accounting is the quantitative expression of economic phenomena. Accounting emerged from a need for a framework for recording, classifying, and communicating economic phenomena. Contemporary accounting practice reflects modifications in response to changing social, cultural, and economic demands.

The accounting function is carried out at two levels. One is the **recording function.** This involves the mechanics of recording and summarizing transactions and economic events in a quantifiable manner. The second is the **measurement and reporting function.** This function is arguably more complex and subject to greater managerial discretion. It governs the methods, procedures, and principles determining how companies measure and report accounting data. This section considers the recording function, while subsequent chapters take up the practices and principles governing accounting measurement and reporting.

The **principle of double-entry** governs the recording function in accounting. Understanding double-entry accounting aids our analysis of financial statements. Users find an understanding of double-entry accounting assists them with reconstructing business transactions from financial statements. The double-entry system uses the duality of every business transaction. For example, if a company borrows $1,000, it acquires both an asset (cash) and a claim against assets (a liability) in equal amounts. This duality and balance prevail in all transactions and provide order, consistency, and control. Exhibit 2.2 describes these counterbalancing effects for assets, liabilities, revenues, and expenses. At all times, a company's assets equal the sum of the claims from creditors and owners (this is the accounting equation discussed in Chapter 1). Under the double-entry system, all transactions are recorded, classified, and summarized using appropriate account designations. Financial statements are formal, condensed presentations of data derived from these accounts.

Relevance of Accounting Information

Business decisions, like choosing equity investments or extending credit, require a variety of data with varying reliability and relevance. These data include information on economic conditions and industry trends, as well as information on intangible items like the integrity and motivations of management. Financial statements represent measurable indices of past performance and financial conditions. While the importance of nonquantifiable intangibles vis-à-vis quantified financial statements varies, financial statements users do not make any serious, well-grounded decisions without analysis of the quantifiable data in financial statements.

**Exhibit 2.2   Counterbalancing Effects of Transactions
             in Financial Statements**

Asset acquisition is counterbalanced with:
- incurrence of a liability;
- increase in ownership claim; and/or
- disposal of another asset.

Liability extinguishment is counterbalanced with:
- disposal of an asset;
- increase in ownership claim; and/or
- incurrence of another liability.

Revenue earned is counterbalanced with:
- increase in assets;
- decrease in liabilities; and/or
- decrease in ownership claim.

Expenses incurred are counterbalanced with:
- decrease in assets;
- increase in liabilities; and/or
- increase in ownership claim.

Financial statements are important because they are objective and report economic consequences of actual events. Moreover, they quantify and measure these consequences. The attribute of measurability endows financial statements with an important characteristic: **common monetary unit.** Since data are expressed in the common denominator of money, it enables us to add and combine data, to relate them to other data, and to manipulate them arithmetically.

Accounting for economic phenomena, however, is imperfect and has limitations. It is easy to become impatient with these imperfections and limitations and search for a substitute. There is no ready substitute. Financial accounting is and remains the only relevant and reliable system for systematic recording, classification, and summarization of business activities. Improvement rests with refinements in this time-tested system. It is thus incumbent on anyone who desires to analyze effectively the financial position and the results of operations of a company to understand accounting, its terminology, and its practices, including its imperfections and limitations.

Analysis of financial statements is an indispensable part of lending, investing, and other financial decisions. We must understand that its relative importance varies considerably in any particular case. Since a lender's return derives primarily from the company, financial statement analysis is an important part of a lending decision. Financial statement analysis plays a different role in the equity investing decision. The equity investor looks to two different sources for a return: dividends and capital appreciation. Dividends depend on profitability, growth, and liquidity—elements lending themselves to evaluation by means of financial statement analysis. However, dividends are but one part, and often the smaller part, of the two sources of investor return. Indeed, many growing and successful companies, like Adaptec, pay no dividends. The often more important return derives from other investors' future willingness to pay more for the stock than we did. While the willingness of investors to pay more for the stock depends on earning power and growth, it can also depend on the psychology of the market, the valuation of earnings retained, and other factors such as rates of return available on alternative investments. Gauging the performance of equity security markets is challenging.

The importance of financial statement analysis for equity investing varies with circumstances and time. Its importance is relatively greater when market valuations are low than when these valuations are subject to general market euphoria. Its relative importance is also greater when

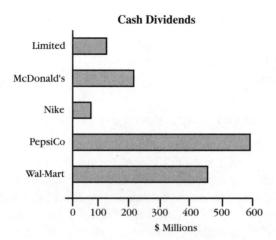

Cash Dividends

Source: Annual reports

directed to risk assessment and the detection of areas of vulnerability. Financial statement analysis is often of greater value for defensive investing and in the avoidance of loss than it is in uncovering investment opportunities.

Information Environment for Financial Statement Analysis

We have discussed the relative importance of financial statement analysis to the total decision effort. The relevant information set a decision maker draws on includes financial statements and various other types of information. The relative importance of each varies from decision to decision. Exhibit 2.3 illustrates the composition of our entire information set. It is important to recognize that financial statements are but a portion of the entire information set available. Companies cannot effectively convey all relevant information in financial statements and better communicate some through other means (e.g., analysts' forecasts or recommendations). Certain information in financial reports is not overseen by accounting regulatory agencies. For example, accounting standards do not extend to Management's Discussion and Analysis. Nevertheless, this additional information is often relevant in our analysis.

ACCOUNTING PRINCIPLES AND LIMITATIONS

We must temper the importance of financial accounting data by the data's limitations for financial statement analysis. This section discusses the more important limitations.

Monetary Expression

An obvious accounting limitation is that information in financial statements must lend itself to quantification in a monetary unit. Not all important economic relations about a company lend themselves to quantification. For example, financial statements convey little if any direct information about the character, motivation, or experience of management or employees. They convey no disaggregate information on the quality of research and development efforts nor the extent of a company's marketing efforts. Nor do they typically convey any detailed information on product lines, machinery efficiency, or future plans. Also absent is information on organization structure, informal communication channels within and outside a company, and assessments on the importance of specific individuals' talents.

Simplification and Summarization

Financial statements simplify and summarize complex and diverse economic activities. Simplification is necessary in classifying the various economic events into a manageable number of categories. Summarization is also necessary to keep the quantity and detail of financial statements within reasonable bounds. Costs of statement preparation further encourage simplification and summarization. Yet simplification and summarization are at the expense of clarity and detail potentially useful in our analysis. Simplification and summarization inherent in accounting make it imperative that we analyze and reconstruct the events and transactions they represent. It is essential we be able to recover from financial statements the economic realities that underlie them or to recognize those realities whose recovery is futile—the latter yield meaningful questions for management and others able to provide additional information.

Judgment and Incentives

Preparation of financial statements requires judgment. Judgment is imperfect, yielding variability in the quality and reliability of accounting numbers.

Exhibit 2.3   Information Set for Financial Statement Analysis

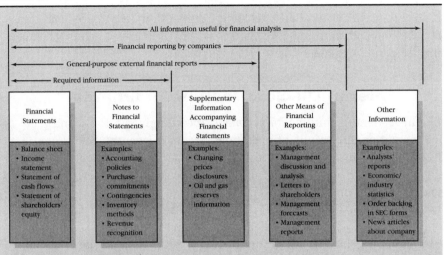

Since financial statements are general-purpose presentations, preparers' judgments are affected by their view of a typical user's requirements and expectations. These requirements and expectations do not necessarily coincide with those of a user with a specific task in mind. Accounting is also a *social science* and, therefore, is at least partially determined by human factors, including incentives. No assessment of financial statement quality or reliability is complete without considering these incentives. While the overriding purpose of accounting is supplying information useful in business decisions, we must recognize many parties are involved in the accounting function, each having their own interest in mind. Exhibit 2.4 lists several examples of how financial reports might reflect insiders' interests. Furthermore, parties external to a company have their own agenda and incentives. Governments want accounting to promote policies encouraging inflation control, good labor relations, continued economic growth, antitrust oversight, and equitable taxes. Accounting practitioners want accounting to increase the market for their services, maintain positive relations with clients, and assist clients in reaching their objectives. These biased interests do not, nor should they, affect objectives of accounting. Accounting regulatory agencies must represent society and ensure that accounting objectives mesh with society. Still, we must be aware of strong personal incentives at stake trying to bend practice to favor other interests. Society's countermeasures include regulatory institutions (e.g., Securities and Exchange Commission), the courts, and the accounting and auditing professions. Each of these institutions can impose punitive damages on the various parties.

Interim Disclosures and Estimates

Useful accounting information is *timely*. Accordingly, disclosure of financial condition and results of operations occurs frequently. But the more frequent the disclosures—especially with an income statement—the greater the need for estimates. This greater need for estimates increases the uncertainty inherent in financial statements. Estimates are required for many items including: (1) amount and timing of cash collections on receivables, (2) expected selling prices and sales volume for inventory items, (3) benefit period and salvage value of depreciable assets, (4) future warranty claims, (5) portion complete and remaining costs of long-term sales contracts, (6) income and property taxes, and (7) loss reserves. The link between frequency of reporting, the length of period covered, and the degree of accounting uncertainty deserves explanation. Namely, many business transactions and events require a long period of time (several quarters or years) for completion and determination of results. For example, long-term depreciable assets benefit several periods extending years into the future. The longer the benefit period, the more tentative are estimates of their salvage value, benefit period, and payback pattern. As another example, the value, if any, of investments in

---

Exhibit 2.4   Transactions or Events in Financial Reports Potentially Affected by Insiders' Interests

- Obtaining credit to ensure a company's survival through difficult events.
- Selling securities in the open market to facilitate company growth.
- Enhancing compensation of executives or employees for personal gain.
- Helping management fend off a hostile takeover attempt.
- Permitting managers to enrich themselves at the expense of owners.
- Increasing wealth of the company's current owners.

mining or exploration ventures is often not apparent until many years subsequent to initial development efforts. Consequently, while we demand and receive interim accounting reports, we must recognize the lower reliability of such disclosures due to the increased need for estimates in interim reports.

Historical Cost Measurement

Accounting systems aim to report *fair and objective* information. Since the value of an asset determined through arm's-length bargaining is usually fair and objective, use of *historical cost* values in financial statements is common. These historical cost values enjoy an objectivity surpassing any other unrealized appraisals of value. Accounting practice adheres, with some exceptions, to this cost concept. The consequence of this objectivity when values subsequently change impairs the usefulness of financial statements. Historical cost balances do not, in most cases, represent current market values. Yet users of financial statements desire a balance between objectively determined values and the most current market values of assets and liabilities. Thus, while we must be aware of and adjust to valuation bases other than cost, historical cost measures represent a pragmatic compromise to a difficult circumstance.

Unstable Monetary Unit

Accounting reports generally deal with items expressed only in monetary terms. However, the purchasing power of money experiences periodic fluctuations with a typically declining trend. The monetary unit has not retained its attribute as a "standard of value" and, consequently, adding account balances across years can yield serious distortions. Practice recognizes this limitation. Yet, no reporting requirements currently exist for adjusting financial statements for changes in purchasing power.

Need to Understand Accounting Measurements and Disclosures

Substantial progress has been made by regulatory agencies in narrowing the range of acceptable accounting practices, in expanding meaningful disclosure, and in improving the quality and creditability of financial statements. This progress notwithstanding, the experienced user of financial statements recognizes continuing limitations and imperfections. We would be naïve and unrealistic in hoping the time is near when we no longer need to "go behind the numbers" underlying financial statements and are able to "go forward from the numbers." Among the more important reasons for this conclusion are:

- Management has a vital interest in financial statements and, hence, exerts influence on accounting for and disclosure of financial results. While auditors increase the objectivity and creditability of financial statements, their influence is limited due to questions of independence and problems inherent in the accounting system. The latter include:

    Application of standards in practice. Accounting standards are rarely so explicit as to eliminate judgment from accounting and auditing practice. Moreover, accounting standards typically apply only to *material* items—yet a standard definition of materiality eludes us.

    Accounting standards are not comprehensive. Several areas of accounting, including business combinations, goodwill, product cost accounting, and allocations, are provided limited guidance from accounting standards. This contributes to diversity and inconsistencies in practice.

    Accounting is slow to change. Emerging transactions, changing business practices, and the ingenuity of "financial engineers" yield an inevitable lag in standards behind practice. Accounting standards generally focus on existing problems vis-à-vis looming or anticipated problems.

- Powerful interest groups have and continue to limit progress on development of uniform and fair accounting standards. These groups exert pressure with regulatory agencies to enact standards in their best interests. An example is the extensive lobbying efforts of certain groups to prevent mandatory expense recognition of costs associated with stock-based compensation.

- Much of the data comprising financial statements is "soft." This is in spite of the precision conveyed by detailed and numeric presentations. Soft data refers to information dependent on subjective evaluations; forecasts of future conditions; and assumptions regarding the integrity, competence, intent, or motives of management.

- We cannot safely abdicate our analysis task of scrutinizing and evaluating the accounting numbers comprising financial statements. A prerequisite to our thorough and intelligent analysis is an understanding of the data relied on. Experience shows us that improvements in accounting standards are accompanied by increased complexity of data measures and disclosures.

Implications of Accounting Risk

Our analysis of financial statements recognizes a number of risks. There are the risks associated with all profit-seeking businesses, including the risk of losses, risk of adversities, risk of contingencies, and risk of information reliability. We must also recognize another type of risk, referred to as **accounting risk**. Accounting risk results from the need for judgments, estimates, and the imprecision inherent in the accounting system. Accounting risk increases our uncertainty in decision making. Accounting risk also involves accounting *conservatism*. Assumptions play an important role in accounting measurements, and these assumptions can be too conservative or optimistic. Thus, the degree of conservatism, or lack thereof, can confound our analysis (we return to this issue in Chapter 8). Partly in recognition of accounting risk, regulators currently require companies to disclose a summary of accounting policies underlying their financial statements. Companies are required to emphasize their accounting choices made from both accepted alternatives and unusual, innovative, or industry-unique practices. Adaptec summarizes its accounting policies in note 1 of its 1996 financial statements.

ANALYSIS VIEWPOINT

YOU ARE THE AUDITOR

You have just been informed your audit firm is the low bidder on a proposed audit engagement and you accept the assignment. How can you use financial statement analysis in your audit engagement of this new client?

ADDITIONAL ANALYSIS TECHNIQUES

Reconstruction of Business Activities and Transactions

An important part of our analysis is the ability to reconstruct business activities and transactions summarized in financial statements. **Accounting reconstruction** is the replication of the financial statement preparers' work in *reverse* order. This role reversal is portrayed as follows:

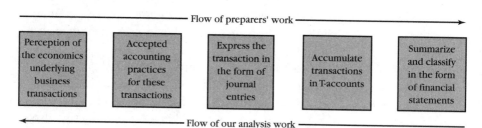

Preparers' efforts and skills are directed at understanding the economics underlying transactions or events. Preparers must then use their accounting knowledge to record the transaction, express it in the form of a journal entry, and carry it to the accounts. These basic concepts of journal entries and T-accounts are particularly useful in our analytical work. Preparers ultimately summarize and report all accounts of a period in the form of financial statements.

Our analysis work is in reverse order. It is important to recognize while preparers' efforts are primarily oriented to past events, our analysis focuses on future expectations. Our analysis works with financial statements made available by the company. Our task is to recapture, to the extent possible, the economics imbedded and summarized in financial statements. This analytical process requires us to visualize the journal entries made and reconstruct, in summary fashion, all or selected accounts in the financial statements. This task requires an understanding of the economics underlying business transactions and events as well as a knowledge of accounting practice.

Our reconstruction of business activities and transactions gives us insight into the changes in balance sheet accounts and the consequences of given transactions or events. It also permits us to answer questions like the following:

- What is the reason for an increase or decrease in investments?
- What are the consequences of debt refunding for working capital and cash?
- What amount of long-term debt is repaid this period?
- What is the effect of income taxes and how much tax is actually paid?

Reconstruction of business transactions and events requires accounting knowledge—the ability to know how a transaction is recorded and what kinds of activities or events increase or decrease specific accounts. It also requires the ability to read carefully, understand, and interpret financial statements and their notes. We need knowledge of what information is available in financial statements, where it is found, and how to reconstruct transactions (including the making of reasonable assumptions). Reconstruction depends on our knowledge of related disciplines—such as accounting, economics, finance, and psychology—and on our skills of derivation and inference. It also demands a degree of detective work based on marshaling all known facts while using the limited and incomplete data available. In reconstructing transactions and events, we work with known information in deducing unknown facts. The degree of accuracy expected in our reconstruction and analysis is not at nor need it approach the accuracy expected in the accounting and recording function.

The **T-account** is a very important analytical tool and we use it often. Our emphasis here is *not* on accounting mechanics but on the use of the T-account to reconstruct and understand transactions and events. Yet we must recognize that our understanding of the accounting function is a useful analytical technique. Use of T-account analysis depends on our ability to visualize transactions in journal form and summarize them in T-accounts. Illustration 2.1 shows us how a T-account is used to derive cash collections.

When there is inadequate information, we often must combine accounts and analyze them together. Having identified the missing information, we can pose informed questions to management or shareholder relations departments to obtain the desired information. We must also recognize what information is not available in financial statements, and attempt to secure it if sufficiently important. For example, specific information on commitments, lines of credit, and order backlogs is usually unavailable. A notes payable account or a loan-to-officers account can show little or no change in year-end balances but might have experienced significant interim balances liquidated during the year.

Illustration 2.1

Our financial statement analysis of Campbell Soup Company needs to determine the amount of cash collected from customers during Year 11. We decide to reconstruct Accounts Receivable to answer this question. We find accounts receivable on the balance sheet and know that reconstruction is key to determining the cash collected from customers (see the financial statements in Supplement A). We also need knowledge of the usual entries determining accounts receivable. Our first step is to establish the accounts receivable T-account with beginning and ending balances (details are in note 13 of Campbell's financial statements):

Accounts Receivable (net)			
Beginning balance	534.1		
Net sales	6,204.1		Cash collections
		6,276.5	(plug & balance)
Ending balance	461.7		

Our second step is to determine the aggregate debits to this account. We must work with aggregates from financial statements rather than the detailed entries comprising them. Knowing debits to assets represent the counterpart of sales (a revenue item increasing equity), we debit the asset Accounts Receivable for the total sales of $6,204.1 (in millions). We know not all sales are for cash, but to arrive at cash collections from customers it does not matter whether the charges are cash sales or credit sales. The amount needed to balance the accounts receivable T-account is $6,276.5. This is our best estimate of cash collections from customers. We know this amount is overstated because it includes credits to customers for cash discounts and bad debts. Yet, to reconstruct the Allowance for Bad Debts account we would need at least the amount of bad debt expense charged to income during the year—an amount not always reported in financial statements. These residual accounts are, however, small relative to total collections and are not likely to materially affect our cash collection estimate.

Indirect Evidence and Evaluation

Financial statement analysis can provide indirect evidence bearing on important questions. For instance, analysis of past statements of cash flows can offer evidence as to the financing and investing tendencies of management. Moreover, analysis of operating statements offers evidence on management's skill in coping with fluctuations in a company's business activities. While indirect evidence and evaluation are often not precise or quantifiable, they provide insight into managerial decisions and preferences. Indirect evidence and evaluation are facilitated through **contrast**

analysis. Contrast analysis rests on the proposition that no number by itself is meaningful but rather acquires meaning only in contrast to a comparable quantity. Contrast analysis focuses on *exceptions and variations,* and saves us the need to formulate individual norms and expectations. It also serves as an attention-directing and control device. Contrast analysis is accomplished by examining:

- External data from competitors or industry publications (i.e., external contrasts).
- Company performance over time (i.e., internal contrasts).
- Yardsticks compiled from standards, budgets, or forecasts.

Advantages of external data are their (1) objectivity and independence, (2) value as standards if derived from similar companies, and (3) comparability when derived from companies subject to similar economic and industry conditions. Reliable contrasts enjoy a consistent basis of compilation, comparable periods of analysis, and source credibility.

Industry Comparability Analysis
of Financial Statements

One of the most popular and effective contrast tests is **industry comparability analysis.** Comparing financial statements of companies within an industry presents a number of challenges. We discuss the more significant challenges below.

Differing Reporting Periods

While the majority of companies use a calendar year-end, some use non-calendar year-ends for reporting purposes. Adjustment for differing year-ends depends on the extent of the year-end time difference. If the year-end time difference is under three months, adjustments are typically not necessary. If the year-end time difference exceeds three months, financial statement users can use quarterly reports to make data comparable for a reliable financial statement analysis. Through the addition of any four consecutive quarters, we can adjust year-ends for comparison purposes. The need to adjust for year-end time differences and the magnitude of adjustments depend on whether extraordinary events, like strikes or property damage, occur in a quarter. Moreover, the effects of seasonal and cyclical influences on comparability of time periods need careful evaluation.

Differing Accounting Principles

As we stress throughout, use of alternative accounting principles or methods renders data of companies noncomparable. This lack of comparability must be corrected by means of data adjustments before performing a reliable financial statement analysis. The following list is a sampling of alternative accounting principles requiring our attention:

Alternative Accounting Principles

Leases (operating, capital)
Inventory valuation (acquisition cost, standard cost, lower of cost or market)
Inventory cost flow assumption (FIFO, LIFO, weighted average)
Investments in securities (trading, available for sale, held to maturity)
Depreciation method (straight line, accelerated)
Corporate acquisitions (purchase, pooling of interests)
Foreign currency translation (all current, temporal method)
Revenue recognition (percentage of completion, completed contract)

Restatement and Reclassification Requirements

Several cases require restatement of financial statements including:

- The merger of companies under the pooling method of accounting requires restating prior years' statements as if the companies had been merged from inception. As a practical matter only financial statements reported when the merger is announced are in restated form.

- Discontinuances or disposals of a segment of a business require that companies classify revenues and expenses of these segments, and any losses expected on disposal, in the income statement under discounted operations. Similarly, net assets of these segments appear separately on the balance sheet. Financial statements that include discontinuances are restated accordingly.

- Certain changes in accounting principles (e.g., changes in inventory cost flow assumptions or changes in income recognition on long-term contracts) require that companies restate any reported prior years' financial statements to reflect the newly adopted principle.

Difficulties often arise because the available restated period is less than the preferred time period for analysis. This is because companies typically report balance sheets for two years and income statements and statements of cash flow for three years. These are the periods for which restated financial statements are likely available, although restatements for longer periods are sometimes found in SEC filings (e.g., registration statements). We must also recognize any account classification differences across companies' financial statements. Some classification differences are easier to adjust for than others. For example, if one company includes depreciation expense in cost of goods sold while another shows this expense as a separate item, we can easily make adjustments to put analytical measures (like ratios) on a comparable basis.

Analytical Use of Accounting Standards and Assumptions

We review many accounting standards and assumptions underlying financial statements in this book. Our purpose is to examine their financial statement consequences when applied to similar transactions and circumstances, as well as the managerial latitude in interpretation and application of accounting standards. These consequences must be understood before making a meaningful analysis or reliable comparison. We highlight the importance of standards and assumptions in accounting determinations in Illustration 2.2.

In Illustration 2.2, our prospective buyer has at least two questions about this income statement: Can reliance be placed on the income statement numbers? What adjustments are necessary for a reliable net income number in computing price?

Assurance about the fairness of financial statements is provided by an independent auditor. We assume an audit assures the financial statements accurately portray results of operations and financial position in accordance with generally accepted principles. An answer to our second question is more difficult. While an auditor's assurance extends to the fairness of the income statement, it does *not* imply income is the relevant figure to use in computing the price of the apartment building. Let us examine the information our buyer needs and what assumptions are necessary to arrive at a reliable income number for computing price. We pursue the following specific analyses:

Illustration 2.2

The owner of Lakeside Apartment Complex has an interested buyer. How is the price set? How is a buyer reassured in the soundness and profitability of this investment at a set price? There is more than one approach to set price, including analysis of comparable current values and reproduction costs. One of the most widely accepted methods for valuation of income-producing properties or investments is *capitalization of earnings*. If earnings is our major consideration, we focus on the income statement. Our prospective buyer is provided the income statement for the apartment (we have excluded income taxes because they depend on our owner's tax status):

LAKESIDE APARTMENT COMPLEX
Income Statement
For the Year Ending December 31

Revenue:		
Rental revenue	$46,000	
Garage rentals	2,440	
Other income from washer and dryer concession	300	
Total revenue		$48,740
Expenses:		
Real estate taxes	4,900	
Mortgage interest	2,100	
Electricity and gas	840	
Water	720	
Superintendent's salary	1,600	
Insurance	680	
Repairs and maintenance	2,400	13,240
Income before depreciation		$35,500
Depreciation		9,000
Net income*		$26,500

*Taxes are excluded.

Rental income. Does the $46,000 figure represent 100 percent occupancy during the year? If so, should we make an allowance for possible vacancies? What are rental trends in the area? What are rental expectations for the next five years? Next 10 years? Are demand factors for apartments in the area stable, improving, or deteriorating? Our aim is to adjust the yearly rental income number to approximate a level that, on average, we expect to prevail for the foreseeable future. Prior years' data are useful in judging this.

Real estate taxes. The trend of taxes over the years is important. This depends on the taxing authority and its tax demands and tendencies.

Mortgage interest. This item is relevant only if our buyer plans to assume the existing mortgage. Otherwise, substitute the interest expense related to our buyer's new financing.

Utilities. This item is scrutinized with a view to ascertaining whether they are at a representative level of future costs.

Superintendent's salary. Is this pay adequate to secure acceptable services? Can the services of the superintendent be retained?

Insurance. Are all foreseeable risks insured for? Is coverage adequate?

Repairs and maintenance. We must review these expenses over a number of years to determine a representative level. Is this level of expenses sufficient to afford proper maintenance of the property or is the expense account "starved" to show a higher net income?

Depreciation. This figure is not likely relevant to our buyer's decision unless the buyer's cost approximates the seller's. If cost to the buyer differs, then we compute depreciation using that cost and an acceptable method of depreciation over the building's useful life.

Our buyer must also ascertain whether any expenses expected are omitted from this income statement. An auditor's unqualified opinion does not diminish the importance of addressing these type of questions. For example, while accepted accounting principles require that insurance expense include accruals for the entire year, they do *not* attest to adequacy of insurance coverage. Nor are accounting principles concerned with a company's maintenance policy, or a superintendent's pay, or with any *expected* revenues and expenses.

Recognizing the many complex questions and problems in this simple income statement provides us with a sense of the complexities in a complete analysis of financial statements of a large business enterprise. It is essential that a reliable analysis includes an appreciation of what financial statements portray and what they do not or cannot portray. There are items that properly belong in statements and there are items that, because of an inability to quantify them or to determine them objectively, cannot be included. Our illustration of the apartment buyer shows, despite their limitations, financial statements are indispensable to business decisions. While our potential buyer can use the income statement without these assumptions and adjustments, our buyer is at a great disadvantage without them.

Traditional Market Measures

Analyses in practice use a variety of measures to evaluate the price and yield behavior of a company's securities. The **price-earnings ratio** measures the multiple at which the market is capitalizing the earnings per share of a company. The **earnings yield,** the inverse of the price-earnings ratio, represents the income-producing power of a share of common stock at the current price. The **dividend yield** is the cash return accruing to an investor on a share of stock based on the current dividend rate and current price. Recall that all or part of a company's earnings can be distributed as dividends and the balance retained. The **dividend payout ratio** measures the proportion of earnings currently paid out as common stock dividends.

GUIDANCE ANSWERS TO ANALYSIS VIEWPOINTS

YOU ARE THE DIRECTOR

As a member of a company's board of directors, you are responsible for oversight of management and the safeguarding of shareholders' interests. Accordingly, a director's interest in the company is broad and risky. To reduce risk, a director uses financial statement analysis to monitor management and assess company profitability, growth, and financial condition. Because of a director's unique position, there is near unlimited access to internal financial and other records. Analysis of financial statements assists our director in (1) recognizing causal relations among business activities and events, (2) "seeing the forest through the trees," that is, helping directors focus on the company, and not on a maze of financial details, and (3) encouraging proactive and not reactive measures in confronting changing financial conditions.

YOU ARE THE AUDITOR

An auditor's primary objective is an expression of an opinion on the fairness of financial statements according to generally accepted accounting principles. As auditor, you desire assurance on the absence of errors and irregularities in financial statements. Financial statement analysis can help identify any errors and irregularities affecting the statements. Also, this analysis compels our auditor to understand the company's operations and its performance in light of prevailing economic and industry conditions. Application of financial statement analysis is especially useful as a preliminary audit tool, directing the auditor to areas of greatest change and unexplained performance.

Accounting Principles Underlying Financial Statements

GENERALLY ACCEPTED ACCOUNTING PRINCIPLES

Generally accepted accounting principles (GAAP) are the rules and operative guidelines of accounting. These rules, or more accurately standards, determine such matters as how assets are measured, when liabilities are incurred, when income is recognized as earned, and when expenses and losses accrue. To the user of accounting data and statements, an understanding of these rules is essential. A user cannot undertake a reliable analysis of financial statements without ascertaining the accounting principles used in their preparation and how they are applied.

How Accounting Standards Are Established

Accounting principles have been long in developing and are subject to continual innovation, modification, and change. Accounting principles have changed in response to developments in, and the needs of, society and its requirements and expectations. It is generally accepted that primary responsibility for fair financial statements rests with management. However, responsibility for development of accounting standards that govern these statements is borne primarily by the accounting profession and the Securities and Exchange Commission (SEC) and, to a lesser extent, the American Accounting Association (AAA) and organized securities exchanges.

Influence of Accounting Profession

Reasons for the accounting profession's early leadership in development of accounting principles are readily apparent. One of the profession's major and unique functions is attesting to the fairness of financial statements. Yet, the term fairness requires a frame of reference. Accepted principles are intended to provide this frame of reference, and the accounting profession is presumed to have both the independence and the technical competence for their development. In pursuing the development of accounting principles, the profession is not only performing a vital public service but is also catering to its own self-interests.

The AICPA initially attempted to place the effort of developing accounting principles with a Committee on Accounting Procedure (CAP). Its purpose was to reduce the areas of difference in accounting and to narrow the choices available in the area of alternative accounting principles. This committee considered numerous accounting problems and issued pronouncements in the form of 51 *Accounting Research Bulletins (ARBs)*. The authority of *ARBs*, except where the CAP asks and secures formal adoption by the AICPA membership, rests on the general acceptability of its opinions. The Committee on Accounting Procedure was subsequently replaced with the Accounting Principles Board (APB). The APB, vested with greater authority and supported by an enlarged research staff, was charged with further narrowing the areas of differences in accounting principles and in promoting the written expression of generally accepted accounting principles. The APB issued 31 *Opinions;* some improved accounting practice (pension accounting), some inadequately changed practice (leasing), and some confused practice (earnings per share).

Currently, the Financial Accounting Standards Board (FASB), composed of seven full-time paid members, functions as the standard-setting body of the accounting profession. Board members are appointed by a group of trustees, including AICPA members and representatives from private industry, security analysts, and others. In spite of its limitations, the FASB is an improvement over its predecessors. Before issuing an accounting standard, the board issues, in most cases, a *discussion memorandum* for public comment. Written comments are filed with the board, and oral comments can be voiced at public hearings that generally precede the issuance of an Exposure Draft for a *Statement of Financial Accounting Standards (SFAS)*. After further exposure and comment, the FASB usually issues a final *SFAS*. It also issues interpretations of previously issued pronouncements from time to time. Another improvement in procedure is the inclusion in most *SFASs* of careful and elaborate explanations of the rationale of the board for the statements it issues, explanations of how comments to the board are dealt with, as well as examples of actual applications. The Financial Accounting Foundation (the FASB's parent body) also adopted a number of changes in the FASB structure to include greater participation by financial statement users in rule making.

Influence of the Securities and Exchange Commission

The SEC, an independent quasi-judicial government agency, administers the Securities Act of 1933 and the Securities Exchange Act of 1934. The primary purpose of the 1933 act is to ensure that a potential purchaser of a security offered for public sale is provided all material facts relating to it. A registration statement, which companies must file with the SEC, discloses these facts. The function of the SEC regarding a registration statement under the 1933 act is to ensure that a company makes full and accurate disclosure of all pertinent information relating to a company's business, its securities, its financial position and earnings, and the underwriting arrangements. Until the SEC approves this statement, amended as necessary, it can prevent the registration statement from becoming effective and the securities from being sold. The SEC is not, however, concerned with the merits of any security registered with it. The 1934 act prescribes disclosure requirements for issuers of securities listed and registered for public trading on our national securities exchanges. Following registration of their securities, registrants must file annual, quarterly, and other periodic reports.

Since its inception, the SEC has encouraged development and improvement of accounting and auditing practice. The commission has issued specific rules and regulations concerning the preparation of financial statements and the degree of detail they contain. The commission's prosecution of numerous accounting and auditing infractions of its rules results in a form of "case law" providing important clues and precedents in the area of accounting principles and auditing procedures. While many SEC positions on accounting and auditing matters confront specific instances and applications, the commission recognizes the impossibility of issuing rules to cover all possible scenarios. An important part of the SEC's influence on matters of accounting takes the form of conferences between companies, their accountants, and SEC staff, and the numerous unpublished rulings and guidelines that result.

The SEC has grown in competence and experience. It has considerable regulatory authority in accounting and the ability to enforce it. It recognizes the great difficulties and complexities involved in finding universally acceptable principles. It also recognizes that certification of financial statements with the commission places a heavy responsibility on the accounting profession. At the same time, the commission does not hesitate to criticize and prod, to take exception to accounting presentations, and to discipline members of the profession when circumstances warrant. The commission exemplifies not a rigid and arbitrary exercise of government authority but the sparing use of this authority.

The SEC approach toward accounting practice is, in large measure, determined by current public attitudes toward, and confidence in, financial reporting—and to some extent by the aggressiveness of its chief accountant. All of these influences change over the years and we see differing and sometimes unique approaches. In recent years, the SEC forced audit firms to consent to quality reviews of their practice by committees of peers, and confronted the FASB with numerous new SEC requirements in areas it considers as being under its jurisdiction. The SEC is increasingly aggressive in modifying FASB standards. The aggressive and constructive influence of these organizations in the development of accounting principles must not mislead us into believing that financial statements filed with the commission are more reliable than others. Less than effective methodologies and limited staffing weaken the SEC's ability to review thoroughly all documents submitted.

Influence of Other Organizations

Two other organizations are influential in formation of accounting principles: the American Accounting Association (AAA) and the organized securities exchanges, particularly the New York Stock Exchange. The AAA is comprised primarily of accounting educators. Being one step removed from practice, they have a more detached point of view and, by the very nature of their calling, a more scholarly and theoretical one. While AAA statements on accounting theory are influential in shaping accounting thought, they have no official standing and are not binding. The role of organized securities exchanges in formulating accounting theory is limited. Like the SEC, organized securities exchanges have the power to enforce adherence to standards. The basic instrument by which an exchange secures compliance to its standards is the listing agreement. This agreement defines, among other things, the minimum accounting disclosure required in the financial statements of the listed company. One important way the organized securities exchanges support efforts to the AICPA in the area of accounting improvements is by urging listed companies to comply with specific professional pronouncements.

ACCOUNTING OBJECTIVES AND CONCEPTS

Objectives of Financial Statements

While there is some degree of agreement with the proper accounting in specific areas, agreement on the basic bedrock objectives of accounting has, so far, eluded us. There is no broad consensus on objectives that help practitioners settle differences. Accounting is not an exact science. It is a social science—its concepts, rooted in the value system of our society, are socially determined and socially expressed. Consequently, broad agreement on useful generalizations regarding basic objectives is difficult to achieve. The setting of accounting standards is basically a political process involving many parties expressing their self-interests.

Concepts Underlying Financial Statements

The FASB has devised a **conceptual framework** whose purpose is establishing a coherent system of interrelated objectives and concepts for consistent measurement and reporting. These objectives and concepts are expected to guide selection of the events accounted for, the measurement of events, and the means of their summarization and communication to users. Without conceptual underpinnings, measures and reports provided by accountants are arguably matters of judgment and personal opinion. The more precise the conceptual framework, the less subjectivity involved.

The conceptual framework is represented by *Statements of Financial Accounting Concepts (SFACs)*. Several *SFACs* are relevant to financial statement analysis. *SFAC No. 1,* "Objectives of Financial Reporting by Business Enterprises," establishes the objectives of general-purpose external financial reporting by business enterprises. This *Statement* asserts financial reporting best serves us by helping us predict the amount, timing, and uncertainty of future cash flows. Moreover, it asserts financial reporting should provide information about the economic resources of an enterprise, the claims to those resources, and the effects of transactions, events, and circumstances that change its resources and claims to those resources. A primary focus of financial reporting is information about earnings and its components. Financial reporting is also expected to provide information about an enterprise's financial performance during a period and about how management has discharged its stewardship responsibility to owners.

SFAC No. 2, "Qualitative Characteristics of Accounting Information," identifies the characteristics of accounting information that make it useful. Exhibit 2.5 illustrates these characteristics as a hierarchy of qualities where usefulness for decision making is first in importance. The hierarchy of accounting qualities separates user-specific qualities (e.g., understandability) from qualities inherent in the information. Information cannot be useful to decision makers unless they understand it regardless of how relevant it is.

Relevance and **reliability** are the primary qualities making accounting information useful for decision making. Information is relevant if it has the capacity to confirm or change a decision maker's expectations. If information is received by a user too late to have an effect on a decision, it is uninformative. Hence, *timeliness* is an important aspect of relevance. So is *predictive value,* usefulness as an input into a predictive process, and *feedback value,* information helping to confirm or adjust earlier predictions. Information is reliable if it is *verifiable*—that is, independent observers using the same measurement methods arrive at the same results. Reliability is enhanced when accounting numbers and disclosures represent what actually exists or happened (*representational faithfulness*). Reliability also implies *neutrality* of information—standard setters should not be swayed if proposed standards cause undesirable economic effects for a particular industry or company. Accounting information must be truthful and unbiased.

Comparability, including consistency, interacts with relevance and reliability to contribute to the usefulness of information. Comparison is one of the most basic and important tools of analysis for decision making. Almost all evaluations and alternative-choice judgments involve comparisons. The ability to compare sets of accounting data of the same company over time, or those of one company with another, is crucial.

Overriding these qualitative characteristics are *pervasive constraints* like **benefits versus costs** and **materiality.** Information is costly to gather, process, interpret, and use. As with other services, information is supplied only if its benefits exceed its costs. *Materiality* is defined as "the magnitude of an omission or misstatement of accounting information that, in the light

Exhibit 2.5   Hierarchy of Accounting Qualities

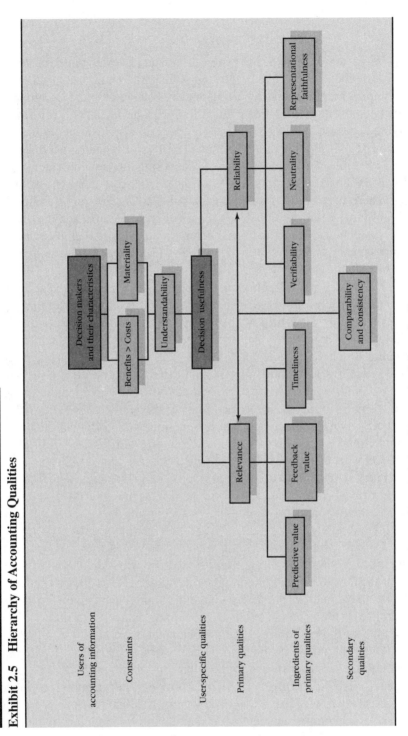

Source: FASB, *FAC No. 2*, "Qualitative Characteristics of Accounting Information."

of surrounding circumstances, makes it possible that the judgment of a reasonable person relying on the information would be changed or influenced by the omission or misstatement." In accounting, the concept of materiality assumes special significance because, by its nature, accounting information is not comprehended easily by readers. The main problem of materiality rests on the allegation that some preparers of financial statements and their auditors use it to avoid disclosing what they do not wish to. This aspect makes the concept significant to users of accounting data who must realize accountants do omit, reclassify, or ignore data and information on the basis of what they consider is material. There are no set criteria guiding either the accountant or user of information in distinguishing between what is material and what is not.

SFAC No. 3, "Elements of Financial Statements of Business Enterprises," describes 10 elements comprising financial statements (see Exhibit 2.6). Items qualifying as elements of financial statements and meeting criteria for recognition and measurement are accounted for and included in financial statements using accrual accounting. Accrual accounting and related concepts include the following processes:

- **Accrual accounting** recognizes noncash events and circumstances as they occur; specifically, accrual is the accounting process of recognizing assets, liabilities, and components of comprehensive income for amounts companies expect to receive or pay, usually in cash, in the future.

- **Deferral** is the accounting system process of recognizing a liability from a current cash receipt or an asset resulting from a current cash payment, with deferred recognition of components of comprehensive income.

- **Allocation** is the accounting process of (1) reducing a liability recorded as a result of a cash receipt by recognizing revenues or (2) reducing an asset recorded as a result of a cash payment by recognizing expenses or cost production payment.

- **Realization** is the process of converting noncash resources and rights into money and is most precisely used in accounting and financial reporting to refer to sales of assets for cash or claims to cash. The related terms, *realized* and *unrealized,* therefore, identify revenues or gains or losses on assets sold and unsold, respectively.

Exhibit 2.6   Financial Statement Elements

- **Assets** are probable future economic benefits obtained or controlled by a particular entity as a result of past transactions or events. Once acquired, an asset continues as an asset of the enterprise until the enterprise collects it, transfers it to another entity, or uses it, or some other event or circumstance destroys the future benefit or removes the enterprise's ability to obtain it. Valuation accounts that reduce or increase the carrying amount of an asset are sometimes found in financial statements; these are part of the related assets and are neither assets in their own right nor liabilities.

- **Liabilities** are probable future sacrifices of economic benefits arising from present obligations of a particular entity to transfer assets or provide services to other entities in the future as a result of past transactions or events. Once incurred, a liability continues as a liability of the enterprise until the enterprise settles it, or another event or circumstance discharges it or removes the enterprise's responsibility to settle it.

- **Equity** is the residual interest in the assets of an entity that remains after deducting its liabilities. In a business enterprise, the equity is the ownership interest (owners' equity).

- **Investments by owners** are increases in net assets of a particular enterprise resulting from transfers to it from other entities of something valuable to obtain or increase equity (ownership interests). What the enterprise receives includes most commonly assets, but may also include services or satisfaction or conversion of liabilities of the enterprise. Investments by owners increase equity (ownership interests).

- **Distributions to owners** are decreases in net assets of a particular enterprise resulting from transferring assets, rendering services, or incurring liabilities by the enterprise to owners. Distributions to owners decrease equity (owners' interest). When an enterprise declares dividends, it incurs a liability to transfer assets to owners in the future, resulting in an equity reduction and a liability increase. Reacquisition by an entity of its own equity securities by transferring assets or incurring liabilities to owners is a distribution to owners.

- **Comprehensive income** is the change in equity (net assets) of an enterprise during a period from transactions and other events and circumstances from nonowner sources. It includes all changes in equity during a period except those resulting from investment by owners and distributions to owners (i.e., the clean surplus relation). Over the life of a business enterprise, its comprehensive income equals the net of its cash receipts and cash outlays (excluding cash investments by owners and cash distributions to owners).

- **Revenues** are inflows or other enhancements of assets of an entity or settlements of its liabilities (or a combination of both) during a period of delivering or producing goods, rendering services, or other activities that constitute

---

Exhibit 2.6   *continued*

the entity's ongoing major or central operations. Revenues represent actual or expected cash inflows (or the equivalent) that have occurred or will eventuate as a result of the enterprise's ongoing major or central operations during the period.

- **Expenses** are outflows or other using up of assets or incurrences of liabilities (or a combination of both) during a period of delivering or producing goods, rendering services, or carrying out other activities that constitute the enterprise's ongoing major or central operations. Expenses represent actual or expected cash outflows (or the equivalent) that have occurred or will eventuate as a result of the enterprise's ongoing major or central operations during the period.

- **Gains** are increases in equity (net assets) from peripheral or incidental transactions of an entity and from all other transactions and other events and circumstances affecting the entity during a period except those resulting from revenues or investments by owners.

- **Losses** are decreases in equity (net assets) from peripheral or incidental transactions of an entity and from all other transactions and other events and circumstances affecting the entity during a period except those that result from expenses or distributions to owners.

- **Recognition** is the process of formally recording or incorporating an item in the financial statements of an entity. Thus, an asset, liability, revenue, expense, gain, or loss may be recognized (recorded) or unrecognized (unrecorded). *Realization* and *recognition* should not be used as synonyms, as they sometimes are in accounting and financial literature.

SFAC No. 5, "Recognition and Measurement in Financial Statements of Business Enterprises," endorses current recognition and measurement practices while allowing for gradual, evolutionary change. The basic approach to recognition is identification of information that financial statements report. Recognition of an item in financial statements is required when the item meets the following four criteria:

- Meets the definition of a financial statement element.
- Is measurable.
- Is relevant—it is capable of making a difference in users' decisions.

- Is reliable—it is representationally faithful, verifiable, and neutral.

This *Statement* fails to resolve the major measurement dilemma of current value versus historical cost. Several measurement attributes are used in practice, and the board expects the use of different attributes to continue. However, the board gives itself an option to pursue more extensive use of current values, stating that: "Information based on current prices should be recognized if it is sufficiently relevant and reliable to justify the costs involved and more relevant than alternative information."

Analysis Implications of Accounting Objectives and Concepts

The conceptual framework is an attempt to establish a logical and coherent structure of interrelated objectives and concepts to enhance the theoretical foundations of accounting standards and to promote confidence in and acceptance of these standards. We are understanding of the profession's efforts to establish a sound framework and are supportive of its goals, which are, ultimately, in our best interests. At the same time, we must be aware previous attempts at establishing conceptual frameworks have not yielded universally accepted concepts or "truths." The board admitted that *SFAC No. 5* "would not produce instant, indisputable answers to questions about whether a particular event should be recognized and when, and what amount best measures it." The board took the cautious position that establishing objectives and identifying concepts do not solve accounting and reporting problems. Rather, objectives give direction, and concepts are tools for solving problems. The board has seemingly concluded that change in accounting is an evolutionary process and is not the product of a conceptual framework.

The conceptual framework does contribute to a healthy debate on the objectives of accounting and the primary users of financial statements. It identifies qualitative characteristics of accounting information and the qualities that make it useful. It defines elements of financial statements, such as assets, liabilities, owners' equity, revenues, expenses, gains, losses, and comprehensive income. It presents superior definitions of accounting-related concepts. It can even contribute to a higher degree of internal consistency in promulgated standards. Nevertheless, it disappoints those who hoped it would provide a structure for resolving today's and tomorrow's vexing accounting problems. By relying on gradual change and evolution, the board admits it cannot meet the expectations of the conceptual framework. From the point of view of users of financial statements, this admission is a healthy development giving the board a more realistic view of what can and cannot be accomplished in accounting standard setting. Change in accounting comes mostly as a process where standard setters address problems demanding immediate action. Motivations for diligent effort and compromise were pressing and solutions found. This process is likely to continue. Resolution of these problems is always influenced by the cries and protests of those most affected by them. Many observers expect this. Social sciences do not have codified conceptual frameworks. There are none for law, economics, or finance. Board members who have experienced firsthand how difficult it is to settle even limited problems of practice—such as those of foreign operations, pensions, or taxes— realize developing a framework to settle important issues of accounting in advance is futile. Addressing accounting problems requires compromises and adjustments. In using financial statements, we must be alert to the practical considerations of self-interest governing accounting as much as logic and rational processes.

Additional Tools and Sources for Financial Statement Analysis

TECHNOLOGY-BASED FINANCIAL ANALYSIS TOOLS

The major emphasis throughout this book is on the application of thoughtful and logical analysis using reliable and relevant data. Financial statement analysis does, however, involve significant work of a computational nature as well. We can utilize technology to our advantage here. Judicious use of technology in financial analysis depends on thorough understanding of its limitations. Technology lacks the ability to generate intuitive judgments or keen insights—capabilities that are essential to a competent and discerning financial analysis. We must always remember there is nothing technology adds that a competent user cannot. Yet technology significantly enhances the efficiency of our analysis, especially in statistical analysis.

With the exception of databases offering on-line access to complete financial statements, most databases for technological analysis do not include all information necessary to adjust accounting numbers to render them comparable or conforming to our specific needs. Reasons for this include the following:

- Databases often lack information on a company's accounting policies and principles. This information is essential to reliable comparisons and interpretations of data.
- Notes and other explanatory information are usually missing or incomplete.

- Lack of retroactive adjustments in the data—even if the data are subsequently revealed as erroneous or misleading.
- Lapses or omissions often occur when examining large masses of financial data on a uniform basis. Data can also be classified inconsistently across companies.
- Aggregation of dissimilar or noncomparable data yields a loss of vital distinctions and diminishes its meaning and value in our analysis.

While technology has its limitations, there are several significant uses to which it can be effectively and efficiently applied in financial analysis.

Data Storage, Retrieval, and Computation

An accessible and comprehensive database is essential to effective use of technology in most phases of our analysis. Technology allows us to store and easily access vast amounts of important data. It has the ability to probe these data, to manipulate them mathematically, to update and modify them, and to select from among them using various criteria (e.g., sales levels, returns, growth rates).

Specialized Financial Analyses

Technology is useful for financial analysis in credit extension and security analysis. In credit extension, technology assists financial analysis with:
- Storage of data for comparison and decision making.
- Projection of enterprise cash requirements under a variety of assumptions.
- Projection of financial statements under various assumptions, showing the impact of changes on key variables. Known as *sensitivity analysis,* this technique allows the user to explore the effect of systematically changing a variable by a predetermined amount.
- Inclusion of probabilistic inputs. We can insert data as probability distributions, either normally shaped or skewed, or random probability distributions, otherwise known as Monte Carlo trials.

In security analysis, technology assists with:
- Calculations using past data.
- Trend computations.

- Predictive models.
- Projections and forecasts.
- Sensitivity analysis.
- Probabilistic analysis.

An understanding of technology, both its capabilities and limitations, is increasingly important in the analysis of financial statements.

SOURCES OF RELEVANT ANALYSIS INFORMATION

For company data, and for comparative industry data, financial statements are often the best and most readily available source. This section presents a list of information sources on financial and operating data. These data, while valuable, must be used with care and with as complete a knowledge as possible of the basis of their compilation. A realistic and sometimes superior alternative for us to use as a basis of comparison is financial statements of one or more comparable industry competitors.

Annual reports to shareholders contain an increasing amount of information required by either GAAP or specific SEC rulings. Company filings with the SEC—such as registration statements pursuant to the Securities Act of 1933, supplemental and periodic reports requiring filing (e.g., Forms 8-K, 10-K, 10-Q, 14-K, and 16-K), or proxy statements—contain a wealth of useful information for our analysis. Additional information is often available through alternative mechanisms. Some companies offer "investor services" or supplementary data on request. Federal or state regulatory agencies require publicly available filings for certain industries. Those able to exert a degree of influence have other avenues available. Bond rating agencies are often given financial and operating details beyond that in published financial statements. Major lenders and investors often have similar access to more detailed information.

To achieve familiarity with the wide variety of available financial and operating data, we classify some popular sources by type of agency compiling the data. This list is intended to exemplify the type of materials available and is *not* a comprehensive list:

Professional Commercial Organizations

Dun & Bradstreet, Business Economics Division, New York.

- Industry norms and key business ratios.
- Key business ratios. Important operating and financial ratios in numerous lines.
- Selected operating expense figures for many retailing, wholesaling, and manufacturing lines, as well as for contract construction; service/transportation/communication; finance/insurance/real estate; agriculture/forestry/fishing; mining.
- Cost-of-Doing Business Series. Typical operating ratios for numerous lines of business, showing national averages. They represent a percentage of business receipts reported by a representative sample of the total of all federal tax returns. Published irregularly.

Moody's Investor Service, New York, NY. Moody's manuals contain financial and operating ratios on the individual companies covered.

Nelson's Directory of Investment Research, Port Chester, NY. W. R. Nelson & Co./Nelson Publications, annual.

Robert Morris Associates, *Annual Statement Studies*. Financial and operating ratios for about 300 lines of business—manufacturers, wholesalers, retailers, services, and contractors—based on information obtained from member banks of RMA. Data are broken down by company size.

Standard & Poor's Corporation.

- *Analysts Handbook.* "Composite corporate per share data—by industries," for over 90 industries. Statistics and percentages cover several components, including sales, operating profits, depreciation, earnings, and dividends.
- *Industry Surveys.* Basic data on many important industries, with financial comparisons of the leading companies in each industry. Includes a "Basic Analysis" for each, revised annually, and a "Current Analysis" for each industry, published quarterly. A monthly "Trends and Projections" includes tables of economic and industry indicators.

Almanac of Business and Industrial Financial Ratios by Leo Troy. Englewood Cliffs, NJ: Prentice Hall. A compilation of corporate performance ratios (operating and financial). Explains the significance of these ratios. Covers all industries in the study, each industry subdivided by asset size.

Value Line Investment Survey, New York: Value Line Publishing, Inc., weekly updating.

Federal Government

Small Business Administration. Publications containing industry statistics (published sporadically—may not be up to date): *Small Marketers Aid, Small Business Management Series;* and *Business Service Bulletins.*

U.S. Department of Commerce. Census of business—wholesale trade—summary statistics, monthly wholesale trade report. Ratio of operating expenses to sales.

Department of the Treasury. Statistics of income, corporation income tax returns. Operating statistics based on income tax returns.

Federal Trade Commission—Securities and Exchange Commission. *Quarterly Financial Report for Manufacturing, Mining, and Trade Corporations.* Contains operating ratios and balance sheet ratios as well as the balance sheet in ratio format.

U.S. Internal Revenue Service, Washington, DC: U.S. Government Printing Office.

- *Source Book: Statistics of Income: Corporation Income Tax Returns.* Annual. Balance sheet, income statement, tax and investment credit items by major and minor industries, broken down by size of total assets.
- *Statistics of Income: Corporation Income Tax Returns.* Annual. Balance sheet and income statement statistics from a sample of corporate returns. Includes tables by major industry, by asset size, and so on. Includes historical summaries.

Industry Associations

Many retail and wholesale trade associations compile and publish periodic statistics. Few manufacturing associations compile statistics available to the public; and so we must rely on general sources or annual reports of specific companies.

American Meat Institute, *Annual Financial Review of the Meat Packing Industry,* Washington, DC. Includes operating ratios.

Federal Deposit Insurance Corporation, *Banking Operating Statistics,* annual.

Institute of Real Estate Management, Experience Exchange Committee, *A Statistical Compilation and Analysis of Actual (year) Income and Expenses Experienced in Apartment, Condominium and Cooperative Building Operation,* annual.

Discount Merchandiser, *The True Look of the Discount Industry,* June issue each year. Includes operating ratios.

National Electrical Contractors Association, *Operation Overhead,* annual.

National Farm & Power Equipment Dealers Association, *Cost of Doing Business Study,* annual.

National Retail Hardware Association, *Lumber/Building Material Financial Report,* Indianapolis, annual.

Journal of Commercial Bank Lending, "Analysis of Year End Composite Ratios of Installment Sales Finance and Small Loan Companies."

National Association of Music Merchants, *Merchandising and Operating Statistics,* New York, annual.

National Decorating Products Association, *NDPA's Annual Cost of Doing Business Survey,* St. Louis. Taken from *Decorating Retailer.*

National Office Products Association, *NOPA Dealers Operating Results,* Alexandria, VA, annual.

National Restaurant Association, *Restaurant Industry Operations Report for the United States,* Washington, DC, annual.

Computerized Databases

ABI/Inform, Ann Arbor, MI: University Microfilms International, weekly (on-line), monthly (CD-ROM).

Corporate Information Research Reports (CIRR), East Chester, NY: J. A. Micropublishing. Microfiche collection, on-line database, and CD-ROM database. Monthly.

Compact Disclosure, Bethesda, MD: Disclosure Incorporated. CD-ROM database. Monthly.

Compustat, New York: Standard & Poor's Compustat Services, Inc. Computer tape files and CD-ROM database. Weekly.

Lotus OneSource, Cambridge, MA: Lotus Development Corporation. CD-ROM database. Monthly.

Financial Analysis Application and Interpretation

CHAPTER 3: SHORT-TERM LIQUIDITY

This chapter begins our application and interpretation of financial analysis. Our analysis tools explore accounting numbers for insights into company operations and future performance. We learn about and describe several measures of liquidity. In our reading you must assume the role of a banker to make a decision on a loan application and consult on estimated cost savings with improved inventory management.

CHAPTER 4: FORECASTING AND PRO FORMA ANALYSIS

In this chapter we study forecasting and pro forma analysis of cash flows and their implications for liquidity. We explain how cash circulates through a company's business activities. While studying forecasting and pro forma analysis, we must decide how to use forecasts in processing a loan application and analyze the disparity between cash and earnings forecasts for an initial public offering of stock.

CHAPTER 5: CAPITAL STRUCTURE AND SOLVENCY

Capital structure and solvency are considered in this chapter. We learn how financial leverage affects both risk and return. We describe earnings coverage measures, as well as analytical adjustments to book values and their interpretation. Along the way we assume the role of an entrepreneur to make a decision on whether to expand through debt financing, and we serve as an analyst who assesses preferred equity risk of two alternative investments.

CHAPTER 6: RETURN ON INVESTED CAPITAL

This chapter describes return on invested capital and its relevance for financial analysis. Attention is directed at *return on assets* and *return on equity*. We disaggregate these return measures, describe their importance, and evaluate the impact of financial leverage. During our reading we assume the role of an auditor to use returns analysis for substantive testing and we also serve as a management consultant in a review of company performance

CHAPTER 7: PROFITABILITY ANALYSIS

This chapter emphasizes returns analysis as applied to profitability and its components, including sales, cost of sales, taxes, selling, and financing expenses. We learn about break-even analysis and its relevance for profitability. Along the way, we decide on component information disclosure requirements as a securities listing director, we assess the relative strength of two loan applicants who differ on their level of diversification, and we scrutinize tax benefits granted to companies as a political activist.

CHAPTER 8: EARNINGS-BASED ANALYSIS AND VALUATION

This chapter concludes returns analysis by focusing on earnings-based analysis and valuation. Earnings-based analysis looks at earnings quality, persistence, and power. Earnings-based valuation focuses on forecasting earnings and estimating company value. In our reading we assess earnings quality as a member of the board of directors, and we analyze earnings persistence in preparing an earnings forecast for publication in an online forecasting service.

CHAPTER 3

Short-Term Liquidity

A LOOK BACK

We focused our attention in the first two chapters on overviewing financial statement analysis and learning the objectives, uses, and approaches to analysis. We discussed how financial statements report on financing, investing, and operating activities.

A LOOK AT THIS CHAPTER

We begin our study of the application and interpretation of analysis tools using financial statement numbers. Analysis tools exploit the accounting numbers to yield useful insights into company operations and future performance. This chapter highlights tools for assessing short-term liquidity. We explain liquidity and describe analysis tools capturing different aspects of it. Attention is directed at accounting-based ratios, turnover, and operating activity measures of liquidity.

A LOOK AHEAD

Chapter 4 extends our focus on analysis tools to cash flow prediction and analysis. We illustrate both short- and long-term forecasting procedures and discuss their reliability. Consideration is given to special cash-based measures in assessing companies' cash requirements.

THIS CHAPTER WILL:

- Explain the importance of liquidity in analyzing business activities.
- Describe working capital measures of liquidity and their components.
- Interpret the current ratio and cash-based measures of liquidity.
- Analyze operating cycle or turnover measures of liquidity and their interpretation.
- Describe other short-term liquidity measures and their usefulness for analysis.
- Illustrate what-if analysis for evaluating changes in company conditions and policies.

PREVIEW OF CHAPTER 3

Liquidity refers to the availability of company resources to meet short-term cash requirements. A company's short-term liquidity risk is affected by the timing of cash inflows and outflows along with its prospects for future performance. Our analysis of liquidity is aimed at companies' operating activities, their ability to generate profits from sale of products and services, and working capital requirements and measures. This chapter describes several financial statement analysis tools used to assess liquidity risk. We begin with a discussion of the importance of liquidity and its link to working capital. We explain and interpret useful ratios of both working capital and a company's operating cycle for assessing liquidity. We also discuss potential adjustments to these analysis tools and the underlying financial statement numbers. What-if analysis of changes in a company's conditions or strategies concludes our discussion. The content and organization of this chapter are as follows:

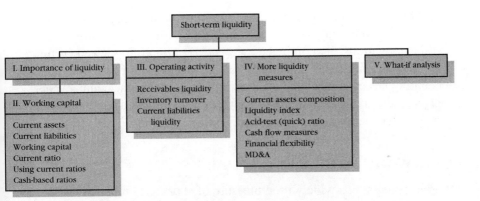

IMPORTANCE OF SHORT-TERM LIQUIDITY

A company's **short-term liquidity** refers to its ability to meet short-term obligations. *Liquidity* is the ability to convert assets into cash or to obtain cash. *Short term* is conventionally viewed as a period up to one year, though it is identified with the normal operating cycle of a company (the time period encompassing the buying-producing-selling-collecting cycle).

The importance of short-term liquidity is best seen by considering repercussions stemming from a company's inability to meet short-term obligations. Liquidity is a matter of degree. Lack of liquidity can signify a company unable to take advantage of favorable discounts or profitable opportunities. It also implies limited opportunities and constraints on management actions. More extreme liquidity problems reflect a company's inability to cover current obligations. This can lead to forced sale of investments and assets and, in its most severe form, to insolvency and bankruptcy.

For a company's shareholders, a lack of liquidity often precedes lower profitability and opportunity. It can foretell a loss of owner control or loss of capital investment. When a company's owners possess unlimited liability (proprietorships and certain partnerships), a lack of liquidity endangers their personal assets. To creditors of a company, a lack of liquidity can yield delays in collecting interest and principal payments or the loss of amounts due them. A company's customers and suppliers of products and services are affected by short-term liquidity problems. Implications include a company's inability to execute contracts and damage to important customer and supplier relationships.

These scenarios highlight why measures of liquidity are of great importance in our analysis of a company. If a company fails to meet its current obligations, its continued existence is doubtful. Viewed in this light, all other measures of analysis are of secondary importance. While accounting measurements assume indefinite existence of the company, our analysis must always assess the validity of this assumption using liquidity and solvency measures.

ANALYZING WORKING CAPITAL

Working capital is a widely used measure of short-term liquidity. **Working capital** is defined as the excess of current assets over current liabilities. A working capital deficiency exists when current liabilities exceed current assets. When current assets exceed current liabilities, there is a working capital surplus.

Working capital is important as a measure of liquid assets providing a safety cushion to creditors. It is also important in measuring the liquid reserve available to meet contingencies and the uncertainties surrounding a company's balance of cash inflows and outflows. The importance attached by creditors, investors, and other users to working capital as a measure of liquidity and solvency causes some companies to stretch the definition of a current asset or a current liability. Our analysis must therefore evaluate the classification of items included in working capital.

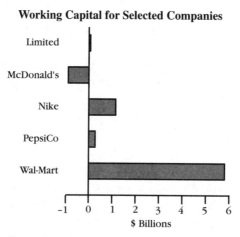

Working Capital for Selected Companies

Source: Annual reports

Current Assets

Current assets are cash and other assets reasonably expected to be (1) realized in cash, or (2) sold or consumed, during the normal operating cycle of the company (or within one year if the operating cycle is less than a year). Note that the principle regarding ability to convert assets into cash within a year is subject to important qualifications. The most important qualification relates to the operating cycle. As we discussed in prior chapters, an operating cycle comprises the time period between acquisition of materials and services for operating activities until final cash realization of proceeds from sale of a company's products or services. This time period can be quite extended in industries requiring a long inventory holding period (e.g., tobacco, distillery, lumber) or for those selling on an installment plan. When a defined operating cycle is not evident, the one-year rule prevails. Common categories of current assets are briefly reviewed in this section.

Cash is the ultimate current asset since most current liabilities are paid off in cash. Cash marked for specific purposes like plant expansion should not be considered a current asset, and compensating balances under bank loan agreements should not, in most cases, be regarded as available cash. *Cash equivalents* are temporary investments of excess cash often made for purposes of earning a return. These investments must be short term and of high quality to ensure their sale without loss. *Marketable securities* are debt or equity securities held as investments. These securities are classified as current assets when (1) management intends to sell them in the near future (e.g., trading and available-for-sale securities), and/or (2) they are comprised of debt securities scheduled to mature in the next period. *Accounts receivable,* net of provisions for uncollectible accounts, are current assets. An exception is when they represent receivables from sales not in the ordinary course of business and are due beyond one year. Installment receivables from routine sales usually fall within the operating cycle of a company. Our analysis must be alert to the valuation and validity of receivables. This is especially important when those "sales" are on consignment or subject to return privileges. Receivables from affiliated companies or employees are current only if collectible in the ordinary course of business and within one year—or for installment receivables, within the operating cycle.

Inventories are current assets except when they are in excess of current production/sale requirements. These excess inventories should be shown as noncurrent and must be distinguished from typical inventories. The variations in practice are considerable and our analysis must carefully scrutinize them. Our analysis must pay special attention to inventory valuation. For example, measurement of inventories using LIFO can understate working capital. *Prepaid expenses* are also current assets. This is not because they can be converted to cash, but rather because they reflect advance payments for services and supplies that otherwise require current cash outlays.

Certain trucking companies include tires on their trucks as current assets. These companies presumably justify this practice on the basis the tires are used up during the company's normal operating cycle.

The mere ability of a company to convert an asset to cash is not the sole determinant of its classification as current. It is both management's intent and normal industry practice that govern classification. Intent is not always sufficient. For example, the cost of fixed assets intended for sale is included in current assets only if a company has a contractual commitment from a buyer to purchase these assets at a specific price within the year or operating cycle. Champion International Corporation classified "operations held for disposition" as current assets and reported it as shown on this page.

The company has entered into an agreement to sell three paperboard mills, its corrugated box manufacturing operations, and all but one of its bag manufacturing operations to Stone Container Corporation ("Stone") for cash and Stone common stock. Upon consummation of the sale to Stone, the company expects to receive $372,900,000 in cash, subject to adjustment in certain circumstances.

Attempts by management to stretch the definition of a *current asset* reinforces the importance that our analysis does not rely exclusively on financial statements. Rather, we need to exercise vigilance in our use of ratios and other analytical measures to render our own judgments. Attempts by management to stretch the rules to present a situation as better than it is serve as a warning of added risk.

Current Liabilities

Current liabilities are obligations expected to be satisfied with either (1) use of current assets, or (2) creation of other current liabilities, within a relatively short period of time, usually one year. Current liabilities include accounts payable, notes payable, short-term bank (and other) loans, taxes payable, accrued expenses, and the current portion of long-term debt. As with current assets, our analysis must not assume current liabilities are always properly classified.

Penn Central Company excluded current maturities of long-term debt from current liabilities and included them in long-term debt. This treatment resulted in an excess of current assets over current liabilities of $21 million. Alternatively, including current debt maturities in current liabilities would have yielded a working capital deficit of $207 million. This disclosure decision by management foreshadowed Penn Central's financial collapse.

Our analysis must assess whether all current obligations with a reasonably high probability of eventual payment are reported in current liabilities. Their exclusion from current liabilities handicaps analysis of working capital. Three examples are:

- Contingent liabilities associated with loan guarantees. We need to assess the likelihood of this contingency materializing when we compute working capital.

- Future minimum rental payments under noncancelable operating lease agreements.

- Contracts for construction or acquisition of long-term assets often call for substantial progress payments. These obligations for payments are reported as "commitments" and *not* as liabilities. When computing working capital, our analysis should often include these commitments.

We should recognize that current deferred tax assets (debits) are no more current assets than current deferred tax liabilities (credits) are current liabilities. Current deferred tax assets do not always represent expected cash inflows in the form of tax refunds. These assets usually serve to reduce future cash payments to taxing authorities. An exception is the case of net operating loss carrybacks. Similarly, current deferred tax liabilities do not always represent future cash outflows. Examples are temporary differences of a recurring nature (such as depreciation) that do not necessarily result in payment of taxes because their reversing differences are offset by equal or larger originating differences.

Many companies with fixed assets as their main "working assets," like certain trucking and leasing companies, carry as current assets their prospective receipts from billings—from which their current equipment purchase obligations are met. Also, certain companies do not distinguish between current and noncurrent on their balance sheets (e.g., real estate companies, banks, insurance companies). These reporting policies are attempts by these companies to convey "special" financing and operating circumstances. They claim the current versus noncurrent distinction is not applicable and that there is no parallel with manufacturing or merchandising companies. While some of these special circumstances are likely valid, they do not necessarily change the relation between current obligations and the liquid funds available or expected to be available to meet them. It is this relation that our analysis, confronted with evaluating liquidity, must focus attention on.

Working Capital Measure of Liquidity

The working capital measure of liquidity and of short-term financial strength is a common analytical tool. Credit grantors regularly rely on the difference between current assets and current liabilities. Loan agreements and bond indentures often contain stipulations for maintenance of minimum working capital levels. Financial analysts assess the magnitude of working capital for investment decisions and recommendations. Government agencies compute aggregates of companies' working capital for regulatory and policy actions. And nearly all published financial statements distinguish between current and noncurrent assets and liabilities in response to these and other user needs.

Yet the amount of working capital is more relevant to users' decisions when related to other key financial variables like sales or total assets. It is of limited value for direct comparative purposes and for assessing the adequacy of working capital. This is seen in Illustration 3.1.

Current Ratio Measure of Liquidity

Illustration 3.1 below highlights the need to consider *relative* working capital. That is, a $200,000 working capital excess yields a different

Illustration 3.1

	Company A	Company B
Current assets	$300,000	$1,200,000
Current liabilities	100,000	1,000,000
Working capital	$200,000	$200,000

These companies have an equal amount of working capital. Yet even a quick comparison of the relation of current assets to current liabilities indicates Company A's working capital position is superior to Company B's.

conclusion for a company with $300,000 in current assets than one with $1,200,000 in current assets. A common relative measure in practice is the current ratio. The **current ratio** is defined as:

$$\text{Current ratio} = \frac{\text{Current assets}}{\text{Current liabilities}}$$

In our illustration, the current ratio is 3:1 ($300,000/$100,000) for Company A and 1.2:1 ($1,200,000/$1,000,000) for Company B. This ratio reveals different pictures for companies A and B, and this ability to differentiate between companies results in the widespread use of the current ratio for assessing a company's short-term liquidity.

Relevance of the Current Ratio
Reasons for the current ratio's widespread use as a measure of liquidity include its ability to measure:

- *Current liability coverage.* The higher the amount (multiple) of current assets to current liabilities, the greater assurance we have in current liabilities being paid.
- *Buffer against losses.* The larger the buffer, the lower the risk. The current ratio shows the margin of safety available to cover shrinkage in noncash current asset values when ultimately disposing or liquidating them.
- *Reserve of liquid funds.* The current ratio is relevant as a measure of the margin of safety against uncertainties and random shocks

to a company's cash flows. Uncertainties and shocks, such as strikes and extraordinary losses, can temporarily and unexpectedly impair cash flows.

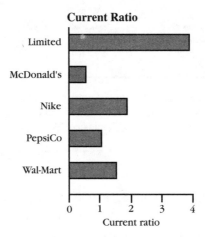

Source: Annual reports

While the current ratio is a relevant and useful measure of liquidity and short-term solvency, it is subject to certain limitations we must be aware of. Consequently, before we describe the usefulness of the current ratio for our analysis, we discuss its limitations.

Limitations of the Current Ratio

A first step in critically evaluating the current ratio as a tool for liquidity and short-term solvency analysis is for us to examine both its numerator and denominator. If we define *liquidity* as the ability to meet cash outflows with adequate cash inflows, including an allowance for unexpected decreases in inflows or increases in outflows, then it is appropriate for us to ask: Does the current ratio capture these important factors of liquidity? Specifically, does the current ratio:

- Measure and predict the pattern of future cash inflows and outflows?
- Measure the adequacy of future cash inflows to outflows?

The answer to both these questions is generally no. The current ratio is a static (or "stock") measure of resources available at a point in time to meet current obligations. The current reservoir of cash resources does not have a logical or causal relation to its future cash inflows. Yet future cash inflows are the greatest indicator of liquidity. These cash inflows depend on factors excluded from the ratio, including sales, cash expenditures, profits, and changes in business conditions. To clarify these limitations, we need to examine more closely the individual components of the current ratio.

Numerator of the Current Ratio

We discuss each individual component comprising current assets and its implications for our analysis using the current ratio.

Cash and Cash Equivalents   Cash held by a well-managed company is primarily of a precautionary reserve intended to guard against short-term cash imbalances. For example, sales can decline more rapidly than cash outlays for purchases and expenses in a business downturn requiring availability of excess cash. Since cash is a nonearning asset and cash equivalents are usually low-yielding securities, a company's investment in these assets is minimized. The cash balance has little relation to the existing level of business activity and is unlikely to convey predictive implications. Further, many companies rely on cash substitutes in the form of open lines of credit not entering into the computation of the current ratio.

Marketable Securities   Cash in excess of the precautionary reserve is often spent on investment securities with returns exceeding those for cash equivalents. These investments are reasonably viewed as available to discharge current liabilities. Since investment securities are reported at their fair values, much of the guesswork from estimating their net realizable value is removed. Our analysis must recognize that the further removed the balance sheet date, the greater likelihood for unrecorded changes in these investments' fair values.

Accounts Receivable   A major determinant of accounts receivable is sales. The relation of accounts receivable to sales is governed by credit policies and collection methods. Changes in receivables correspond to changes in sales, though not necessarily on a directly proportional basis. Our analysis of accounts receivable as a source of cash must recognize, except in liquidation, the revolving nature of this asset. The collection of one account is succeeded by a new extension of credit. Accordingly, the level of receivables is not a measure of future net cash inflows.

Inventories   Like receivables, the major determinant of inventories is sales or expected sales—not the level of current liabilities. Since sales are a function of demand and supply, methods of inventory management (e.g., economic order quantities, safety stock levels, and reorder points) maintain inventory increments varying not in proportion to demand but by lesser amounts. The relation of inventories to sales is underscored by the observation that sales initiate the conversion of inventories to cash. Determination of future cash inflows from the sale of inventories depends on the profit margin that can be realized since inventories are reported at the lower of cost or market. The current ratio does not recognize sales level or profit margin, yet both are important determinants of future cash inflows.

Prepaid Expenses   Prepaid expenses are expenditures for future benefits. Since these benefits are typically received within a year or the company's operating cycle, they preserve the outlay of current funds. Prepaid expenses are usually small relative to other current assets. However, our analysis must be aware of the tendency of companies with weak current positions to include in prepaid expenses deferred charges and other items of dubious liquidity. We should exclude such items from our computation of working capital and the current ratio.

Denominator of the Current Ratio
Current liabilities are the focus of the current ratio. They are a source of cash in the same way receivables and inventories use cash. Current liabilities are primarily determined by sales, and a company's ability to meet them when due is the object of working capital measures. For example, since purchases giving rise to accounts payable are a function of sales, payables vary with sales. As long as sales remain constant or are rising, the payment of current liabilities is a refunding activity. In this case the components of the current ratio provide little, if any, recognition to this activity or to its effects on future cash flows. Also, current liabilities entering into the computation of the current ratio do not include prospective cash outlays—examples are commitments under construction contracts, loans, leases, or pensions.

Using the Current Ratio for Analysis

From our discussion of the current ratio we can draw at least three conclusions.

1. Liquidity depends to a large extent on *prospective* cash flows and to a lesser extent on the level of cash and cash equivalents.

2. No direct relation exists between balances of working capital accounts and likely patterns of future cash flows.

3. Managerial policies regarding receivables and inventories are directed primarily at efficient and profitable asset utilization and secondarily at liquidity.

These conclusions do not bode well for the current ratio as an analysis tool and we might question why it enjoys widespread use in analysis. Reasons for using the current ratio include its understandability, its simplicity in computation, and its data availability. Its use also derives from the creditor's (especially banker's) propensity in viewing credit situations as conditions of last resort. They ask themselves: What if there were a complete stoppage of cash inflows? Would current assets meet current liabilities? This extreme analysis is not always a useful way of assessing liquidity. Two other points are also pertinent. First, our analysis of short-term liquidity and solvency must recognize the relative superiority of cash flow projections and pro forma financial statements versus the current ratio. These analyses require information not readily available in financial statements, including product demand estimation. Second, should our analysis use the current ratio as a static measure of the ability of current assets to satisfy current liabilities, we must recognize this is a different concept of liquidity from the one described above. In our context, liquidity is the readiness and speed that current assets are convertible to cash and the extent conversion results in shrinkage in current asset values.

It is not our intent to reject the current ratio as an analysis tool. But it is important for us to know its relevant use. Our consideration of the current ratio's limitations indicates any analysis process of "adjusting" for them is not feasible. Consequently, to what valuable use can our analysis apply the current ratio? The relevant use of the current ratio is recognizing its limitations and restricting its use to appropriate situations. This means limiting its use to measuring the ability of current assets to discharge existing current liabilities. Second, we can consider the excess of current assets, if any, as a liquid surplus available to meet imbalances in the flow of funds and other contingencies. These two applications are applied with our awareness that the ratio assumes company liquidation. This is in contrast to the usual going-concern situation where current assets are of a revolving nature (e.g., collecting receivables is replaced with new receivables) and current liabilities are of a refunding nature (e.g., covering payables is met with new payables).

Provided we apply the current ratio in the manner described, there are two components that we must evaluate and measure before the current ratio can usefully form a basis of analysis:

1. Quality of both current assets and current liabilities entering into the ratio's computation.
2. Turnover rate of both current assets and current liabilities—that is, time period necessary for converting receivables and inventories into cash and for paying current liabilities.

Several adjustments, ratios, and other analysis tools are available to accomplish these tasks and enhance our use of the current ratio (see below). The remainder of this section describes relevant applications of the current ratio in practice.

Comparative Analysis

Analyzing the trend in the current ratio is often enlightening. Two tools of analysis described in Chapter 1 are useful here. One is *trend analysis,* where components of working capital and the current ratio are converted to indexes and examined over time. The other is *common-size analysis,* where the composition of current assets is examined over time. These comparative time analyses, along with intra-industry comparisons of these trends, are useful for our analysis.

Changes in the current ratio over time must be interpreted with caution. Changes in this ratio do not necessarily imply changes in liquidity or operating performance. For example, during a recession a company might continue to pay current liabilities while inventory and receivables accumulate, yielding an increase in the current ratio. Conversely, in a successful period, increases in taxes payable can lower the current ratio. Company expansion often accompanying operating success can create larger working capital requirements. This "prosperity squeeze" in liquidity decreases the current ratio and is illustrated in the case of company expansion unaccompanied by an increase in working capital. See Illustration 3.2.

Inflation can produce a similar effect by increasing the balances of current assets and current liabilities.

Ratio Management

Our analysis must look for "management" of the current ratio, also known as *window dressing.* Toward the close of a period, management will occa-

Illustration 3.2

Technology Resources, Inc., experiences a doubling of current assets and a quadrupling of current liabilities with *no change* in its working capital. This yielded a prosperity squeeze evidenced by a 50 percent decline in the current ratio.

	Year 1	Year 2
Current assets	$300,000	$600,000
Current liabilities	100,000	400,000
Working capital	$200,000	$200,000
Current ratio	3:1	1.5:1

sionally press the collection of receivables, call in advances to officers for temporary repayment, reduce inventory below normal levels, and delay normal purchases. Proceeds from these activities are then used to pay off current liabilities. The effect of these activities is to increase the current ratio, as shown in Illustration 3.3.

Illustration 3.3

Technology Resources, Inc., increases its current ratio by making an earlier-than-normal payoff of $50,000 of current liabilities:

	Before Payoff	After Payoff
Current assets	$200,000	$150,000
Current liabilities	100,000	50,000
Working capital	$100,000	$100,000
Current ratio	2:1	3:1

In a related situation, given management's desire to offset liabilities against assets, practice restricts offsets to situations where the legal right to offset exists. Our analysis should also go beyond annual measures and use interim measures of the current ratio. Interim analysis makes it more difficult for management to window dress and allows us to gauge seasonal effects on the ratio. For example, a strong current ratio in December can be misleading if a company experiences a credit squeeze at its seasonal peak in July.

Rule of Thumb Analysis

A frequently heard rule of thumb is if the current ratio is 2:1 or better, then a company is financially sound, while a ratio below 2:1 suggests increasing liquidity risks. At one time this "norm" was 2.5:1. This change in the rule of thumb may reflect lenders', and particularly bankers', reduced conservatism. It might also reflect better accounting, allowing bankers and lenders to reduce the "cushion" acceptable as their minimum protection. The 2:1 norm implies there are $2 of current assets available for every $1 of current liabilities or, alternatively viewed, the value of current assets can in liquidation shrink by as much as 50 percent and still cover current liabilities. A current ratio much higher than 2:1, while implying superior coverage of current liabilities, can signal inefficient use of resources and a reduced rate of return. Our evaluation of the current ratio with any rule of thumb is of dubious value for two reasons:

1. Quality of current assets, and the composition of current liabilities, are more important in evaluating the current ratio (e.g., two companies with identical current ratios can present substantially different risks due to variations in the quality of working capital components).
2. Working capital requirements vary with industry conditions and the length of a company's net trade cycle.

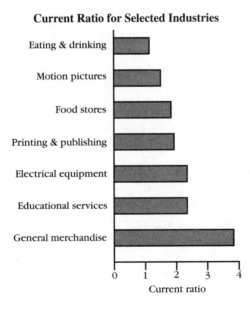

Current Ratio for Selected Industries

Net Trade Cycle Analysis

A company's working capital requirements are affected by its desired inventory investment and the relation between credit terms from suppliers and those extended to customers. These considerations determine a company's **net trade cycle.** Computation of a company's net trade cycle is shown in Illustration 3.4.

Illustration 3.4

Selected financial information from Technology Resources, Inc., for the end of Year 1 is reproduced below:

Sales for Year 1	$360,000
Receivables	40,000
Inventories*	50,000
Accounts payable†	20,000
Cost of goods sold (including depreciation of $30,000)	320,000

*Beginning inventory is $100,000.
†We assume these relate to purchases included in cost of goods sold.

We estimate Technology Resources' purchases per day as:

Ending inventory	$ 50,000
Cost of goods sold	320,000
	$ 370,000
Less: Beginning inventory	(100,000)
Cost of goods purchased and manufactured	$ 270,000
Less: Depreciation in cost of goods sold	(30,000)
Purchases	$ 240,000

Purchases per day = $240,000 ÷ 360 = $666.67

The net trade cycle for Technology Resources is computed as (in days):

$$\text{Accounts receivable} = \frac{\$40,000}{\$360,000 \div 360} = 40.00 \text{ days}$$

$$\text{Inventories} = \frac{\$50,000}{\$320,000 \div 360} = 56.24 \text{ days}$$

$$96.24 \text{ days}$$

$$\text{Less: Accounts payable} = \frac{\$20,000}{\$666.67} = 30.00 \text{ days}$$

$$\text{Net trade cycle (days)} = 66.24 \text{ days}$$

Notice the numerator and denominator are adjusted on a consistent basis. Specifically, accounts receivable reported in sales dollars are divided by sales per day, inventories reported at cost are divided by cost of goods sold per day, and accounts payable reported in dollars of purchases are divided by purchases per day. Consequently, while the day measures are expressed on different bases, our estimation of the net trade cycle is on a consistent basis. Our analysis shows Technology Resources has 40 days of sales tied up in receivables, maintains 56.24 days of goods available in inventory, and receives only 30 days of purchases as credit from its suppliers. The longer the net trade cycle, the larger is the working capital requirement. Reduction in the number of days' sales in receivables or cost of sales in inventories lowers working capital requirements. An increase in the number of days' purchases as credit received from suppliers lowers working capital needed. Working capital requirements are determined by industry conditions and practices. Comparisons using industry current ratios, and analysis of working capital requirements using net trade cycle measures, are useful in our analysis of the adequacy of a company's working capital.

Sales Trend Analysis

Our analysis of the liquidity of current assets should include a review of the trend in sales. Since sales are necessary to convert inventory into receivables or cash, an upturn in sales implies the conversion of inventories into liquid assets is more likely than when sales are stable. Declining sales delay the conversion of inventories into liquid assets.

ANALYSIS VIEWPOINT

YOU ARE THE BANKER

International Machines Corporation (IMC) calls on you for a short-term one-year $2 million loan to finance expansion in the United Kingdom. As part of your loan analysis of IMC you compute a 4:1 current ratio on current assets of nearly $1.6 million. Analysis of industry competitors yields a 19:1 average current ratio. What is your decision on IMC's loan application using this limited information? Would your decision change if IMC's application is for a 10-year loan?

Cash-Based Ratio Measures of Liquidity

Cash and cash equivalents are the most liquid of current assets. In this section, we examine cash-based ratio measures of liquidity.

Cash Ratio

The ratio of "near-cash" assets to the total of current assets is a measure of the degree of current asset liquidity. This measure, known as the **cash ratio,** is computed as:

$$\frac{\text{Cash} + \text{Cash equivalents} + \text{Marketable securities}}{\text{Current assets}}$$

The larger this ratio, the more liquid are current assets. This ratio has minimal danger of loss in value in case of liquidation and there is nearly no waiting period for conversion of these assets into usable cash. Our analysis should recognize possible restrictions on these near-cash assets. For example, lenders sometimes expect borrowers to maintain compensating balances. While these balances are relevant, the analyst must assess the effect on a company's credit standing and credit availability, and its banking relationship, of a breach of this tacit agreement not to draw on a compensating cash balance. Two additional factors bearing on our evaluation of the cash ratio should be recognized. One relates to cash management practices leading to efficient use of cash by companies and a lower threshold for cash required. The other is open lines of credit and standby credit arrangements that are effective substitutes for cash and should be considered in our analysis.

Cash to Current Liabilities Ratio

Another ratio measuring cash adequacy is the **cash to current liabilities ratio.** It is computed as:

$$\frac{\text{Cash} + \text{Cash equivalents} + \text{Marketable securities}}{\text{Current liabilities}}$$

This ratio measures the cash available to pay current obligations. This is a severe test ignoring the refunding nature of current assets and current liabilities. It supplements the cash ratio in measuring cash availability from a different perspective. To view this ratio as an extension of the quick ratio (see below) is, except in extreme cases, a too severe test of short-term liquidity. Nevertheless, the importance of cash as the ultimate form of liquidity should not be underestimated. The record of business failures provides many examples of insolvent companies with sizable noncash assets (both current and noncurrent) and an inability to pay liabilities or to operate.

OPERATING ACTIVITY ANALYSIS OF LIQUIDITY

Operating activity measures of liquidity are important in our analysis. This section considers three operating activity measures based on accounts receivable, inventory, and current liabilities.

Accounts Receivable Liquidity Measures

For most companies selling on credit, accounts and notes receivable are an important part of working capital. In assessing liquidity, including the quality of working capital and the current ratio, it is necessary to measure the quality and liquidity of receivables. Both quality and liquidity of accounts receivable are affected by their turnover rate. *Quality* refers to the likelihood of collection without loss. A measure of this likelihood is the proportion of receivables within terms of payment set by the company. Experience shows that the longer receivables are outstanding beyond their due date, the lower is the likelihood of their collection. Their turnover rate is an indicator of the age of receivables. This indicator is especially useful when compared with an expected turnover rate computed using the permitted credit terms. *Liquidity* refers to the speed in converting accounts receivable to cash. The receivables turnover rate is a measure of this speed.

Accounts Receivable Turnover
The **accounts receivable turnover** ratio is computed as:

$$\frac{\text{Net sales on credit}}{\text{Average accounts receivable}}$$

The most direct way for us to determine *average* accounts receivable is to add beginning and ending accounts receivable for the period, and divide by two. Using monthly or quarterly figures yields more accurate estimates. The more sales fluctuate, the more likely distorted is this ratio. We should include notes receivable from normal sales when computing accounts receivable turnover. We should also include only credit sales when computing this ratio because cash sales do not create receivables. Since finan-

Receivables Turnover for Selected Industries

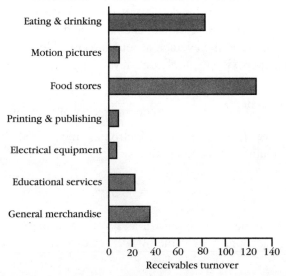

Receivables turnover

cial statements rarely disclose both cash and credit sales, our analysis often must compute this ratio using total net sales (i.e., assuming cash sales are insignificant). If they are not insignificant, then this ratio is less useful. However, if the proportion of cash sales to total sales is relatively stable, year-to-year comparisons of changes in the receivables turnover ratio are more relevant. The receivables turnover ratio indicates how often, on average, receivables revolve—that is, are received and collected during the year. An example of the computation is provided in Illustration 3.5.

Illustration 3.5

Consumer Electronics, Inc., reports sales of $1,200,000, beginning receivables of $150,000, and year-end receivables of $250,000. Its receivables turnover ratio is computed as:

$$\frac{\$1,200,000}{(\$150,000 + \$250,000) \div 2} = \frac{\$1,200,000}{\$200,000} = 6$$

Accounts Receivable Collection Period

While the receivables turnover ratio measures the speed of collections and is useful for comparison purposes, it is not directly comparable to the terms of trade a company extends to its customers. This latter comparison is made by converting the turnover ratio into days of sales tied up in receivables. The **receivables collection period** measures the number of days it takes, on average, to collect accounts (and notes) receivable. It is computed by dividing the average accounts receivable turnover ratio into 360 days (the approximate number of days in a year):

$$\text{Collection period} = \frac{360}{\text{Accounts receivable turnover}}$$

Using the figures from Consumer Electronics, Inc., in the above illustration, the receivables collection period is:

$$\frac{360}{6} = 60 \text{ days}$$

An alternative computation, known as **days' sales in receivables,** is to divide *ending* accounts receivable by average daily sales as follows:

$$\text{Accounts receivable} \div \frac{\text{Sales}}{360}$$

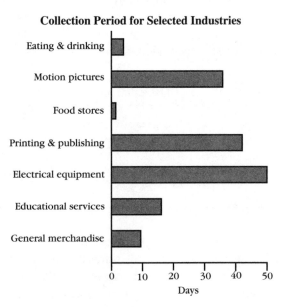

Collection Period for Selected Industries

This measure differs from the foregoing collection period computation. The accounts receivable collection period uses *average* accounts receivable, while the latter alternative computation uses *ending* accounts receivable. Using data from Consumer Electronics, Inc., the alternative computation yields:

$$\text{Average daily sales} = \frac{\text{Sales}}{360} = \frac{\$1,200,000}{360} = \$3,333$$

$$\frac{\text{Accounts receivable}}{\text{Average daily sales}} = \frac{\$250,000}{\$3,333} = 75 \text{ days}$$

Interpretation of Receivables Liquidity Measures

Accounts receivable turnover rates and collection periods are usefully compared with industry averages or to the credit terms given by the company. When the collection period is compared with the terms of sale allowed by the company, we can assess the extent of customers paying on time. For example, if usual credit terms of sale are 40 days, then an average collection period of 75 days reflects one or more of the following conditions:

- Poor collection efforts.
- Delays in customer payments.
- Customers in financial distress.

The first condition demands corrective managerial action, while the other two reflect on both the quality and liquidity of accounts receivable and demand judicious managerial action. An initial step is to determine whether accounts receivable are representative of company sales activity. For example, receivables may be sheltered in a captive finance subsidiary of the company. In this case, bad debts may also relate to receivables not on the company's books. It is also possible an average figure is not representative of the receivables population it represents. For example, the 75-day average collection period might not represent an across-the-board delay in payment by customers, but rather is due to the extreme delinquency of one or two customers. An excellent tool to investigate an extreme collection period is to *age* accounts receivable, listing the distribution of each account by the number of days past due. An aging schedule like the one shown below reveals whether the delay is widespread or concentrated:

| | | Days Past Due | | | |
	Current	*0–30*	*31–60*	*61–90*	*Over 90*
Accounts receivable	$ ____	$ ____	$ ____	$ ____	$ ____

An aging analysis of receivables leads to more informed conclusions regarding the quality and liquidity of receivables. It also improves managerial decisions to take action necessary to remedy the situation. However, information to perform an aging analysis is often unavailable to us. Another measure of receivables quality is the credit rating from agencies like Dun & Bradstreet who often have access to other data.

Certain other areas deserve our attention. We must scrutinize notes receivable because, while they are normally more negotiable than open accounts, they are sometimes of lower quality. This is especially the case if they originate as a means to extend the payment period of an unpaid open account. Our analysis should also recognize that converting receivables into cash, except for their use as collateral for borrowing, cannot be achieved without a cutback in sales volume. The sales policy aspect of a collection period evaluation must be kept in mind. A company might be willing to accept slow-paying customers who provide overall profitable business. In this case, profit on sales compensates for the extended use by the customer of the company's funds. This circumstance can alter our analysis regarding the quality of receivables but not their liquidity. A company might also extend more liberal credit in cases where (1) a new product is launched, (2) sales are made to utilize excess capacity, or (3) special competitive conditions prevail. Accordingly, we must consider the relations between receivables, sales, and profits when evaluating the collection period.

Certain trend analyses also merit our study. The trend in collection period over time is important in assessing the quality and liquidity of receivables. Another trend to watch is the relation between the provision for doubtful accounts and gross accounts receivable, computed as:

$$\frac{\text{Provision for doubtful accounts}}{\text{Gross accounts receivable}}$$

Increases in this ratio over time suggest a decline in the collectibility of receivables. Conversely, decreases in this ratio suggest improved collectibility or the need to reevaluate the adequacy of the doubtful accounts provision. Overall, accounts receivable liquidity measures are important in our analysis. They are also important as measures of asset utilization, a subject we address in Chapter 6.

Inventory Turnover Measures

Inventories often comprise a substantial proportion of current assets. The reasons for this often have little to do with a company's need to maintain adequate liquid funds. Reserves of liquid funds are seldom kept in the form of inventories. Inventories are investments made for purposes of obtaining a return. This return is derived from the expected profits resulting from sales to customers. In most companies, a certain level of inventory must be kept. If inventory is inadequate, sales volume declines below an attainable level. Conversely, excessive inventories expose a company to storage costs, insurance, taxes, obsolescence, and physical deterioration. Excessive inventories also tie up funds used more profitably elsewhere. Due to risks in holding inventories, and given inventories are further removed from cash compared to receivables, they are normally considered the least liquid current asset. This is not always the case since items like commodities and raw materials enjoy ready markets and can usually be sold with little effort, expense, or loss. Yet fashion merchandise, special components, or perishable items can rapidly lose value unless sold on a timely basis. Our evaluation of short-term liquidity and working capital, which includes inventories, must include an evaluation of the quality and liquidity of inventories. Measures of inventory turnover are excellent tools for this analysis.

Inventory Turnover

The **inventory turnover ratio** measures the average rate of speed inventories move through and out of a company. Inventory turnover is computed as:

$$\frac{\text{Cost of goods sold}}{\text{Average inventory}}$$

Consistency in valuation requires we use cost of goods sold in the numerator like inventories, it is reported typically at cost. Sales, in contrast, includes a profit margin. Cost of goods sold is regularly reported in income statements. Yet our analysis is occasionally confronted with the unavailability of cost of sales figures. In this case, sales is often used as the numerator in a "modified" ratio. Dun & Bradstreet reports modified inventory turnover ratios. While use of sales impairs the usefulness of the turnover ratio, this modified ratio can be used for comparative (trend) analysis, especially if used consistently and where changes in profit margins are small. Average inventory is computed by adding the opening and closing inventory balances, and dividing by 2. This averaging computation can he refined by averaging quarterly or monthly inventory figures. When we are interested in evaluating the level of inventory at a specific date, such as year-end, we compute the inventory turnover ratio using the inventory balance at this date as the denominator. Our analysis must also examine composition of inventory and make any necessary adjustments (e.g., from LIFO to FIFO).

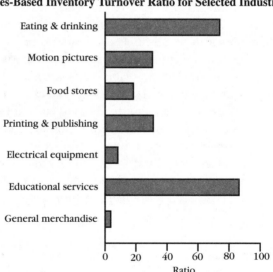

Sales-Based Inventory Turnover Ratio for Selected Industries

Days to Sell Inventory

Another measure of inventory turnover useful in assessing purchasing/production policy is the number of days to sell inventory. The **days to sell inventory ratio** is computed as:

$$\frac{360}{\text{Inventory turnover}}$$

This ratio tells us the number of days a company takes in selling *average* inventory for that year. An alternative computation, referred to as the **days' sales in inventory,** is computed as:

$$\frac{\text{Ending inventory}}{\text{Cost of average day's sales}}$$

This alternative ratio tells us the number of days required to sell *ending* inventory, assuming a given rate of sales. The cost of average day's sales is computed as:

$$\frac{\text{Cost of goods sold}}{360}$$

These computations are shown in Illustration 3.6.

Illustration 3.6

Selected financial information from Macon Resources, Inc., for the end of Year 8 is reproduced below:

Sales	$1,800,000
Cost of goods sold	1,200,000
Beginning inventory	200,000
Ending inventory	400,000

Inventory turnover ratios using *average* inventory are computed as:

$$\text{Inventory turnover ratio} = \frac{\$1,200,000}{(\$200,000 + \$400,000) \div 2} = 4$$

$$\text{Days to sell inventory ratio} = \frac{360}{4} = 90 \text{ days}$$

Inventory turnover ratios based on *ending* inventory equal:

$$\text{Cost of average day's sales} = \frac{\$1,200,000}{360} = \$3,333$$

$$\text{Days' sales in inventory} = \frac{\$400,000}{\$3,333} = 120 \text{ days}$$

Interpreting Inventory Turnover

The current ratio views current asset components as sources of funds to potentially pay off current liabilities. Viewed similarly, inventory turnover ratios offer measures of both the quality and liquidity of the inventory

Sales-Based Days to Sell Inventory for Selected Industries

component of current assets. *Quality of inventory* refers to a company's ability to use and dispose of inventory. When our analysis assumes inventory liquidation, then cost recovery is the objective. Yet in the normal course of business, inventory is usually sold at profit. Assuming this usual state, the normal profit margin is important since funds obtained and deemed available for paying current liabilities include *both* profit and cost components. Our analysis of inventory under either liquidation or normal sales must reduce proceeds by any costs of selling inventory. We should also recognize a continuing company does not use inventory for paying current liabilities since any serious reduction in normal inventory levels likely cuts into sales volume.

When inventory turnover decreases over time, or is less than the industry norm, it suggests slow-moving inventory items attributed to obsolescence, weak demand, or nonsalability. These conditions question the feasibility of a company recovering inventory costs. We need further analysis to see if decreasing inventory turnover is due to inventory buildup in anticipation of sales increases, contractual commitments, increasing prices, work stoppages, inventory shortages, or other legitimate reason. We also must be aware of inventory management (e.g., just-in-time systems) aimed at keeping inventory levels low by integrating ordering, producing, selling, and distributing. Effective inventory management increases inventory turnover.

We can improve our evaluation of inventory turnover by computing separate turnover rates for major inventory components like raw materials, work in process, and finished goods. Similarly, computing department or division turnover rates yields more useful inferences concerning inventory quality. We should not forget that inventory turnover is an aggregate of varying turnover rates for diverse inventory groupings. One problem confronting our analysis when computing inventory turnover ratios by various groupings is availability of data. Companies do not frequently report inventory component data in financial statements. Certain companies are willing to provide these data when requested.

Inventory turnover is also a gauge of liquidity in measuring the speed with which inventory is converted to cash. A useful inventory liquidity measure is its **conversion period** or **operating cycle.** This measure combines the collection period of receivables with the days to sell inventories to obtain the time interval to convert inventories to cash. Using results computed from our two independent illustrations above, we compute the conversion period as:

Days to sell inventory	90
Collection period	60
Operating cycle	150

This implies it takes 150 days to sell inventory on credit and to collect receivables.

In evaluating inventory turnover, our analysis must be alert to the influence of alternative accounting principles for valuing the ratio's components. Use of the LIFO method of inventory valuation can seriously impair the usefulness of both turnover and current ratios. For example, inventory valuation affects both the numerator and denominator of the current ratio—the latter through its effect on taxes payable. Information is often available in the financial statements enabling us to adjust unrealistically low LIFO inventory values in times of rising prices, making these values useful for inclusion in turnover and current ratios. Notice if two companies use the LIFO method for inventory valuation, their inventory-based ratios are likely *not* comparable because their LIFO inventory pools (bases) are almost certainly acquired in different years with different price levels. We must also remember companies using a "natural year" may have at year-end an atypically low inventory level. This can increase a turnover ratio to an abnormally high level.

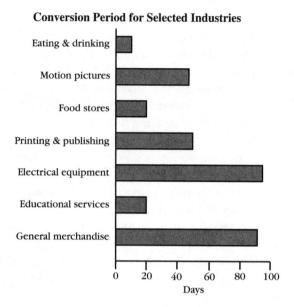

Conversion Period for Selected Industries

Liquidity of Current Liabilities

Current liabilities are important in computing both working capital and the current ratio for two related reasons:

- Current liabilities are used in determining whether the excess of current assets over current liabilities affords a sufficient margin of safety.
- Current liabilities are deducted from current assets in arriving at working capital.

In using working capital and the current ratio, our point of view is one of liquidation and *not* of continuing operations. This is because in normal operations current liabilities are not paid off but are of a refunding nature. Provided sales remain stable, both purchases and current liabilities will remain steady. Increasing sales usually yield increasing current liabilities. The trend and direction of sales are good indicators of future current liabilities.

Quality of Current Liabilities

The quality of current liabilities is important in our analysis of working capital and the current ratio. Not all current liabilities represent equally urgent or forceful payment demands. At one extreme, we find liabilities

ANALYSIS VIEWPOINT

YOU ARE THE CONSULTANT

King Entertainment, Inc., engages your services as a management consultant. One of your tasks is to streamline costs of inventory. After studying prior performance and inventory reports, you propose to strategically reduce inventories through improved inventory management. Your proposal expects the current inventory turnover of 20 will increase to 25. Money not invested in inventory can be used to decrease current liabilities—the costs of holding current liabilities average 10 percent per year. What is your estimate of cost savings if predicted sales are $150 million and predicted cost of sales is $100 million?

for various taxes that must be paid promptly regardless of current financial pressures. Collection powers of federal, state, and local government authorities are formidable. At the other extreme are current liabilities to suppliers with whom a company has a long-standing relationship and who depend on and value its business. Postponement and renegotiation of these liabilities in times of financial pressures are both possible and common.

The quality of current liabilities must be judged on their degree of urgency in payment. We should recognize if fund inflows from current revenues are viewed as available for paying current liabilities, then labor and similar expenses requiring prompt payment have a first call on revenues. Trade payables and other liabilities are paid only after these outlays are met. We examine this aspect of funds flow in the next chapter.

Our analysis must also be aware of unrecorded liabilities having a claim on current funds. Examples are purchase commitments and certain postretirement and lease obligations. When long-term loan acceleration clauses exist, a failure to meet current installments can render the entire debt due and payable.

Days' Purchases in Accounts Payable

A measure of the extent accounts payable represent current and not overdue obligations is obtained by calculating the **days' purchases in accounts payable ratio.** This ratio is computed as:

$$\text{Days' purchases in accounts payable} = \frac{\text{Accounts payable}}{\text{Purchases} \div 360}$$

One difficulty we often encounter when computing this ratio is purchases are usually not separately reported in financial statements. For merchandising companies, an approximation of purchases is obtained by adjusting cost of goods sold for depreciation, other noncash charges, and changes in inventories as follows:

Purchases = Adjusted cost of goods sold + Ending inventory − Beginning inventory

If cost of goods sold contains significant cash charges, this can reduce the reliability of computations based on our approximation of purchases on credit.[1]

ADDITIONAL SHORT-TERM LIQUIDITY MEASURES

Current Assets Composition

Composition of current assets is an indicator of working capital liquidity. Use of common-size percentage comparisons facilitates our evaluation of comparative liquidity, regardless of the dollar amounts. Consider a case example, Illustration 3.7.

Illustration 3.7

Texas Electric Corp.'s current assets along with their common-size percentages are reproduced below for Years 1 and 2:

	Year 1		Year 2	
Current assets:				
Cash	$ 30,000	30%	$ 20,000	20%
Accounts receivable	40,000	40	30,000	30
Inventories	30,000	30	50,000	50
Total current assets	$100,000	100%	$100,000	100%

Our analysis of Texas Electric's common-size percentages reveals a marked deterioration in current asset liquidity in Year 2 relative to Year 1. This is evidenced by the 10 percent decline in both cash and accounts receivable.

---

[1] Another useful measure is **accounts payable turnover.** It is computed as: Purchases ÷ Average Accounts Payable. This ratio indicates the speed at which a company pays for purchases on account.

Liquidity Index

Our assessment of the liquidity of current assets is aided by use of a **liquidity index.** Computation of the liquidity index is shown in Illustration 3.8. The liquidity index is expressed in days and its computation is a weighting mechanism. Its usefulness depends on the validity of assumptions implicit in the weighting process. Increases in the index signify a dete-

---

Illustration 3.8

Using the financial data of Texas Electric Corp. reported in the illustration above, along with additional data, we find their conversion of inventories into accounts receivable takes 50 days (on average) and their conversion of receivables into cash takes 40 days (on average). The liquidity index for Texas Electric is computed as:

Year 1:

	Amount	×	Days Removed from Cash	=	Product Dollar × Days
Cash	$ 30,000		—		—
Accounts receivable	40,000		40 days		1,600,000
Inventories	30,000		90 days		2,700,000
Total	$100,000 *(a)*				4,300,000 *(b)*

$$\text{Liquidity index} = \frac{b}{a} = \frac{4,300,000}{\$100,000} = 43 \text{ days}$$

Year 2:

	Amount	×	Days Removed from Cash	=	Product Dollar × Days
Cash	$ 20,000		—		—
Accounts receivable	30,000		40 days		1,200,000
Inventories	50,000		90 days		4,500,000
Total	$100,000				5,700,000

$$\text{Liquidity index} = \frac{5,700,000}{\$100,000} = 57 \text{ days}$$

Computation of the liquidity indexes of Texas Electric for Years 1 and 2 is consistent with results from the common-size analysis of current assets composition—liquidity has deteriorated in Year 2 relative to Year 1.

rioration in liquidity, while decreases signify improved liquidity. The liquidity index must be interpreted with caution. The index is a number without direct meaning. It becomes meaningful when comparing one index number with another. It is best used as a measure of period-to-period change in liquidity or as a company-to-company comparison of relative liquidity.

Acid-Test (Quick) Ratio

A stringent test of liquidity uses the **acid-test (quick) ratio.** This ratio includes those assets most quickly convertible to cash and is computed as:

$$\frac{\text{Cash} + \text{Cash equivalents} + \text{Marketable securities} + \text{Accounts receivable}}{\text{Current liabilities}}$$

Inventories are often the least liquid of current assets and are removed from the acid-test ratio. Another reason for excluding inventories is their valuation typically involves more managerial discretion than required for other current assets. Yet we must remember certain inventories are more liquid than slow-paying receivables. Interpretation of the acid-test ratio is similar to that of the current ratio. The acid-test ratio is a more stringent test of liquidity, and our analysis must assess the merits of excluding inventories in evaluating liquidity.

"Quick Ratio" for Selected Industries
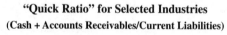
(Cash + Accounts Receivables/Current Liabilities)

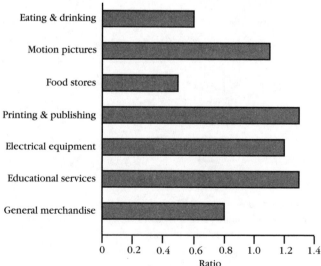

Cash Flow Measures

The static nature of the current ratio and its inability (as a measure of liquidity) to recognize the importance of cash flows in meeting maturing obligations has led to a search for a dynamic measure of liquidity. Since liabilities are paid with cash, a comparison of operating cash flow to current liabilities is important. A ratio comparing operating cash flow to current liabilities overcomes the static nature of the current ratio since its numerator reflects a flow variable. For analysis purposes, operating cash flow for a period should be compared with current liabilities for that period. This **cash flow ratio** is computed as:

$$\frac{\text{Operating cash flow}}{\text{Current liabilities}}$$

The cash flow ratio computation for Campbell Soup in Year 11 is (data taken from financial statements reproduced in Supplement A):

$$\frac{\$805.2}{\$1,278} = 0.63$$

A ratio of operating cash flow to current liabilities of 0.40 or higher is common for healthy companies.

Financial Flexibility

In addition to the usual analysis tools for short-term liquidity, there are important *qualitative* considerations bearing on short-term liquidity. These are usefully characterized as depending on the financial flexibility of a company. **Financial flexibility** is the ability of a company to take steps to counter unexpected interruptions in the flow of funds. It can mean the ability to borrow from various sources, to raise equity capital, to sell and redeploy assets, or to adjust the level and direction of operations to meet changing circumstances. A company's capacity to borrow depends on several factors and is subject to change. It depends on profitability, stability, size, industry position, asset composition, and capital structure. It also depends on credit market conditions and trends. A company's capacity to borrow is important as a source of cash and in turning over short-term debt. Prearranged financing or open lines of credit are reliable sources of cash. Additional factors bearing on our assessment of a company's financial flexibility are (1) ratings of its commercial paper, bonds, and preferred stock, (2) any restrictions on its sale of assets, (3) the extent expenses are discretionary, and (4) ability to respond quickly to changing conditions (e.g., strikes, demand shifts, breaks in supply sources).

Management's Discussion and Analysis

As we discussed in Chapter 1, the Securities and Exchange Commission requires companies to include in their annual reports an expanded management discussion and analysis of financial condition and results of operations (MD&A). The financial condition section requires a discussion of liquidity—including known trends, demands, commitments, or uncertainties likely to impact on the company's ability to generate adequate cash. If a material deficiency in liquidity is identified, management must discuss the course of action it has taken or proposes to take to remedy the deficiency. Internal and external sources of liquidity and any material unused sources of liquid assets must be identified and described. Our analysis benefits from management's discussion and analysis. Adaptec includes a discussion titled Liquidity and Capital Resources in its MD&A section (see Supplement A).

WHAT-IF ANALYSIS

What-if analysis is a useful technique to trace through the effects of changes in conditions or policies on the cash resources of a company. What-if analysis is illustrated in this section using the following selected financial data from Consolidated Technologies, Inc., at December 31, Year 1:

	Debit	Credit
Cash	$ 70,000	
Accounts receivable	150,000	
Inventory	65,000	
Accounts payable		$130,000
Notes payable		35,000
Accrued taxes		18,000
Fixed assets	200,000	
Accumulated depreciation		43,000
Capital stock		200,000

The following additional information is reported for Year 1:

Sales	$750,000
Cost of sales	520,000
Purchases	350,000
Depreciation	25,000
Net income	20,000

Consolidated Technologies anticipates 10 percent growth in sales for Year 2. All revenue and expense items are expected to increase by 10 percent, except for depreciation, which remains the same. All expenses are paid in cash as they are incurred, and Year 2 ending inventory is projected at $150,000. By the end of Year 2, Consolidated Technologies expects to have notes payable of $50,000 and a zero balance in accrued taxes. The company maintains a minimum cash balance of $50,000 as a managerial policy.

Case 3.1   Consolidated Technologies is considering a change in credit policy where ending accounts receivable reflect 90 days of sales. What impact does this change have on the company's cash balance? Will this change affect the company's need to borrow? Our analysis of this what-if situation is as follows:

Cash, January 1, Year 2			$ 70,000
Cash collections:			
Accounts receivable, January 1, Year 2		$150,000	
Sales		825,000	
Total potential cash collections		$975,000	
Less: Accounts receivable, December 31, Year 2		(206,250) *(a)*	768,750
Total cash available			$838,750
Cash disbursements:			
Accounts payable, January 1, Year 2	$130,000		
Purchases	657,000 *(b)*		
Total potential cash disbursements	$787,000		
Accounts payable, December 31, Year 2	(244,000) *(c)*	$543,000	
Notes payable, January 1, Year 2	$ 35,000		
Notes payable, December 31, Year 2	(50,000)	(15,000)	
Accrued taxes		18,000	
Cash expenses *(d)*		203,500	749,500
Cash, December 31, Year 2			$ 89,250
Cash balance desired			50,000
Cash excess			$ 39,250

Explanations:

(a) $825.000 \times \dfrac{90}{360} = \$206,250.$

(b)
Year 2 cost of sales*: $520,000 × 1.1 =	$572,000
Ending inventory (given)	150,000
Goods available for sale	$722,000
Beginning inventory	(65,000)
Purchases	$657,000

*Excluding depreciation.

(c) Purchases $\times \dfrac{\text{Beg. accounts payable}}{\text{Year 1 purchases}} = \$657,000 \times \dfrac{\$130,000}{\$350,000} = \underline{\$244,000}$

(d)
Gross profit ($825,000 − $572.000)		$253,000
Less: Net income	$ 24,500*	
Depreciation	25,000	(49,500)
Other cash expenses		$203,500

*110 percent of $20,000 (Year 1 N.I.) + 10 percent of $25,000 (Year 1 depreciation).

This change in credit policy would yield an excess in cash and no required borrowing.

Case 3.2   What if Consolidated Technologies worked to achieve an *average* accounts receivable turnover of 4.0 (instead of using *ending* receivables as in the previous case)? What impact does this change have on the company's cash balance? Our analysis of this what-if situation follows:

Excess cash balance as computed above		$39,250
Change from *ending* to *average* accounts receivable turnover increases year-end accounts receivable to:		
Average A.R. $= \dfrac{\$825,000}{4} = \$206,250$		
Ending A.R. $= [\$206,250 \times 2] - \$150,000 = $ $262,500^{a}$		
Less: Accounts receivable balance from Case 3.1 $\underline{206,250}$		$\underline{56,250}$ (cash decrease)
Cash required to borrow		$\underline{\underline{\$17,000}}$

[a] $\dfrac{Sales}{Average\ A.\,R.\ turnover} = Average$ A.R.; Ending A.R. $= [(Average\ A.R.) \times 2] - Beginning$ A.R.

Consolidated Technologies would be required to borrow funds to achieve expected performance under the conditions specified.

Case 3.3   What if, in addition to the conditions prevailing in Case 3.2, the company's suppliers require payment within 60 days? What is the effect of this payment requirement on the cash balance? Our analysis of this case is as follows:

Cash required to borrow (from Case 3.2)		$ 17,000
Ending accounts payable (from Case 3.1)	$244,000	
Ending accounts payable under 60-day payment:		
Purchases $\times \dfrac{60}{360} = \$657,000 \times \dfrac{60}{360} = $	$\underline{109,500}$	
Additional disbursements required		$\underline{134,500}$
Cash to be borrowed		$\underline{\underline{\$151,500}}$

This more demanding payment schedule from suppliers would place additional borrowing requirements on Consolidated Technologies.

GUIDANCE ANSWERS TO ANALYSIS VIEWPOINTS

YOU ARE THE BANKER

Your decision on IMC's one-year loan application is positive for at least two reasons. First, your analysis of IMC's short-term liquidity is assuring. IMC's current ratio of 4:1 suggests a considerable margin of safety in its ability to meet short-term obligations. Second, IMC's current assets of $1.6 million and current ratio of 4:1 implies current liabilities of $400,000 and a working capital excess of $1.2 million. This working capital excess totals 60 percent of the loan amount. The evidence supports approval of IMC's loan application. However, if IMC's application is for a 10-year loan, our decision is less optimistic. While the current ratio and working capital suggest a good safety margin, there are indications of inefficiency in operations. First, a 4:1 current ratio is in most cases too excessive and characteristic of inefficient asset use. Second, IMC's current ratio is more than double that of its competitors. Our decision regarding a long-term loan is likely positive, *but* substantially less optimistic than a short-term loan.

YOU ARE THE CONSULTANT

Cost savings are assumed to derive from paying off current liabilities with money not invested in inventory. Accordingly, cost savings equal inventory reduction $\times$ 10%. Under the old system, inventory equaled $5 million. This is obtained using the inventory turnover ratio: 20 = $100 million/average inventory. With the new system inventory equals $4 million, computed using the new inventory turnover: 25 = $100 million/average inventory. The cost savings are $100,000—computed from $5 million $-$ $4 million $\times$ 10%.

Forecasting and Pro Forma Analysis

A LOOK BACK

Chapter 3 began our study of the application and interpretation of financial statement analysis tools. We described analysis tools using financial data for assessing short-term liquidity. We defined accounting-based, turnover, and activity measures of liquidity and explained their relevance for analyzing different aspects of liquidity.

A LOOK AT THIS CHAPTER

We focus on forecasting and pro forma analysis of financial statements in this chapter. We explain the flow of cash through a company's business activities and its implications for liquidity. Both short- and long-term forecasting of cash flows are described. We direct special attention at applying these analysis tools.

A LOOK AHEAD

Chapter 5 expands our analysis of a company to capital structure and long-term solvency. We analyze capital structure and interpret its implications for future company performance and solvency. Several useful analysis tools are described and illustrated for the interpretation of financial statements.

THIS CHAPTER WILL:

- Describe cash flow patterns in a company's business activities.
- Explain short-term forecasting and pro forma analysis of financial statements.
- Analyze cash flow patterns for long-term forecasting.
- Describe forecasting of operating, investing, and financing cash flows.
- Explain what-if forecasting scenarios and their relevance.
- Interpret specialized cash flow adequacy and reinvestment ratios.

PREVIEW OF CHAPTER 4

Future liquidity is as important to our analysis of financial statements as our assessment of past and current liquidity. This chapter shows how our analysis of future liquidity benefits from forecasts of cash inflows and outflows. For long-term cash forecasting horizons, we show the usefulness of forecasts framed by the statement of cash flows. The forecast tools described in this chapter are extremely useful in analyzing a company's future liquidity, solvency, and financial flexibility. We demonstrate these tools with actual financial statements. Our analysis relies on a more *dynamic* representation of liquidity than traditional static ratio analysis based on past financial statement data. The static nature of traditional analysis, relying on financial reports listing claims against an enterprise and the resources available to meet these claims, fails to capture the dynamic nature of liquidity. We show how the analysis techniques in this chapter build on reliable patterns of past performance, incorporate estimates of future plans and conditions, and forecast the future availability and disposition of cash. These techniques are subject to feasibility tests using pro forma analysis and the discipline inherent in the accounting system. The content and organization of this chapter are as follows:

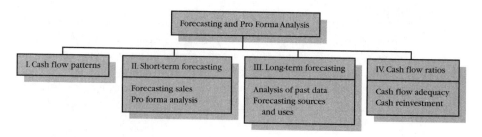

CASH FLOW PATTERNS

It is important for us to review the nature of cash flow patterns before examining models for cash flow analysis and projection. Cash and cash equivalents (hereafter simply *cash*) are the most liquid of assets. Nearly all management decisions to invest in assets or pay expenses require the immediate or eventual use of cash. This results in management's focus on cash rather than on other concepts of liquid funds, although some users (like creditors) sometimes consider assets like receivables and inventories part of liquid assets given their near-term conversion into cash.

Holding cash provides little or no return and, in times of rising prices, cash (like all monetary assets) is exposed to purchasing power loss. Nevertheless, holding cash represents the least exposure to risk. Management is responsible for the decisions to invest cash in assets or to pay immediate costs. These *cash conversions* increase risk because the ultimate recovery of cash from these activities is less than certain. Risks associated with these cash conversions are of various types and degrees. For instance, risk in converting cash into temporary investments is less than the risk in committing cash to long-term payout assets like plant and equipment. Investing cash in assets or costs aimed at developing and marketing new products carries often more serious risks of cash recovery. Both short-term liquidity and long-term solvency depend on the recovery and realizability of cash outlays.

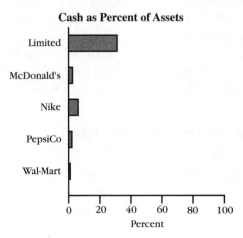

Cash as Percent of Assets

Source: Annual reports.

Cash inflows and outflows are interrelated. A failure of any aspect of the company's business activities to successfully carry out its assigned task affects the entire cash flow system. A lapse in sales affects the conversion of finished goods into receivables and cash, leading to a decline in cash availability. A company's inability to replace this cash from sources like equity, loans, or accounts payable can impede production activities and produce losses in future sales. Conversely, restricting expenditures on items like advertising and marketing can slow the conversion of finished goods into receivables and cash. Long-term restrictions in either cash outflows or inflows can lead to company insolvency.

Our analysis must recognize the interrelations between cash flows, accruals, and profits. Sales is the driving source of operating flows. When finished goods representing the accumulation of many costs and expenses are sold, the company's profit margin produces an inflow of liquid funds through receivables and cash. The higher the profit margin, the greater the growth of liquid funds. Profits often primarily derive from the difference between sales and cost of sales (gross profit) and have enormous consequences to cash flows. Many costs, like those flowing from utilization of plant and equipment or deferred charges, do not require cash outlays. Similarly, items like long-term installment sales of land create noncurrent receivables limiting the relevance of accruals for cash flows. Our analysis must appropriately use these measures in assessing cash flow patterns.

Cash flows are limited in another respect. As cash flows into a company, management has certain discretion in its disbursement. This discretion depends on commitments to outlays like dividends, inventory accumulation, capital expenditures, or debt repayment. Cash flows also depend on management's ability to draw on sources like equity and debt. With noncommitted cash inflows, referred to as free cash flows, management has considerable discretion in their use. It is this noncommitted cash component that is of special interest and importance for our analysis.

SHORT-TERM CASH FORECASTING

In our analysis of short-term liquidity, one of our most useful tools is **short-term cash forecasting.** Short-term cash forecasting is of interest to internal users like management and auditors in evaluating a company's current and future operating activities. It is also of interest to external users like short-term creditors who need to assess a company's ability to repay short-term loans. Our analysis stresses short-term cash forecasting when a company's ability to meet current obligations is in doubt. The accuracy of cash flow forecasting is inversely related to the *forecast horizon*—the longer the forecast period, the less reliable the forecasts. This is due to the number and complexity of factors influencing cash inflows and outflows that cannot be reliably estimated in the long term. Even in the case of short-term cash forecasting, the information required is substantial. Since cash flow forecasting often depends on publicly available information, our objective is "reasonably accurate" forecasts. By studying and preparing cash flow forecasts, our analysis should achieve greater insights into a company's cash flow patterns.

Importance of Forecasting Sales

The reliability of our cash forecast depends importantly on the *quality of the sales forecast.* With few exceptions, such as funds from financing or funds used in investing activities, most cash flows relate to and depend on sales. Our forecasting of sales includes an analysis of:

- Directions and trends in sales.
- Market share.
- Industry and economic conditions.
- Productive and financial capacity.
- Competitive factors.

These components are typically assessed along product lines potentially affected by forces peculiar to their markets. Later examples illustrate the importance of sales forecasts.

Cash Flow Forecasting
with Pro Forma Analysis

The reasonableness and feasibility of short-term cash forecasts are usefully checked by means of **pro forma financial statements.** We accomplish this by using assumptions underlying cash forecasts to construct a pro forma income statement for the forecast period and a pro forma balance sheet for the end of the forecast period. Financial ratios and other relations are derived from these pro forma financial statements and checked for feasibility against historical relations. These comparisons must recognize adjustments for factors expected to affect them during the cash forecast period.

ANALYSIS VIEWPOINT

YOU ARE THE LOAN OFFICER

As a recently hired loan officer at Intercontinental Bank you are processing a loan application for a new customer, DEC Manufacturing. In their application materials DEC submits short-term sales forecasts for the next three periods of $1.1, $1.25, and $1.45 million, respectively. You notice the most recent two periods' sales are $0.8 and $0.65 million, and you ask DEC management for an explanation. DEC's response is twofold: (1) recent sales are misleading due to a work stoppage and an unusual period of abnormally high raw material costs due to bankruptcy of a major supplier; and (2) recent industry volatility tied to consumer demand. Do you use their forecasts in your loan analysis?

We illustrate cash flow forecasting using financial data from IT Technologies, Inc. IT Technologies recently introduced a new electronic processor that has enjoyed excellent market acceptance. IT's management estimates sales ($ thousands) for the next six months ending June 30, Year 1, as: $100, $125, $150, $175, $200, and $250 (see the bar graph). The current cash balance at January 1, Year 1, is $15,000. In light of the predicted increase in sales, IT's treasurer hopes to maintain *minimum* monthly cash balances of $20,000 for January; $25,000 for February; $27,000 for March; and $30,000 for April, May, and June. The treasurer foresees a need for additional funds to finance sales expansion. The treasurer expects new equipment valued at $20,000 will be purchased in February by giving a note payable to the seller. The note is paid, beginning in February, at the rate of $1,000 per month. The new equipment is not planned to be operational until August of Year 1.

The treasurer plans several steps to fund these financing requirements. First, she obtains a financing commitment from an insurance company to acquire $110,000 of IT's long-term bonds (less $2,500 issue costs). These bond sales are planned for April ($50,000) and May ($60,000). She plans to sell real estate for additional financing, including $8,000 in May and $50,000 in June, and will sell equipment (originally costing $25,000 with a book value of zero) for $25,000 in June. The treasurer approaches IT's banker for approval of short-term financing to cover additional funding needs. The bank's loan officer requires the treasurer to prepare a *cash forecast* for the six months ending June 30, Year 1, along

IT's Forecasted Sales ($ in thousands)

January	100
February	125
March	150
April	175
May	200
June	250

$ Thousands

with *pro forma financial statements* for that period, to process her request. The loan officer also requests IT Technologies to specify its uses of cash and its sources of funds for loan repayment. The treasurer recognizes the importance of a cash forecast and proceeds to compile data necessary to comply with the loan officer's request.

As one of her first steps, the treasurer estimates the pattern of receivables collections. Prior experience suggests the following collection pattern:

Collections	Percent of Total Receivables
In month of sale	40%
In second month	30
In third month	20
In fourth month	5
Written off as bad debts	5
	100%

This collection pattern along with expected product sales allows the treasurer to construct estimates of cash collections shown in Exhibit 4.1.

Analyzing expense patterns in prior periods' financial statements yields expense estimates based on either sales or time. Exhibit 4.2 shows these expense relations. IT Technologies pays off these expenses (excluding

Exhibit 4.1

Estimates of Cash Collections
For Months January–June, Year 1

	January	February	March	April	May	June
Sales	$100,000	$125,000	$150,000	$175,000	$200,000	$250,000
Collections of sales:						
1st month—40%	$ 40,000	$ 50,000	$ 60,000	$ 70,000	$ 80,000	$100,000
2nd month—30%		30,000	37,500	45,000	52,500	60,000
3rd month—20%			20,000	25,000	30,000	35,000
4th month—5%				5,000	6,250	7,500
Total cash collections	$ 40,000	$ 80,000	$117,500	$145,000	$168,750	$202,500
Write-offs—5%				5,000	6,250	7,500

Exhibit 4.2

Expense Estimates
For Months January–June, Year 1

Materials	30% of sales
Labor	25% of sales
Manufacturing overhead:	
Variable	10% of sales
Fixed	$8,000 per month (includes $1,000 depreciation per month)
Selling expenses	10% of sales
General and administrative expenses:	
Variable	8% of sales
Fixed	$7,000 per month

the $1,000 monthly depreciation) when incurred. The only exception is for purchases of materials, where 50 percent is paid in the month of purchase and 50 percent in the following month. Materials inventory on January 1, Year 1, is $57,000. The treasurer estimates materials inventory for the end of each month from January to June of Year 1 as: $67,000, $67,500, $65,500, $69,000, $67,000, and $71,000, respectively. She also estimates the pattern of payments on accounts payable for these materials. Exhibit 4.3 shows these expected payments. Since the electronic processor is manufactured to specific order, no finished goods inventories are expected to accumulate.

Exhibit 4.3

	January	February	March	April	May	June
Estimates of Cash Payments for Materials **For Months January–June, Year 1**						
Materials purchases*	$40,000	$38,000	$43,000	$56,000	$58,000	$79,000
Payments:						
1st month—50%	$20,000	$19,000	$21,500	$28,000	$29,000	$39,500
2nd month—50%		20,000	19,000	21,500	28,000	29,000
Total payments	$20,000	$39,000	$40,500	$49,500	$57,000	$68,500

*These reconcile with material costs and changes in inventories.

The treasurer's resulting cash forecast for each of the six months ending June 30, Year 1, is shown in Exhibit 4.4. Exhibit 4.5 shows IT technologies' pro forma income statement for the six months ending June 30, Year 1. Both actual and pro forma balance sheets of IT Technologies as of January 1 and June 30, respectively, of Year 1 are shown in Exhibit 4.6.

Our cash flow analysis should critically examine the pro forma statements and submit them to *feasibility tests* on both their forecasts and their assumptions. We should evaluate both ratios and relations revealed in pro forma financial statements and compare them to historical ratios to

IT's Forecasted Cash ($ thousands)
(from Exhibit 4.4)

Exhibit 4.4

IT TECHNOLOGIES, INC.
Cash Forecast
For Months January–June, Year 1

	January	February	March	April	May	June	Six-Month Totals
Cash balance—beginning	$ 15,000	$ 20,000	$ 25,750	$ 27,250	$ 30,580	$ 30,895	$ 15,000
Add cash receipts for:							
Cash collections (Exh. 4.1)	40,000	80,000	117,500	145,000	168,750	202,500	753,750
Sale of real estate‡					8,000	50,000	58,000
Sale of bonds‡				47,500	60,000		107,500
Sale of equipment‡						25,000	25,000
Total cash available	$ 55,000	$100,000	$143,250	$219,750	$267,330	$308,395	$959,250
Less disbursements for:							
Materials (Exh. 4.3)	$ 20,000	$ 39,000	$ 40,500	$ 49,500	$ 57,000	$ 68,500	$274,500
Labor†	25,000	31,250	37,500	43,750	50,000	62,500	250,000
Fixed overhead†	7,000	7,000	7,000	7,000	7,000	7,000	42,000
Variable overhead†	10,000	12,500	15,000	17,500	20,000	25,000	100,000
Selling expenses†	10,000	12,500	15,000	17,500	20,000	25,000	100,000
General and administrative†	15,000	17,000	19,000	21,000	23,000	27,000	122,000
Taxes§						19,000	19,000
Purchase of fixed assets‡		1,000	1,000	1,000	1,000	1,000	5,000
Total cash disbursements	87,000	120,250	135,000	157,250	178,000	235,000	912,500
Tentative cash balance (deficit)	$(32,000)	$ (20,250)	$ 8,250	$ 62,500	$ 89,330	$ 73,395	$ 46,750
Minimum cash required‡	20,000	25,000	27,000	30,000	30,000	30,000	
Borrowing required	$ 52,000	$ 46,000	$ 19,000			—	$117,000
Repayment of loan				$ 30,000	$ 58,000	$ 29,000	(117,000)
Interest paid on balance*				1,920	435	145	2,500
Ending cash balance	$ 20,000	$ 25,750	$ 27,250	$ 30,580	$ 30,895	$ 44,250	$ 44,250
Loan balance	$ 52,000	$ 98,000	$117,000	$ 87,000	$ 29,000	—	—

*Interest is computed at the rate of ½ percent per month and paid at month-end. Any loan is taken out at the beginning of a month.
†Estimates computed using information from Exhibit 4.2.
‡Treasurer's expectations taken from information on prior pages.
§Taxes total a 40 percent combined state and federal rate. Taxes of $19,000 are paid in June, with the balance accrued.

Exhibit 4.5

IT TECHNOLOGIES, INC.
Pro Forma Income Statement
For Six Months Ending June 30, Year 1

		Source of Estimate
Sales	$1,000,000	Forecasted sales
Cost of sales:		
Materials	$ 300,000	Exhibit 4.2
Labor	250,000	Exhibit 4.2
Overhead	148,000	Exhibit 4.2
	$ 698,000	
Gross profit	$ 302,000	
Selling expense	$ 100,000	Exhibit 4.2
Bad debts expense	18,750	Exhibit 4.1
General and administrative expense	122,000	Exhibit 4.2
	$ 240,750	
Operating income	$ 61,250	
Gain on sale of equipment	25,000	Treasurer
Interest expense	(2,500)	Exhibit 4.4 note
Income before taxes	83,750	
Income taxes (40% rate)	33,500	
Net income	$ 50,250	

determine their reasonableness and feasibility. As an example, IT Technologies' current ratio increases from 2.6 on January 1, Year 1, to 3.5 in the pro forma balance sheet of June 30, Year 1. In addition, for the six months ended June 30, Year 1, the projected return on average equity exceeds 8 percent. These and other measures such as turnover, trends, and common-size comparisons should be evaluated. Unexpected variations in important relations should be either explained or adjustments made to assumptions and expectations if errors are identified. These steps increase the reliability of pro forma statements for our analysis.

We should recognize that electronic spreadsheet programs are available to assist us in pro forma analysis. The ease of changing variables for sensitivity tests improves the usefulness of pro forma statements. Nevertheless, we should not confuse the ease and flexibility of these programs with the crucial need to develop and verify estimates and assumptions underlying their output. The reasonableness of important estimates and

Exhibit 4.6

IT TECHNOLOGIES, INC.
Balance Sheets

	Actual *January 1, Year 1*		*Pro Forma* *June 30, Year 1*	
Assets				
Current assets:				
Cash	$ 15,000		$ 44,250	
Accounts receivable (net)	6,500		234,000	
Inventories—materials	57,000		71,000	
Total current assets		$ 78,500		$349,250
Real estate	$ 58,000		—	
Fixed assets	206,400		$201,400	
Accumulated depreciation	(36,400)		(17,400)	
Net fixed assets		228,000		184,000
Other assets		3,000		3,000
Deferred bond issue costs		—		2,500
Total assets		$309,500		$538,750
Liabilities and Equity				
Current liabilities:				
Accounts payable	$ 2,000		$ 41,500	
Notes payable	28,500		43,500	
Accrued taxes	—		14,500	
Total current liabilities		$ 30,500		$ 99,500
Long-term debt	$ 15,000		$125,000	
Common stock	168,000		168,000	
Retained earnings	96,000		146,250	
		279,000		439,250
Total liabilities and equity		$309,500		$538,750

assumptions, and the usefulness of this analysis, depend on our critical evaluation and judgment and *not* on our technology.

LONG-TERM CASH FORECASTING

Short-term cash forecasting using pro forma statements is a very useful and reliable aid in assessing liquidity. However, the reliability and feasibility of cash forecasting using pro forma statements decline in longer time horizons. When the time horizon exceeds two or three years, the uncertainties in using pro forma analysis likely preclude detailed and accurate cash forecasts. **Long-term cash forecasting,** instead of focusing on items like receivables collections and payments for labor and materials, focuses on projections of income, operating cash flows, and other sources and uses of cash. Long-term forecasting of cash flows often involves two steps. First, we analyze prior periods' cash flow statements. Second, we introduce adjustments to cash flow data based on relevant information and estimates about future uses and sources of cash to generate our forecasts. This section describes both of these tasks.

Analysis of Prior Cash Flows for Forecasting

We previously analyzed the principles underlying preparation of the statement of cash flows (SCF) and identified useful inferences from this statement. We now focus further on analysis of the statement of cash flows—paying special attention to its use in projecting future cash flows. In our analysis of financial statements, recent years' data are likely the most relevant since they represent a company's prevailing business activities. Since there is inherent continuity in business activities, recent performance is likely most relevant for forecasting purposes.

While we emphasize recent performance, it is important we obtain financial statements for several prior years if possible. This is especially important when analyzing the statement of cash flows. This is because planning and execution of plant expansions, modernization strategies, working capital changes, and financing policies likely involve multiyear horizons. For our analysis of management's plans and their execution, it is useful to analyze several prior years' statements of cash flows. This enables us to perform a more comprehensive analysis of management's strategies and their performance.

Since conditions vary from company to company, it is difficult to formulate a "standard" analysis of cash flows. Nevertheless, certain commonalities exist. First, our analysis must establish the prior *major* sources of cash and their uses. A common-size analysis of the statement of cash flows aids in this year-to-year comparison. In assessing trends, it is useful to total the major sources and uses of cash over a period of years since annual or quarterly reporting periods are often too short for meaningful inferences. For example, financing of major projects often spans several years. In evaluating sources and uses of cash, the analyst should focus on questions like:

- Are asset replacements financed from internal or external funds?
- What are the financing sources of expansion and business acquisitions?
- Is the company dependent on external financing?
- What are the company's investing demands and opportunities?
- What are the requirements and forms of financing?
- Are managerial policies (e.g., dividends) highly sensitive to cash flows?

Case Analysis of Cash Flows for Forecasting

We illustrate the analysis of prior years' statements of cash flows for Campbell Soup Company in the Comprehensive Case following Chapter 8. Our analysis covers the six-year period ending July 28, Year 11. Exhibit CC.15 presents these statements in common-size format.

Our analysis of these statements reveals several insights. During this six-year period the major sources of cash are operations ($3,010 million), long-term debt ($854 million), and short-term debt ($737 million)—see Exhibit CC.14 and Campbell's statements in Supplement A. Major uses are plant purchases (net of sales) of $1,647 million, business acquisitions (net of sales) of $718 million, and cash dividends of $649 million. During this six-year period, cash and cash equivalents increased by $24 million. Sources of cash from operations as a percent of total sources average 55.7 percent, with a low of 31.3 percent in Year 9. Year 11 is the most profitable of the six, reflecting a recovery after two years of poor performance and restructuring activities. For this six-year period, cash from operations covered net cash used in investing activities and nearly all dividends paid. Cash flows are partially insulated from the sharp declines in earnings for Years 9 and 10 because restructuring charges of $682 million involved no cash outlays.

Our analysis of prior years' statements of cash flows is a useful basis for cash flow forecasting. A forecast of future cash flows must consider the above-mentioned relations—including the relation between cash and income, the components of the income to operating cash flow conversion, asset acquisitions, and the relation of sales to growth in operating cash flows. Noncash adjustments like depreciation depend on future depreciation and acquisition policies. Acquisition policies and write-offs for tax purposes partially determine deferred tax adjustments. The more we know about these and other factors, the more reliable our cash flow forecasts.

Major Sources of Cash for Campbell Soup (Years 6–11)

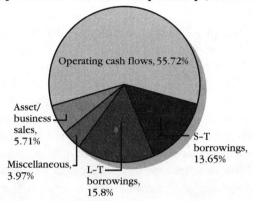

Operating cash flows, 55.72%

Asset/business sales, 5.71%

S-T borrowings, 13.65%

Miscellaneous, 3.97%

L-T borrowings, 15.8%

Major Uses of Cash for Campbell Soup (Years 6–11)

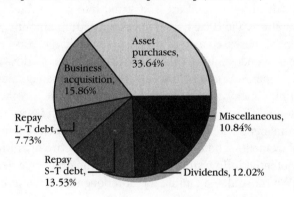

Asset purchases, 33.64%

Business acquisition, 15.86%

Repay L-T debt, 7.73%

Miscellaneous, 10.84%

Repay S-T debt, 13.53%

Dividends, 12.02%

Forecasting Inferences from Analysis of Cash Flows

Our analysis of the statement of cash flows is, as the previous case suggests, an important step in forecasting cash flows. The Campbell Soup case illustrates the range of useful insights drawn from our analysis of cash flows. We must remember our analysis of the statement of cash flows is performed within the framework of our overall analysis of financial statements. Accordingly, inferences from our analysis of cash flows are corroborated or refuted through analysis of other financial statements.

Nevertheless, there are useful generalizations we can make about potential inferences from analysis of the statement of cash flows. First, our analysis of the statement of cash flows enables us to appraise the quality of management's decisions over time and their impact on the company's results of operations and financial position. When our analysis covers a long time period, it can yield insights into management's success in responding to changing business conditions and their ability to seize opportunities and overcome adversities.

Inferences from our analysis of cash flows include where management committed its resources, where it reduced investments, where additional cash derived from, and where claims against the company are reduced. Inferences also pertain to the disposition of earnings and the investment of discretionary cash flows. Analysis also enables us to infer the size, composition, pattern, and stability of operating cash flows.

We previously described patterns of cash flows through a company. Cash flows are used for labor, material, and overhead. They are also used for long-term assets like plant and equipment where conversion through the product-cost stream is at a slower rate. But eventually all uses of cash enter the sales process and are converted into receivables or cash. Profitable operations yield cash recoveries exceeding amounts invested and, consequently, increase cash inflows. Losses yield a reverse effect.

Our inferences must explain the variation in cash flow segmentation. Most view operating cash flows as an index of management's ability to redirect funds away from unprofitable opportunities to those of greater profit potential. Yet not all operating cash flows can be so judged because of commitments for items like debt retirements, stock redemptions, equipment replacements, and dividend payments. Nor are operating cash flows the only potential inflow since management can draw on external financing sources. We must also examine the components of operating cash flows. Components often hold important clues about the stability of cash sources. For example, depreciation is a stable component representing a "recovery" of investments in fixed assets from sales. Cash recovered from depreciation is normally reinvested in maintaining productive assets. Similarly, while goodwill amortization is also a stable component, any recovered amount of this noncash charge is not typically reinvested in those assets. Our inferences from analysis of cash flows include earnings quality assessment. One factor in the quality of earnings is the impact of changes in business conditions for cash flows. The statement of cash flows also reveals noncash income components bearing on our inferences of earnings quality. Inferences can involve assessments of future earnings potential implying demands for additional financing. Our analysis of the statement of cash flows can provide us insights into likely sources of this needed cash and its potential impacts, including any dilution of earnings per share.

Forecasting Sources and Uses of Cash Flows

Our analysis of prior periods' cash flows enables us to prepare estimates of future sources and uses of long-term cash flows. Credible cash forecasts of all business activities, especially investing and financing activities, improve the reliability of our long-term cash forecasting. We desire dependable forecasts of the cash needed for carrying out the operating activities planned and of the cash sources required to support planned activities. For example, if we forecast a company's expansion of sales and profits, we must assess whether the company has the "financial horse-power" to support this expansion. We do this by analyzing the likelihood and costs for both internal and external sources of future cash.

The statement of cash flows is a good analytical structure to assist us in long-term forecasting. Forecasting the statement of cash flows begins with a careful estimate of expected changes in individual asset categories and the cash acquired or used by these changes. Important factors for us to consider when performing this task include:

- Net income forecasts need adjusting for noncash items like depreciation, depletion, deferred income taxes, and nonremitted earnings of subsidiaries and investees for reliable estimates of operating cash flows.
- Forecasts of operating working capital are obtained by estimating required levels of working capital components like receivables, inventories, and payables. If necessary, working capital needed to support forecasted sales is also estimated on an aggregate (net) basis—often using the relation between incremental sales and working capital requirements.
- Estimates of cash sources from items like asset disposals, investment sales, and issuance of stock and bonds are required.
- Capital expenditure forecasts are based on current operations adjusted for productive capacity, forecasts of activity implied by profit projections, and estimates of asset replacement costs.
- Estimates of debt retirements and dividend payments are required.

Forecasting the Statement of Cash Flows: A Case Analysis

This section illustrates our forecasting of the statement of cash flows for Campbell Soup Company for Years 12 and 13. We use our analysis of both prior years' cash flows and the other financial statements in the Comprehensive Case following Chapter 8. Results of other analyses and important assumptions underlying our forecasts include the following ($ millions):

1. Sales forecasts are $6,350 in Year 12 and $6,800 in Year 13.
2. Forecast of net income for Year 12 is taken from our Year 12 forecasted income statement (see Exhibit CC.16). Forecast of net income for Year 13 is 7.9 percent of forecast sales.
3. Net income for Years 9 and 10 is used in our forecasting procedures *before* the net effects of divestitures, restructurings, and unusual charges totaling $260.8 in Year 9 and $301.6 in Year 10.
4. Forecasts of depreciation and amortization for Years 12 and 13 are based on their relation to net income. We use the relation of average depreciation and amortization for Years 9 through 11 to the average net income over the same period.
5. Deferred income taxes in Year 12 are estimated using the relation of total deferred taxes to total net income for Years 10 and 11. It changes in Year 13 by the percent change in Year 13 forecasted net income relative to Year 12 forecasted net income.
6. Forecast of "Other, net" in Year 12 reflects the relation of "Other, net" to net income from Years 9 through 11. Its forecast changes in Year 13 by the percent change in Year 13 forecasted net income relative to Year 12 forecasted net income.
7. Operating working capital items like accounts receivable, inventory, and payables (excluding cash and temporary investments) for Years 12 and 13 are forecasted as follows:
    a. Compute the percent relation between operating working capital items and sales for Year 11.
    b. Multiply the percent relation in (*a*) by forecasted sales in Years 12 and 13.
8. Forecasts of cash and temporary investments reflect their relation to forecasted sales in Years 12 and 13 using the relation of cash and temporary investments to sales from Year 11.
9. Other amounts in our forecast of the statement of cash flows are estimated (marked by est.) using available information. This includes items where we use the moving average of the prior six years' data.

Using these analyses and assumptions we compute forecasts for Years 12 and 13 in the structure of the statement of cash flows for Campbell Soup. Exhibit 4.7 shows our forecasted statements. Calculations underlying these

Exhibit 4.7

CAMPBELL SOUP COMPANY
Forecasted Statements of Cash Flows
($ millions)

	Year 13	Year 12
Cash flows from operating activities:		
Net earnings[a]	$ 540.0	$ 480.0
To reconcile net earnings to net cash from operations:		
Depreciation and amortization[b]	331.1	294.3
Deferred taxes[c]	30.0	26.7
Other, net[d]	65.5	58.3
(Increase) decrease in accounts receivable[e]	(38.2)	(12.4)
(Increase) decrease in inventories[f]	(51.2)	(16.6)
Net change in other current assets and liabilities[g]	85.9	27.9
Net cash provided by operating activities	$ 963.1	$ 858.2
Cash flows from investing activities:		
Purchases of plant assets[h]	$ (443.1)	$ (400.0)
Sale of plant assets (est.)[i]	31.5	28.4
Businesses acquired (est.)[i]	(85.3)	(77.0)
Sale of businesses (est.)[i]	25.5	23.0
Increase in other assets (est.)[i]	(53.9)	(48.6)
Net change in other short-term investments (est.) [i]	12.3	11.1
Net cash used in investing activities	$ (513.0)	$ (463.1)
Cash flows from financing activities:		
Long-term borrowings (est.)	$ 132.0	$ 142.3
Repayments of long-term borrowings[j]	(218.9)	(227.7)
Increase (decrease) in short-term borrowings[k]	(200.3)	(95.7)
Other short-term borrowings (est.)	131.2	122.9
Repayments of other short-term borrowings (est.)[l]	(140.4)	(200.0)
Dividends paid (est.)	(108.8)	(108.2)
Treasury stock purchases (est.)	(49.4)	(42.4)
Treasury stock issued (est.)	15.6	14.2
Other, net (est.)	9.1	10.4
Net cash provided (used in) financing activities	$ (429.9)	$ (384.2)
Effect of exchange rate changes on cash (est.)	$ (7.5)	$ (6.7)
Net increase (decrease) in cash and cash equivalents[m]	12.7	4.2
Cash and cash equivalents at the beginning of year[m]	183.1	178.9
Cash and cash equivalents at the end of year[m]	$ 195.8	$ 183.1

Notes:

[a]Projected net income for Year 12 is 7.6% of projected sales, and for Year 13 is 7.9% of projected sales. These projections are corroborated in the *Value Line Investment Survey*.

[b]Average percent of depreciation and amortization to net income in Years 9–11:

$$\frac{\text{Total depreciation and amortization}}{\text{Total net income}^*} = \frac{\$601.8}{\$981.4} = 61.32\%$$

Exhibit 4.7 *continued*

Depreciation and amortization for Year 12 = $480.0 × 0.6132 = $294.3
Depreciation and amortization for Year 13 = $540.0 × 0.6132 = $331.1

(c) Average percent of deferred taxes to net income in Years 10–11:

$$\frac{\text{Total deferred taxes}}{\text{Total net income}^*} = \frac{\$39.4 \boxed{59}}{\$707.5} = 5.57\%$$

Deferred taxes for Year 12 = $480.0 × 0.0557 = $26.7
Percent change of Year 13 net income to Year 12 net income = $540.0 / $480.0 = 112.5%
Deferred taxes for Year 13 = $26.7 × 1.125 = $30.0

(d) Average percent of "Other, net" to net income in Years 9–11:

$$\frac{\text{Total "Other, net"}}{\text{Total net income}^*} = \frac{\$119.1 \boxed{60}}{\$981.4} = 12.14$$

"Other, net" for Year 12 = $480.0 × 0.1214 = $58.3
Percent change of Year 13 net income to Year 12 net income = 112.5%
"Other, net" for Year 13 = $58.3 × 1.125 = $65.5

(e) Percent of year-end accounts receivable to sales in Year 11:

$$\frac{\text{A.R. } \boxed{33}}{\text{Sales } \boxed{13}} = \frac{\$527.4}{\$6,204.1} = 8.5\%$$

Fiscal year-end A.R. in Year 12 = $6,350.0 × 0.085 = $539.8
Fiscal year-end A.R. in Year 13 = $6,800.0 × 0.085 = $578.0
Change in A.R. in Year 12 = $539.8 − $527.4 = $12.4 increase
Change in A.R. in Year 13 = $578.0 − $539.8 = $38.2 increase

Data in the Comprehensive Case indicate that over a 10-year period A.R. had year-to-year increases over 9 years.

(f) Percent of year-end inventories to sales in Year 11:

$$\frac{\text{Inventories } \boxed{34}}{\text{Sales } \boxed{13}} = \frac{\$706.7}{\$6,204.1} = 11.39\%$$

Fiscal year-end inventories in Year 12 = $6,350.0 × 0.1139 = $723.3
Fiscal year-end inventories in Year 13 = $6,800.0 × 0.1139 = $774.5
Change in inventories in Year 12 = $723.3 − $706.7 = $16.6 increase
Change in inventories in Year 13 = $774.5 − $723.3 = $51.2 increase

(g) Percent of year-end net other current assets and liabilities (NOCACL) to sales in Year 11:

$$\frac{\text{Total current liabilities } \boxed{45} - \text{Prepaid expenses } \boxed{35}}{\text{Sales } \boxed{13}} = \frac{\$1,278.0 - \$92.7}{\$6,204.1} = 19.11\%$$

Fiscal year-end NOCACL in Year 12 = $6,350.0 × 0.1911 = $1,213.2
Fiscal year-end NOCACL in Year 13 = $6,800.0 × 0.1911 = $1,299.1
Change in NOCACL in Year 12 = $1,213.2 − $1,185.3 = $27.9 increase in liabilities
Change in NOCACL in Year 13 = $1,299.1 − $1,213.2 = $85.9 increase in liabilities

(h) For Year 12 see item $\boxed{11}$ of MD&A under "statements of cash flows" within investing activities. For Year 13 we compute percent change in capital expenditures from Year 11 to Year 12:

$$\frac{\$400.0}{\$361.1 \boxed{65}} = 110.8\%$$

Projected capital expenditures = $400.0 × 110.8% = $443.1

(i) From (b), a percent of 110.8% of last year's balance is used also in relatively similar areas.

(j) See item $\boxed{172}$ and $\boxed{173}$, for maturity dates of LTD. For Year 13, $100.0 million is due in Year 16 at interest rate of 10.5%, but is redeemable in Year 13. If interest rates continue to fall, it may call for refinancing.

continued

Exhibit 4.7 *concluded*

[k]Net amount needed to balance the statement.
[l]For Year 12, see item $\boxed{170}$, 13.99% notes due Year 12. For Year 13, estimated using average of Years 7–12.
[m]Cash and cash equivalents balance is assumed related to net sales of that year.

$$\text{For Year 11} = \frac{\$178.9\,\boxed{31}}{\$6,204.1\,\boxed{13}} = 2.88\%$$

For Year 12 = $6,350.0 × 0.0288 = $183.1
For Year 13 = $680.0 × 0.0288 = $195.8

Income Numbers	*For Year 11*	*For Year 10*	*For Year 9*		
Total net income =	$401.5	+ $(4.4 + 301.6)	+ $(13.1 + 260.8)	=	$981.4
For Year 10 and Year 11 =	$401.5	+ $(4.4 + 301.6)		=	$707.5

forecasts are reported in the notes to this exhibit. More refined relations and computations underlying forecasts are possible with more detailed analysis and understanding of company and industry performance.

What-If Forecasting of Cash Flows

Our use of forecasts from the statement of cash flows extends to our ability to assess the impact of unexpected changes or adversities confronting a company—a variation on traditional *what-if analysis.* Unexpected events usually manifest themselves through a significant change in cash inflows or outflows. These events include recessions, strikes, loss of a major customer, and market shifts. Forecasting the statement of cash flows is often a first step in assessing the defensive posture and capabilities of a company. The basic question addressed by this analysis is: What are the company's options and what resources (internal and external) are available to

ANALYSIS   VIEWPOINT

YOU ARE THE STOCKBROKER

You are analyzing the long-term cash forecasts of Boston Biotech, Inc., that are reported along with a scheduled initial public offering (IPO) of its common stock for next month. You notice Boston Biotech's forecasts of net cash flows are zero or negative for the next five years. During this same time period, Boston Biotech is forecasting net income at more than 10 percent of shareholders' equity. Your co-workers at the securities firm question the reliability of these forecasts. Can you identify potential explanations for the disparity between the five-year forecasts of cash flows and income?

respond to unexpected changes in cash flows? This analysis is relevant for assessing a company's financial flexibility. We can use forecasts of the statement of cash flows to assess resources available to meet adversities and pursue opportunities. We can trace through the effects of these events for operating cash flows and on the sources and uses of cash. Forecasts of this statement are also useful in planning changes in managerial strategies to confront changing business environments. Forecasting is also a valuable tool for creditors in assessing risk exposures.

SPECIALIZED CASH FLOW RATIOS

The following two ratios are often useful in analyzing a firm's flow of funds.

Cash Flow Adequacy Ratio

The **cash flow adequacy ratio** is a measure of a company's ability to generate sufficient cash from operations to cover capital expenditures, investments in inventories, and cash dividends. To remove cyclical and other random influences, a five-year total is typically used in computing this ratio. The cash flow adequacy ratio is calculated as:

$$\frac{\text{Five-year sum of cash from operations}}{\text{Five-year sum of capital expenditures, inventory additions, and cash dividends}}$$

Investment in other important working capital items like receivables is omitted because they are financed primarily by short-term credit (e.g., growth in accounts payable). Accordingly, only additions to inventories are included. Note in years where inventories decline, the downward change is treated as a zero change in computing the ratio. Using the financial statement data from Campbell Soup Company in Supplement A we compute its (five-year) cash flow adequacy ratio:

$$\frac{\$2,545.8^{(a)}}{\$2,418.5^{(b)} + \$117.1^{(c)} + \$544.8^{(d)}} = 0.83$$

[a] Cash from operations—item $\boxed{64}$.

[b] Property additions—items $\boxed{65}$ and $\boxed{67}$.

[c] Inventory additions—item $\boxed{62}$.

[d] Cash dividends—item $\boxed{77}$.

Proper interpretation of the cash flow adequacy ratio is important. A ratio of 1 indicates the company exactly covered these cash needs without a need for external financing. A ratio below 1 suggests internal cash sources are insufficient in maintaining dividends and current operating growth levels. For Campbell Soup Company the ratio indicates that for the five years ending in Year 11, Campbell's operating cash flows fell short of covering dividends and operating growth. While not illustrated here, if we computed a six-year ratio, a more favorable ratio results. The cash flow adequacy ratio also reflects inflationary effects for funding requirements of a company. As with other analyses, inferences drawn from this ratio should be supported with further analysis and investigation.

Cash Reinvestment Ratio

The **cash reinvestment ratio** is a measure of the percent of investment in assets representing operating cash retained and reinvested in the company for both replacing assets and growth in operations. This ratio is computed as:

$$\frac{\text{Operating cash flow} - \text{Dividends}}{\text{Gross plant} + \text{Investment} + \text{Other assets} + \text{Working capital}}$$

A reinvestment ratio in the area of 7 to 11 percent is generally considered satisfactory. Using the financial statements of Campbell Soup Company, we compute the cash reinvestment ratio for Year 11:

$$\frac{\$805.2^{(e)} - \$137.5^{(f)}}{(\$2,921.9 + \$477.6)^{(g)} + \$404.6^{(h)} + (\$1,518.5 - \$1,278.0)^{(i)}} = 16.5\%$$

[e] Cash from operations–item $\boxed{64}$.

[f] Cash dividends–item $\boxed{77}$.

[g] Gross plant assets–items $\boxed{158}$ through $\boxed{161}$; plus: intangibles–items $\boxed{163}$ and $\boxed{164}$.

[h] Other assets–item $\boxed{39}$.

[i] Total current assets–item $\boxed{36}$; less: total current liabilities–item $\boxed{45}$.

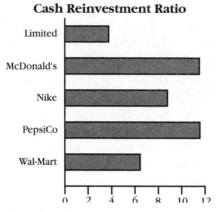

Cash Reinvestment Ratio

Source: Annual reports.

GUIDANCE ANSWERS TO ANALYSIS VIEWPOINTS

YOU ARE THE LOAN OFFICER

Your first step is to corroborate or refute management's explanation for decreased sales in recent years. If their explanations are *not* validated with objective evidence, then you should reject DEC's application—hint of unscrupulous behavior is reason enough for immediate nonapproval. If you are able to verify management's explanations, your next step is to assess the *level and uncertainty* of DEC's sales forecasts. Your analysis of sales forecasts should consider important economic factors, including consumer demand, industry competition, supplier costs, and DEC's productive capacity/quality. Perhaps more important under DEC's circumstances is your assessment of uncertainty with sales. For example, sales might be objectively forecasted at $1 million, but the range of likely sales might extend anywhere from $0.5 to $1.5 million. Recent turmoil in consumer demand, material costs, and supplier relations suggests substantially greater risk than normal. Your assessment of increased risk can yield a response extending from a slight increase in interest rates or increased collateral demands to ultimate loan rejection. Consequently, while DEC's sales forecasts might be unbiased, we must recognize differences in uncertainty associated with sales forecasts in practice.

YOU ARE THE STOCKBROKER

The disparity in Boston Biotech's forecasts of cash flows and income is not necessarily of concern. Many growing companies experience little to no positive cash flows in the near term. Of course, these low near-term cash flows are expected to yield above-average cash flows in the future. Boston Biotech could potentially be recording substantial operating cash flows that are offset by large cash outflows in new investments, debt retirements, or dividends. Our analysis must look to the components of both cash flows and income to address our potential interest in Boston Biotech's IPO of common stock. Instead of spurning the stock of Boston Biotech, we might find it a lucrative and underpriced security due to our superior knowledge of accounting in financial statements.

Capital Structure and Solvency

A LOOK BACK

The prior two chapters focused on analysis tools for evaluating a company's liquidity. We described both turnover and activity-based measures and their relevance for analysis. We also explained how forecasting and pro forma analysis are useful in statement analysis.

A LOOK AT THIS CHAPTER

This chapter focuses on capital structure, or a company's financing, and its implications for solvency. We analyze the importance of financial leverage and its effects on risk and return. Analytical adjustments to accounting book values are evaluated for solvency assessments. We also describe earnings coverage measures and their interpretation for financial statement analysis.

A LOOK AHEAD

In Chapter 6 our analysis shifts to the concept of return. We analyze return on investment, asset utilization, and other measures of performance that are relevant to a wide class of financial statement users. We describe several tools of analysis to assist in evaluation of company performance.

THIS CHAPTER WILL:

- Describe capital structure and its relation to solvency.
- Explain financial leverage and its implications for company performance and analysis.
- Analyze adjustments to accounting book values to assess capital structure.
- Describe analysis tools for evaluating and interpreting capital structure composition and assessing solvency.
- Analyze asset composition and coverage for solvency analysis.
- Explain earnings-coverage analysis and its relevance in evaluating solvency.
- Describe capital structure risk and return and its relevance to financial statement analysis.
- Interpret ratings of organizations' debt obligations (Appendix 5A).
- Describe prediction models of financial distress (Appendix 5B).

PREVIEW OF CHAPTER 5

Solvency is an important factor in our analysis of a company's financial statements. **Solvency** refers to a company's long-run financial viability and its ability to cover long-term obligations. All business activities of a company—financing, investing, and operating—affect a company's solvency. One of the most important components of solvency analysis is the composition of a company's capital structure. **Capital structure** refers to a company's sources of financing and its economic attributes. This chapter describes capital structure and explains its importance to solvency analysis. Since solvency depends on success in operating activities, the chapter examines earnings and the ability of earnings to *cover* important and necessary company expenditures. This chapter also describes various tools of solvency analysis, including leverage measures, analytical accounting adjustments, capital structure analysis, and earnings-coverage measures. We demonstrate these analysis tools with data from financial statements. We also discuss the relation between risk and return inherent in a company's capital structure and its implications for financial statement analysis. The content and organization of this chapter are as follows:

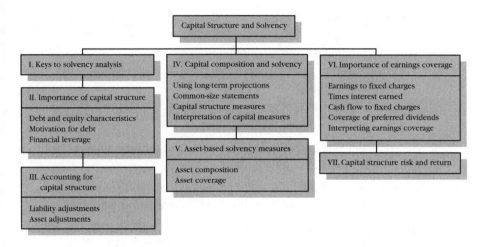

KEYS TO SOLVENCY ANALYSIS

Analyzing long-term solvency of a company is markedly different from analyzing short-term liquidity. In liquidity analysis, the time horizon is sufficiently short for reasonably accurate forecasts of cash flows. Long-term forecasts are less reliable and, consequently, our analysis of long-term solvency uses less precise but more encompassing analytical measures.

Our analysis of solvency involves several key elements. Analysis of capital structure is one of these. *Capital structure* refers to the sources of financing for a company. Financing forms range from relatively permanent equity capital to more risky or temporary short-term financing sources. Once a company obtains financing, it subsequently invests it in various assets. Assets represent secondary sources of security for lenders and range from loans secured by specific assets to assets available as general security to unsecured creditors. These and other factors yield different risks associated with different assets and financing sources.

Another key element of long-term solvency is *earnings* or *earning power*—implying the recurring ability to generate cash from operations. Earnings-based measures are important and reliable indicators of financial strength. Earnings is the most desirable and reliable source of cash for long-term payment of interest and debt principal. As a measure of cash inflows from operations, earnings is the gauge in covering interest and other fixed charges. A stable earnings stream is an important measure of a company's ability to borrow in times of cash shortage. It is also a measure of the likelihood of a company rebounding from conditions of financial distress.

Lenders guard themselves against company insolvency and financial distress by including in the lending agreements loan *covenants* or *pledges* of specific assets as security. Loan covenants define *default* (and the legal remedies available when it occurs), often defined using accounting data, to allow a lender the opportunity to collect on the loan before severe financial distress. Covenants are often designed to (1) emphasize key measures of financial strength like the current ratio and debt to equity ratio, (2) prohibit the issuance of additional debt, or (3) ensure against disbursement of company resources through excessive dividends or acquisitions. Covenants cannot assure lenders against operating losses—invariably the source of financial distress. Covenants and protective provisions also cannot substitute for our alertness and monitoring of a company's results of operations and financial condition.[1] The enormous amount of both public and private debt financing has led to standardized approaches to its analysis and evaluation. While this chapter explains many of these approaches, Appendix 5A discusses the analysis of debt securities by rating agencies, and Appendix 5B describes the use of ratios as predictors of financial distress.

IMPORTANCE OF CAPITAL STRUCTURE

Capital structure is the equity and debt financing of a company. It is often measured in terms of the relative magnitude of the various financing sources. A company's financial stability and risk of insolvency depend on its financing sources and the types and sizes of various assets it owns. Exhibit 5.1 portrays a typical company's asset distribution and its financing sources. This exhibit highlights the potential variety in investing and financing items comprising a company—depicted within the accounting framework of assets equal liabilities plus equity.

---

[1]Lenders must recognize that senior positions in the debt hierarchy do not always ensure the safety they seem to afford. Subordinated (junior) debt is not like capital stock because subordinated creditors have a voice in determining whether a debtor should be rescued or thrown into bankruptcy. This interdependence between junior and senior lenders leads some to buy the highest *yielding* obligation of a company under the presumption any situation affecting the value of junior securities is likely to affect senior securities.

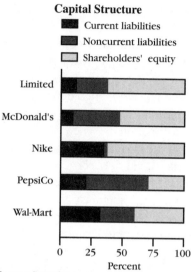

Capital Structure

■ Current liabilities
■ Noncurrent liabilities
☐ Shareholders' equity

Limited

McDonald's

Nike

PepsiCo

Wal-Mart

0   25   50   75   100
Percent

Source: Annual reports

Exhibit 5.1   A Typical Company's Asset Distribution and Capital Structure

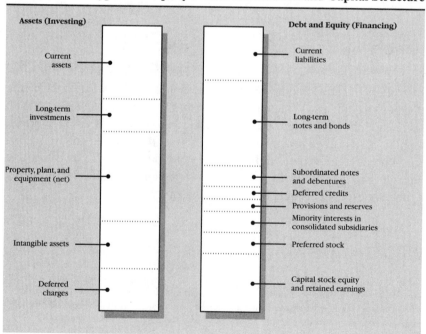

Characteristics of Debt and Equity

The importance of analyzing capital structure derives from several perspectives, not the least is the difference between debt and equity. **Equity** refers to the *risk capital* of a company. Characteristics of equity capital include its uncertain or unspecified return and its lack of any repayment pattern. Capital that can be withdrawn at the contributor's option is *not* equity capital and has, instead, characteristics of debt capital. Equity capital contributes to a company's stability and solvency. It is usually characterized by a degree of permanence, persistence in times of adversity, and a lack of any mandatory dividend requirement. A company can confidently invest equity financing in long-term assets and expose them to business risks without threat of recall. Loss of equity capital for whatever reason does not necessarily jeopardize a company's ability to pay its fixed claims.

Unlike equity capital, both short-term and long-term **debt** capital must be repaid. The longer the debt repayment period and the less demanding its repayment provisions, the easier it is for a company to service debt capital. Still, debt must be repaid at specified times regardless of a company's financial condition, and so too must periodic interest on most debt. Failure to pay principal or interest typically results in proceedings where common shareholders can lose control of the company and all or part of their investment. If a company's equity capital is entirely taken by losses, creditors can also lose part or all of the principal and interest due them. When the proportion of debt in the total capital structure of a company is larger, the higher are the resulting fixed charges and repayment commitments. This also increases the likelihood of a company's inability to pay interest and principal when due.

For investors in common stock, debt reflects a risk of loss of the investment, balanced by the potential of profits from financial leverage. **Financial leverage** is the use of debt to increase earnings. Leverage magnifies both managerial success (profits) and failure (losses). It increases risks due to factors like commodity price fluctuations or technological obsolescence. Excessive debt limits management's initiative and flexibility for pursuing profitable opportunities. For creditors, increased equity capital is preferred as protection against losses from adversities. Lowering equity capital as a proportionate share of a company's financing decreases creditors' protection against loss and consequently increases risk.

While there is debate over whether the *cost of capital* for a company varies with different capital structures (mixes of debt and equity), the issue is relatively clear from an analysis perspective (creditors or investors). When analyzing companies, creditors expose themselves to increased risk if lending to a company with a greater proportion of debt financing, all else equal. Using the *Modigliani-Miller hypothesis,* a company's cost of capital in a perfect market is, except for the tax deductibility of interest, unaffected by the debt-to-equity relation. This result is due to the assertion that a shareholder can introduce personal risk preferences through portfolio management of stock. Under this hypothesis, the advantage of debt is offset by a company's lower price-earnings ratio.

Whatever one's perspective on the relation between cost of capital and debt, every company possesses a risk of loss for our investment. Our analysis task is to measure the degree of risk resulting from a company's capital structure. The remainder of this section looks at the motivation for debt capital and measuring its effects.

Motivation for Debt Capital

A primary motivation for a company financing its business activities through debt is its potential for lower cost. From a shareholder's perspective, debt is *less expensive* than equity financing for at least two reasons:

- Interest on most debt is fixed, and provided interest is less than the return earned from debt financing, the excess return goes to the benefit of equity investors.
- Interest is a tax-deductible expense whereas dividends are not.

We discuss each of these factors in this section due to their importance for debt financing and our risk analysis.

Concept of Financial Leverage

Companies' capital structures are typically comprised of both debt and equity financing. Creditors are generally unwilling to provide financing without protection provided by equity financing. Financial leverage refers to the amount of debt financing that pays a fixed return in a company's capital structure. Companies with financial leverage are said to be **trading on the equity.** This indicates a company is using equity capital as a borrowing base in a desire to reap excess returns.

Exhibit 5.2 illustrates trading on the equity. This exhibit computes the returns achieved for two companies referred to as Risky, Inc., and Safety, Inc. These two companies have identical assets and earnings before

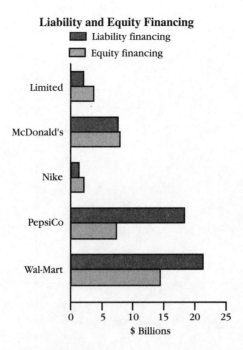

Liability and Equity Financing

Source: Annual reports

interest expense. Risky, Inc., derives 40 percent of its financing from debt while Safety, Inc., is debt-free, or *unlevered.* For Year 1, when the average return on total assets is 12 percent, the return on stockholders' equity of Risky, Inc., is 16 percent. This higher return to stockholders is due to the excess return on assets over the *after-tax* cost of debt (12 percent versus 6 percent, the latter computed as 10 *[1 − 0.40]*). Safety, Inc.'s return on equity always equals the return on assets since there is no debt. For Year 2, the return on assets of Risky, Inc., equals the after-tax cost of debt and, consequently, the effects of leverage are neutralized. For Year 3, leverage is shown to be a double-edged sword. Specifically, when the return on assets is *less* than the after-tax cost of debt, Risky, Inc.'s return on equity is lower than the return of equity for debt-free Safety, Inc. To generalize from this example: (1) an unlevered company's return on assets is identical to its return on equity, (2) a levered company is *successfully* trading on the equity when return on assets exceeds the after-tax cost of debt (alternatively stated, return on assets is less than return on equity), (3) a levered company is *unsuccessfully* trading on the equity when return on assets is

Exhibit 5.2 Trading on the Equity—Returns for Different Earnings Levels ($ thousands)

		Financing Sources		Income before Interest and Taxes	10 Percent Debt Interest	Taxes*	Net Income	Net Income + [Interest × (1 − Tax Rate)]	Return on	
	Assets	Debt	Equity						Assets†	Equity‡
Year 1:										
Risky, Inc.	$1,000,000	$400,000	$ 600,000	$200,000	$40,000	$64,000	$ 96,000	$120,000	12.0%	16.0%
Safety, Inc.	1,000,000	—	1,000,000	200,000	—	80,000	120,000	120,000	12.0	12.0
Year 2:										
Risky, Inc.	1,000,000	400,000	600,000	100,000	40,000	24,000	36,000	60,000	6.0	6.0
Safety, Inc.	1,000,000	—	1,000,000	100,000	—	40,000	60,000	60,000	6.0	6.0
Year 3:										
Risky, Inc.	1,000,000	400,000	600,000	50,000	40,000	4,000	6,000	30,000	3.0	1.0
Safety, Inc.	1,000,000	—	1,000,000	50,000	—	20,000	30,000	30,000	3.0	3.0

*Tax rate is 40 percent.

†Return on assets = Net income + Interest (1 − 0.40)/Assets.

‡Return on equity = Net income/Shareholders' equity.

less than the after-tax cost of debt (alternatively stated, return on assets exceeds return on equity), and (4) effects of leveraging are magnified in both good *and* bad years (for example, when return on assets drops below the after-tax cost of debt, a levered company's return on equity drops even farther).

Tax Deductibility of Interest

One reason for the advantageous position of debt is the *tax deductibility of interest.* We illustrate this tax advantage by extending the case in Exhibit 5.2. Let us reexamine the two companies' results for Year 2:

Year 2 Financials	*Risky, Inc.*	*Safety, Inc.*
Income before interest and taxes	$100,000	$100,000
Interest (10% of $400,000)	40,000	—
Income before taxes	$ 60,000	$100,000
Taxes (40%)	24,000	40,000
Net income	$ 36,000	$ 60,000
Add back interest paid to bondholder	40,000	—
Total return to security holders (debt and equity)	$ 76,000	$ 60,000

Recall the leverage effects are neutral in this year. But notice even when the return on assets equals the after-tax cost of debt, the total amount available for distribution to debt and equity holders of Risky, Inc., is $16,000 higher than the amount available for the equity holders of Safety, Inc. This is due to the lower tax liability for Risky, Inc. We must remember the value of tax deductibility of interest depends on having sufficient earnings (unrecovered interest charges can be carried back and carried forward as part of tax loss carryovers permitted by tax law). To generalize from this example: (1) interest is tax deductible while cash dividends to equity holders are not, (2) because interest is tax deductible the income available to security holders can be much larger, and (3) nonpayment of interest can yield bankruptcy whereas nonpayment of dividends does not.

Other Effects of Leverage

Beyond advantages from excess return to financial leverage and the tax deductibility of interest, a long-term debt position can yield other benefits to equity holders. For example, a growth company can avoid earnings dilution through issuance of debt. In addition, if interest rates are increasing, a leveraged company paying a fixed lower interest rate is more profitable than its nonleveraged competitor. However, the reverse is also true. Strategically increasing debt capital prior to adverse operating performance is often advantageous to the borrower because availability or cost of debt financing likely changes. Finally, in times of inflation, monetary liabilities (like most debt capital) yield price-level gains.

Measuring Effects of Financial Leverage

As we saw in our examples above, the effect of financial leverage on operating results is positive when the return on equity capital exceeds the return on assets. This difference in returns isolates the return on borrowed money from the return on equity capital. We can use the measures in this section to effectively assess the effects of financial leverage.

Financial Leverage Index

One measure of the effect of financial leverage is the **financial leverage index** and is computed as:

$$\frac{\text{Return on common equity}}{\text{Return on assets}}$$

A financial leverage index greater than 1.0 indicates favorable effects from leverage, a value less than 1.0 suggests unfavorable effects from leverage, and a value of exactly 1.0 suggests neither favorable nor unfavorable effects. Using the financial data in Exhibit 5.2, we compute the financial leverage indexes of Risky, Inc., for Years 1, 2, and 3:

$$\text{Year 1: } \frac{16.0\%}{12.0\%} = 1.33 \quad \text{Year 2: } \frac{6.0\%}{6.0\%} = 1.00 \quad \text{Year 3: } \frac{1.0\%}{3.0\%} = 0.33$$

For Year 1, when return on equity exceeds the return on assets, the financial leverage index equals 1.33, implying favorable effects of leverage. In Year 2, when return on equity equals the return on assets, the index is 1.00. This index of 1.00 reflects a neutralization of financial leverage. For Year 3, the index equals 0.33, well below 1.0. This suggests unfavorable effects of financial leverage in Year 3. We further discuss return on investment in Chapter 6.

Financial Leverage Index

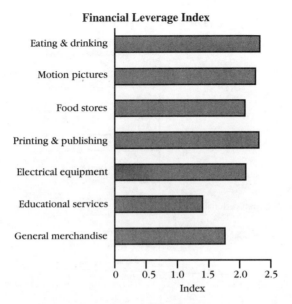

Financial Leverage Ratio

The **financial leverage ratio** measures the relation between total assets and the common equity capital that finances assets. It is expressed as:

$$\frac{\text{Total assets}}{\text{Common equity capital}}$$

The greater the proportion of assets financed by common equity capital, the lower the financial leverage ratio. For a company successfully utilizing leverage, a higher financial leverage ratio enhances return on equity. Concurrently, the risk inherent in a change in profitability is greater when the financial leverage ratio is higher. The financial leverage ratio of Risky, Inc., (see Exhibit 5.2) at the end of Year 3 is:

$$\frac{\$1,000,000}{\$600,000} = 1.67$$

This financial leverage ratio indicates that every dollar of common equity commands $1.67 in assets for the company. We show in Chapter 6 how the financial leverage ratio can be viewed as a component of the analytical disaggregation of return on equity.

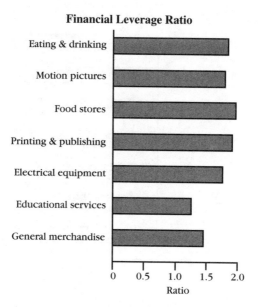

Financial Leverage Ratio

ANALYSIS VIEWPOINT

YOU ARE THE ENTREPRENEUR

You are the entrepreneur and sole shareholder of a small, start-up restaurant. Your business is unlevered and doing well. The most recent year's return on assets is 9 percent, on assets of $200,000 (the tax rate is 40%). You are considering expanding your business but need to take on debt to finance expansion. What is your criterion in deciding whether to expand by adding debt?

ACCOUNTING IMPLICATIONS FOR CAPITAL STRUCTURE ANALYSIS

Measurement and disclosure of liability (debt) and equity accounts in financial statements are governed by the application of accepted accounting principles. Our analysis must remember these principles when analyzing capital structure and its implications for solvency.

Adjustments to Book Values of Liabilities

The relation between liabilities and equity capital, the two major sources of a company's financing, is an important factor in assessing long-term solvency. An understanding of this relation is therefore essential in our analysis. There exist liabilities not fully reflected in balance sheets and there are financing-related items whose accounting classification as debt or equity must not be blindly accepted in our analysis. Our identification and classification of these items depend on a thorough understanding of their economic substance and the conditions to which they are subject.

Deferred Income Taxes

Deferred income taxes is a deferred liability that is both significant in size and important to our analysis. Deferred taxes is not a liability in the usual sense because the government does not have a definite short-term or even long-term claim against a company for these taxes. Yet we showed how deferred taxes represent the aggregate exhaustion in tax deductibility of assets and other items over and above that recorded in financial statements. This means at some point in the future the Deferred Tax liability account (credit) is used to reduce the higher income tax expense corresponding to the *increased* tax liabilities. Even if the likelihood of the Deferred Tax account "reversing" in the foreseeable future is high, there remains the question of whether the present value of future expected reversals should be used instead of the nominal face value amount of the deferred credit. Most other liabilities on the balance sheet (including pensions and leases) are carried at present value. The higher the borrowing rate (cost of debt) applicable to a company, the more significant the impact of discounting for present value. Accounting standard setters considered requiring the discounting of deferred taxes but decided against it.

For our analysis, an important question is whether we treat deferred taxes as a liability, as equity, or as part debt and part equity. Our answer depends on the nature of the deferral, past experience of the account (e.g., its growth pattern), and the likelihood of future reversals. In reaching our decision, we must recognize, under normal circumstances, deferred taxes reverse and become payable when a company's size declines. A company declining in size is usually accompanied by losses rather than by positive taxable income. In this case the drawing down of deferred taxes likely involves credits to tax loss carrryforwards or carry-backs rather than payments in cash. To the extent future reversals are a remote possibility, as conceivable with timing differences from acceler-ated depreciation, deferred taxes should be viewed like long-term financ-ing and treated like equity. However, if the likelihood of a drawing down of deferred taxes in the foreseeable future is high, then deferred taxes (or part of them) should be treated like long-term liabilities. As an example, if we decide the proper treatment of deferred tax credits is as equity (either in whole or in part), we can make the following type of *analytical* entry:

Deferred Income Taxes—Current	xx	
Deferred Income Taxes—Noncurrent	xx	
Shareholders' Equity		xx

There are other deferred credits (e.g., bond premiums) that represent allocation accounts designed to aid in measuring income. These types of deferred credits are typically insignificant in size and unimportant for our analysis. However, *deferred income* items like "subscription income received in advance" represent obligations for future services and are properly treated as liabilities.

Operating Leases

Current accounting practice requires most financing long-term non-cancelable leases be shown as debt. Yet companies have certain opportu-nities to structure leases in ways to avoid reporting them as debt. For example, if our analysis encounters noncancelable operating leases that should be capitalized, we can make the following analytical entry using data from Quaker Oats:

Leasehold Assets[2]	93.8	
Liabilities under Long-Term Leases		93.8

---

[2] This capitalized amount is the present value of Quaker's rentals on noncancelable operating leases (computed as: $93.8 = \$16.5/1.1 + \$16.5/1.1^2 + \$15.7/1.1^3 + \$15.2/1.1^4 + \$15.0/1.1^5 + 66.8/1.1^{7.2}$ (or $93.8 = \$15 + \$13.6 + \$11.8 + \$10.4 + \$33.6$). We assume a 10 percent discount rate. We also assume rentals after Year 16 continue at the Year 16 level of $15. This means the $66.8 is paid over the next 4.45 years ($66.8/\$15.0) or, on average, it is paid in 2.2 years (4.45/2) after Year 16. Therefore, the discount factor for the *average* rental in the $66.8 is $1.1^{7.2}$, which is 7.2 years from Year 11. This adjustment affects subsequent analyses (e.g., see Appendix 5C).

Off-Balance-Sheet Financing

In determining the debt for a company, our analysis must be aware that some managers attempt to understate debt, often with new and sometimes complex means. There are several means for doing this including take or pay contracts, sales of receivables, and inventory repurchase agreements. Our critical reading of notes and management comments, along with inquiries to management, can often shed light on existence of unrecorded liabilities.

Pensions and Postretirement Benefits

Current accounting practice recognizes that if the fair value of pension assets falls short of the accumulated pension benefit obligation, a liability for pensions exists. This liability does not consider the projected benefit obligation, which recognizes estimates of future pay increases for pension plans using future pay formulas. Our analysis must be aware of this potential understatement, and estimate its impact on the pension liability when appropriate.

Companies can recognize the unfunded obligation on other postretirement employee benefits immediately or over as many as 20 years. Under the latter amortization option a company is, unlike with pensions, not required to record a minimum liability. Our analysis needs to assess the present value of this unrecorded liability related to postretirement benefits.

There is an important distinction between pension (and probably postretirement) liabilities and many other types of liabilities in that pensions are not often an immediate threat to a company's solvency. While the *Pension Benefit Guaranty Corporation* has authority to take control of an underfunded plan and place a lien on company assets for the protection of employee benefits, it moves very cautiously in this area. Also, the Internal Revenue Service has established procedures where companies in financial difficulty can obtain waivers to defer their pension fund contributions.

Unconsolidated Subsidiaries

From our analysis perspective we prefer consolidated statements. Separate financial statements of the consolidated entities are useful in certain cases like when utilization of assets of a subsidiary is not subject to the full discretion of the parent. Information on unconsolidated subsidiaries is also useful in our analysis when bondholders of subsidiaries must rely on subsidiaries' assets as security. Also, bondholders of a parent company (particularly holding companies) sometimes derive a significant portion of their fixed-charge coverage from the dividends of unconsolidated subsidiaries. The parent's bondholders can also be in a junior position to the subsidiary's bondholders, which is important in the event of a subsidiary's bankruptcy. When financial statements of a subsidiary are *not* consolidated with a parent, consolidation can be effected as an analytical adjustment:

Subsidiary's Assets	xx	
Subsidiary's Liabilities		xx
Parent's Investment in Subsidiary		xx

If a subsidiary has unrecorded lease or pension liabilities, they too are consolidated for purposes of our analysis.

Contingent Liabilities

Contingencies such as product guarantees and warranties represent obligations to offer future services or goods that are classified as liabilities. Typically, reserves created by charges to income are also considered liabilities. Our analysis must make a judgment regarding the likelihood of commitments or contingencies becoming actual liabilities and then treat these items accordingly. For example, guarantees of indebtedness of subsidiaries or others that are likely to become liabilities should be treated as liabilities.

Minority Interests

Minority interests in consolidated financial statements represent the book value of ownership interests of minority shareholders of subsidiaries in the consolidated group. These are *not* liabilities similar to debt because they have neither mandatory dividend payment nor principal repayment requirements. Capital structure measurements concentrate on the mandatory payment aspects of liabilities. From this point of view, minority interests are more like outsiders' claims to a portion of equity or an offset representing their proportionate ownership of assets. Minority interests are currently reported at book value. If our analysis wants to assess what a parent company must pay to acquire the minority interest, market rather than book value is the relevant measure.

Convertible Debt

Convertible debt is usually reported among liabilities. If conversion terms imply this debt will be converted into common stock, then it can be classified as equity for purposes of our capital structure analysis.

Preferred Stock

Most preferred stock requires no obligation for payment of dividends or repayment of principal. These characteristics are similar to those of equity. However, preferred stock with a fixed maturity or subject to sinking fund requirements should from our analytical perspective be considered debt. Preferred stock with mandatory redemption requirements is also similar to debt and we should consider it as debt in our analysis. This is in spite of certain cases where default by a company on redemption provisions does not carry repercussions as severe as those from nonpayment of debt. An example of financing with redeemable preferred stock is B.F. Goodrich:

B.F. Goodrich has issued 250,000 shares of $7.85 Cumulative Preferred Stock, Series A. In order to comply with sinking-fund requirements, each year on August 15, B.F. Goodrich must redeem 12,500 shares. . . . The redemption price is $100 per share, plus dividends accrued at the redemption date.

Adjustments to Book Values of Assets

Because shareholders' equity of a company is measured by the excess of assets over liabilities, analytical revisions of asset book values necessarily change the amount of equity. For this reason, in assessing capital structure our analysis must evaluate whether book values of assets are sufficiently reliable. We describe several examples of potential adjustments. Different or additional adjustments are sometimes necessary depending on circumstances.

Recognition of Market Values

In certain industries like mining, petroleum, timber, and real estate, the market value of assets can significantly differ from the book values reported on companies' balance sheets. Adjustments of book values to market values for these assets have a corresponding effect on equity. The adjusted values of these assets are reflected in a company's earning power *and* in a company's fixed-charge coverage measure—an effect that does not depend on our analytical adjustments discussed here. These adjustments assume market value is better reflective of a company's financial condition than its current accounting procedures. We discuss market adjustments to three important asset categories. These adjustments should be viewed as representative of other asset adjustments often required in our analysis of financial statements.

Inventories

Inventories reported using the LIFO costing method are typically understated in times of rising prices. Companies usually disclose (often in notes) the amount by which inventories computed using FIFO (which are more similar to replacement cost) exceed inventories computed using LIFO. This difference is referred to as the **LIFO reserve.** This reserve enables us to adjust inventory amounts and corresponding equity amounts (after tax) to reflect current values.

Marketable Securities

Current practice requires marketable securities be reported at market value (except for held-to-maturity securities). However, for fiscal years beginning *before* December 16, 1993, marketable securities were often stated at cost when their book value was below market value. When examining

ANALYSIS RESEARCH INSIGHT 5.1

LIFO RESERVE AND COMPANY VALUE

What is the relation between the LIFO reserve and company value? A common assumption is that the LIFO reserve represents an unrecorded asset. Under this view, the magnitude of the LIFO reserve reflects the current value adjustment to inventory. Analysis research has investigated this issue, with interesting results.

Contrary to the "unrecorded asset theory," evidence from practice is consistent with a *negative* relation between the LIFO reserve and company market value. This implies the higher is the LIFO reserve, and the lower is company value. Why this negative relation? An "economic effects theory" suggests that companies adopt LIFO if the present value of expected tax savings exceeds the costs of adoption (e.g., administrative costs). If we assume the present value of tax savings is related to the anticipated effect of inflation on inventory costs (a reasonable assumption), a negative relation might reflect the decline in the real value of a company due to anticipated inflation. Our analysis must therefore consider the possibility that companies using LIFO and companies using FIFO are inherently different and that any adjustments using the LIFO reserve reflect this difference.

financial statements from these earlier periods, our analysis should use parenthetical, footnote, or other information to make an analytical adjustment—increasing both the securities to market and equity (after tax) by a corresponding amount.

Intangible Assets

Intangible assets and deferred asset items reported on the balance sheet affect computation of a company's equity. To the extent our analysis cannot assess or form a reliable opinion on the value or future utility of these assets, they should probably be excluded from our consideration. This conservative adjustment reduces equity (after tax) by the book values of these assets. The arbitrary exclusion of all intangible assets from equity is an unjustified exercise in overconservatism. Similarly, if our analysis yields information suggesting revisions in asset book values, our analysis should make these analytical revisions to both assets and equity.

ANALYSIS VIEWPOINT

YOU ARE THE ANALYST

You are an analyst for a securities firm. Your supervisor asks you to assess the relative risk of two potential *preferred equity* investments. Your analysis indicates these two companies are identical on all aspects of both returns and risks with the exception of their financing composition. The first company is financed 20 percent by debt, 20 percent from preferred equity, and 60 percent from common equity. The second is financed 30 percent by debt, 10 percent from preferred equity, and 60 percent from common equity. Which company presents the greater preferred equity risk?

CAPITAL STRUCTURE COMPOSITION AND SOLVENCY

The fundamental risk with a leveraged capital structure is the risk of inadequate cash under conditions of adversity. Debt involves a commitment to pay fixed charges in the form of interest and principal repayments. While certain fixed charges can be postponed in times of cash shortages, the fixed charges related to debt cannot be postponed without adverse repercussions to a company's shareholders and creditors. A leveraged capital structure also runs a risk from loss of financing flexibility. A company's ability to raise needed funds is impaired when it has a highly leveraged capital structure, especially in periods of adverse market conditions.

Long-Term Projections in Analyzing Solvency

Having sufficient cash to service debt is important for a levered company's continued viability. A direct and relevant risk measure of a levered company's capital structure is the *projection of future cash resources and inflows* available to meet debt requirements. These projections typically assume the worst possible economic conditions. This "bad news" analysis is a valuable safety test from the creditor's perspective. If we examine only prosperous or normal conditions, creditors would not need their senior position to equity, *and* would be better off with an equity position where potential rewards are higher.

We typically consider short-term horizons as involving periods of up to one year. Long-term horizons cover a wide range of periods exceeding one year. Examples include solvency analysis covering a three-year term loan and the evaluation of risk with a 30-year bond issue. Meaningful long-term projections covering interest and principal of a three-year loan are reasonable. Yet projections of funds flow for the 30-year bond issue are unrealistic. This is one reason why long-term debt often contains **sinking fund provisions** to reduce risk from long-term horizons, and often stipulates additional security in the form of assets pledged as collateral. Long-term debt also often contains provisions requiring maintenance of minimum working capital levels or restrictions on dividend payments. Both of these help protect creditors against severe deterioration in a company's financial position. However, these provisions cannot prevent adverse operating performance—the most serious cause of cash flow deficiencies.

We described in the previous chapter detailed long-term cash flow projections. We showed how the statement of cash flows can be effectively used and that it requires less detail than projections of *all* cash flows. Nevertheless, projections for long time horizons are less reliable than short-term horizons even when using the statement of cash flows. Since long-term cash flow projections are less reliable, several measures of long-term solvency are available to assist our analysis. These long-term solvency measures are typically static and include analysis of capital structure and both asset and earnings coverage.

Common-Size Statements
in Solvency Analysis

A common measure of financial risk for a company is its capital structure composition. **Composition analysis** is performed by constructing a **common-size statement** of the liabilities and equity section of the balance sheet. Exhibit 5.3 illustrates a common-size analysis for Tennessee Teletech, Inc. An advantage of common-size analysis of capital structure is in revealing the relative magnitude of financing sources for a company. We see Tennessee Teletech is primarily financed from common (35.6%) and preferred (17.8%) stock and liabilities (41.2%)—and a small amount of earnings is retained in the company (4.5%). Common-size analysis also lends itself to direct comparisons across different companies. A variation of common-size analysis is to perform the analysis using ratios. Another variation focuses only on long-term financing sources, excluding current liabilities.

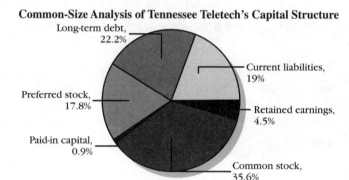

Common-Size Analysis of Tennessee Teletech's Capital Structure

Exhibit 5.3   Tennessee Teletech's Capital Structure: Common-Size Analysis

Current liabilities	$ 428,000	19.0%
Long-term debt	$ 500,000	22.2
Equity capital:		
Preferred stock	$ 400,000	17.8
Common stock	800,000	35.6
Paid-in capital	20,000	0.9
Retained earnings	102,000	4.5
Total equity capital	$1,322,000	58.8
Total liabilities and equity capital	$2,250,000	100.0%

Capital Structure Measures
for Solvency Analysis

Capital structure ratios are another means of solvency analysis. Ratio measures of capital structure relate components of capital structure to each other or their total. In this section we describe the most common of these ratios. We must take care before applying any measure or ratio that we understand its meaning and computation.

Total Debt to Total Capital

A comprehensive ratio is available to measure the relation between total debt (Current debt + Long-term debt + Other liabilities determined by our analysis, e.g., deferred taxes and redeemable preferred) and total capital (Total debt + Stockholders' equity [including preferred]). The **total debt to total capital ratio** (also called **total debt ratio**) is expressed as

$$\frac{\text{Total debt}}{\text{Total capital}}$$

The total debt to total capital ratio for Quaker Oats Company is computed as:

$$\frac{\$926.9^{(a)} + \$701.2^{(b)} + \$115.5^{(c)} + \$366.7^{(d)}}{\$99.3^{(e)} + \$806.5^{(f)} + \$2,100.3^{(g)}} = \frac{\$2,110.3}{\$3,016.1} = 0.70$$

$^{(a)}$Current liabilities.
$^{(b)}$Long-term debt.
$^{(c)}$Other liabilities.
$^{(d)}$Deferred income taxes.
$^{(e)}$Preferred stock outstanding.
$^{(f)}$Shareholders' equity,
$^{(g)}$Total debt (numerator).

This measure is often expressed in ratio form, 0.70, or described as debt comprising 70 percent of Quaker Oats' capital structure.

Total Debt to Equity Capital

Another measure of the relation of debt to capital sources is the ratio of total debt (as defined above) to *equity* capital. The **total debt to equity capital ratio** is computed as:

$$\frac{\text{Total debt}}{\text{Shareholders' equity}}$$

The total debt to equity capital ratio for Quaker Oats is computed as:

$$\frac{\$2,110.3}{\$99.3 + \$806.5} = 2.33$$

This ratio implies that Quaker Oats' total debt is 2.33 times its equity capital. Alternatively stated, Quaker Oats' credit financing equals $2.33 for every $1 of equity financing.

Creditors often prefer the reciprocal measure of this ratio. This ratio, the **equity capital to total debt ratio,** is computed as:

$$\frac{\text{Shareholders' equity}}{\text{Total debt}}$$

Computation of this ratio for Quaker Oats equals:

$$\frac{\$905.8}{\$2,110.3} = 0.43$$

Creditors interpret this ratio as implying every dollar of debt is backed by 43 cents of equity capital. This ratio emphasizes that owners contribute a smaller share of the financing of Quaker Oats than do creditors.

Total Debt to Equity Ratio

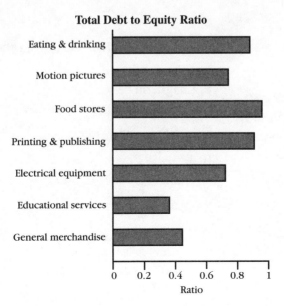

Long-Term Debt to Equity Capital

The **long-term debt to equity capital ratio** measures the relation of long-term debt (usually defined as all noncurrent liabilities) to equity capital. A ratio in excess of 1:1 indicates greater long-term debt financing compared to equity capital.

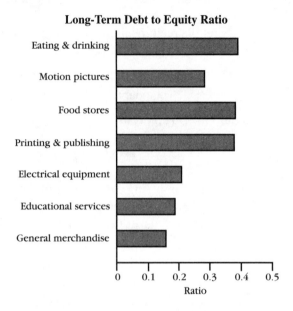

Long-Term Debt to Equity Ratio

This ratio is commonly referred to as the **debt to equity ratio** and it is computed as:

$$\frac{\text{Long-term debt}}{\text{Shareholders' equity}}$$

For Quaker Oats the long-term debt to equity ratio equals:

$$\frac{\$2,110.3^{(a)} - \$926.9^{(b)}}{\$905.8^{(c)}} = 1.31$$

[a]Total debt.
[b]Total current liabilities.
[c]Shareholders' equity.

Short-Term Debt to Total Debt

The ratio of debt maturing in the short term relative to total debt is an important indicator of the short-run cash and financing needs of a company. Short-term debt, as opposed to long-term debt or sinking fund requirements, is an indicator of enterprise reliance on short-term (primarily bank) financing. Short-term debt is usually subject to frequent changes in interest rates.

Equity Capital at Market Value

Accounting practice emphasizes historical costs rather than market values. Since shareholders' equity is the residual of assets minus liabilities, equity book values can substantially differ from market values. This difference is especially meaningful when equity book values enter into the computation of important ratios. A common means of adjusting equity book values is to restate asset values from historical cost to market value. While company disclosures sometimes include replacement cost data, information on market value data is difficult to construct. One solution to this problem is computing equity capital at current (or average) market value of the stock comprising it. This technique assumes the securities market recognizes current values of assets and their earning power. The resulting *market value of equity* is then used in ratio computations that use equity values.

This method is less useful when stock prices fluctuate widely and when, in times of overspeculation or market uncertainty, prices may not be representative of a company's "fundamentals." Motivation for using stock prices derives from evidence that the marketplace provides a good approximation (or at least as good as any other judgmental process) of equity values. Also, use of *average* market prices diminishes the impact of transitory price changes. Use of reliable equity values can improve certain ratio analyses and provide more realistic measures of asset protection for creditors.

Evidence of equity book values consistently in excess of equity market values is usually interpreted as financial weakness and restricted financial capabilities. This affects a company's ability to issue additional equity or debt capital. Conversely, evidence of equity market values exceeding equity book values is interpreted as protection for creditors. This implies a company's ability to obtain capital at favorable prices and is an indicator of financial strength. Use of market values introduces a notion inherent in earnings coverage measures. We discuss earnings coverage measures later in this chapter; such measures benefit from a focus on the earning power of assets and not on asset book values. Equity market values also recognize the earning power of a company's assets. In this way, ratio measures using equity market values are consistent with earnings coverage ratios.

We can compute the total debt to equity ratio of Quaker Oats using the average common stock market price for the year:

$$\frac{\text{Total debt}}{\text{Common equity at market value} + \text{Preferred equity at book value}}$$

$$\frac{\$2,110,300,000}{\$73,328,721^{(a)} \times \$53.32^{(b)} + \$4,800,000^{(c)}} = 0.52$$

[a]Number of shares of common stock outstanding.

[b]Average stock price for year (range is 41.75–64.88).

[c]Preferred stock at book value (market value unavailable).

Equity market values reflect the earning power of assets and possess a long-term perspective. If we compare the 0.52 we get when using equity market value to the 2.33 computed using book value, our interpretation is that the market value ratio is more favorable.

Interpretation of Capital Structure Measures

Common-size and ratio analyses of capital structure are primarily measures of the *risk* of a company's capital structure. The higher the proportion of debt, the larger the fixed charges of interest and debt repayment, and the greater the likelihood of insolvency during periods of earnings decline or hardship. Capital structure measures serve as *screening devices.* For example, when the ratio of debt to equity capital is relatively small (10 percent or less), there is no apparent concern with this aspect of a company's financial condition—our analysis is probably better directed elsewhere. Should our analysis reveal debt is a significant part of capitalization, then further analysis is necessary. Extended analysis should focus on several different aspects of a company's financial condition, results of operations, and future prospects.

Analysis of short-term liquidity is always important because before we assess long-term solvency we want to be satisfied about the near-term financial survival of the company. We described various analyses of short-term liquidity in the two previous chapters, and we would also assess the size of working capital to that of long-term debt. Loan and bond indenture covenants requiring maintenance of minimum working capital levels attest to the importance of current liquidity in ensuring a company's long-term solvency. Additional analytical tests of importance include our examination of debt maturities (as to size and timing), interest costs, and risk-bearing factors. The latter factors include a company's earnings stability or persistence, industry performance, and composition of assets.

Adjustments of Long-Term Debt to Equity Ratio

There are certain analytical adjustments we can make in our analysis of financial statements when using the debt to equity ratio. We illustrate these adjustments in Appendix 5C.

Event and Other Risk Factors

There are additional risk-bearing factors for creditors that are not easily measured and must be recognized in protective bond-indenture provisions or similar means. One risk factor is the possibility the company issues additional debt of equal or higher priority. This risk is referred to as **event risk** and occurs most often with leveraged buyouts, tender offers, and going-private transactions. These transactions typically yield serious declines in the value of outstanding debt. Additional risk of loss arises when a company increases shareholders' dividends to unreasonable levels, invests in riskier assets, or pursues business activities increasing risk of debt.

ASSET-BASED MEASURES OF SOLVENCY

This section describes two categories of asset-based analyses of a company's solvency.

Asset Composition in Solvency Analysis

The assets a company employs in its operating activities determine to some extent the sources of financing. For example, fixed and other long-term assets are typically not financed with short-term loans. These long-term assets are usually financed with equity capital. Debt capital is also a common source of long-term asset financing, especially in industries like utilities where revenue sources are stable.

    Asset composition analysis is an important tool in assessing the risk exposure of a company's capital structure. Asset composition is typically evaluated using common-size statements of asset balances. Exhibit 5.4 shows our common-size analysis of Tennessee Teletech's assets (its liabilities and equity were analyzed in Exhibit 5.3). Judging by the distribution of assets and the related capital structure, it appears that since a relatively high proportion of assets is current (61 percent), a 41 percent total liabilities position is not excessive. Further analysis and measurements might alter or reinforce this preliminary interpretation.

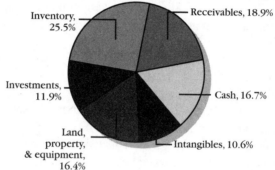

Common-Size Analysis of Tennessee Teletech's Asset Composition

Asset Coverage in Solvency Analysis

Asset coverage is an important factor in evaluating long-term solvency. Assets provide protection to creditors both because of their earning power and liquidation value. Assets represent the base a company relies upon for additional financing requirements. The relation between asset groups and

Exhibit 5.4   Tennessee Teletech's Asset Composition: Common-Size Analysis

Current assets		
Cash	$ 376,000	16.7%
Accounts receivable (net)	425,000	18.9
Merchandise inventory	574,000	25.5
Total current assets	$1,375,000	61.1
Investments	$ 268,000	11.9
Land, property, and equipment (net)	368,000	16.4
Intangibles	239,000	10.6
Total assets	$2,250,000	100.0%

selected items of capital structure is often usefully expressed in ratio form for our analysis. The **fixed assets to equity capital** ratio measures the relation between long-term assets and equity. A ratio in excess of 1:1 implies a portion of fixed assets are financed with debt. The ratio of **net tangible assets to long-term debt** is a measure of asset coverage for long-term obligations. It is a conservative measure—it excludes assets of sometimes doubtful realizability or value (intangibles). This ratio is interpreted as a measure of safety for creditors assuming asset liquidation at book values. The **total liabilities to net tangible assets** ratio (including net working capital) is a measure of the relation between debt and a company's investment in operating assets. This analysis tool measures the property collateral enjoyed by creditors. This ratio is especially useful when analyzing companies whose book values are understated.

IMPORTANCE OF EARNINGS COVERAGE

Our discussion of capital structure measures recognizes their usefulness as screening devices. They are a valuable means of deciding whether risk inherent in a company's capital structure requires further analysis. One limitation of capital structure measures is their inability to focus on availability of cash flows to service a company's debt. As debt is repaid, capital structure measures typically *improve* whereas annual cash requirements for paying interest or sinking funds remain *fixed* or *increase* (examples of the latter include level payment debt with balloon repayment provisions or zero coupon bonds). This limitation highlights our important emphasis on a company's **earnings coverage,** or *earning power,* as the source of interest and principal repayments. While highly profitable companies can in the short term face liquidity problems because of asset composition, we must remember that long-term earnings are the major source of liquidity, solvency, and borrowing capacity.

Relation of Earnings to Fixed Charges

The relation of earnings to fixed charges is part of **earnings coverage analysis.** Earnings coverage measures focus on the relation between debt-related fixed charges and a company's earnings available to meet these charges. These measures are important factors in debt ratings (see Appendix 5A). Bond indentures often specify minimum levels of earnings coverage for additional issuance of debt. Securities and Exchange

Commission regulations require the ratio of *earnings to fixed charges* be disclosed in the prospectus of all debt securities registered. The typical measure of the **earnings to fixed charges** ratio is:

$$\frac{\text{Earnings available for fixed charges}}{\text{Fixed charges}}$$

The concept underlying this measure is straightforward. Yet application of this measure is complicated by what is included in both "earnings available for fixed charges" and "fixed charges."

Computing Earnings Available for Fixed Charges

We previously discussed differences between income determined using accrual accounting and cash from operations. For example, certain revenue items like undistributed subsidiary earnings and sales on extended credit terms do not generate immediate cash inflows (although a parent can determine dividends for controlled subsidiaries). Similarly, certain expenses like depreciation, amortization, depletion, and deferred tax charges do not require cash outflows. These distinctions are important since fixed debt charges are paid out of cash, not earnings. Our analysis must recognize that unadjusted net income is not necessarily a good measure of cash available for fixed charges. Using earnings as an approximation of cash from operations is sometimes appropriate while in others it can misstate the amount available for servicing fixed charges. Our approach to this problem lies not with generalizations but in careful analysis of noncash revenue and expense items comprising income. For example, in analyzing depreciation as a noncash expense, we must remember the long-run necessity of a company replacing plant and equipment. Our analysis of the earnings available for fixed charges requires consideration of several of these important factors that are discussed below.

Extraordinary Gains and Losses   Extraordinary gains and losses enter into the determination of long-term average earning power. They must be recognized as a factor that can over the long term contribute to or reduce cash available to pay fixed charges. Our computation of earnings coverage measures using average earnings must recognize extraordinary gains and losses. This is especially true of earnings coverage ratios where we measure the risk of loss of cash sources for paying fixed charges.

Preferred Dividends   Preferred dividends are not deducted from income because paying these dividends is not mandatory. In consolidated financial statements, preferred dividends of a subsidiary whose income is consolidated are deducted because they represent a charge having priority over the distribution of earnings to the parent.

Earnings Attributed to Minority Interests   These earnings are usually deducted from earnings available for fixed charges even though minority shareholders can rarely enforce a cash claim. An exception arises when a consolidated subsidiary has fixed charges. In this case, the coverage ratio should be computed using earnings before deducting minority interests. Another case arises when a subsidiary (having a minority interest) reports a loss. In this case, the credit to income from the minority's share in the loss should be excluded from consolidated earnings in computing our coverage ratio. The parent in most cases meets fixed charges obligations of its subsidiary to protect its own credit standing, whether or not legally obligated.

Income Taxes   Income taxes in the computation of earnings coverage ratios demand careful scrutiny. For example, since interest is tax deductible, it is paid from pre-tax earnings. In contrast, preferred dividends or sinking fund payments are not tax deductible and are paid from after-tax earnings.

Adding Back Fixed Charges   To determine pre-tax earnings available for fixed charges, the fixed charges deducted in arriving at pre-tax earnings must be added back to pre-tax earnings in the numerator of earnings coverage ratios.

Income Level   The income level used in computing earnings coverage ratios deserves attention. We must consider the question: What level of income is most representative of the amount actually available in future periods for paying debt-related fixed charges? Average earnings from continuing operations that span the business cycle and are adjusted for likely future changes are probably a good approximation of the average cash available from future operations to pay fixed charges. If one objective of an earnings coverage ratio is to measure a creditor's maximum exposure to risk, an appropriate earnings figure is one that occurs at the low point of the company's business cycle.

Computing Fixed Charges

The second major component in the earnings to fixed charges ratio is fixed charges. In this section we examine the fixed charges typically included in the computation. Analysis of fixed charges requires us to consider several important components.

Interest Incurred   Interest incurred is the most direct and obvious fixed charge arising from debt. Yet reported interest expense includes amortization of any discount or premium. *Discount* and issuance expenses represent an amount by which par value exceeded proceeds from the debt issuance. Discount amortization increases reported interest expense. *Premium* is the reverse of a discount and represents proceeds exceeding par value. Premium amortization reduces reported interest expense. Both discount and premium amortization do not typically affect cash flows. They reflect expense or revenue allocations over the debt period. Another probable adjustment is when low coupon bonds are near maturity and it is likely they will be refinanced with higher coupon bonds. In this case the fixed charges should probably be adjusted to include the expected higher interest costs. Another issue arises from lack of information. When information is so limited as to preclude our computation of interest incurred from interest capitalized, we can approximate the amount of interest incurred by referring to the mandatory disclosure of *interest paid* in the statement of cash flows. Interest incurred differs from the reported interest paid due to reasons that include (1) changes in interest payable, (2) interest capitalized being netted, and (3) discount and premium amortization. In the absence of information, interest paid is a good approximation of interest incurred.

Capitalized Interest   Current practice requires capitalization of certain interest costs. We must use care in dealing with capitalized interest in computing both the numerator and denominator of the earnings to fixed charges ratio. To begin, let's clarify the role of interest in reported income. Interest paid or obligated to be paid by a company for a period is *interest incurred*. This is the amount we focus on as needing coverage with earnings. Interest incurred that is charged to an asset is *interest capitalized*. Interest incurred less interest capitalized equals *interest expense*. Since interest expense is subtracted in computing pre-tax earnings, it should be added back to pre-tax earnings of the ratio's numerator to arrive at pre-tax pre-interest earnings. The ratio's denominator includes as a fixed charge the interest incurred whether capitalized or not. Interest capitalized in one period finds its way into the income statements of subsequent periods in the form of expenses like depreciation or amortization of assets capitalized. This amortized interest previously capitalized should be added back to pre-tax income. Failure to add back this interest yields earnings in the numerator computed *after* interest expenses rather than *before* interest expenses, understating the earnings to fixed charges ratio. Since the amount of previously capitalized interest that is amortized in a period does not require disclosure, our analysis must obtain this amount voluntarily from companies or derive it from other disclosures like those relating to deferred taxes.

Interest Implicit in Lease Obligations   When a lease is capitalized, the interest portion of the lease payment is included in interest expense on the income statement, while most of the balance is usually considered repayment of the principal obligation. A question arises when our analysis discovers certain leases that should be capitalized but are not. This question goes beyond the accounting question of whether capitalization is appropriate or not. We must remember a long-term lease represents a fixed obligation that must be given recognition in computing the earnings to fixed charges ratio. Long-term leases that conceptually need not be capitalized can consist of fixed charges requiring inclusion in the earnings to fixed charges ratio. One problem is extracting the interest portion from the long-term lease payment. Our analysis can sometimes obtain the rate of interest implicit in a lease from note disclosures. Absent this, a rule of thumb (e.g., interest is approximately one-third of rental payments) might be our only solution. The Securities and Exchange Commission accepts this rule of thumb by registrants if management believes it represents a reasonable approximation of the interest factor. .

Preferred Stock Dividend Requirements of Majority-Owned Subsidiaries   These are viewed as fixed charges because they have priority over the distribution of earnings to the parent. Items that would be or are eliminated in consolidation should not be viewed as fixed charges. We must remember that all fixed charges not tax deductible must be tax adjusted. This is done by increasing them by an amount equal to the income tax required to yield an after-tax income sufficient to cover these fixed charges. The preferred stock dividend requirements of majority-owned subsidiaries are an example of a non-tax-deductible fixed charge. We make an adjustment to compute the "grossed-up" amount:

$$\frac{\text{Preferred stock dividend requirements}}{1 - \text{Income tax rate}}$$

The tax rate used should be based on the relation between income tax expense on income from continuing operations and the amount of pre-tax income from continuing operations (this is a company's *effective tax rate*). We use the effective tax rate rather than the statutory rate since this is the SEC's requirement.

Principal Repayment Requirements   Principal repayment obligations are from a cash outflow perspective as onerous as interest obligations. In the case of rental payments a company's obligations to pay principal and interest must be met simultaneously. Several reasons are advanced as to why requirements for principal repayments are not given recognition in earnings to fixed charges ratio calculations, including:

- The earnings to fixed charges ratio is based on income. It assumes if the ratio is at a satisfactory level, a company can refinance obligations when they become due or mature. Accordingly, they need not be met by funds from earnings.
- If a company has an acceptable debt to equity ratio it should be able to reborrow amounts equal to principal repayments.
- Inclusion can result in double counting. For example, funds recovered by depreciation provide for debt repayment. If earnings reflect a deduction for depreciation, then fixed charges should not include principal repayments. There is some merit to this argument if debt is used to acquire depreciable fixed assets and if there is some correspondence between the pattern of depreciation and principal repayments. We must recognize depreciation is recovered typically only from profitable or at least break-even operations. Therefore, this argument's validity is subject to these conditions. We must also recognize the definition of *earnings* in the earnings to fixed charges ratio emphasizes cash from operations as that available to cover fixed charges. Using this concept eliminates the double-counting problem since

noncash charges like depreciation would be added back to net income in computing earnings coverage.

- A problem with including debt repayment requirements in fixed charges is not all debt agreements provide for sinking funds or similar repayment obligations. Any arbitrary allocation of indebtedness across periods would be unrealistic and ignore differences in pressures on cash resources from actual debt repayments across periods. In the long run, maturities and balloon payments must all be met. One solution rests with our careful analysis of debt repayment requirements. This analysis serves as the basis in judging the effect of these requirements for long-term solvency. Assuming debt can be refinanced, rolled over, or otherwise paid from current operations is risky. Rather, we must recognize debt repayment requirements and their timing in analysis of long-term solvency. Including sinking fund or other early repayment requirements in fixed charges is a way of recognizing these obligations. Another way is applying debt repayment requirements over a period of 5 to 10 years into the future and relating these to after-tax funds expected to be available from operations.

Guarantees to Pay Fixed Charges   Guarantees to pay fixed charges of unconsolidated subsidiaries or of unaffiliated persons (suppliers) should be added to fixed charges if the requirement to honor the guarantee appears imminent.

Other Fixed Charges   While interest payments and principal repayment requirements are the fixed charges most directly related to the incurrence of debt, there is no reason to restrict our analysis of long-term solvency to these charges or commitments. A thorough analysis of fixed charges should include all long-term rental payment obligations[3] (not only the interest portion), and especially those rentals that must be met under noncancelable leases. The reason short-term leases can be excluded from consideration in fixed charges is they represent obligations of limited duration, usually less than three years. Consequently, these leases can be discontinued in a period of financial distress. Our analysis must evaluate how

---

[3] Capitalized long-term leases affect income by the interest charge implicit in them and by the amortization of the property right. To consider the "principal" component of these leases as fixed charges (after income is reduced by amortization of the property right) can yield double counting.

essential these leased items are to the continued operation of the company. Additional charges not directly related to debt, but considered long-term commitments of a fixed nature, are long-term noncancelable purchase contracts in excess of normal requirements.

Computing Earnings to Fixed Charges

The conventional formula, and one adopted by the SEC, for computing the earnings to fixed charges ratio is:

(a) Pre-tax income from continuing operations *plus* (b) Interest expense *plus* (c) Amortization of debt expense and discount or premium *plus* (d) Interest portion of operating rental expenses *plus* (e) Tax-adjusted preferred stock dividend requirements of majority-owned subsidiaries *plus* (f) Amount of previously capitalized interest amortized during the period *minus* (g) Undistributed income of less than 50-percent-owned subsidiaries or affiliates

(h) Total interest incurred *plus* (c) Amortization of debt expense and discount or premium *plus* (d) Interest portion of operating rental expenses *plus* (e) Tax-adjusted preferred stock dividend requirements of majority-owned subsidiaries

Individual components in this ratio are labeled *a* through *h* and are explained in detail below:

a. Pre-tax income before discontinued operations, extraordinary items, and cumulative effects of accounting changes.
b. Interest incurred less interest capitalized.
c. Usually included in interest expense.
d. *Financing leases* are capitalized so the interest implicit in these is already included in interest expense. However, the interest portion of *long-term operating leases* is included on the assumption many long-term operating leases narrowly miss the capital lease criteria, but have many characteristics of a financing transaction.
e. Excludes all items eliminated in consolidation. The dividend amount is increased to pre-tax earnings required to pay for it.[4]
f. Applies to *non*utility companies. This amount is not often disclosed.
g. Minority interest in income of majority-owned subsidiaries having fixed charges can be included in income.
h. Included whether expensed or capitalized.

---

[4] Computed as [Preferred stock dividend requirements]/[1 − income tax rate]. The income tax rate is computed as [Actual income tax provision]/[Income before income taxes, extraordinary items, and cumulative effect of accounting changes].

For ease of presentation, two items (provisions) are left out of the ratio above:

1. Losses of majority-owned subsidiaries should be considered in *full* when computing earnings.
2. Losses on investments in less than 50-percent-owned subsidiaries accounted for by the equity method should not be included in earnings *unless* the company guarantees subsidiaries' debts.

The SEC requires that if the earnings to fixed charges ratio is less than 1.0, the amount of earnings insufficient to cover fixed charges should be reported (rather than the ratio).

Case Illustration of Earnings to Fixed Charges Ratio

This section illustrates actual computation of the earnings to fixed charges ratio. Our first case focuses on CompuTech Corp., whose income statement is reproduced in Exhibit 5.5 along with additional financial information. Using the financial data of CompuTech ($ thousands) we compute the earnings to fixed charges ratio as (letter references are to the ratio definition):

$$\frac{\$2{,}200\ (a) + \$700\ (b\ \text{and}\ c) + \$300\ (d) + \$80\ (f) - \$600\ (g) + \$200^*}{\$840\ (h) + \$60\ (c) + \$300\ (d)} = 2.40$$

Note: The SEC permits including in income the minority interest in the income of majority-owned subsidiaries having fixed charges. This amount is added to reverse a similar deduction from income.

Our second case uses the financial statements of Quaker Oats ($ millions). The earnings to fixed charges ratio for Quaker Oats is computed as (letter references are to the ratio definition):

$$\frac{(a)\ \$411.5^{(1)} + (b)\ \$101.9^{(2)} + (d)\ \$14.8^{(3)}}{(h)\ \$103.8^{(4)} + (d)\ \$14.8^{(3)}} = 4.45$$

(1) Income from continuing operations before taxes.
(2) Interest expense.
(3) One-third of operating lease rentals or one-third of $44.5 = $14.8.
(4) Interest incurred $101.9 + $1.9 = $103.8.

Pro Forma Computation of Earnings to Fixed Charges

In situations where fixed charges not yet incurred are recognized in computing the earnings to fixed charges ratio (e.g., interest costs under a prospective debt issuance), it is acceptable to estimate offsetting benefits expected from these future cash inflows and include them in pro forma earnings. Benefits derived from prospective debt can be measured in several ways, including interest savings from a planned refunding operation, income from short-term investments where proceeds can be invested, or other reasonable estimates of future benefits. When the effect of a prospective refinancing plan changes the ratio by 10 percent or more, the SEC usually requires a pro forma computation of the ratio reflecting changes to be effected under the plan.

Times Interest Earned Analysis

Another earnings coverage measure is the **times interest earned ratio.** This ratio considers interest as the only fixed charge needing earnings coverage:

$$\frac{\text{Income} + \text{Tax expense} + \text{Interest expense}}{\text{Interest expense}}$$

The times interest earned ratio is a simplified measure. It ignores most adjustments to both the numerator and denominator that we discussed with the earnings to fixed charges ratio. While its computation is simple, it is potentially misleading and not as effective an analysis tool as the earnings to fixed charges ratio.

Relation of Cash Flow to Fixed Charges

Accrual accounting for net income does not always give us a good measure of the cash provided by operations that is available to cover fixed charges. Companies must pay fixed charges in cash while net income includes earned revenues and incurred expenses that do not necessarily generate or require immediate cash. This section describes a cash-based measure of fixed-charges coverage to address this limitation.

Exhibit 5.5

COMPUTECH CORPORATION

Income Statement

Net sales		$13,400,000
Income of less than 50%-owned affiliates (all undistributed)		600,000
Total revenue		$14,000,000
Cost of goods sold	$7,400,000	
Selling, general, and administrative expenses	1,900,000	
Depreciation (excluded from above costs)[3]	800,000	
Interest expense[1]—net	700,000	
Rental expense[2]	800,000	
Share of minority interests in consolidated income[4]	200,000	11,800,000
Income before taxes		$ 2,200,000
Income taxes:		
Current	$ 800,000	
Deferred	300,000	1,100,000
Income before extraordinary items		$ 1,100,000
Extraordinary gain (net of $67,000 tax)		200,000
Net income		$ 1,300,000
Dividends:		
On common stock	$ 200,000	
On preferred stock	400,000	600,000
Earnings retained for the year		$ 700,000

Selected notes to the financial statements:

[1]Interest expense is composed of the following:

Interest incurred (except items below)	$740,000
Amortization of bond discount	60,000
Interest portion of capitalized leases	100,000
Interest capitalized	(200,000)
Interest expense	$700,000

[2]Interest implicit in noncapitalized leases amounts to $300,000.

[3]Depreciation includes amortization of previously capitalized interest of $80,000.

[4]These subsidiaries have fixed charges.

Additional information (during the income statement period):

Increase in accounts receivable	$310,000
Increase in inventories	180,000
Increase in accounts payable	140,000
Decrease in accrued taxes	20,000

Cash Flow to Fixed Charges Ratio

The **cash flow to fixed charges ratio** is computed using *cash from operations* rather than earnings in the numerator of the earnings to fixed charges ratio. Cash from operations is reported in the statement of cash flows. The cash flow to fixed charges ratio is computed as:

$$\frac{\text{Pre-tax operating cash flow } + \text{ Adjustments } (b) \text{ through } (g) \text{ on previous pages}}{\text{Fixed charges}}$$

Using financial data from CompuTech in Exhibit 5.5 we can compute pre-tax cash from operations for this ratio as:

Pre-tax income	$2,200,000
Add (deduct) adjustments to cash basis:	
Depreciation	800,000
Deferred income taxes (already added back)	—
Amortization of bond discount	60,000
Share of minority interest in income	200,000
Undistributed income of affiliates	(600,000)
Increase in receivables	(310,000)
Increase in inventories	(180,000)
Increase in accounts payable	140,000
Decrease in accrued tax	(20,000)
Pre-tax cash from operations	$2,290,000

Fixed charges needing to be added back to pre-tax cash from operations are:

Pre-tax cash from operations	$2,290,000
Interest expensed (less bond discount added back above)	640,000
Interest portion of operating rental expense	300,000
Amount of previously capitalized interest amortized during period*	—
Total numerator	$3,230,000

*Assume included in depreciation (already added back).

Notice the numerator does not reflect a deduction of $600,000 (undistributed income of affiliates) because it, being a noncash source, is already deducted in arriving at pre-tax cash from operations. Also the "share of minority interests in consolidated income" is already added back in arriving at pre-tax cash from operations. Fixed charges for the ratio's denominator are:

Interest incurred	$ 900,000
Interest portion of operating rentals	300,000
Fixed charges	$1,200,000

CompuTech's cash flow to fixed charges ratio is computed as:

$$\frac{\$3,230,000}{\$1,200,000} = 2.69$$

As another example, we compute Quaker Oats' pre-tax cash from operations plus fixed charges for the numerator in the cash flow to fixed charges ratio as:

Numerator of cash flow to fixed charges ratio	*$ millions*
Cash from operations	532.4
Add back:	
Income tax expense (except deferred)[a]	161.4
Interest expense	101.9
One-third of operating lease rentals of 44.5[c]	14.8
Amortization of previously capitalized interest (already added back)	——
Total numerator of ratio	810.5

We then compute Quaker Oats' cash flow to fixed charges ratio as:

$$\frac{\$810.5}{\$103.8^{(b)} + \$14.8^{(c)}} = 6.83$$

[a]Deferred tax already added back in computing cash from operations.
[b]Interest incurred ($101.9 + $1.9).
[c]One-third of operating lease rentals of $44.5.

Permanence of Cash from Operations

The relation of a company's cash flows from operations to fixed charges is important to our analysis of long-term solvency. Because of this relation's importance, we assess the "permanence" of operating cash flows. We typically do this in evaluating the components comprising operating cash flows. For example, the depreciation add-back to net income is more permanent than net income because recovery of depreciation from sales precedes receipt of any income. For all businesses, selling prices must (in the long run) reflect the cost of plant and equipment used in production. The depreciation add-back assumes cash flow benefits from recovery of depreciation are available to service debt. This assumption is true only in the short run. In the long run, the cash recovery must be dedicated to replacing plant and equipment. An exception can occur with add-backs of items like amortization of goodwill that are not necessarily replaced or depleted. Permanence of changes in the operating working capital (operating current assets less operating current liabilities) component of operating cash flows is often difficult to assess. Operating working capital is linked more with sales than with pre-tax income and therefore is often more stable than operating cash flows.

Earnings Coverage of Preferred Dividends

Our analysis of preferred stock often benefits from measuring the earnings coverage of preferred dividends. This analysis is similar to our analysis of how earnings cover debt-related fixed charges. The SEC requires disclosure of the ratio of combined fixed charges and preferred dividends in the prospectus of all preferred stock offerings. Computing the earnings coverage of preferred dividends must include in fixed charges all expenditures taking precedence over preferred dividends.[5] Since preferred dividends are not tax deductible, after-tax income must be used to cover them. Accordingly, the **earnings coverage of preferred dividends** ratio is computed as:

$$\frac{\text{Pre-tax income} + \text{Adjustments } (b) \text{ through } (g) \text{ on previous pages}}{\text{Fixed charges} + \left(\dfrac{\text{Preferred dividends}}{1 - \text{Tax rate}}\right)}$$

Using the financial data from CompuTech Corp. in Exhibit 5.5 we compute the earnings coverage of preferred dividends ratio. This is identical to using CompuTech's ratio of earnings to fixed charges (computed earlier)

---

[5] Care must be exercised in comparing coverage ratios because some analysts and financial services include only the preferred dividend requirements in fixed charges.

and adding the tax-adjusted preferred dividend requirement. Computation of the earnings coverage to preferred dividends ratio is ($ thousands):

$$\frac{\$2{,}200\ (a) + \$700\ (b \text{ and } c) + \$300\ (d) + \$80\ (f) - \$600\ (g) + \$200^{*}}{\$840\ (h) + \$60\ (c) + \$300\ (d) + \dfrac{\$400^{\dagger}}{1 - 0.50}} = 1.44$$

Note: Letters refer to individual components in the earnings to fixed charges ratio (see prior pages).
    *Minority interest in income of majority-owned subsidiaries (see prior discussion).
    †Tax-adjusted preferred dividend requirement.

If there are two or more preferred issues outstanding, this coverage ratio is usually computed for each issue by omitting dividend requirements of junior issues and including all prior fixed charges and senior issues of preferred dividends.

Interpreting Earnings Coverage Measures

Earnings coverage measures provide us insight into the ability of a company to meet its fixed charges out of current earnings. There exists a high correlation between earnings coverage measures and the default rate on debt—the higher the coverage, the lower the default rate. A study of creditor experience[6] with debt revealed the following default and yield rates for debt classified according to times interest earned ratios:

Times Interest Earned	Default Rate	Promised Yield	Realized Yield	Loss Rate
3.0 and over	2.1%	4.0%	4.9%	-0.9%
2.0–2.9	4.0	4.3	5.1	-0.8
1.5–1.9	17.9	4.7	5.0	-0.3
1.0–1.4	34.1	6.8	6.4	0.4
Under 1.0	35.0	6.2	6.0	0.2

Our attention on earnings in coverage measures is sensible since creditors place considerable reliance on the ability of a company to meet its obligations and continue operating. An increased yield rate on debt seldom compensates creditors for the risk of losing principal. If the likelihood of a

---

[6] See H. B. Hickman, *Corporate Bond Quality and Investor Experience* (Princeton, NJ: Princeton University Press, 1958).

company meeting its obligations through continuing operations is not high, creditors' risk is substantial.

Importance of Earnings Variability and Persistence for Earnings Coverage

An important factor in evaluating earnings coverage measures is the behavior of earnings and cash flows across time. The more stable the earnings pattern of a company or industry, the lower is the acceptable earnings coverage measure. For example, a utility experiences little in the way of economic downturns or upswings and therefore we accept a lower earnings coverage ratio. In contrast, cyclical companies like machinery manufacturers can experience both sharp declines and increases in performance. This uncertainty leads us to impose a higher earnings coverage ratio on these companies. Both *earnings variability* and *earnings persistence* are common measures of this uncertainty across time. Our analysis can use one or both of earnings measures in determining the accepted standard for earnings coverage. Earnings persistence is usually measured as the (auto) correlation of earnings across time.

Importance of Measurements and Assumptions for Earnings Coverage

Determining an accepted standard for earnings coverage depends on the method of computing an earnings coverage measure. We described several earnings coverage measures in the chapter. Many of these measures assume different definitions of *earnings* and *fixed charges*. We expect lower standards for earnings coverage measures employing the most demanding and stringent definitions. Both the SEC and our computation of the earnings to fixed charges coverage ratio use earnings *before* discontinued operations, extraordinary items, and cumulative effects of accounting changes. While excluding these three items yields a less variable earnings stream, it also excludes important components that are part of a company's business activities. Accordingly, we suggest these components be included in computing the *average* coverage ratio over several years. The accepted standard also varies with the measure of earnings—for example, earnings measured as the average, worst, best, or median performance. The quality of earnings is another important factor that we examine in Chapter 8. We should not compute earnings coverage ratios using shortcuts or purposefully conservative means. For example, using after-tax income in computing coverage ratios where fixed charges are tax deductible is incorrect and uses conservatism improperly. Our accepted standard of coverage must ultimately reflect our willingness and ability to incur risk (relative to our expected return). Appendix 5A refers to accepted standards of coverage ratios used by rating agencies in analyzing debt securities.

CAPITAL STRUCTURE RISK AND RETURN

It is useful for us to consider recent developments in "financial innovations" for risk inherent in a company's capital structure. A company can increase risks (and potential returns) of equity holders by increasing leverage. A leveraged buyout of a company uses increased leverage and often other factors (undervalued assets saleable for cash) favorable to buyers. Specifically, a *leveraged buyout* uses debt to take a company private by "buying out" equity holders. The acquirers rely on future cash flows to service the increased debt and on anticipated asset sales to reduce debt. Another benefit of leverage is the tax deductibility of interest while dividends paid to equity holders are not tax deductible.

Substitution of debt for equity yields a riskier capital structure. This is why bonds used to finance certain leveraged buyouts are called *junk bonds*. A junk bond, unlike its high-quality counterpart, is part of a high-risk capital structure where its interest payments are minimally covered by earnings. Economic adversities rapidly jeopardize interest payments and principal of junk bonds. Junk bonds possess the risk of equity more so than the safety of debt.

Financial experience continually reminds us of those who forget the relation between risk and return. It is no surprise that highly speculative financial periods spawn risky securities. Our surprise is the refusal by some to appreciate the adjective *junk* when applied to bonds. Similarly, zero coupon bonds defer all payment of interest to maturity and offer several advantages over standard debt issues. However, when issued by companies with less than outstanding credit credentials, the risk with zero coupon bonds is substantially higher than with standard debt—due to the uncertainty of receiving interest and principal many years into the future. Another financial innovation called *payment in kind (PIK) securities* pays interest by issuing additional debt. The assumption is a debtor, possibly too weak to pay interest currently, will subsequently be successful enough to pay it later. While innovations in financing companies' business activities continue, and novel terms are coined, our analysis must focus on substance over form. The basic truth about the relation between risk and return in a capital structure remains.

Factors contributing to risk and our available tools of analysis discussed in this and preceding chapters point to our need for thorough and sound financial analysis. Relying on credit ratings or others' rankings is a delegation of our analysis and evaluation responsibilities. It is risky for us to place partial or exclusive reliance on these sources of analysis. No matter how reputable, these sources cannot capture our unique risk and return expectations. We need to exercise and improve our abilities to analyze risk and return in a company's capital structure to avoid situations like the following:

World of Wonder, Inc., raised $80 million from selling convertible debentures through the reputable investment banking firm of Smith Barney, Inc. Before paying its first coupon on these debentures, World of Wonder filed for protection from its creditors under Chapter 11 of the Bankruptcy Act. These debenture bonds, initially selling for $1,000 each, were trading at $75 each after this filing.

Rating Debt Obligations

A comprehensive and complex system for rating debt securities is established in the world economy. Ratings are available from several highly regarded investment research firms: Moody's, Standard & Poor's (S&P), Duff and Phelps, and Fitch Investors Service. Many financial institutions also develop their own in-house ratings.

BOND CREDIT RATINGS

The bond credit rating is a composite expression of judgment about the *creditworthiness* of the bond issuer and the quality of the specific security being rated. A rating measures credit risk, where *credit risk* is the probability of developments unfavorable to the interests of creditors. This judgment of creditworthiness is expressed in a series of symbols reflecting degrees of credit risk. Specifically, the top four rating grades from Standard & Poor's are:

AAA Bonds rated AAA are highest-grade obligations. They possess the highest degree of protection as to principal and interest. Marketwise, they move with interest rates and provide maximum safety.

AA Bonds rated AA also qualify as high-grade obligations, and in the majority of instances differ little from AAA issues. Here, too, prices move with the long-term money market.

Treasury and Company Bond Yield Rates (One-Year Maturity)

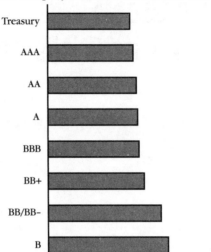

Source: Standard & Poor's, December 1996.

A   Bonds rated A are regarded as upper-medium grade. They have considerable investment strength but are not free from adverse effects of changes in economic and trade conditions. Interest and principal are regarded as safe. They predominantly reflect money rates in their price behavior, and to some extent economic conditions.

BBB   Bonds rated BBB, or medium-grade category, are borderline between sound obligations and those where the speculative element begins to predominate. These bonds have adequate asset coverage and normally are protected by satisfactory earnings. Their susceptibility to changing conditions, particularly economic downturns, necessitates constant monitoring. Marketwise, these bonds are more responsive to business and trade conditions than to interest rates. This grade is the lowest qualifying for commercial bank investment.

There is a lower selection of ratings, including **BB,** lower-medium grade to marginally speculative; **B,** very speculative; and **D,** bonds in default.

	Bond Quality Ratings	
Rating Grades	*Standard & Poor's*	*Moody's*
Highest grade	AAA	Aaa
High grade	AA	Aa
Upper medium	A	A
Lower medium	BBB	Baa
Marginally speculative	BB	Ba
Highly speculative	B	B, Caa
Default	D	Ca, C

A major reason why debt securities are widely rated while equity securities are not is because there is far greater uniformity of approach and homogeneity of analytical measures in analyzing creditworthiness than in analyzing future market performance of equity securities. This wider agreement on what is being measured in credit risk analysis has resulted in acceptance of and reliance on published credit ratings for several purposes.

Criteria determining a specific rating are never precisely defined. They involve both *quantitative* (ratio and comparative analyses) and *qualitative* (market position and management quality) factors. Major rating agencies refuse to disclose their precise mix of factors determining ratings (which are usually a committee decision). They wish to avoid arguments about the validity of qualitative factors in ratings. These rating agencies use the analysis techniques discussed throughout this book. The following description of factors determining ratings is based on published sources and from discussions with officials of rating agencies.

RATING COMPANY BONDS

In rating an industrial bond issue the rating agency focuses on the issuing company's asset protection, financial resources, earning power, management, and specific provisions of the debt. Also important are company size, market share, industry position, cyclical influences, and general economic conditions.

Asset protection refers to the extent a company's debt is covered by its assets. One measure is net tangible assets to long-term debt. One rating agency uses a rule of thumb where a bond needs a net tangible asset to long-term debt value of 5:1 for a AAA rating; 4:1 for a AA rating; 3 to 3.5:1 for a A rating; and 2.5:1 for a BBB rating. Concern with undervalued assets, especially with companies in the natural resources or real estate industries, leads to adjustments to these rating levels. Another rule of thumb suggests the long-term debt to total capital ratio be under 25 percent for a AAA, near 30 percent for a AA, near 35 percent for a A, and near 40 percent for a BBB rating. Additional factors entering rating agencies' consideration of asset protection include book value; composition of working capital; the quality and age of property, plant, and equipment; off-balance-sheet financing; and unrecorded liabilities.

Financial resources refer to liquid resources like cash and working capital accounts. Analysis measures include the collection period of receivables and inventory turnover. Their values are assessed relative to industry and absolute standards. Raters also analyze the issuer's use of both short-term and long-term debt, and their mix.

Future earning power and the issuer's cash-generating ability are important factors in rating debt securities because the level and quality of future earnings determine a company's ability to meet its obligations. Earning power is usually a more reliable source of protection than are assets. One common measure of protection due to earning power is the earnings to fixed charges coverage ratio. A rule of thumb suggests an acceptable earnings to fixed charges ratio is 5:1 to 7:1 for a AAA rating, over 4:1 for a AA rating, over 3:1 for a A rating, and over 2:1 for a BBB rating. Another measure of debt servicing potential is cash flow from operations to long-term debt. A rule of thumb suggests this ratio be over 65 percent for a AAA, 45 to 60 percent for a AA, 35 to 45 percent for a A, and 25 to 30 percent for a BBB rating.

Management's abilities, foresight, philosophy, knowledge, experience, and integrity are important considerations in rating debt. Through interviews, site visits, and other analyses, the raters probe management's goals, strategies, plans, and tactics in areas like research and development, product promotion, product planning, and acquisitions.

Specific debt provisions are usually written in the bond indenture. Raters analyze the specific provisions in the indenture designed to protect interests of bondholders under a variety of conditions. These include analysis of stipulations (if any) for future debt issuances, security provisions like mortgaging, sinking funds, redemption provisions, and restrictive covenants.

RATING MUNICIPAL BONDS

Buyers and raters of municipal bonds analyze different factors from those of company debt. Municipal bonds are issued by state and local governments and are of several types. Many are *general obligation bonds* backed by the government unit issuing them. *Special tax bonds* are limited in protection to a particular tax used to service and retire them. *Revenue bonds* are protected by revenues of municipal enterprises. Others include *housing authority bonds* and *tax anticipation notes*. The amount of information disclosed to buyers of municipal bonds is of diverse quality, but legislative actions are attempting to remedy this.

Raters require a variety of information from issuers of municipal debt. With general obligation bonds, the debt relies on the issuer's ability and willingness to repay it from general revenues. The major revenue source is the taxing power of the municipality. Accordingly, raters' information needs include current population, trend and composition of population, largest taxpayer listing, market values of taxable properties, gross indebtedness, net indebtedness (e.g., deducting self-sustaining obligations and sinking funds), annual reports, budgets, estimates of capital improvements, future borrowing programs, and description of the area's economy. Rating techniques have similar objectives to those with company bonds. Yet the ratios are adapted to the unique factors associated with municipal debt. Consequently, the debt to market value of real estate ratio is important, where 10 percent is viewed as high and 3 to 5 percent as low. Moreover, annual debt expense of 10 percent of revenue is acceptable whereas percentages exceeding the upper teens are not. Another measure is per capita debt, where $400 or less is viewed as low and $900 to $1,000 is considered high (unfavorable). Raters also desire tax delinquencies not exceeding 3 to 4 percent. Additional factors include unfunded pension liabilities and the trend of indebtedness. An increase in indebtedness is undesirable. Management of the municipality is equally important for rating debt.

LIMITATIONS IN THE RATINGS GAME

Debt ratings are useful to a large proportion of debt issuances. Yet we must understand the inherent limitations of the standardized ratings procedures of rating agencies. As with equity security analysis, our analysis can improve on these ratings. Debt issuances reflect a wide range of characteristics. Consequently, they present us with opportunities to identify differences within rating classes and assess their favorable or unfavorable impact within their ratings class. Also, there is evidence that rating changes lag the market. This lag effect presents us with additional opportunities to identify important changes prior to their being reported by rating agencies.

Predicting Financial Distress

A common use of financial statement analysis is in identifying areas needing further investigation and analysis. One of these applications is **predicting financial distress.** Research has made substantial advances in suggesting various ratios as predictors of distress. This research is valuable in providing us additional tools in analyzing long-term solvency. Models of financial distress, commonly referred to as **bankruptcy prediction models,** examine the trend and behavior of selected ratios. Characteristics of these ratios are used in identifying the likelihood of future financial distress. Models presume evidence of distress appears in financial ratios and we can detect it sufficiently early for us to take actions to avoid risk of loss or to capitalize on this information.

ALTMAN'S Z-SCORE

Probably the most well-known model of financial distress is **Altman's Z-score.** Altman's Z-score uses multiple ratios to generate a predictor of distress.[7] Altman's Z-score uses a statistical technique (multiple discriminant analysis) to produce a predictor that is a linear function of several

---

[7] See E. Altman, "Financial Ratios, Discriminant Analysis, and the Prediction of Corporate Bankruptcy," *Journal of Finance* 22 (September 1968), pp. 589–609. Also see J. Begley, J. Ming, and S. Watts, "Bankruptcy Classification Errors in the 1980s: An Empirical Analysis of Altman's and Ohlson's Models," *Review of Accounting Studies* (1997).

explanatory variables. This predictor classifies or predicts the likelihood of bankruptcy or nonbankruptcy. Five financial ratios are included in the Z-score: X_1 = Working capital/Total assets, X_2 = Retained earnings/Total assets, X_3 = Earnings before interest and taxes/Total assets, X_4 = Shareholders' equity/Total liabilities, and X_5 = Sales/Total assets. We can view $X_1, X_2, X_3, X_4,$ and X_5 as reflecting (1) liquidity, (2) age of firm and cumulative profitability, (3) profitability, (4) financial structure, and (5) capital turnover rate, respectively. The Altman Z-score is computed as:

$$Z = 0.717\,X_1 + 0.847\,X_2 + 3.107\,X_3 + 0.420\,X_4 + 0.998\,X_5$$

A Z-score of less than 1.20 suggests a high probability of bankruptcy, while Z-scores above 2.90 imply a low probability of bankruptcy. Scores between 1.20 and 2.90 are in the gray or ambiguous area.[8]

DISTRESS MODELS AND FINANCIAL STATEMENT ANALYSIS

Research efforts identify a useful role for ratios in predicting financial distress. However, we must *not* blindly apply this or any other model without informed and critical analysis of a company's fundamentals. There is no evidence to suggest computation of a Z-score is a better means of analyzing long-term solvency than is the integrated use of the analysis tools described in this book. Rather, we assert the use of ratios as predictors of distress is best in complementing our rigorous analysis of financial statements. Evidence does suggest the Z-score is a useful screening, monitoring, and attention-directing device.

---

[8] The model shown is from Altman [*Corporate Financial Distress*, New York: John Wiley, 1983, pp. 120–124]. This model is more generalizable than his earlier 1968 model which can only be applied to publicly traded companies. The earlier model is: $Z = 1.2\,X_1 + 1.4\,X_2 + 3.3\,X_3 + 0.6\,X_4 + 1.0\,X_5$. But X_4 in the earlier model requires the market value of preferred and common equity be available. The new model can be applied to BOTH publicly traded and nonpublicly traded companies with no measurable affect on prediction performance. Use of the earlier model is fine provided it is only applied to publicly traded companies.

Analytical Adjustments to the Long-Term Debt to Equity Ratio

The conventional long-term debt to equity ratio is expressed as:

$$\frac{\text{Long-term debt}}{\text{Shareholders' equity}}$$

We can make useful analytical adjustments to increase its reliability:

$$\frac{\text{LTD} + \text{NFL}}{\text{SE} + \text{NDT} + \text{LR} + \text{MSA}}$$

LTD = Long-term debt consisting of all long-term liabilities inclusive of (1) noncurrent deferred taxes *likely* to reverse, and (2) other noncurrent liabilities.

NFL = Estimated present value of noncapitalized financial leases.

SE = Shareholders' equity, including minority interests.

NDT = Noncurrent deferred taxes assessed as *unlikely* to reverse in the foreseeable future.

LR = LIFO reserve (excess of disclosed FIFO value of ending inventory over reported LIFO amount).

MSA = Excess of market value of marketable securities over cost (for analysis of financial statements prior to 1994).

Using the financial data of Quaker Oats, we compute this ratio as:

$$\frac{\$701.2^{(a)} + \$115.5^{(d)} + \$147^{(c)} + \$93.8^{(h)}}{\$806.5^{(d)} + \$99.3^{(g)} + \$220^{(e)} + \$18.9^{(f)}} = 0.92$$

[a]Long-term debt.
[b]Other liabilities.
[c]40% of deferred income taxes, assumed liability portion.
[d]Shareholders' equity.
[e]60% of deferred income taxes, assumed equity portion.
[f]Excess of mostly average cost over LIFO.
[g]Preferred stock outstanding.
[h]See discussion and footnote in Chapter 5's section titled "Adjustments to Book Values of Liabilities."

GUIDANCE ANSWERS TO ANALYSIS VIEWPOINT

YOU ARE THE ENTREPRENEUR

The primary criterion in your analysis is to compare the restaurant's return on assets to the after-tax cost of debt. If your restaurant can continue to earn 9 percent on assets, then the *after-tax* cost of debt must be less than 9 percent for you to successfully trade on the equity. Since the tax rate is 40 percent, you could successfully trade on the equity by adding new debt with an interest rate of 15 percent or less (9%/[1 − 0.40]). The lower the interest rate is from 15 percent, the more successful is your trading on the equity. You must recognize that taking on debt increases the riskiness of your business (due to the risk of unsuccessfully trading on the equity). This is because if your restaurant's earnings decline to where return on assets falls below the after-tax cost of debt, then return on equity declines even further. Accordingly, your assessment of earnings stability, or *persistence*, is a crucial part of the decision to add debt.

YOU ARE THE ANALYST

The preferred equity risk is greater for the second company. For the first company, senior securities (to preferred equity) comprise 20 percent of financing. However, for the second company, senior securities comprise 30 percent of financing. In a situation of bankruptcy, 30 percent of residual value must be paid to debtors prior to payments to preferred equity holders. In addition, financial leverage for the second company is potentially greater, although precise assessment of leverage risk depends on the features of preferred stock (e.g., features like fixed return, cumulative, nonparticipating, redeemable, and nonvoting make preferred stock more like debt).

CHAPTER 6

Return on Invested Capital

A LOOK BACK

The previous three chapters focused primarily on risk. We analyzed a company's ability to cover both short- and long-term obligations. We described several useful analytical tools and applied them to illustrate their relevance for risk analysis. We also explained how capital structure affects the returns to shareholders.

A LOOK AT THIS CHAPTER

This chapter focuses on return. We emphasize return on invested capital and explain variations in its measurement. Special attention is directed at return on assets and return on common shareholders' equity. We explore disaggregations of both these return measures and describe their relevance to our analysis. Financial leverage is explained and analyzed using the return measures in this chapter.

A LOOK AHEAD

Chapter 7 extends our analysis of return to focus on profitability. We analyze operating activities using several techniques, including component analysis, break-even analysis, gross profit analysis, and income tax analysis. We describe operating leverage and its implications for profitability.

THIS CHAPTER WILL:

- Describe the usefulness of return measures in financial statement analysis.
- Explain return on invested capital and variations in its computation.
- Analyze return on total assets and its relevance in our analysis.
- Describe disaggregation of return on assets and the importance of its components.
- Analyze return on common shareholders' equity and its role in our analysis.
- Describe disaggregation of return on common shareholders' equity and the relevance of its components.
- Explain financial leverage and how to assess a company's success in trading on the equity by individual financing sources.

PREVIEW OF CHAPTER 6

Return on invested capital is important in our analysis of financial statements. Financial statement analysis involves our assessing both risk and return. The prior three chapters focused primarily on risk, whereas this chapter extends our analysis to return. *Return on invested capital* refers to a company's earnings relative to both the level and source of financing. It is a measure of a company's success in using financing to generate profits, and is an excellent measure of a company's solvency risk. This chapter describes return on invested capital and its relevance to financial statement analysis. We also explain variations in measurement of return on invested capital and their interpretation. We also disaggregate return on invested capital into important components for additional insights into company performance and future operations. The role of financial leverage and its importance for returns analysis are examined. This chapter demonstrates each of these analysis techniques using financial statement data. The content and organization of this chapter are as follows:

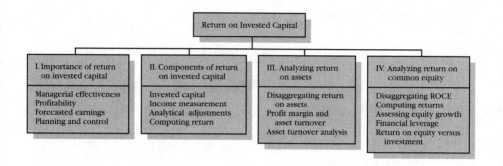

IMPORTANCE OF RETURN ON INVESTED CAPITAL

We can analyze company performance in several possible ways. Revenue, gross profit, and net income are performance measures in common use. Yet none of these measures *individually* are useful as a comprehensive measure of company performance. The reason stems from their interdependency and the interdependency of business activities. For example, increases in revenue are desirable only if they increase profits. The same applies to sales volume. To assess gross profit or net income we must relate them to invested capital. For example, a profit of $1 million is assessed differently if a company's invested capital is $2 million or $200 million.

Analysis of company performance demands *joint* analysis, where we assess one measure relative to another. The relation between income and invested capital, referred to as **return on invested capital** or *return on investment (ROI),* is probably the most widely recognized measure of company performance. It allows us to compare companies on their success with invested capital. It also allows us to assess a company's return relative to its capital investment risk, and we can compare the return on invested capital to returns of alternative investments. Government treasury bonds reflect a minimum return due to their low risk. Riskier investments are expected to yield higher returns. Analysis of return on invested capital compares a company's income, or other performance measure, to the company's level and source of financing. It determines a company's ability to succeed, attract financing, repay creditors, and reward owners. We use return on invested capital in several areas of our analysis including: (1) managerial effectiveness, (2) level of profitability, (3) earnings forecasting, and (4) planning and control.

Measuring Managerial Effectiveness

The level of return on invested capital depends primarily on the skill, resourcefulness, ingenuity, and motivation of management. Management is responsible for a company's business activities. It makes financing, investing, and operating decisions. It selects actions, plans strategies, and executes plans. Return on invested capital, especially when computed over intervals of a year or longer, is a relevant measure of a company's managerial effectiveness.

Measuring Profitability

Return on invested capital is an important indicator of a company's long-term financial strength. It uses key summary measures from both the income statement (profits) and the balance sheet (financing) to assess profitability. This profitability measure has several advantages over other long-term measures of financial strength or solvency that rely on only balance sheet items (e.g., debt to equity ratio). It can effectively convey the return on invested capital from varying perspectives of different financing contributors (creditors and shareholders). It is also helpful in short-term liquidity analysis.

Measure of Forecasted Earnings

Return on invested capital is useful in earnings forecasting. This measure effectively links past, current, and forecasted earnings with total invested capital. Its use in our analysis and forecasting of earnings adds discipline and realism. It identifies overly optimistic or pessimistic forecasts relative to competitors' returns on invested capital, and it yields managerial assessments of financing sources when forecasts are different from expectations. Expectations are determined from historical and incremental rates of return, projected changes in company and business conditions, and expected returns for new projects. Return on invested capital is used as either a primary or supplementary means of earnings forecasting and to evaluate the reasonableness of forecasts from other sources.

Measure for Planning and Control

Return on invested capital serves an important role in planning, budgeting, coordinating, evaluating, and controlling business activities. This return is comprised of the returns (and losses) achieved by the company's segments or divisions. These segment returns are also comprised of the returns achieved by individual product lines, projects, and other components. A well-managed company exercises control over returns achieved by each of its profit centers and rewards its managers on these results. In evaluating investing alternatives, management assesses performance relative to expected returns. Out of this assessment come strategic decisions and action plans for the company.

ANALYSIS VIEWPOINT

YOU ARE THE AUDITOR

You are the audit manager responsible for substantive audit tests of a manufacturing client. Your analytical procedures reveal a 3 percent increase in sales from $2 to $2.06 (millions) and a 4 percent decrease in total expenses from $1.9 to $1.824 (millions). Both changes are within your "reasonableness" criterion of ± 5 percent. Accordingly, you do not expand audit tests of these accounts. The audit partner in charge questions your lack of follow-up on these deviations and expressly mentions *joint* analysis. What is the audit partner referring to?

COMPONENTS OF RETURN ON INVESTED CAPITAL

Analyzing company performance using return on invested capital is conceptually sound and appealing. **Return on invested capital** is computed as:

$$\frac{\text{Income}}{\text{Invested capital}}$$

There is, however, not complete agreement on the computation of either the numerator or denominator in this relation. These differences are valid and stem from the diverse perspectives of financial statement users. This section describes these differences and explains how different computations are relevant to different users or analyses. We begin with a discussion of invested capital, followed by consideration of income.

Defining Invested Capital

There is no universal measure of invested capital from which to compute rate of return. Return on invested capital reflects fundamental and

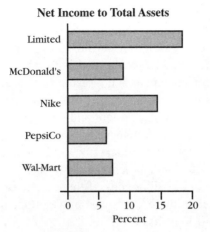

Net Income to Total Assets

Source: Annual reports.

accepted concepts of income and financing levels. The different measures of invested capital used reflect users' different perspectives. In this section we describe different measures of invested capital and explain their relevance to different users and interpretations.

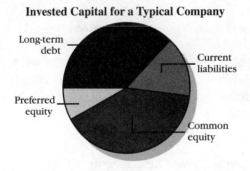

Invested Capital for a Typical Company

Total Debt and Equity Capital

A company's return can be assessed from the perspective of its total financing base—*liabilities plus equity,* or simply *total assets.* This **return on total assets** is a relevant measure of operating efficiency. It reflects a company's return from all assets (or financing) entrusted to it. This measure does not distinguish return by financing sources. By removing the effect of financing of assets, our analysis can concentrate on evaluating or forecasting operating performance. The total asset base for computing return on invested capital is sometimes subject to adjustments. We describe three types of adjustments.

Unproductive Asset Adjustment   One type of adjustment relates to unproductive assets. The *unproductive asset adjustment* removes idle plant, facilities under construction, surplus plant, surplus inventories, surplus cash, and deferred charges from the invested capital base. These exclusions assume management is not responsible for earning a return on invested capital not in operations. While this argument is sometimes valid for internal analysis as a management and control tool, it is not justified when used to evaluate overall management effectiveness. Management is entrusted with funds by shareholders and creditors, and it has discretion over their investment. Management can dispose of assets with no return and repay creditors or pay dividends. If there are reasons for maintaining these investments, then there is no reason to exclude them from invested capital. Moreover, if long-run profitability benefits by maintaining these assets, then longer-term return reflects these benefits. Accordingly, our external analysis should not typically remove assets from invested capital because they are unproductive or fail to earn a return.

Intangible Asset Adjustment   Another type of adjustment excludes intangible assets from invested capital. This adjustment derives from skepticism regarding their value or earnings contribution to a company. In practice, intangibles are reported at amortized cost. If this cost exceeds their future utility, they are written down or sometimes reported with an "uncertainty reference" regarding their value in the auditor's report. Similar to our discussion for unproductive assets, this adjustment lacks merit. Excluding intangible assets from invested capital must be justified on substantive evidence and not lack of information or unsupported suspicion on their value.

Accumulated Depreciation Adjustment   A third adjustment relates to whether the invested capital base includes an addback for accumulated depreciation on depreciable assets (note that earnings are still reported *net* of depreciation). This adjustment is sometimes referred to as the *Du Pont method* due to its endorsement from that same company as an internal management tool. Advocates argue that since plant assets are maintained in prime working condition during their useful life, it is inappropriate to assess return relative to *net* assets. They also argue if accumulated depreciation is not added back, earnings in succeeding periods relate to an ever-decreasing investment base. Accordingly, even with stable earnings, return on investment continually rises and would fail to reveal true company performance. Relating earnings to invested capital that is stable would arguably offer a sound basis for comparing profitability of assets employed across years. This addback also compensates for the effects of inflation on assets expressed at historical cost. Price-level adjustments are usually valid only with a complete restatement of financial statements. Crude adjustments like these are likely misleading and often worse than no adjustment.

In evaluating the Du Pont method we must remember its focus on the internal control of separate productive units and of operating management. Our analysis is different, focusing on the operating performance of an entire company. For analysis of an entire company, it is better to not add back accumulated depreciation to invested capital. This is consistent with computation of income net of depreciation expense. The increase in return due to decreasing depreciable assets is offset by the acquisition of new depreciable assets through capital recovered from depreciation. These new assets must also earn a return. We must also recognize that maintenance and repair costs commonly increase as assets age, tending to offset the reduction (if any) in the invested capital base.

Long-Term Debt Plus Equity Capital

Another computation of invested capital includes long-term debt capital and equity capital, often referred to as long-term capitalization. This computation differs from total debt and equity capital by excluding current liability financing. The aim of this calculation is to focus on the two main suppliers of long-term financing—long-term creditors and equity shareholders.

Equity Capital

Our use of equity capital as the definition of invested capital gives us a measure of the return on shareholders' equity. This implies a focus on the return to equity holders. As we discussed in the context of financial leverage in the previous chapter, return on equity captures the effect of leverage (debt) capital on shareholders' return. Since preferred stock typically receives a fixed return, we exclude it from our calculation of equity capital.

Book versus Market Value of Invested Capital

Return on invested capital is typically computed using reported values from financial statements rather than market values. Yet market values are

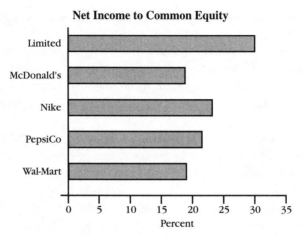

Net Income to Common Equity

Source: Annual reports.

sometimes more relevant for our analysis because certain assets are not recognized in financial statements (patents, trademarks, reputation, human resources). Additionally, earnings by companies are sometimes delayed due to overly conservative accounting recognition criteria. One adjustment is to use the market value of invested capital. This adjustment substitutes the market value of invested capital (debt and equity) for its reported value in computing return.

Investor versus Company Invested Capital

In computing return on invested capital, we must distinguish between a company's invested capital and an investor's invested capital. An investor's invested capital is the price paid for a company's securities. Except when an investor acquires securities at book value, an investor's invested capital differs from the company's invested capital. Our analysis of return on invested capital focuses on the company and not on individual shareholders. Later in this chapter we come back to this issue and focus on shareholder return.

Computing Invested Capital for the Period

Regardless of our *invested capital* definition, we compare the return for the period with its investment base. The invested capital for the period is typically computed using the *average* capital available to a company during the period. An average is used to reflect changes in invested capital during the period. The most common method is adding beginning and ending year invested capital and dividing by 2. We must use care in applying averaging. Companies in certain industries choose a "natural" rather than calendar business year. For example, in retailing the natural business year ends when inventories and sales are low (e.g., January 31 after the holiday season). In this case, averaging year-ends yields the lowest rather than the average invested capital during the period. A more accurate method is to average interim amounts—for example, adding month-end invested capital amounts and dividing by 12.

Defining Income

Our analysis of return on invested capital requires a measure of **income.** The definition of *income,* or *return,* depends on our definition of *invested capital.* If *invested capital* is defined as total debt and equity capital, then income *before* interest expense is used. Excluding interest from income is necessary because interest is viewed as payment to suppliers of debt capital. Similar reasoning is used to exclude dividends—viewed as payments to suppliers of equity capital. Hence, income *before* interest expense and dividends is used when computing both return on assets and return on long-term debt plus equity capital (assuming interest expense is from long-term debt).

The income of a consolidated company that includes a subsidiary that is partially owned by a minority interest typically reflects a deduction for the minority's share of income. The company's consolidated balance sheet, however, includes the subsidiary's assets. Since invested capital (denominator) includes assets of the consolidated company, income (numerator) should include total company income (or loss), not just the parent's share. For this reason we add back the minority's share of earnings (or loss) to income when computing return on assets. When we define *invested capital* (denominator) as equity capital excluding minority interest, we need *not* add back the minority's share of earnings (or loss) to income.

Return on common equity capital uses income defined as net income *after* deductions for interest and preferred dividends. If preferred dividends are cumulative, they are deducted in computing income whether these dividends are declared or not. This is because common shareholders' claims are junior to preferred shareholders.

Measures of income in computing return on invested capital must reflect all applicable expenses including income taxes. Some users exclude income taxes in their computations. These users claim it is to isolate the effects of tax management from operating performance. Others claim changes in tax rates affect comparability across years. Still others claim companies with tax loss carryforwards add confusion and complications to return on invested capital computations. We must recognize that income taxes reduce a company's income and we should include them in measuring income, especially for the return on shareholders' equity. Later in the chapter we disaggregate return on invested capital where one component reflects the company's tax situation.

Adjustments to Invested Capital and Income

Our analysis of return on invested capital uses reported financial statement numbers as a starting point. As we discussed in several prior chapters, certain accounting numbers call for analytical adjustment. Also certain numbers not reported in financial statements need to be included. Much of our discussion in Chapter 5 regarding accounting adjustments is applicable here. Some adjustments, like those relating to inventory, affect both the numerator and denominator of return on invested capital, moderating their effect.

Computing Return on Invested Capital

This section applies our discussion to an analysis of return on invested capital. We illustrate the different measures of both income and invested capital for the computations. For this purpose, we draw on the financial statements of Excell Corporation reproduced in Exhibits 6.1 and 6.2. Our return on invested capital computations below are for Year 9 and use amounts rounded to the nearest million.

Return on Total Assets
Return on assets (both debt and equity capital) of Excell Corporation for Year 9 is computed as:

$$\frac{\text{Net income} + \text{Interest expense } (1 - \text{Tax rate}) + \text{Minority interest in income}}{(\text{Beginning total assets} + \text{Ending total assets}) \div 2}$$

$$\frac{\$64{,}569 + \$20{,}382\ (1 - 0.40) + \$0}{(\$1{,}333{,}982 + \$1{,}371{,}621) \div 2} = 5.677\%$$

Exhibit 6.1

EXCELL CORPORATION
Income Statement
For Years Ended December 31, Year 8, and Year 9
($ thousands)

	Year 8	Year 9
Net sales	$1,636,298	$1,723,729
Costs and expenses	1,473,293	1,579,401
Operating income	$ 163,005	$ 144,328
Other income, net	2,971	1,784
Income before interest and taxes	$ 165,976	$ 146,112
Interest expense*	16,310	20,382
Income before taxes	$ 149,666	$ 125,730
Less federal and other income taxes	71,770	61,161
Net income	$ 77,896	$ 64,569
Less cash dividends:		
Preferred stock	2,908	2,908
Common stock	39,209	38,898
Net income reinvested in the business	$ 35,779	$ 22,763

*In Year 9, interest on long-term debt is $19,695.

Our tax adjustment of interest expense recognizes interest is tax deductible. This implies that if interest expense is excluded, the related tax benefit must be excluded from income. We assume a *marginal* corporate tax rate of 40 percent—the tax incidence with respect to any one item (like interest expense) can be measured by the marginal tax rate. There is no minority interest in the income of Excell, and the assets are averaged using year-end figures.

Return on Long-Term Debt Plus Equity

Return on long-term debt plus equity, also called *return on long-term capitalization,* of Excell Corporation for Year 9 is computed as:

$$\frac{\text{Net income} + \text{Interest expense} (1 - \text{Tax rate}) + \text{Minority interest in income}}{(\text{Average long-term debt} + \text{Average equity})}$$

$$\frac{\$64{,}569 + \$20{,}382 \, (1 - 0.40) + \$0}{(\$437{,}088 + \$715{,}901 + \$437{,}346 + \$740{,}455) \div 2} = 6.59\%$$

Exhibit 6.2

EXCELL CORPORATION
Balance Sheet
at December 31, Year 8, and Year 9
($ thousands)

	Year 8	Year 9
Assets		
Current assets:		
Cash	$ 25,425	$ 25,580
Marketable securities	38,008	28,910
Accounts and notes receivable—net	163,870	176,911
Inventories	264,882	277,795
Total current assets	$ 492,185	$ 509,196
Investments in and receivables from nonconsolidated		
subsidiaries	33,728	41,652
Miscellaneous investments and receivables	5,931	6,997
Funds held by trustee for construction	6,110	—
Land, buildings, equipment, and timberlands—net	773,361	790,774
Deferred charges to future operations	16,117	16,452
Goodwill and other intangible assets	6,550	6,550
Total assets	$1,333,982	$1,371,621
Liabilities		
Current liabilities:		
Notes payable to banks	$ 7,850	$ 13,734
Accounts payable and accrued expenses	128,258	144,999
Dividends payable	10,404	10,483
Federal and other taxes on income	24,370	13,256
Long-term indebtedness payable within one year	9,853	11,606
Total current liabilities	$ 180,735	$ 194,078
Long-term indebtedness	350,565	335,945
Deferred taxes on income	86,781	101,143
Total liabilities	$ 618,081	$ 631,166
Equity		
Preferred, 7% cumulative and noncallable, par value $25 per		
share; authorized 1,760,000 shares	$ 41,538	$ 41,538
Common, par value $12.50 per share; authorized		
30,000,000 shares	222,245	222,796
Capital in excess of par value	19,208	20,448
Retained earnings	436,752	459,515
Less: Common treasury stock	(3,842)	(3,842)
Total equity	$ 715,901	$ 740,455
Total liabilities and equity	$1,333,982	$1,371,621

Decisions of how to classify items like deferred taxes between debt and equity must be made following our discussion in Chapter 5. For Excell, deferred taxes are included in long-term liabilities. In computing return on long-term debt plus equity, there is no need to classify deferred taxes because this computation includes both debt and equity. A classification problem does arise when computing return on shareholders' equity. In the cases that follow, deferred taxes possess characteristics more like a long-term liability than equity. Yet we must always assess this in practice since its classification can significantly affect return.

Return on Common Shareholders' Equity

Return on common equity typically excludes from invested capital all but common shareholders' equity. The **return on common equity** of Excell Corporation for Year 9 is computed as:

$$\frac{\text{Net income} - \text{Preferred dividends}}{\text{Average common shareholders' equity}}$$

$$\frac{\$64,569 - \$2,908}{(\$674,363 + \$698,917) \div 2} = 8.98\%$$

Excell's higher return on common shareholders' equity as compared to its return on total assets reflects the favorable effects of financial leverage. Excell is successfully trading on the equity. There is another method to compute the return on common shareholders' equity using a ratio of two often reported figures as follows:

$$\frac{\text{Basic earnings per share}}{\text{Book value per share}}$$

The return from this latter computation is often slightly different due to rounding. When *convertible* debt sells at a substantial premium above par and is held by investors primarily for its conversion feature, there is justification for treating it as an equivalent of equity capital. This is especially true when a company has the right to force conversion by calling it in.

ANALYZING RETURN ON ASSETS

Return on invested capital is useful in management evaluation, profitability analysis, earnings forecasting, and planning and control. Our use of return on invested capital for these tasks requires a thorough understanding of this return measure. This is because the return measure includes components with the potential to contribute to our understanding of company performance. This section examines this return when invested capital is viewed independently of its financing sources, using debt and equity capital (total assets), commonly referred to as **return on assets (ROA).**

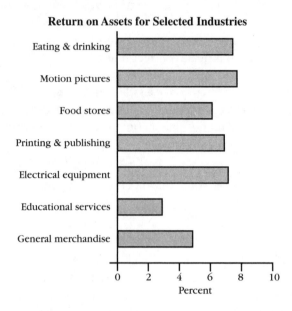

Return on Assets for Selected Industries

Disaggregating Return on Assets

Recall that the return on assets (or return on total capital) in its most *simplified form* is computed as:

$$\frac{\text{Income}}{\text{Assets}}$$

We can disaggregate this return into meaningful components relative to sales. We do this because these component ratios are useful in our analysis of company performance. Sales is an important criterion to judge company profitability and is a major indicator of company activity. This disaggregation of return on assets is:

Return on assets = Profit margin × Asset turnover

$$\frac{\text{Income}}{\text{Assets}} = \frac{\text{Income}}{\text{Sales}} \times \frac{\text{Sales}}{\text{Assets}}$$

The income to sales relation is called **profit margin** and measures a company's profitability relative to sales. The sales to assets relation is called **asset turnover** or **utilization** and measures a company's effectiveness in generating sales from assets. This decomposition highlights the role of these components, profit margin and asset turnover, in determining return on assets. Profit margin and asset turnover are useful measures that require our analysis to gain further insights into a company's profitability. We describe the major components determining return on assets in Exhibit 6.3. The "first level" of analysis focuses on the interaction of profit margin and asset turnover. The "second level" of analysis highlights other important factors determining profit margin and asset turnover. This section emphasizes the first level of analysis. The next two chapters explore the second level—Chapter 7 with analysis of operating results, and Chapter 8 with analysis and forecasting of earnings.

Exhibit 6.3   Disaggregating Return on Assets

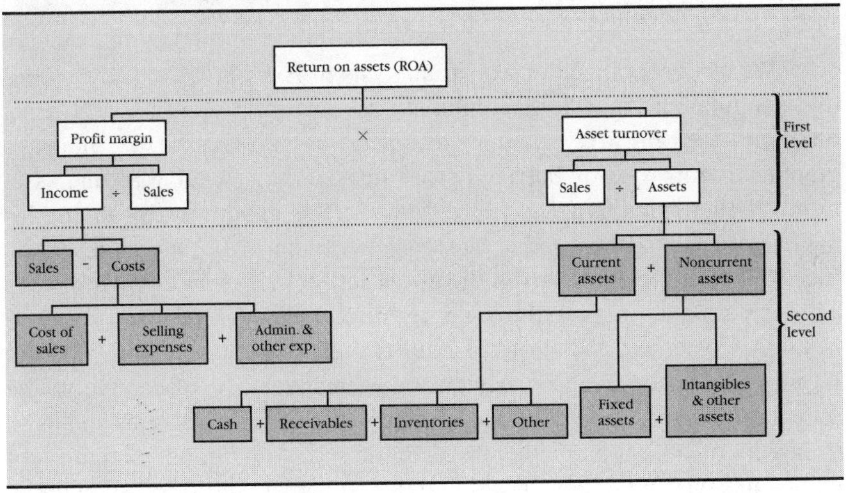

Relation between Profit Margin and Asset Turnover

The relation between profit margin and asset turnover is illustrated in Exhibit 6.4. As defined, return on assets (in percent) equals profit margin (in percent) multiplied by asset turnover. As Exhibit 6.4 shows, Company X achieves a 10 percent return on assets with a relatively high profit margin and a low asset turnover. In contrast, Company Z achieves the same return on assets but with a low profit margin and high asset turnover. Company Y's return is between these two companies, a 10 percent return with a profit margin one-half that of Company X and an asset turnover double that of Company X. This exhibit indicates there are many combinations of profit margins and asset turnovers yielding a 10 percent return on assets.

Exhibit 6.4   Analysis of Return on Assets

	Company X	Company Y	Company Z
Sales	$5,000,000	$10,000,000	$10,000,000
Income	$ 500,000	$ 500,000	$ 100,000
Assets	$5,000,000	$ 5,000,000	$ 1,000,000
Profit margin	10%	5%	1%
Asset turnover	1	2	10
Return on assets	10%	10%	10%

We can generalize the returns analysis of Exhibit 6.4 to show a continuous range of possible combinations of profit margins and asset turnovers yielding a 10 percent return on assets. Exhibit 6.5 portrays graphically this relation between profit margin (horizontal axis) and asset turnover (vertical axis). The curve drawn in this exhibit traces all combinations of profit margin and asset turnover yielding a 10 percent return on assets. This curve slopes from the upper left corner of low profit margin and high asset turnover to the lower right corner of high profit margin and low asset turnover. We plot the data from Companies X and Y (from Exhibit 6.4) in Exhibit 6.5—designated points X and Y, respectively. The remaining points A through P are combinations of profit margins and asset turnovers of other companies in a sample industry. Graphing returns of companies within an industry around the 10 percent return on asset curve (or other applicable return curve) is a valuable method of comparing profitability. More important, graphing reveals the relation between profit margin and asset turnover determining ROA and is extremely useful in our company analysis.

Disaggregating return on assets as in Exhibit 6.5 is useful in assessing companies' strategic actions to increase returns. Companies B and C must concentrate on restoring profitability. Assuming the industry represented in Exhibit 6.5 has a representative profit margin and asset turnover,

Exhibit 6.5   Relation between Profit Margin, Asset Turnover, and Return on Assets

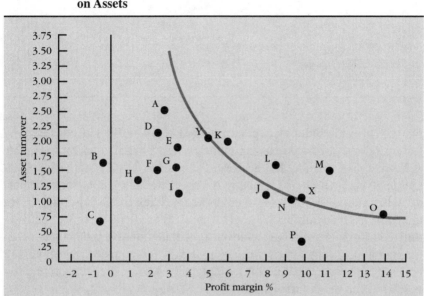

the evidence suggests Company P should focus on improving asset turnover while Company D should focus on increasing profit margin. Other companies like H and I best concentrate on both profit margin and asset turnover. Our analysis to this point treats profit margin and asset turnover as independent. Yet profit margin and asset turnover are *interdependent.* As we stress in our discussion of break-even analysis in Chapter 7, when fixed expenses are substantial, a higher level of asset turnover increases profit margin. This is because in a certain range of activity, costs increase proportionally less than sales. In comparing companies in an industry, we must consider companies with low asset turnovers having potential to increase return through increased asset turnover (sales expansion).

Analysis of return on assets can reveal additional insights into strategic activity. As another example, consider two companies (AA and BB) in the same industry with identical returns on assets. Both companies' returns on assets are poor. Strategically, corrective action for each is different. Our analysis must evaluate the likelihood of managerial success and other factors in improving performance. Company AA has a 10 percent profit

	Company AA	Company BB
Sales	$ 1,000,000	$20,000,000
Income	$ 100,000	$ 100,000
Assets	$10,000,000	$10,000,000
Profit margin	10%	0.5%
Asset turnover	0.1	2
Return on assets	1%	1%

margin (near the industry average) while Company BB's is considerably lower. A dollar invested in assets supports only $0.10 in sales for Company AA, whereas Company BB achieves $2 in sales for each dollar invested. Our analysis focuses on Company AA's assets, asking questions such as: Why is turnover so low? Are there assets yielding little or no return? Are there idle assets requiring disposal? Are assets inefficiently or ineffectively utilized? Company AA can achieve immediate improvements by concentrating on increasing turnover (by increasing sales, reducing investment, or both). It is likely more difficult for Company AA to increase profit margin much beyond the industry norm.

Company BB confronts a much different scenario. Our analysis suggests Company BB should focus on correcting the low profit margin. Reasons for low profit margins are varied but often include inefficient equipment or production methods, unprofitable product lines, excess capacity with high fixed costs, or excessive selling and administrative expenses. Companies with low profit margins sometimes discover that changes in tastes and technology require increased investment in assets to finance sales. This implies that to maintain its return on assets, a company must increase its profit margin or else production is no longer moneymaking.

There is a tendency to view a high profit margin as a sign of high earnings quality. Yet we must emphasize the importance of return on invested capital (however defined) as the ultimate test of profitability. A supermarket is content with a profit margin of 1 percent or less because of its high asset turnover owing to a relatively low asset investment and a high proportion of leased assets (like stores and fixtures). Similarly, a discount store accepts a low profit margin to generate high asset turnover (primarily in inventories). In contrast, capital-intensive industries like steel, chemicals, and automobiles having large asset investments and low asset turnovers must achieve high profit margins to be successful. Exhibit 6.6 portrays graphically the relation between profit margin and asset

Exhibit 6.6   Profit Margin, Asset Turnover, and Return on Assets for Selected Industries

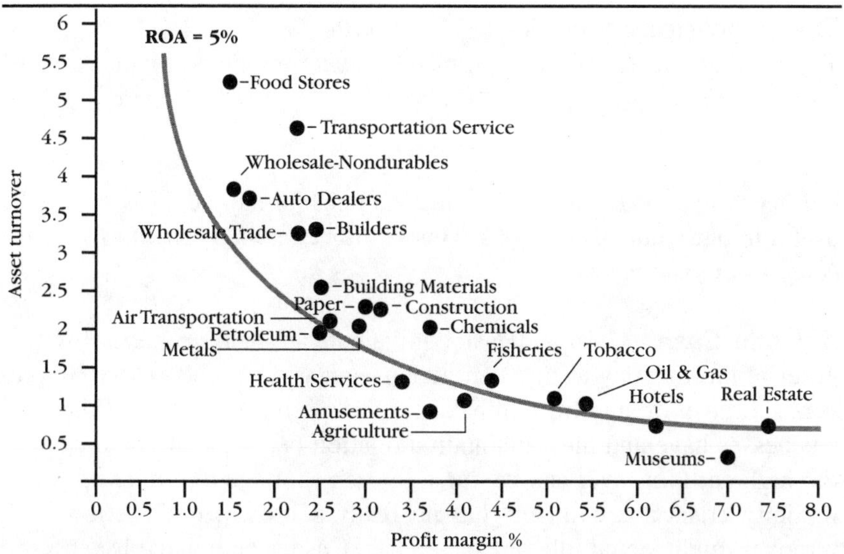

turnover. This figure extends Exhibit 6.5 to show components for actual industries. We graph the 5 percent return on assets curve in Exhibit 6.6 as a reference point for analysis.

We must remember that analysis of returns for a single year is potentially misleading. The cyclical nature of many industries yields swings in profit margins where some years' profits can be excessive while others are not. Companies must be analyzed using returns computed over several years and spanning a business cycle.

Asset Turnover Analysis

Asset turnover measures the intensity with which companies utilize assets. The most relevant measure of asset utilization is the amount of sales generated because sales are essential to profits. In special cases like start-up or development companies, our analysis of turnover must recognize that most assets are committed to future business activities. Also, unusual supply problems or work stoppages are conditions affecting asset utilization and require special evaluation and interpretation. This section describes various analyses using disaggregation of asset turnover.

Disaggregation of Asset Turnover

The standard measure of asset turnover in determining return on assets is:

$$\frac{\text{Sales}}{\text{Assets}}$$

Further evaluation of changes in turnover rates for individual assets can be useful in our company analysis. This section examines asset turnover for *component asset accounts*.

Sales to Cash   Cash and cash equivalents are held primarily for purposes of meeting day-to-day transactions and as a liquidity reserve to prevent shortages arising from imbalances in cash inflows and outflows. All businesses have and must maintain a relation between sales and cash. A too high cash turnover can be due to a cash shortage that might signal a liquidity crisis if a company has no ready source of cash. A low cash turnover might signal idle or excess cash. Cash accumulated for specific purposes or known contingencies often yields temporary decreases in turnover. The basic trade-off is between liquidity and accumulation of funds yielding little or no return.

Sales to Receivables   A company selling on credit knows that the level of its receivables is a function of sales. A low receivables turnover is likely due to overextending credit, an inability of customers to pay, or poor collection activity. A high receivables turnover can imply a strict credit policy, or a reluctance or inability to extend credit. Receivables turnover often involves a trade-off between increased sales and accumulation of funds in receivables.

Sales to Inventories   Maintaining sales typically requires inventories. The sales to inventories relation varies across industries depending on the variety of types, models, colors, sizes, and other inventory classes necessary to lure and retain consumers. Both the length of the production cycle and the type of item (luxury versus necessity, or perishable versus durable) have a bearing on inventories turnover. A low inventory turnover often suggests overstocked, slow-moving, or obsolete inventories. It can also signal overestimation of sales. Temporary conditions like work stoppages or slowdowns with important customers can yield low turnover. A high turnover can imply underinvestment in inventory, threatening customer relations and future sales. Inventory turnover involves a trade-off between funds accumulated in inventory and the potential loss of customers and future sales.

Sales to Fixed Assets   The relation between sales and property, plant, and equipment is long term and fundamental to most companies. There are temporary conditions affecting this relation. Temporary conditions include excess capacity, inefficient plants, obsolete equipment, demand changes, and interruptions in raw materials supply. Our analysis must remember increases in fixed assets are typically *not* gradual, but occur in large increments. This process can create changes in fixed asset turnover. Leased facilities and equipment, often not appearing on the balance sheet, can distort this turnover. The fixed asset turnover involves a trade-off between fixed asset investments having high break-even points vis-à-vis more efficient, productive capacity with high sales potential.

Sales to Other Assets   Other assets often include patents, deferred charges, or other miscellaneous deferred expenditures. While a relation between other assets and sales is not always evident, no assets should be held unless they contribute to sales or income. For example, deferred R&D costs should reflect potential for future sales. Our analysis of other assets turnover must consider these potentialities.

Sales to Current Liabilities   The relation between sales and current trade liabilities is a predictable one. A company's short-term trade liabilities depend on its sales (demand for its goods and services). Short-term credit is relatively cost free and reduces a company's funds accumulated in working capital. Also, a company's available credit line depends on its sales and income.

Factors in Asset Turnover
Our analysis of return on assets involves several additional factors. In Chapter 8 we consider extraordinary gains and losses and how our analysis adjusts for them. The effect of discontinued operations must be similarly evaluated. Our analysis of the trend in return on assets must consider the effects of acquisitions accounted for as poolings of interest and their

likelihood of recurrence. An internal analysis (by managers, auditors, consultants) can often obtain return data by segments, product lines, and divisions. These disaggregated data increase the reliability of and insights from our analysis. Where bargaining power or position permits, an external analysis can sometimes obtain and analyze disaggregated data. A problem arises when the level of individual assets (or total assets) changes during a period and adversely affects turnover computation. Accordingly, we use averages of individual and total asset levels. Specifically, the *denominator in computing asset turnover is an average of beginning and ending balances.* Provided data are available, an average can be computed using monthly or quarterly balances.

A consistently high return on assets is the earmark of effective management. Such management can distinguish a growth company from one experiencing merely a cyclical or seasonal pickup in business. Examining all factors comprising return on assets usually reveals the source and limitations of a company's return. Neither profit margin nor asset turnover can increase indefinitely. Increasing assets through external financing and/or internal earnings retention is necessary for further earnings growth.

ANALYZING RETURN ON COMMON EQUITY

Return on common shareholders' equity (ROCE), or simply return on common equity, is of great interest to the shareholders of a company. Return on common shareholders' equity differs from return on assets due primarily to what is excluded from invested capital. Return on common shareholders' equity excludes assets financed by creditors and preferred shareholders. Creditors usually receive a fixed return on their financing or in some cases no return. Preferred shareholders usually receive a fixed dividend. Yet common shareholders are provided no fixed or promised returns. These shareholders have claims on the *residual* earnings of a company only after all other financing sources are paid. Accordingly, the return on shareholders' equity is most important to common shareholders. The relation between return on shareholders' equity and return on assets is also important as it bears on the analysis of a company's success with financial leverage.

Return on common shareholders' equity serves a key role in equity valuation. Recall the accounting-based stock valuation formula from Chapter 2:

Return on Shareholders' Equity for Selected Industries

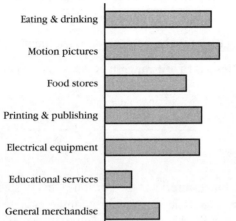

$$V_t = BV_t + \frac{NI_{t+1} - (k \times BV_t)}{(1 + k)} + \frac{NI_{t+2} - (k \times BV_{t+1})}{(1 + k)^2} + \ldots + \frac{NI_{t+n} - (k \times BV_{t+n-1})}{(1 + k)^n} + \ldots$$

Through algebraic simplification, the formula can be restated in terms of *future* returns on common shareholders' equity:

$$V_t = BV_t + \frac{(ROCE_{t+1} - k)BV_t}{(1 + k)} + \frac{(ROCE_{t+2} - k)BV_{t+1}}{(1 + k)^2} + \ldots + \frac{(ROCE_{t+n} - k)BV_{t+n-1}}{(1 + k)^n} + \ldots$$

where ROCE is equal to net income available to common shareholders (i.e., *after* preferred dividends) divided by the beginning-of-period balance of common equity. This formula is intuitively appealing. Namely, it implies that companies with ROCE greater than the investors' required rate of return (k) increase value in excess of that implied by book value alone.

Disaggregating Return on Common Equity

While ROCE in the above formula is computed using the beginning-of-period balance of common equity, in practice we use the *average* balance during the period under analysis. Like with return on assets, disaggregating return on common equity into components is extremely useful for our analysis. Recall that the return on common shareholders' equity is computed as:

$$\frac{\text{Net income} - \text{Preferred dividends}}{\text{Average common shareholders' equity}}$$

We can disaggregate return on common shareholders' equity to obtain:

ROCE = Adjusted profit margin × Asset turnover × Leverage

$$\frac{\begin{array}{c}\text{Net income} - \\ \text{Preferred dividends}\end{array}}{\begin{array}{c}\text{Average common} \\ \text{equity}\end{array}} = \frac{\begin{array}{c}\text{Net income} - \\ \text{Preferred dividends}\end{array}}{\text{Sales}} \times \frac{\text{Sales}}{\begin{array}{c}\text{Average} \\ \text{assets}\end{array}} \times \frac{\begin{array}{c}\text{Average} \\ \text{assets}\end{array}}{\begin{array}{c}\text{Average} \\ \text{common equity}\end{array}}$$

Adjusted profit margin reflects the portion of every sales dollar remaining for common shareholders after providing for all costs and claims (including preferred dividends). Asset turnover is exactly as defined above for return on assets, and **leverage** (or *common leverage*) is the common shareholders' leverage ratio measuring the proportion of assets financed by common shareholders. The larger the leverage ratio, the smaller the proportion of assets financed by common shareholders and the greater the financial leverage. These components are useful in both our analysis of company performance and in assessing returns to shareholders.[1]

Drawing on the financial statements of Excell Corporation in Exhibits 6.1 and 6.2, we can compute the disaggregated ROCE for Year 9 as (in $ millions):

---

[1]An alternative disaggregation of return on common equity is a variant of the return on assets (ROA). This disaggregation is:

ROCE = ROA × Earnings leverage × Common leverage

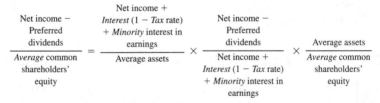

Return on assets reflects return independent of financing sources. The two leverage components reflect the effect of using both creditor and preferred shareholder financing to increase return to common shareholders. **Earnings leverage** is the proportion of income available to common shareholders (*after* removing costs of both creditor [interest] and preferred [dividend] financing) relative to income available to creditor and equity financing sources (*before* removing these costs). **Common leverage** reflects the proportion of assets financed by common shareholders.

$$\frac{\$65 - \$3}{(\$674 + \$699) \div 2} = \frac{\$65 - \$3}{\$1,724} \times \frac{\$1,724}{(\$1,334 + \$1,372) \div 2} \times \frac{(\$1,334 + \$1,372) \div 2}{(\$674 + \$699) \div 2}$$

or

$$\begin{array}{ccccccc} \text{ROCE} & = & \text{Adjusted profit margin} & \times & \text{Asset turnover} & \times & \text{Leverage} \\ 8.98\% & = & 3.577\% & \times & 1.274 & \times & 1.970 \end{array}$$

We can compute additional variations on the disaggregated ROCE of Excell Corporation to provide us further insights into different aspects of its business. One way is to merge asset turnover and leverage. In Excell's operations, every dollar of common equity is used to obtain an *incremental* $0.97 of non-common equity financing (e.g., creditor and preferred equity). The *total* financing of $1.97 generates $2.51 in sales. We obtain this insight from recognizing that assets (equaling total debt and equity financing) are turning over (generating sales) at a rate of 1.274—in formula form, $1.97 \times 1.274 = \$2.50$. This highlights that $2.51 in sales earns an adjusted profit margin (*after* all costs and preferred dividends) of 3.577 percent, yielding a return on common shareholders' equity of 8.98 percent ($2.51 \times 3.577\%$).

Another variation of this analysis disaggregates adjusted profit margin into its pre-tax and tax retention components. When *pre-tax* adjusted profit margin is multiplied by (1 − Effective tax rate), or **retention rate,** of the company, we get adjusted profit margin:

Adjusted profit margin = Pre-tax adjusted profit margin × Retention rate

$$\frac{\text{Net income } - \text{ Preferred dividends}}{\text{Sales}} = \frac{\text{Pre-tax earnings } - \text{ Preferred dividends}}{\text{Sales}} \times \frac{\text{Net income } - \text{ Preferred dividends}}{\text{Pre-tax earnings } - \text{ Preferred dividends}}$$

The purpose of this profit margin disaggregation is to separate pre-tax margin, a measure of *operating effectiveness,* from retention rate, a measure of *tax-management effectiveness.* In the case of Excell Corporation, the adjusted profit margin of 3.6 percent is disaggregated as:

$$3.577\% = \frac{\$126 - \$3}{\$1,724} \times \frac{\$65 - \$3}{\$126 - \$3} = 7.125\% \times 50.204\%$$

ANALYSIS VIEWPOINT

YOU ARE THE CONSULTANT

You are the management consultant to a client seeking a critical review of its performance. As part of your analysis you compute ROCE and its components (industry norms in parenthesis): asset turnover = 1.5 (1.0); leverage = 2.1 (2.2); pre-tax adjusted profit margin = 0.05 (0.14); and retention rate = 0.40 (0.24). What does your preliminary analysis of these figures suggest?

Computing Return on Invested Capital

This section applies our analysis of return on invested capital to the financial statements of Campbell Soup Company reproduced in Supplement A.

Return on Assets

Return on assets is measured as (including reference to Campbell's relevant financial statement items):

$$\frac{\text{Net income } \boxed{28} + [\text{Interest expense } \boxed{18} \times (1 - \text{Tax rate})] + \text{Minority interest in earnings } \boxed{25}}{\text{Average assets } \boxed{39A}}$$

Computation of this return for Year 11 of Campbell yields ($ millions):

$$\frac{\$401.5 + \$116.2(1 - 0.34) + \$7.2}{(\$4,149.0 + \$4,115.6)/2} = \frac{\$485.4}{\$4,132.3} = 11.75\%$$

Disaggregated Return on Assets

We can disaggregate Campbell's Year 11 return on assets (ROA) into its profit margin and asset turnover components:

$$\text{Return on assets} = \text{Profit margin} \times \text{Asset turnover}$$

$$= \frac{\text{Net income} + \text{Interest}(1 - \text{Tax rate}) + \text{Minority interest in earnings}}{\text{Sales}} \times \frac{\text{Sales}}{\text{Average assets}}$$

$$11.75\% = \frac{\$485.4}{\$6,204.1} \times \frac{\$6,204.1}{\$4,132.3} = 7.8\% \times 1.5$$

Return on Common Equity

Return on common shareholders' equity is defined as (including reference to Campbell's relevant financial statement items):

$$\frac{\text{Net income } \boxed{28} - \text{Preferred dividends}}{\text{Average common equity}^* \; \boxed{54} \; \boxed{176}}$$

*Includes 50 percent of deferred taxes we assume as equity.

Computation of return on common equity for Year 11 of Campbell yields ($ millions):

$$\frac{\$401.5}{[(\$1,793.4 + \$129.3) + (\$1,691.8 + \$117.5)]/2} = \frac{\$401.5}{\$1,866} = 21.52\%$$

Disaggregated Return on Common Equity

We disaggregate Campbell's Year 11 return on common equity into its components:

$$ROCE = \text{Adjusted profit margin} \times \text{Asset turnover} \times \text{Leverage}$$

$$ROCE = \frac{\text{Net income } - \text{Preferred dividends}}{\text{Sales } \boxed{13}} \times \frac{\text{Sales}}{\text{Average assets}} \times \frac{\text{Average assets}}{\text{Average common equity}}$$

$$= \frac{\$401.5}{\$6,204.1} \times \frac{\$6,204.1}{\$4,132.3} \times \frac{\$4,132.3}{\$1,866.0}$$

$$21.52\% = 6.47\% \times 1.50 \times 2.22$$

Further disaggregation of Campbell's adjusted profit margin into its *pre-tax* and *tax retention* components yields:

$$\text{Adjusted profit margin} = \text{Pre-tax adjusted profit margin} \times \text{Retention rate}$$

$$= \frac{\text{Pre-tax earnings}}{\text{Sales}} \times \frac{\text{Net earnings}}{\text{Pre-tax earnings}}$$

$$= \frac{\$667.4 \; \boxed{26}}{\$6,204.1} \times \frac{\$401.5 \; \boxed{28}}{\$667.4}$$

$$6.5\% = 10.8\% \times 60.2\%$$

We conduct a comparative analysis of these ratios across time in our analysis of return on invested capital section of the Comprehensive Case chapter. Analysis of return on invested capital measures across time is often revealing of company performance. If ROCE declines, it is important for us to identify the component(s) responsible for this decline to assess past and future company performance. We can also assess areas of greatest potential improvement in ROCE and the likelihood of a company successfully pursuing this strategy. For example, if leverage is high and not likely to increase, our analysis focuses on adjusted profit margin and asset turnover. Our analysis of company strategies and potential for improvements depends on industry and economic conditions. We ask questions like: Is profit margin high or low in comparison with the industry? What is the potential improvement in asset turnover in this industry? Evaluating returns using the structured approach described in this chapter and interpreting them in their proper context can greatly aid our analysis.

Further Disaggregation of Return on Common Equity

Further disaggregation of return on common equity is sometimes useful for our analysis. Specifically, we can separate both *interest* and *tax* components from net income as follows:

EBIT [$783.6] = Net income [$401.5] + Interest [$116.2] + Taxes [$265.9 $\boxed{27}$]

where EBIT is earnings (income) *before* interest and taxes (and *before* preferred dividends, if applicable). We use these net income components and merge them into the ROCE disaggregation formula as follows:

$$ROCE = [(\textbf{EBIT profit margin} \times \textbf{Asset turnover}) -$$
$$\textbf{Interest turnover}] \times \textbf{Leverage} \times \textbf{Retention rate}$$

where EBIT profit margin equals EBIT divided by sales, interest turnover equals interest expense divided by average assets, and the other components are as defined above. Interest turnover is referred to as *interest burden*. This derives from the notion that the higher the interest burden, the lower the ROCE. Also, the higher the tax retention, the higher the ROCE. Computation of the disaggregation of ROCE for Year 11 of Campbell yields ($ millions):

$$ROCE = \left[\left(\frac{\$783.6}{\$6,204.1} \times \frac{\$6,204.1}{\$4,132.3} \right) - \frac{\$116.2}{\$4,132.3} \right] \times \frac{\$4,132.3}{\$1,866.0} \times (1.000 - 0.398)$$

$$21.52\% = \quad [(0.126 \times 1.50) - 0.028] \quad \times \quad 2.22 \quad \times 0.602$$

This disaggregation highlights *both* effects of interest and taxes on Campbell's ROCE.

Assessing Growth in Common Equity

Equity Growth Rate

We can assess the common equity growth rate of a company through earnings retention. This analysis emphasizes equity growth *without* resort to external financing. To assess equity growth we assume earnings retention *and* a constant dividend payout over time. The **equity growth rate** is computed as:

$$\text{Equity growth rate} = \frac{\text{Net income} - \text{Preferred dividends} - \text{Dividend payout}}{\text{Average common stockholders' equity}}$$

The equity growth rate for Year 9 of Excell Corporation, using its financial statements reproduced in Exhibits 6.1 and 6.2, is computed as:

ANALYSIS RESEARCH INSIGHT 6.1

RETURN ON COMMON SHAREHOLDERS' EQUITY

How does a company's return on common shareholders' equity (ROCE) behave across time? Do certain companies consistently have high or low ROCE? Do companies' ROCEs tend to move toward an average ROCE? Analysis research has addressed these important questions. *On average,* a company's ROCE for the current period is a good predictor of its ROCE for the next period. However, as the time horizon increases, a company's ROCE tends to converge toward the average economy-wide ROCE. This is usually attributed to the effects of competition. Companies that are able to sustain high ROCEs typically command large premiums over book value.

A large portion of the variability in companies' ROCEs is due to changes in ROA. This is because, on average, leverage factors do not vary significantly over time. Two factors are important in predicting ROCE. First, disaggregating net income into operating and nonoperating components improves forecasts. Second, the conservatism inherent in accounting practice must eventually "reverse." This accounting reversal predictably yields an increase in ROCE.

$$3.35\% = \frac{\$65 - \$3 - \$39^*}{(\$674 + \$699) \div 2}$$

*Common stock dividend payout.

This measure implies Excell Corporation can grow 3.35 percent per year without increasing its current level of financing.

Sustainable Equity Growth Rate

The **sustainable equity growth rate,** or simply sustainable equity growth, recognizes that internal growth for a company depends on *both*: (1) earnings retention and (2) return earned on the earnings retained. Specifically, the **sustainable equity growth rate** is computed as:

Sustainable equity growth rate = ROCE × (1 − Payout rate)

For Excell Corporation (see Exhibits 6.1 and 6.2), we find the dividend payout rate for Year 9 equals 65 percent ($41,806/$64,569). We then compute Excell's sustainable equity growth rate for Year 9 as:

3.17% = 8.98% × (1 − 0.647)

Excell experienced an earnings decline from Year 8 ($77,896) to Year 9 ($64,569). This along with a constant dividend payout produced a declining sustainable growth rate. When estimating future equity growth rates it is often advisable to average (or otherwise recognize) sustainable growth rates for several recent years. We should also recognize potential changes in earnings retention and forecasted ROCE.

Financial Leverage and Return on Common Equity

This section analyzes effects of financial leverage for the return on common equity. *Financial leverage* refers to the extent of invested capital from other than common shareholders. For purposes of our analysis, we use financial statements of Excell Corporation. Our first step is to list the *average* amounts of all financing sources for Excell Corporation taken from its December 31, Year 9 and Year 8, balance sheets ($ thousands):

Current liabilities (excluding current portion of long-term debt)		$ 176,677
Long-term debt	$343,255	
Current portion of long-term debt	10,730	353,985
Deferred taxes		93,962
Preferred stock		41,538
Common shareholders' equity		686,640
Total financing		$1,352,802

We also reproduce relevant financial data from Excell's income statement for Year 9 ($ thousands):

Income before taxes	$125,730
Income taxes	61,161
Net income	$ 64,569
Preferred dividends	2,908
Income accruing to common shareholders	$ 61,661
Total interest expense	$ 20,382
Assume interest on short-term notes (5%)	687
Balance of interest on long-term debt	$ 19,695

We can compute Excell Corporation's return on assets as:

$$ROA = \frac{\text{Net income} + \text{Interest} \times (1 - \text{Tax rate})}{\text{Average assets}}$$

$$5.677\% = \frac{\$64,569 + \$20,382\,(1 - 0.40)}{\$1,352,802}$$

Excell's 5.677 percent return on assets is relevant for assessing the effects of financial leverage. This implies that if suppliers of capital (other than the common shareholders) receive a less than 5.677 percent return, then common shareholders benefit. The reverse occurs when suppliers of capital receive more than a 5.677 percent return. The greater the difference in returns between common equity and other capital suppliers, the more successful (or unsuccessful) is the trading on the equity.

A thorough analysis of Excell's financial leverage appears in Exhibit 6.7. This exhibit shows an analysis of the relative contribution and return for each of the major financing suppliers. It also shows the influence of each financing supplier's returns on ROCE. A few findings deserve mention. The $9,618 accruing to common shareholders from use of current liabilities is largely due to them being free of interest costs. The $8,279 accruing to shareholders from long-term debt is primarily due to tax deductibility of interest. The value of tax deferrals is evident where Excell's use of cost-free funds yields an annual advantage of $5,334. Since preferred dividends are *not* tax deductible, the low return on assets (5.677 percent) yields a leverage disadvantage to common shareholders of $550.

We can further extend our analysis of leverage to its component parts. Excell's return on common shareholders' equity is ($ thousands):

$$\frac{\text{Net income} - \text{Preferred dividends}}{\text{Average common equity}} = \frac{\$61,661^*}{\$686,640} = 8.98\%$$

*Identical to income accruing to common shareholders in Exhibit 6.7.

We know the net benefit to common shareholders from financial leverage is $22,681 (see Exhibit 6.7). As a percent of common equity, this benefit is computed as:

$$\frac{\substack{\text{Earnings in excess of return} \\ \text{to suppliers of funds}}}{\text{Average common equity}} = \frac{\$22,681}{\$686,640} = 3.303\%$$

Our analysis of return on common equity can view return as comprised of two components:

Return on assets	5.677%
Leverage advantage accruing to common equity	3.303
Return on common equity	8.980%

Return on Common Shareholders' Equity versus Investment

Return on common shareholders' equity measures the relation of net income (attributable to common shareholders) to common shareholders' equity. Common shareholders' equity is measured using book values

Exhibit 6.7   Analyzing Leverage on Common Equity ($ thousands)

Financing Supplier	Average Funds Supplied	Earnings on Funds Supplied at Rate of 5.677 Percent	Payment to Suppliers of Funds	Accruing to (Detracting from) Return on Common Equity
Current liabilities	$ 176,677	$10,030	$ 412[a]	$ 9,618
Long-term debt	353,985	20,096	11,817[b]	8,279
Deferred taxes	93,962	5,334	none	5,334
Preferred stock	41,538	2,358	2,908[c]	(550)
Earnings in excess of return to suppliers of funds				$22,681
Add: Common equity	686,640	38,980	—	38,980
Totals	$1,352,802	$76,798	$15,137	
Total return to shareholders				$61,661

[a]Short-term interest expenses of $687 less 40 percent tax (from Exhibit 6.1).
[b]Long-term interest expense of $19,695 less 40 percent tax (from Exhibit 6.1).
[c]Preferred dividends (from Exhibit 6.1)—not tax deductible.

reported in the balance sheet. These values do not necessarily reflect how individual shareholders like us might fare in terms of return on our personal investment (price we pay for common stock). This is important since shareholders do not typically buy common stock at book value—they often pay a multiple of book value. The price we pay for stock plays an important role in determining **return on shareholders' investment (ROSI),** computed as (using all per share figures):

$$ROSI = \frac{\text{Dividends} + \text{Market value of earnings reinvested}}{\text{Share price (cost)}}$$

To illustrate, consider the following financial data from Austin Technics, Inc. (per share rounded to nearest dollar):

Net income	$ 6
Cash dividends to common	(2)
Earnings reinvested	$ 4
Book value of common equity	$60
Ratio of market value to book value	2:1
Market valuation of earnings reinvested	$ 4

The return on common shareholders' equity for Austin Technics is 10 percent ($6/$60). However, since a shareholder must pay the market share price (2 × $60), the shareholders' ROSI is only 5 percent—computed as:

$$5\% = \frac{\$2 + \$4}{2 \times \$60}$$

One component in computing shareholders' return on investment is the assumption that the market uses earnings reinvested at their reported amount. It is important for the shareholder to consider how the market values earnings reinvested and make an informed assumption. In the case of Austin Technics' earnings of $6 per share, shareholders benefit from: (1) earnings paid out as dividends [$2], and (2) the value the market places on the earnings reinvested [$4]. If we assume the market value of earnings reinvested is valued at more than their reported value, say $5.2 per share, then we can compute a **shareholder multiple** as (per share):

$$\frac{\$2 \text{ (dividend)} + \$5.2 \text{ (market valuation of \$4 earnings reinvested)}}{\$6 \text{ (earnings)}} = \frac{\$7.2}{\$6} = 1.20$$

This shareholder multiple implies a dollar earned and reinvested by the company enriches shareholders by $1.20 (ignoring tax effects). Evidence in practice suggests a wide variation in the shareholder multiple across companies, where earnings do not always yield increased dividends or higher stock values. There is some evidence that the correlation between ROCE and ROSI is low (recall ROCE does not include the market's valuation of earnings reinvested or other measures).[2] The ROSI critically depends on market valuation. As we discussed in Chapter 2, our valuation of equity securities must include analysis of both financial statements *and* market prices. This distinction between the value of a company and its stock is extremely important. For example, our financial statement analysis might reveal a company is well managed and fundamentally sound. Yet this company might be a poor investment because its stock is overvalued (unless we can sell it short). Conversely, a poor performing company can be a good investment because its stock is undervalued.

---

[2]See B. Ball, "The Mysterious Disappearance of Retained Earnings," *Harvard Business Review* (July–August 1987).

GUIDANCE ANSWERS TO ANALYSIS VIEWPOINTS

YOU ARE THE AUDITOR

Joint analysis is where one measure of company performance is assessed relative to another. In the case of our manufacturing client, both *individual* analyses yield percent changes within the ±5 percent acceptable range. However, a joint analysis would suggest a more alarming situation. Consider a joint analysis using profit margin (net income/sales). The client's profit margin is 11.46 percent ($2,060,000 − $1,824,000/$2,060,000) for the current year compared with 5.0 percent ($2,000,000 − $1,900,000/$2,000,000) for the prior year—a 129 percent increase in profit margin! This is what the audit partner is concerned with, and encourages expanded audit tests including joint analysis to verify or refute the client's figures.

YOU ARE THE CONSULTANT

Your preliminary analysis highlights deviations from the norm in (1) asset turnover, (2) pre-tax adjusted profit margin, and (3) retention rate. Asset turnover for your client is better than the norm. Your client appears to efficiently use its assets. One note of warning: we need to be assured all assets are accounted for and properly valued, and we want to know if the company is sufficiently replacing its aging assets. Your client's pre-tax adjusted profit margin is 60 percent lower than the norm. This is alarming, especially in light of the positive asset turnover ratio. Our client has considerably greater costs than the norm, and we need to direct efforts to identify and analyze these costs. Retention rate is also considerably worse than competitors. Our client is paying a greater proportion of its income in taxes than the norm. We need to utilize tax experts to identify and appropriately plan business activities with tax considerations in mind.

Profitability Analysis

A LOOK BACK

The previous chapter described return on invested capital and explained its relevance for analysis. Return on assets and return on common equity were shown to be useful tools of analysis. We disaggregated both return measures and explained their value in assessing financial leverage.

A LOOK AT THIS CHAPTER

This chapter expands our return analysis to emphasize profitability. Our analysis focuses on the components of income and their evaluation. We direct special attention at sales, cost of sales, taxes, and selling and financing expenses. We explain break-even analysis and its relevance. We demonstrate the use of profitability analysis tools, emphasizing interpretation and adjustments.

A LOOK AHEAD

Chapter 8 extends our analysis to earnings quality, persistence, and prediction. We describe how to assess earnings quality and explain analytical adjustments to income. We analyze management's incentives in reporting income and their implications for analysis. Earnings forecasting and its use of accounting disclosures are discussed.

THIS CHAPTER WILL:

- Describe the importance of profitability analysis and the necessity of analyzing and adjusting income.
- Analyze the sources, persistence, measurement, and recognition of revenues for assessing profitability.
- Explain gross profit and its evaluation using volume, price, and costs of sales.
- Analyze operating and nonoperating expenses using common-size, index number, and ratio analyses.
- Describe the effective tax rate and the analysis of income tax disclosures.
- Explain break-even analysis and its relevance in assessing profitability.
- Interpret operating leverage and its implications for profitability.

PREVIEW OF CHAPTER 7

Profitability analysis is important in analyzing financial statements and complements the return analysis discussed in the previous chapter. Profitability analysis goes beyond the accounting measures—such as sales, cost of sales, and operating and nonoperating expenses—to assess their sources, persistence, measurement, and key economic relations. Results from this assessment enable us to better estimate both the return and risk characteristics of a company. Profitability analysis also allows us to distinguish between performance primarily attributed to management (operating decisions) and those results less tied to management decisions (taxes and selling prices). This chapter describes tools of analysis enabling us to make these distinctions. We also describe break-even analysis and its relevance for assessing profitability. Both analytic and graphic analysis of break-even points are explained. We also describe operating leverage and its importance for profitability. Throughout this chapter we emphasize the application of these analysis tools with several illustrative cases. The content and organization of this chapter are as follows:

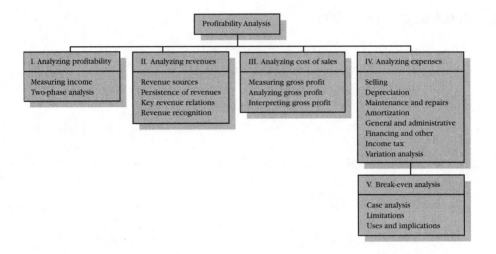

ANALYZING COMPANY PROFITABILITY

Analyzing company profitability is a major part of financial statement analysis. All financial statements are pertinent to profitability analysis, but none is more important than the income statement. The income statement reports a company's operating results over a period of time. Operating results are the primary purpose of a company, and play an important role in determining company value, solvency, and liquidity.

Profitability analysis is critically important for all users but especially for equity investors and creditors. For equity investors, income is often the single most important determinant of changes in security values. Measuring and forecasting income are crucial tasks of investors. For creditors, income and operating cash flows are common and desirable sources of interest and principal repayments. When we evaluate company profitability, our analysis focuses on several questions including:

- What is the company's relevant income measure?
- What is the quality of income?
- What income components are important for income forecasting?
- How persistent (including stability and trend) are income and its components?
- What is a company's earning power?

Factors in Measuring Company Income

Income is defined as revenues less expenses over a reporting period. This presumably simple concept creates many challenges in practice. Users' frustrations are reflected in questions like: Why is it so difficult to determine income under specific circumstances? What is "true income"? Does accounting identify and measure true income? We cannot expect accounting to provide us with a true income measure. Income is not a unique amount awaiting the perfection of a measurement system to precisely value it. We discuss several reasons for this in this section.

Estimation Issues

Income measurement depends on estimates of the outcome of future events. These estimates are a matter of judgment and probabilities. They require allocation of revenues and expenses across current and future periods. They involve determining future usefulness of many asset types and estimation of future liabilities and obligations. While we expect the judgments of skilled and experienced professionals to reveal some consensus (less variability), income measurement requires certain discretion.

Accounting Methods

Accounting standards governing income measurement are the result of professional experience, regulatory agendas, business happenings, and other social influences. They reflect a balance in these factors, including compromises on differing interests and views toward income measurement. There is also latitude in the application of accounting to accommodate different business circumstances as explained in Illustration 7.1.

Illustration 7.1

Our financial analysis uses knowledge of the company and industry to adjust reported income. We adjust income for estimated changes needed for revenue and expense items. These can include adjustments for bad debts, depreciation, research expenses, advertising, and extraordinary or unusual gains and losses. Comparative analysis with other companies demands similar adjustments.

Incentives for Disclosure

Practitioners are ideally concerned with fairly presenting financial statements. This implies accounting would be neutral and give expression and effect to business events without affecting how those events are perceived. Practitioners would choose from alternative principles those most applicable to the circumstances, and disclose relevant information, favorable and unfavorable, affecting users' decisions. However, all of us have opinions, we see the world a little differently, and we experience life from different perspectives. These yield *incentives* that affect much of what we do—and so it is for practitioners. Pressures of management, competition, finances, and family all bear on financial statements and income measurement. Managers bring strong views to the table. Directors expect certain results. Shareholders concentrate on the bottom line. Creditors want safeguards. And the incentives of accounting preparers and auditors are determined by these pressures—especially in gray areas of accounting. These incentives create pressure to choose "acceptable" measures rather than "appropriate" measures given the business circumstances. Our analysis must recognize these incentives and evaluate income accordingly.

Diversity across Users

Financial statements are general-purpose reports serving diverse needs of many users. It is unlikely that one simple income figure is relevant to all users. Certain users value only the bottom line, others value employment opportunities, and still others value social responsibility. This diversity of views implies that our analysis must use income as an initial measure of profitability. We then use information from financial statements and elsewhere to appropriately adjust income consistent with our interests and objectives as shown in Illustration 7.2.

Illustration 7.2

> Consider the case where we wish to purchase an income-producing property. Depreciation expense for the property based on the seller's cost is not relevant to us but is to the seller. Our projection of income from this property must use depreciation based on expected purchase price, not on the seller's cost.

Illustration 7.2 makes clear that the importance of measuring income is *secondary* to our analysis objective of gathering relevant information to adjust income consistent with our needs. This chapter describes analysis tools useful in this task and in evaluating income components. The next chapter considers questions regarding the quality of earnings, usefulness of income components for forecasting, persistence of income, and earning power.

Two-Phase Analysis of Income

Our analysis of income and its components involves two phases. The first phase is our *analysis of accounting and its measurements.* This requires an understanding of the accounting for revenue and expenses. It also requires an understanding of accounting for assets and liabilities since many assets reflect costs deferred and some liabilities represent deferred income. We must understand and assess the implications of using one type of accounting versus another, and its effect on income measurement and comparative analysis.

Our second phase is *applying analysis tools to income (and its components) and interpreting the analytical results.* Applying analysis tools is aimed at achieving our respective objectives in analyzing income. These objectives include income forecasting, assessing income persistence and quality, and estimating earning power. We devote the remainder of this chapter to describing these tools and interpreting their results.

ANALYSIS VIEWPOINT

YOU ARE THE SECURITIES LISTING DIRECTOR

You are responsible for setting companies' listing requirements for a regional securities exchange. Several analyst groups request that you increase information disclosure requirements for income, regarding both income components and note disclosures. You also receive requests from certain labor unions, activist groups, and small investors to streamline and condense financial reports and improve the usefulness of aggregate income. What are some reasons for the apparent differences in these groups' requests? How do you balance their information needs?

ANALYZING COMPANY REVENUES

This section focuses on analyzing a company's revenues (commonly called *sales*). Our analysis of revenues focuses on several questions including:

- What are the major sources of revenue?
- How persistent are revenue sources?
- How are revenues, receivables, and inventories related?
- When is revenue recorded and how is it measured?

Major Sources of Revenues

Knowledge of major sources of revenues is important in our analysis of income. This information is especially important if our analysis is of a *diversified* company. With diversified companies, each market or product line often has its own growth pattern, profitability, and future potential.

PepsiCo's Revenue Sources

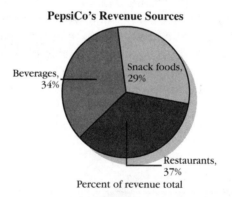

Percent of revenue total

PepsiCo's *Restaurant* Revenue Sources

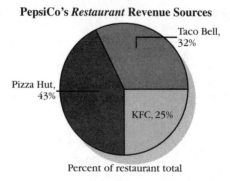

Percent of restaurant total

An excellent means to analyze sources of revenues is common-size analysis. A *common-size analysis* shows the percent of each major class of revenue to its total. A useful tool for this purpose is to portray graphically the sources of revenue on an absolute dollar basis as shown in Exhibit 7.1 for GT Electronics. This graphical analysis is especially useful across periods. Another common approach is to portray revenue sources in a *pie chart* for specific periods or segments. On page 276 we show a pie chart presentation of PepsiCo for (1) total revenues, and (2) restaurant revenues.

Challenges of Diversified Companies

Our analysis of financial statements of diversified companies must separate and interpret the impact of individual business segments on the company as a whole. This is challenging because different segments or divisions can experience varying rates of profitability, risk, and growth opportunities. Their existence is an important reason why our analysis requires considerable detailed information by business segment. Our evaluation, projection, and valuation of earnings require this information be separated into segments sharing characteristics of variability, growth, and risk. Asset composition and financing requirements of segments often vary and demand separate analysis. A creditor is interested in knowing which

Exhibit 7.1   Analysis of GT Electronics' Revenues by Product Line across Periods

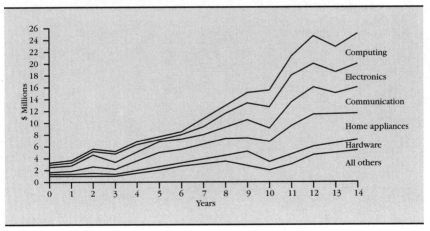

segments provide cash and which are cash users. Knowing the make-up of investing and financing activities, the size and profitability of segments, and the performance of segment management is important information. We show in Chapter 8 that income forecasting benefits from forecasting by segments. Our evaluation of income growth opportunities also benefits from segment information. One analysis tool available to us is the **segmented earnings contribution matrix**. This matrix is useful in assessing earnings quality and growth opportunities, and for valuing aggregate earnings. Examples of variations on this matrix are reported in Exhibits 7.2 and 7.3 for Land's, Ltd. Land's has three major segments that are further subdivided. Both matrixes reveal that leisure goods dominate Land's business, and that its growth opportunities are greatest in this segment.

Reporting by Segments

Information reported on operating results and financial position by segments varies. Full disclosure would provide detailed income statements, balance sheets, and statements of cash flow for each important segment.

Exhibit 7.2   Land's, Ltd., Earnings Contribution and Growth Rates by Segments

Segments	Earnings Contributions ($ thousands)	Growth Rate of Earnings Contribution for Past Three Years
Leisure goods:		
Camping equipment	$100	11%
Fishing equipment	50	2
Boats and accessories	72	15
Sporting goods	12	3
	$234	
Clothing apparel:		
Dress	$ 85	2%
Casual	72	8
Sports	12	15
	$169	
Education:		
Text publishing	$ 40	3%
Papers and supplies	17	6
	$ 57	
Total	$460	

However, full disclosure by segments is rare in practice because of difficulties in separating segments and management's reluctance to release
information that can harm its competitive position.

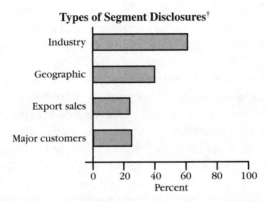

Types of Segment Disclosures†

†Total can exceed 100% because companies can report one
or more types of segments.
Source: *Accounting Trends & Techniques.*

Regulatory agencies have established reporting requirements for
industry segments, international activities, export sales, and major customers. Evaluating risk and return is a major objective of financial statement analysis, and practice recognizes the value of segment disclosures in
this evaluation. Analysis of companies operating across industry segments
or geographic areas, which often have different rates of profitability, risk,
and growth, is aided by segment data. These data assist us in analyzing
uncertainties affecting the timing and amount of expected cash inflows
and outflows.

Exhibit 7.3   Land's, Ltd., Segmented Earnings Contribution Matrix

	Growth Rate (in percent)			
Segment	**0–5**	**5–10**	**10–15**	**Total**
Leisure goods	$ 62	$ 0	$172	$234
Agribusiness	85	72	12	169
Education	40	17	0	57
Total	$187	$89	$184	$460

Practice considers a segment significant if its sales, operating income, *or* identifiable assets comprise 10 percent or more of their relevant total amounts. Companies must disclose information for these segments. To ensure that these segments comprise a substantial portion of a company's operations, the combined sales of all segments reported must be at least 75 percent of the company's total sales. Practice suggests *10 segments* as a practical limit on the number of industry segments reported. For each segment, companies must report annually the following items: (1) sales—both intersegment and to unaffiliated customers, (2) operating income—revenue less operating expenses, (3) identifiable assets, (4) capital expenditures, and (5) depreciation, depletion, and amortization expense. Practice does not prescribe methods of accounting for transfer pricing or cost allocation, but does require their disclosure. Practice also requires that if a company derives 10 percent or more of revenues from sales to a single customer, revenues from this customer must be reported. Guidelines are provided in determining a company's international operations and export sales, and for segmenting operations by geographic areas. Information similar to that required for industry segments (except capital expenditures and depreciation) is reported for these additional segments. The SEC also requires a narrative description of the company's business by segments including information on competition, customer dependence, principal products and services, backlogs, sources and availability of raw materials, patents, research and development costs, number of employees, and the seasonality of its business. Segment information for Adaptec is reported in note 9 of its annual report in Supplement A.

Analysis Implications of Segment Reports

Diversified companies, and the loss of identity for subsidiary companies in consolidated financial statements, create challenges for our analysis. While segment information is available, our analysis must be careful in using this information for profitability tests. The more specific and detailed is segment information, the more dependent it is on accounting allocations of revenues and expenses. Allocation of common costs as practiced in internal accounting is often based on notions of fairness, reasonableness, and acceptability to managers. These notions are of little relevance to our profitability analysis. Allocations of joint expenses are often arbitrary and limited in their validity and precision. Examples are research and development costs, promotion expenses, advertising costs, interest, pension costs, federal and state income taxes, and general and administrative costs. There are no accepted principles in allocating or transferring costs of one segment to another. We must recognize these limitations when relying on segment reports.

Companies do not typically disclose internal accounting practices unless it is in their interest. Management of Murray Ohio Manufacturing Company felt it advantageous to disclose, in federal court, that its annual report did not reveal the true story in profitability or loss by product line. They admitted to understating losses in its bicycle division by millions of dollars to fend off hostile takeover advances by a Swedish company. Murray Ohio feared that the potential closing of a nonprofitable bicycle division would appeal to a potential acquirer. They therefore chose not to allocate $17 million in overhead to its bicycle division. This case offers us a rare glimpse into the murky area of overhead allocation and the many possibilities companies have to report misleading segment data.

Accounting practice recognizes limitations with segment data. This accounts for companies not being required to disclose segment profit contribution (revenue less those operating expenses *directly* traceable to a segment). The FASB also requires revenues from intersegment sales or transfers be accounted for on *whatever* basis the company uses to price intersegment sales or transfers—no single basis is prescribed. They also recognized certain items of revenues and expenses do not relate to segments or cannot be allocated objectively to segments. Consequently, there is no requirement that income be disclosed by segments. The FASB notes that identifying "segments must depend to a considerable extent on the judgment of the management of the enterprise."

The analysis implications of these limitations in financial statements (lack of firm guidelines and definitions) are serious. Segment reports are and must be analyzed as "soft" information—information subject to manipulation and preinterpretation by management. It must be treated with uncertainty, and inferences drawn from these data must be subjected to alternative sources of verification. Nevertheless, when alternative evidence supports the reliability of segment data, they are extremely useful for our analysis. Specifically, segment data can aid our analysis in:

- *Analyzing sales growth.* Analysis of trends in sales by segments is useful in assessing profitability. Sales growth is often the result of one or more factors including: (1) price changes, (2) volume changes, (3) acquisitions/divestitures, and (4) changes in exchange rates. A company's Management's Discussion and Analysis section usually offers insights into the causes of sales growth.

- *Analyzing asset growth.* Analysis of trends in identifiable assets by segments is relevant for our profitability analysis. Comparing capital expenditures to depreciation can reveal the segments undergoing "real" growth. When analyzing geographic segment reports, our analysis must be alert to changes in foreign currency exchange rates that can significantly affect reported values.

- *Analyzing profitability.* Measures of operating income to sales and operating income to identifiable assets by segment are useful in analyzing profitability. Due to limitations with segment income data, our analysis should focus on trends versus absolute levels.

Exhibit CC.1 in the Comprehensive Case chapter reports a summary of segment information for Campbell Soup Company. Note 2 of Campbell Soup's financial statements also reports Geographic Area Information.

ANALYSIS   RESEARCH   INSIGHT   7.1

USEFULNESS OF SEGMENT DATA

Analysis research provides evidence that segment disclosures are useful in forecasting future profitability. We know that total sales and earnings of a company equals the sum of the sales and earnings of all segments (less any intercompany transactions). As long as different segments are subject to different economic factors, the accuracy of segment-based forecasts should exceed that of forecasts based on consolidated data.

Combining company-specific segment data with industry-specific forecasts improves the accuracy of sales and earnings forecasts. Evidence shows that the introduction of segment reporting requirements increased the accuracy and reduced the dispersion of earnings forecasts made by professional securities analysts. This implies that our profitability analysis can also benefit from segment data.

Persistence of Revenues

The stability and trend, or *persistence,* of revenues are important to our analysis of profitability. To the extent we can assess the persistence of revenues by segments, profitability analysis is enhanced. This section considers two useful analysis tools for assessing persistence in revenues: (1) trend percent analysis, and (2) evaluation of Management's Discussion and Analysis.

Trend Percent Analysis

A useful method in assessing persistence of revenues either in total or by segments is **trend percent analysis.** A five-year trend percent analysis of revenues by product lines for Madison, Inc., is shown in Exhibit 7.4. In this case Year 1 revenues are set equal to 100 percent and all years' revenues compared to it (e.g., Year 2 percent equals Year 2 revenues divided by Year 1 revenues). Revenue indexes by segments are often correlated and compared to industry norms or to similar measures for specific competitors. We can also compute *(auto)correlations* for revenues across periods to measure persistence in revenues. Additional considerations bearing on our analysis of revenues' persistence include:

- Demand sensitivity of revenues to business conditions.
- Ability to anticipate demand with new or revised products and services.
- Customer analysis—concentration, dependence, and stability.
- Revenues' concentration or dependence on one segment.
- Revenues' reliance on sales staff.
- Geographical diversification of markets.

As an illustration, our analysis of Micron Products, Inc., yields concern with overreliance on a few major customers.

Sales to three major customers amounted to approximately 32 percent, 25 percent, and 11 percent of the Company's net sales.

—Micron Products, Inc.

Exhibit 7.4   Trend Percent Analysis of Revenues by Product Line for Madison, Inc. (Year 1 = 100)

Segment	Year 1	Year 2	Year 3	Year 4	Year 5
Bridges	100	110	114	107	121
Roadways	100	120	135	160	174
Landscaping	100	98	94	86	74
Engineering	100	101	92	98	105

Management's Discussion and Analysis

The Management's Discussion and Analysis (MD&A) of a company's financial condition and operating results is often useful in our analysis of persistence in revenues. The SEC requires several disclosures of an interpretative or explanatory nature in MD&A. This information aids us in understanding and evaluating period-to-period changes in financial accounts including revenues. Management is required to report on changes in revenue and expense components relevant for understanding operating activities. These include unusual events affecting operating income, trends or uncertainties affecting or likely to affect operations, and impending changes in revenue and expense relations like increases in material or labor costs. Management must also report on whether they attribute growth in revenues to increases in prices, volume, inflation, or new product introduction. Management is encouraged to describe financial results, report forward-looking information, and discuss trends and forces not evident in the financial statements. The SEC asserts that MD&A provides information relevant to analyzing financial condition and operating results by evaluating the amounts and uncertainty of cash flows.

Reporting guidelines for management in preparing MD&A are few. Management has considerable discretion in communicating relevant information. The aim is meaningful disclosure in narrative form by management, and to supply useful information not typically available in financial statements. Its success in achieving this aim depends on management's attitudes and incentives. While our analysis using information in MD&A is likely "soft," we must remember that management cannot risk being careless or deceptive with this information because of potential SEC-related consequences. Accordingly, our analysis often benefits from this information. It usually provides useful insights, offers us management's perspective, and cannot readily be obtained in other ways. We can use these disclosures as analytical supplements for both the information offered (especially when independently verified) and as insight into management's strategic plans and actions.

Relations between Revenues, Receivables, and Inventories

The relations between revenues and accounts receivable, and revenues and inventories often provide important clues for our evaluation of operating results. They are also often useful in predicting future performance.

Revenues and Accounts Receivable

We discussed the relation between accounts receivable and revenues in Chapter 3 in the context of short-term liquidity. We assessed the quality (collectibility) of receivables and their liquidity (nearness to cash collection). Another important dimension of our analysis is the relation between revenues and receivables in evaluating earnings quality. If accounts receivable grow at a rate exceeding revenues, we need to analyze this to identify the causes. Causes can include revenues being driven by increased incentives, generous extension of credit, or an "in-the-door" strategy in anticipation of future revenue. These conditions bear on future revenues, both favorably and unfavorably. Additionally, such conditions often affect collectibility of receivables. See Illustration 7.3.

Illustration 7.3

The relation between revenues and accounts receivable of Toyland, Inc., for a recent five-year period is reflected in the following chart ($ thousands):

	Year Ended				
	Year 6	Year 5	Year 4	Year 3	Year 2
Net revenues	$199	$227	$175	$198	$290
Percent change	−12.4%	29.7%	−11.3%	−31.9%	—
Accounts receivable	$271	$225	$190	$276	$328
Percent change	20.6%	18.2%	−31.1%	−15.9%	—

In Year 6, revenues declined by 12.4 percent whereas accounts receivable increased by 20.6 percent. This relation contrasts with relations prevailing in preceding years where increases and decreases in revenue or accounts receivables were met with increases and decreases in the other. This negative correlation warrants our special attention and analysis.

Revenues and Inventories

We discussed the relation of inventories to cost of goods sold in Chapter 3 in analyzing short-term liquidity. Also, our discussion in Chapter 6 showed how inventory turnover is related to inventory quality and asset turnover. Our analysis of inventory components often reveals valuable clues to future revenues and operating activity. For example, when increases in finished goods are accompanied by decreases in raw materials and/or work in process, we expect a decline in production. Refer to Illustration 7.4.

Illustration 7.4

The relation between revenues and inventories (and inventory components) for Burroughs Corporation for a recent five-year period is reported in the chart below ($ millions):

	Year 6	Year 5	Year Ended Year 4	Year 3	Year 2
Net revenues	$ 762.7	$ 793.9	$ 689.8	$ 559.0	$ 560.0
Inventories:					
Finished goods	907.1	830.6	631.6	677.9	699.9
Work in process and raw materials	609.0	664.7	561.2	467.7	379.2
Total inventories	$1,516.1	$1,495.3	$1,192.8	$1,145.6	$1,079.1

This table reveals that during the most recent two years, finished goods inventories increase while work in process and raw materials decline. This relation usually foreshadows a production decline. An increase of inventories (especially in finished goods) with a decline in revenues is indicative of a failure of revenues to keep up with production. This is another cause for an expected decline in production.

Revenue Recognition and Measurement

There are various criteria in the recognition and measurement of revenue. We know that certain methods are more conservative than others. Our analysis must recognize the revenue recognition methods used by a company and their implications. We must also be aware of potential differences in revenue recognition methods used by different companies in any comparative analysis. When forecasting revenue, one consideration is whether the revenue recognition method used reflects the relevant measure of business performance and operating activities.

ANALYSIS VIEWPOINT

YOU ARE THE BANKER

You are considering loan requests from two companies. Analysis of both companies' financial statements indicates similar risk and return character-istics, and both are marginal applicants. In discussing these cases with your senior loan officer, she points out that one company's income is dispersed across 10 different segments while the other is concentrated in one industry. How does this additional information influence your loan decision? Does it impact your comparison of these companies?

ANALYZING COMPANY COST OF SALES

Cost of sales or services provided is, as a percent of revenues, the single largest cost item for most companies. There is also, especially in unregu-lated industries, no generally accepted cost classification method yielding a clear distinction between expenses such as cost of sales, administrative, general, selling, and financing. This is particularly true in classifying gen-eral and administrative expenses. Our analysis must be ever alert to meth-ods of cost classification and the effect they have on individual cost assessments and comparative analysis within or across companies.

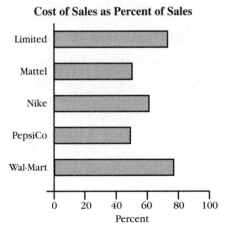

Cost of Sales as Percent of Sales

Source: Annual reports.

Measuring Gross Profit (Margin)

Gross profit, or *gross margin,* is measured as revenues less cost of sales. It is frequently reported and described as a percent. A recent year's gross profit for New York Jewelry, Inc., is ($ thousands):

Sales	$11,950	100%
Cost of sales	8,604	72
Gross profit	$ 3,346	28%

The gross profit or gross profit percent is a key performance measure. New York Jewelry's gross profit is $3,346,000 or 28 percent of sales. All other costs must be recovered from gross profit, and any income earned is the balance remaining after these costs. A company must produce a sufficient gross profit to be profitable. Also, gross profit must be sufficiently large to finance essential future-directed discretionary expenditures like research and development, marketing, and advertising. Gross profits vary across industries depending on factors like competition, capital investment, and the level of costs that must be recovered from gross profit.

Analyzing Changes in Gross Profit

Our analysis of gross profit directs special attention to the factors explaining variations in sales and cost of sales. Analyzing changes in gross profit is usually performed internally because it often requires access to nonpublic data, including number of units sold, unit selling prices, and unit costs. Unless a company sells a single product, this analysis benefits from data by product line. For internal analysis (and for external analysis when data permit), evaluating changes in gross profit is part of a useful analysis.

Case 7.1   This case show us an analysis of changes in gross profit for Pennsylvania Printers, Inc. (PPI). Selected financial data of PPI for the most recent two years are reproduced below:

	Year Ended December 31		Year-to-Year Change	
Item	Year 1	Year 2	Increase	Decrease
1. Sales ($ millions)	$657.6	$687.5	$29.9	
2. Cost of sales ($ millions)	237.3	245.3	8.0	
3. Gross profit ($ millions)	$420.3	$442.2	$21.9	
4. Units sold (in millions)	215.6	231.5	15.9	
5. Sales price per unit (1 ÷ 4)	$ 3.05	$ 2.97		$0.08
6. Cost per unit (2 ÷ 4)	1.10	1.06		0.04

Drawing on these financial data, we prepare an analysis of changes in PPI's gross profit of $21,900,000 from Year 1 to Year 2. Our analysis focuses sequentially on changes in sales and then cost of sales. The following steps underlie our analysis, and the results are reported in Exhibit 7.5.

Step 1. We focus first on year-to-year change in volume assuming unit selling price remains unchanged from Year 1. The volume change (15.9) is then multiplied by the constant unit selling price ($3.05) yielding a positive change in sales ($48.5).

Step 2. We focus next on year-to-year change in selling price assuming volume is constant. This decrease in selling price (−$0.08) is then multiplied by the constant volume (215.6) yielding a decline in sales (−$17.2).

Step 3. We recognize that assumptions in steps 1 and 2—that volume is constant while unit price changes and vice versa—are simplifications to highlight causes for change. Our analysis must recognize these assumptions ignore *joint* changes in volume and unit price. Specifically, the positive volume change (15.9) along with the decrease in unit selling price (−$0.08) yields a net decline in sales (−$1.3).

Step 4. Steps 1 to 3 explain the $30 net increase in sales. Adding the effects on sales due to a (1) volume change (48.5), (2) price change (−17.2), and (3) combined volume and price change (−1.3), we obtain the components explaining the sales increase.

Our analysis of the increase in cost of sales ($8.3) follows the same four steps. Exhibit 7.5 reports results from analysis of both sales and cost of sales components of gross profit.

Exhibit 7.5   Analysis Statement of Changes in Gross Profit

PENNSYLVANIA PRINTERS, INC.
For Year 1 and Year 2 ($ millions)

Analysis of Variation in Sales

1. Change in volume of products sold:

Change in volume (15.9) × Year 1 unit selling price ($3.05). $48.5

2. Change in selling price:

Change in selling price (−$0.08) × Year 1 sales volume (215.6) . . . . −17.2

$31.3

3. Combined change in sales volume (15.9) and unit price (−$0.08) . . . . −1.3

Increase in net sales $30.0*

Analysis of Variation in Cost of Sales

1. Change in volume of products sold:

Change in volume (15.9) × Year 1 cost per unit ($1.10) $17.5

2. Change in cost per unit sold:

Change in cost per unit (−$0.04) × Year 1 sales volume (215.6) . . . . −8.6

$ 8.9

3. Combined change in volume (15.9) and cost per unit (−$0.04) . . . . −0.6

Increase in cost of sales . . . . $ 8.3*

Net variation in gross profit $21.7*

*Differences are due to rounding.

Interpreting Changes in Gross Profit

Analyzing changes in sales and cost of sales is useful in identifying major causes of changes in gross profit. The types of changes often consist of one or a combination of the following factors:

- Increase in sales volume.
- Decrease in sales volume.
- Increase in unit selling price.
- Decrease in unit selling price.
- Increase in cost per unit.
- Decrease in cost per unit.

The potential for a combined change in volume and unit selling price or a combined change in volume and unit cost poses no particular problem for our analysis.

Interpreting the results of our analysis of changes in gross profit requires identifying the major factors responsible for these changes. It also requires assessing the reasons underlying changes in the factors responsible for gross profit changes. We often extend our analysis to focus on strategic business activities to remedy or improve (through volume, price, or cost) gross profit. If we determine the reason for a decrease in gross profit is a decline in unit selling prices and this reflects overcapacity in the industry with necessary price cutting, then our analysis of the company is pessimistic given management's lack of strategic actions when confronting this condition. However, if the reason for a decrease in gross profit is an increase in unit costs, then our analysis is more optimistic yielding a wider range of potential strategic activities for management.

When interpreting cost of sales and gross profit, especially for comparative analysis, we must direct attention to potential distortions arising from accounting methods. While this is applicable to all cost analysis, it is especially important with inventories and depreciation accounting. These two items merit special attention because they represent costs that are usually substantial in amounts and are subject to alternative accounting methods that can substantially affect their measurement.

ANALYZING COMPANY EXPENSES

Most expenses have an identifiable and measurable relation to revenues. This is because revenues are the primary measure of a company's operating activity. Three useful tools for our analysis are based, in part, on the relation between revenues and expenses:

- *Common-size analysis.* Common-size income statements express expenses in terms of their percent relation with revenues. This relation between expenses and sales is then traced over several periods or compared with the experience of competitors. Our analysis of Campbell Soup Company (see the Comprehensive Case chapter) includes common-size income statements spanning several years.

- *Index number analysis.* Index number analysis of income statements expresses income and its components in an index number related to a base period. This analysis highlights relative changes in these items across time allowing us to trace and assess their significance. Changes in expenses are readily compared with changes in both revenues and related expenses. Using index number analysis *with* common-size balance sheets, we can relate percent changes in expenses to changes in assets and liabilities. For example, a change in revenues or revenue-related expenses might explain a change in inventories or accounts receivable. Index number analysis is illustrated in our analysis of Campbell Soup in the Comprehensive Case.

- *Operating ratio analysis.* The operating ratio measures the relation between operating expenses (or its components) and revenues. It equals cost of goods sold plus other operating expenses divided by net revenues. Interest and taxes are normally excluded from this measure due to its focus on operating efficiency (expense control) and not financing and tax management. It is useful for analysis of expenses within or across companies, and can be viewed as an intermediate step in our common-size analysis of income. Properly interpreting this measure requires analysis of the reasons for variations in its components, including gross margin, selling, marketing, general, and administrative expenses.

This section applies these analytical tools in an analysis of a company's expenses.

Selling Expenses

Our analysis of selling expenses focuses on three primary areas:

- Evaluating the relation between revenues and key expenses.
- Assessing bad debts expense.
- Evaluating the trend and productivity of future-directed marketing expenses.

Relation of Selling Expenses to Revenues

The importance of the relation between selling expenses and revenues varies across industries and companies. In certain companies, selling expenses are primarily commissions and are highly variable, while in others they are largely fixed. Our analysis must attempt to distinguish between these variable and fixed components. These components are then usefully analyzed relative to revenues. The more detailed the components, the more meaningful the analysis. A component analysis of selling expenses for Sporting Goods, Inc., is reported in Exhibit 7.6. Our analysis of this exhibit reveals that selling expenses are rising faster than revenues from Year 1 to Year 4. Specifically, selling expenses in Year 4 comprised 5.6 percent more of revenues than in Year 1 ($360/$1,269 versus $180/$791). This is driven by increases, as a percent of revenue, of 1.0 percent in sales staff salaries, 3.6 percent in advertising, and 2.2 percent in branch expenses. Special attention should be directed at the 3.6 percent increase in advertising to determine its cause—for example, is it due to promotion of new products or development of new branches benefiting future sales? The 1.2 percent decline in delivery expense is partially offset with a 0.7 percent increase in freight costs.

When selling expenses as a percent of revenues show an increase, we should focus attention on the increase in selling expense generating the associated increase in revenues. Beyond a certain level of selling expenses

Exhibit 7.6   Component Analysis of Selling Expenses

SPORTING GOODS, INC.
Comparative Statement of Selling Expenses
($ thousands)

	Year 4		Year 3		Year 2		Year 1	
Sales	$1,269		$935		$833		$791	
Sales trend percent								
(Year 1 = 100%)		160.0%		118.0%		105.0%		100.0%
Selling expenses:[†]								
Advertising	$ 84	6.6%	$ 34	3.6%	$ 28	3.4%	$ 24	3.0%
Branch expenses*	80	6.3	41	4.4	38	4.6	32	4.1
Delivery expense								
(own trucks)	20	1.6	15	1.6	19	2.3	22	2.8
Freight-out	21	1.7	9	1.0	11	1.3	8	1.0
Sales staff salaries	111	8.7	76	8.1	68	8.1	61	7.7
Sales staff								
travel expense	35	2.8	20	2.1	18	2.2	26	3.3
Miscellaneous								
selling expenses	9	0.7	9	1.0	8	0.9	7	0.9
Total selling expense	$ 360	28.4%	$204	21.8%	$190	22.8%	$180	22.8%

*Includes rent, regional advertising, and promotion.
[†]Selling expenses are reported in both dollars and as percent of that year's sales amount.

there are lower marginal increases in revenues. This can be due to market saturation, brand loyalty, or increased expense in new territories. It is important for us to distinguish between the percent of selling expenses to revenues for new versus continuing customers. This has implications on our forecasts of profitability. If a company must substantially increase selling expenses to increase sales, its profitability is limited or can decline.

Bad Debts Expense

Bad debts expense is usually regarded as marketing expenses. Since the level of bad debts expense is related to the level of "allowance for doubtful accounts," it is usefully analyzed by examining the relation between the allowance and (gross) accounts receivable. We illustrate this analysis with interim data from Toyland, Inc. ($ thousand):

Item	*Year 3—Quarterly*			
	1st Quarter	**2nd Quarter**	**3rd Quarter**	**4th Quarter**
Allowance for doubtful accounts	$ 13,500	$ 12,900	$ 10,600	$ 15,800
Gross receivables	$343,319	$223,585	$179,791	$305,700
Allowance as percent of gross receivables	3.93%	5.77%	5.90%	5.17%

Item	*Year 2—Quarterly*			
	1st Quarter	**2nd Quarter**	**3rd Quarter**	**4th Quarter**
Allowance for doubtful accounts	$ 16,600	$ 15,000	$ 12,200	$ 18,500
Gross receivables	$331,295	$215,660	$172,427	$285,600
Allowance as percent of gross receivables	5.01%	6.96%	7.07%	6.48%

Notice the significant decline in Toyland's Year 3 allowance for doubtful accounts in relation to gross receivables as compared with Year 2. Potential reasons include improved collectibility of receivables or inadequate allowances resulting in understated bad debts expense. Further analysis is necessary to identify the reasons.

Future-Directed Marketing Expenses

Certain sales promotion expenses, particularly advertising, yield current *and* future benefits. Measuring future benefits from these expenses is extremely difficult. Yet it is reasonable for us to assume a relation between current expenditures for advertising and promotion and current *and* future revenues. Expenditures for these future-directed marketing activities are largely discretionary, and our analysis must consider year-to-year trends in these expenditures. Beyond the ability of these expenditures to influence future sales, they provide insights into management's tendency to "manage" reported earnings. We consider the effect of these and other discretionary expenses on earnings quality in the next chapter.

Depreciation Expense

Depreciation expense is often substantial in amount, especially for manufacturing and many service companies. Depreciation is usually considered a fixed cost in that it is often computed based on elapsed time. If its computation uses operating activity, it is a variable cost. In contrast to most expenses, the relation of depreciation to income is not usually meaningful due to its fixed nature. The relation of depreciation to gross plant and equipment is often more meaningful. A measure of this relation is the ratio of depreciation to depreciable assets:

$$\frac{\text{Depreciation expense}}{\text{Depreciable assets}}$$

The purpose of this ratio is to help us detect changes in the composite rate of depreciation. This is useful in evaluating depreciation levels and in detecting any adjustments (smoothing) to income. It is often useful to compute this ratio by asset categories. Analyzing the age of assets is also important.

Maintenance and Repairs Expenses

Maintenance and repairs expenses vary with investment in plant and equipment and with the level of productive activity. They affect cost of goods sold and other expenses. Maintenance and repairs comprise both variable *and* fixed expenses and therefore do not vary directly with sales. Accordingly, the relation of sales to maintenance and repairs expenses, both across companies and time, must be interpreted with care. To the extent our analysis can distinguish between variable and fixed portions of these expenses, we can better interpret their relation to sales. We also must remember that maintenance and repairs are largely discretionary expenses. Many of these expenses can be timed to not detract from one period's income or to preserve liquid resources. For example, companies can postpone or limit much preventive maintenance and many repairs; there are, of course, certain expenses that cannot be postponed without losses in productivity. Management's decisions in this regard bear on earnings quality. We should also consider a company's maintenance and repairs expenses when evaluating depreciation expense. We estimate assets' useful lives using many assumptions including their upkeep and maintenance. If maintenance and repairs are cut back, assets' useful lives likely decline. We may need to adjust upward the depreciation expense to counter the overstatement in income.

Amortization of Special Costs

Certain companies and industries have special costs related to items like tools, dies, jigs, patterns, and molds. The auto industry has considerable special costs related to frequent style and design changes. How a company amortizes these costs affects reported income and is important to our profitability analysis, including comparative analysis. Measures used to analyze changes in the deferral and amortization policies of these costs focus on the relation of the costs to revenues or asset categories. For example, the annual *expenditure* for special costs can be related to and expressed as a percent of (1) revenues and (2) net property and equipment. Similarly, the annual *amortization* of special costs can be related to (1) revenues, (2) unamortized special costs, and (3) net property and equipment. Comparison of annual trends in these relations can aid our analysis of consistency in reporting of income. Comparisons can be extended to evaluation of the income of two or more companies in an industry.

General and Administrative Expenses

Most general and administrative expenses are fixed. This is largely because these expenses include items like salaries and rent. There is a tendency for increases in these expenses, especially in prosperous times. When analyzing these expenses, our analysis should direct attention at both the trend in these expenses and the percent of revenues they consume.

Financing and Other Expenses

This section describes our analysis of financing expenses and "other" expenses.

Financing Expenses

Financing expenses are largely fixed (an exception is interest on short-term debt). Experience shows most creditor financing is eventually refinanced and not removed unless replaced with equity financing. Interest expense often includes amortization of any premium or discount on the debt along with any issue expenses. A useful tool in our analysis of a company's cost of borrowed money and credit standing is its **average effective interest rate** and is computed as:

$$\frac{\text{Total interest incurred}}{\text{Average interest-bearing indebtedness}}$$

As an example, we compute Quaker Oats' average effective interest rate ($ millions):

$$\frac{(\$43.3 + \$60.5)^{(a)}}{(\$814.7 + \$1,115.8)^{(b)} \div 2} = 10.75\%$$

[a]Total interest costs (before deduction for interest capitalized).

[b]

	Year 10: $	Year 11: $
Short-term debt	343.2	81
Current portion of long-term debt	32.3	33
Long-term debt	740.3	701
Total liabilities subject to interest	$1,115.8	$815

The average effective interest rate is usefully compared across years or companies. Quaker Oats includes a good discussion of debt in the Liquidity and Capital Resources section of its MD&A and in its disclosure on weighted-average interest rates of debt. We can also measure a company's sensitivity of interest rate changes by determining the portion of debt tied to market rates like the prime rate. In periods of rising interest rates, a company with debt tied to market rates is exposed to increased risk through higher interest expenses. Conversely, declining interest rates yield increased returns for these companies.

"Other" Expenses and Revenues

"Other" expenses and revenues are often of limited value in assessing company profitability. They are usually small in relation to a company's total expenses and are nondescript in nature. Yet they sometimes obscure component expenses that are useful in assessing profitability but cannot be extracted from the total. For example, nonrecurring components are sometimes included and are often useful in our analysis. It is useful for us to analyze "other revenues" since they can include income from investments in new ventures and information not available elsewhere. These investments can have future implications, favorable or unfavorable, far exceeding their current revenue or expense. We must be alert to management's tendency to offset other expenses against other revenues. The problem is one of obscuring important information as we attempt to gather data on items comprising these expenses and revenues.

Income Tax Expenses

Income taxes essentially reflect a distribution of profits between a company and governmental agencies. They usually comprise a substantial portion of a company's income before taxes. For this reason our analysis must pay special attention to income taxes.

Volume of Sales Activity by Type of Organization

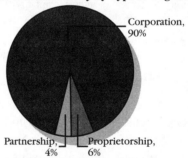

Source: Statistical Abstract of the U.S.

Since corporations conduct nearly 10 times more sales activity than other forms of businesses combined (see pie chart), we focus primarily on *corporate* income taxes in this section.

Measuring Effective Tax Rate

Except for a graduated rate on lower levels of income, corporate income is taxed at a uniform rate determined by tax law (35 percent). Differences in timing of recognition for revenues or expenses between taxable income and accrual income should not influence the effective tax rate. This is because interperiod income tax allocation aims to match tax expense with accrual income regardless of when taxes are paid.

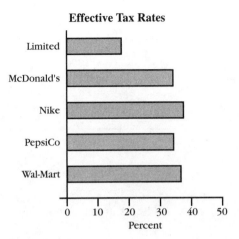

Effective Tax Rates

Source: Annual reports.

The relation between the income tax accrual and the pre-tax income, referred to as the **effective tax rate** or *tax ratio,* is also influenced by *permanent* tax differences. Examples include differences due to state and local taxes, foreign tax rate differentials, various tax credits, untaxed income, and nondeductible expenses. The effective tax rate is computed as:

$$\frac{\text{Income tax expense}}{\text{Income before income taxes}}$$

For Quaker Oats the effective tax rate is computed as:

$$\frac{\$175.7^{(a)}}{\$411.5^{(b)}} = 42.7\%$$

[a] Provision for income taxes.
[b] Income from continuing operations before income taxes.

The 42.7 percent effective tax rate corresponds to the rate computed by the company (see its annual report). Notice the effective tax rate uses income from continuing operations rather than net income. If we want to compute the effective tax rate incurred by the company on *all* items of income during a period, including discontinued operations and extraordinary items, then a different computation is required. We use Quaker Oats to illustrate this:

Income (loss)	Before Tax	Related Tax	After Tax
Income from continuing operations before income taxes and other items	$411.5	$175.7	$235.8
Loss from discontinued operations	(50)	(20)[*]	(30)
Net income	$361.5[*]	$155.7[*]	$205.8

*Derived amount.

The effective tax rate using *all* items in net income is:

$$\frac{\$155.7}{\$361.5} = 43.1\%$$

We might also notice in our analysis of Quaker Oats' income that preferred dividends are reported net of tax. This is an unusual case of preferred dividends yielding a tax benefit of undisclosed amount. We must consider this type of tax effect bypassing net income (similar to tax effects relating to stock options and reported in equity) when reconciling all tax-related accounts to understand a company's tax position and amounts paid. We discuss this later in the chapter.

In evaluating income level, trend, and forecasts, we must identify the reasons why an effective tax rate deviates from the normal or expected rate. Income taxes are of such magnitude that small changes in the effective tax rate can yield major changes in income. Knowledge of the reasons for deviations and changes in the effective tax rate of a company is important to our profitability analysis and income forecasting. Practice requires several disclosures of current and deferred income taxes. Our analysis of these and other aspects of tax disclosures is important and is described next.

Analyzing Income Tax Disclosures

Our analysis of income tax disclosures can be undertaken with specific or general objectives. The more general objectives of our analysis include:

- Assess tax implications on income, assets, liabilities, and cash sources and uses.
- Evaluate tax effects for future income and cash flows.
- Appraise the effectiveness of tax management.

- Identify unusual gains or losses revealed in tax disclosures.
- Signal areas of concern requiring further analysis or management inquiry.
- Analyze the adequacy of tax disclosures.

The following *analytical strategy* is useful in analyzing income tax disclosures.

Step 1   Our first step is to establish a T-account for each tax-related account in the balance sheet and income statement. A current tax liability and/or a current tax receivable (for a refund) should be identifiable. There are also one or two deferred tax accounts (one current and one noncurrent) in the balance sheet. We must take care to identify income taxes (current and possibly deferred) relating to the separate income statement sections: (1) continuing operations, (2) discontinued operations, (3) extraordinary items, and (4) cumulative effect of changes in accounting principles. Their separate income tax effects are sometimes identified outside the income statement—in parenthetical and financial statement notes, in schedules like those reconciling owner's equity, and in sections containing management discussion.

Step 2   Reconstruct the period's summary entry for recording tax expense. It is often helpful to split this into two or more entries: at least one for current tax expense and one for deferred tax expense.

Step 3   Once the opening and closing balances of all tax-related balance sheet T-accounts are entered, post the tax expense entries and income statement accounts to their relevant T-accounts. We should use all available information to reconstruct these accounts. Changes in deferred tax on the balance sheet should agree with the deferred tax expense reported in the income statement or in related footnotes. Information like noncash adjustments to income reported in the statement of cash flows is often useful. If our attempts at reconciliation are unsuccessful, we might look for either a deferred tax account combined with or reported under another caption in the balance sheet or an undisclosed entry for correcting errors or similar adjustment. We can always obtain the necessary balancing amount and enter it. We must realize our conclusions regarding balancing (plugged) amounts in a reconciliation are subject to the assumptions implicit in this balancing. For deferred tax accounts not fully reconciled, we transfer the amounts needed to reconcile them to Current Taxes Payable or to Tax Refunds Receivable. The tax T-accounts are now fully reconstructed.

Step 4   Use taxes paid during the period as a "plug" to the current Taxes Payable account. A credit plug reflects a tax refund.

We must recognize the usefulness of our analysis depends on the quality of disclosures in financial statements. Poor disclosures require more analytical adjustments like combining accounts (e.g., current tax receivable and payable accounts). Our analysis must also be aware that acquisition or disposition of businesses can result in related additions or deductions to balance sheet tax accounts. For example, acquisition of a company can require accepting its tax liabilities.

Illustration of Income Tax Analysis   To illustrate income tax analysis we use Quaker Oats' annual report. Our *first step* is to establish T-accounts for each tax-related balance sheet account and for each income tax expense and tax effect account in Quaker's income statement. We identify income tax payable and deferred income taxes (noncurrent account) in the balance sheet. We also identify the provision for income taxes and accounts below this (reported net of tax) in the income statement (the tax effect of the loss from discontinued operations is ($20)). Quaker Oats' financial statements do not disclose the preferred dividends' tax effect. We therefore compute its tax effect as (where PD is preferred dividends before tax and the assumed marginal tax rate is 34 percent):

$$PD\,(1\,-\,34\%) = \$4.3 \text{ or } PD = \$6.5$$

Then, the preferred dividends' tax effect is simply:

$$\$6.5\,-\,\text{Tax effect} = \$4.3 \text{ or Tax effect} = \$2.2$$

Our *second step* is to enter opening and ending balances in T-accounts. Tax-related accounts in income statements do not have opening balances and their ending balances are closed via the income statement to retained earnings. Opening balances must sometimes be derived using changes reported in the statement of cash flows.

Income Tax Payable		
	36.3	Beg.
(b) 20.0	161.4	(a)
(d) 24.7	2.2	(c)
Assumed paid 110.1		
	45.1	End.

Deferred Income Tax		
	327.7	Beg.
	14.3	(a)
	24.7	(d)
	366.7	End.

Income Tax Expense	
(a) 175.7	

Tax Effect—Discontinued Operations	
	20.0 (b)

Tax Effect—Preferred Dividends	
(c) 2.2	

Our *third step* is to enter the tax-related activity during year into the T-accounts using all available information, especially the tax note. We achieve this by using analytical entries and posting to relevant T-accounts. The tax expense (including tax effects of items shown net of tax) can be combined, but it is often easier to enter them separately as shown here:

Income Tax Expense	175.7	
Income Tax Payable		161.4
Deferred Income Tax		14.3
Income Tax Payable	20.0	
Tax Effect—Discontinued Operation		20.0
Tax Effect—Preferred Dividends	2.2	
Income Tax Payable		2.2

Having entered all tax-related transactions in T-accounts, we then determine whether these entries explain the changes in all tax-related accounts except Tax Payable. For Quaker we find the change in Deferred Income Tax is not explained and requires a plugging entry as follows:

Income Tax Payable	24.7	
Deferred Income Tax (plug)		24.7

Our *fourth step* is to estimate taxes paid during the period and is only made after changes in the balances of all tax-related accounts, except Tax Payable (or Tax Receivable), are accounted for. Once done, as in our example here, we determine the taxes paid (or received) as a balancing figure (plug) in Tax Payable. For Quaker, the plug of $110.1 is on the debit side, indicating a tax payment. The tax paid (or received) should be reconciled (as feasible) to taxes paid as reported in the statement of cash flows. Quaker reports taxes paid of $88.7 million. This is considerably less than the $110.1 million from our analysis. A complete explanation of Quaker's tax policies requires management (or inside) information.

We also explain how a company's tax rate is different from the "legal" rate. In Quaker's case it reports pre-tax income from continuing operations of $411.5. This income yields $175.7 in tax expense, of which $161.4 are current federal income taxes. We explain this as follows:

Reconciliation to Legal Rate	Computation	$ Millions
Expected federal income tax at 34%	$411.5 × 0.34	$139.9
Add: State tax net of federal benefit	$411.5 × 0.041	16.9
		$156.8
Add permanent differences:		
Repatriation of foreign earnings	$4.3	
Non-U.S. tax rate differential	8.2	
Miscellaneous (rounded)	6.4	18.9
		$175.7
Less total deferred taxes		14.3
Total current federal, non-U.S., and state taxes		$161.4

Consideration of Pre-Tax Income

Our focus on net income and earnings per share requires an analysis of changes in the effective tax rate. Pre-tax income is also relevant for certain analyses. This is due to the importance attached to pre-tax operating results. Pre-tax operating results derive from management skills in operating the business as compared with performance due to variations in the effective tax rate. Management is likely to have less control over the company's tax performance relative to its operating activities.

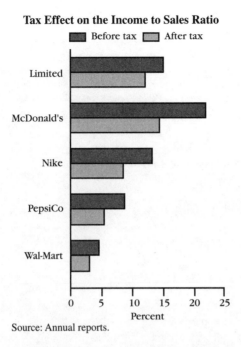

Tax Effect on the Income to Sales Ratio

Source: Annual reports.

Variation Analysis of Income and Its Components

In our analysis of year-to-year changes in income, it is useful to measure components contributing to increases and decreases in income. This analysis is referred to as **variation analysis.** A common method of variation analysis indicating the percent increase or decrease in income components uses the *statement of variations in income and income components.* Exhibit 7.7 presents this statement for Campbell Soup Company using its annual report in Supplement A.

BREAK-EVEN ANALYSIS

Break-even analysis focuses on the relation between a company's revenues and expenses. An important part of break-even analysis is distinguishing among two classes of expenses: variable and fixed. Variable expenses vary directly with revenues while fixed expenses remain essentially constant over a wide range of revenue levels.

Exhibit 7.7

CAMPBELL SOUP COMPANY Statement of Variations in Income and Income Components Three-Year Period Year 6–Year 8 (Average) compared to Three-Year Period Year 9–Year 11 (Average) (in millions)			
			Percent Change
Components Tending to Increase Net Income			
Increase in net sales:			
Net sales (Year 9–Year 11)	$6,027.3		
Net sales (Year 6–Year 8)	4,548.7	$1,478.6	32.5%
Deduct the increase in costs of goods sold:			
Cost of products sold (Year 9–Year 11)	$4,118.4		
Cost of products sold (Year 6–Year 8)	3,218.7	$ 899.7	28.0
Net increase in gross margin		$ 578.9	
Increase (decrease) in interest income:			
Interest income (Year 9–Year 11)	$ 27.3		
Interest income (Year 6–Year 8)	30.0	(2.7)	(9.0)
Total items tending to increase net income		$ 576.2	
Components Tending to Decrease Net Income			
Increase in marketing and sales expenses:			
Marketing and sales expenses (Year 9–Year 11)	$ 918.5		
Marketing and sales expenses (Year 6–Year 8)	634.6	$ 283.9	44.7
Increase in administrative expenses:			
Administrative expenses (Year 9–Year 11)	$ 283.2		
Administrative expenses (Year 6–Year 8)	214.1	$ 69.1	32.3
Increase in R&D expenses:			
R&D expenses (Year 9–Year 11)	$ 52.6		
R&D expenses (Year 6–Year 8)	44.6	$ 8.0	17.9
Increase in interest expenses:			
Interest expenses (Year 9–Year 11)	$ 107.3		
Interest expenses (Year 6–Year 8)	53.9	$ 53.4	99.1
Increase in other expenses:*			
Other expenses (Year 9–Year 11)	$ 32.2		
Other expenses (Year 6–Year 8)	5.0	$ 27.2	544.0
Increase in income tax expenses:			
Income tax (Year 9–Year 11)	$ 178.1		
Income tax (Year 6–Year 8)	160.5	$ 17.6	11.0
Total items tending to decrease net income		$ 459.2	
Change in net effect of equity in earnings of affiliates and minority interests (MI):			
Equity in earnings of affiliates and MI (Year 9–Year 11)	$ 2.7		
Equity in earnings of affiliates and MI (Year 6–Year 8)	3.6	(0.9)	(25.0)
Increase in net income:†			
Net income (Year 9–Year 11)	$ 367.0		
Net income (Year 6–Year 8)	250.9	$ 116.1	46.3

*Includes foreign exchange losses.
†Income before divestitures, restructuring, and unusual charges; and before cumulative effect of change in accounting for income taxes.

ANALYSIS VIEWPOINT

YOU ARE THE POLITICAL ACTIVIST

You are the campaign manager for a first-time candidate running for state representative. The incumbent's campaign is financed almost exclusively by a major forest products company in your district. The incumbent fought for and received state and local logging cost benefits for this company in the past two years. One of your goals is to repeal these benefits if elected. The incumbent counters that this company is the largest employer in the district and points to this company's income *after* these benefits, which is similar to its competition. You look at the financial statements and find gross margin is 40% of sales while the industry norm is 20%. Yet profit margin is at the industry norm of 10%—the difference between gross and profit margin is primarily due to executive compensation. Is this useful information?

Break-Even Analysis Case

Distinguishing between expenses according to their variable or fixed behavior is best understood with a case example. To focus on the information required and the analysis techniques involved, we consider the following scenario:

Case 7.2   A local electronics company placed an ad in the college newspaper announcing an opportunity for an individual to sell compact cassette players with special discount coupons at an upcoming analysts' convention on campus. This position requires that one purchase a $10 vendor's license from the convention organizing committee and to rent a $140 sales booth. The electronics company charges the salesperson $3 for each cassette player with the right to return any that are unsold. The company also specifies an $8 selling price per player. Each cassette player purchase is packaged with discount coupons from the company. You must decide whether to accept this job. You wonder how many cassette players you must sell to break even. We analyze this case scenario using break-even analysis.

Equation-Based Break-Even Analysis

An equation-based analysis of break-even begins with the income equation:

Sales = Variable expenses + Fixed expenses + Profit (or *minus* Loss)

Break-even analysis assumes a zero profit or loss—this reflects common usage of the term break-even. If profit or loss is zero, the income equation is simplified as:

Sales = Variable expenses + Fixed expenses

For the above case, sales can be expressed as $8 multiplied by the number of cassette players sold. Similarly, variable expenses equal $3 multiplied by cassette players sold, and fixed expenses equal the $10 license plus the $140 booth. Substituting these relations into the income equation yields:

$$\$8X = \$3X + \$150$$

where:

$$\text{Sales} = \$8 \text{ (unit selling price)} \times X$$
$$\text{Variable expenses} = \$3 \text{ (unit variable cost)} \times X$$
$$\text{Fixed expenses} = \$10 \text{ (license fee)} + \$150 \text{ (booth fee)}$$

Fixed expenses are incurred regardless of the number of cassette players sold. We can solve the equation for X as follows:

$$(\$8 - \$3)X = \$150$$
$$X = 30 \text{ units to break even}$$

Knowing the number of cassette players necessary to be sold just to break even is important for your decision to accept or reject this job opportunity. Once you have this information you can assess the likelihood of at least selling the break-even number of units. This focus on break-even *units* is primarily limited to *single product* companies.

Companies typically sell multiple products. This would be the case in the scenario above if you sold calculators and headphones along with cassette players. In this case the break-even *units* computation is not appropriate. Rather, we focus on break-even *dollar* sales. Applying the break-even dollar sales analysis to the scenario above using the income equation yields (where Y is the break-even dollar sales):

$$Y = \text{(Variable expense as percent of price)} \times Y + \text{Fixed expenses}$$
$$Y = 0.375Y + \$150$$
$$0.625Y = \$150$$
$$Y = \$240$$

This indicates one must sell $240 of cassette players to break even. The $240 is equivalent to the 30 break-even units calculated above (at $8 per player). The variable expense percent is the ratio of variable expenses ($3) to selling price ($8). This percent is interpreted as a dollar of sales generates $0.375 of variable expenses, or variable expenses comprise 37.5 percent of sales.

Graphic-Based Break-Even Analysis

We can also estimate break-even points using graphic-based analysis. Using information from our cassette player scenario we portray graphically break-even analysis in Exhibit 7.8. A graph drawn to scale yields a solution identical to equation-based analysis, although graphic-based analysis is usually less precise. An especially nice feature of graphic-based analysis is the portrayal of the break-even point *and* a wide range of profitable scenarios above this point and losses below it.

Contribution Margin Break-Even Analysis

Contribution margin analysis is another method to assess break-even points. This method can provide additional insights into the relation between sales, expenses, and profits. **Contribution margin** is what remains after deducting variable expenses from sales. This contribution

---

Exhibit 7.8   Graphic-Based Break-Even Analysis

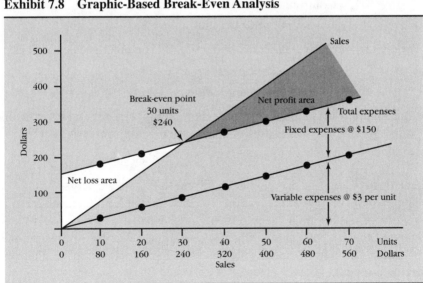

must cover fixed expenses before any profit is earned. Using the cassette player case, *contribution margin per unit* is computed as:

Selling price per cassette player	$8
Variable expenses per cassette player	3
Contribution margin per unit	$5

Since each unit (cassette player) sold contributes $5 to cover fixed expenses, the break-even point in units is:

$$\frac{\text{Fixed expenses}}{\text{Contribution margin per unit}} = \frac{\$150}{\$5} = 30 \text{ units}$$

This implies that after 30 units are sold, fixed expenses are covered and each additional unit sold yields a profit equal to the unit contribution margin, or $5.

Contribution margin analysis can also be performed using sales dollars to compute the break-even point. This analysis uses the contribution margin ratio rather than the contribution margin per unit. The **contribution margin ratio** is computed as:

$$\frac{\text{Contribution margin per unit}}{\text{Selling price per unit}} = \frac{\$5}{\$8} = 0.625$$

For our cassette player case, the dollar break-even point is calculated as:

$$\frac{\text{Fixed expenses}}{\text{Contribution margin ratio}} = \frac{\$150}{0.625} = \$240$$

Contribution margin analysis is an important tool in assessing break-even points. We discuss further uses of contribution margin analysis later in this section.

Further Considerations in Break-Even Analysis

The break-even methods described in this section lend themselves to a variety of assumptions, requirements, and what-if analysis. We reveal some of these advantages in Illustrations 7.5 and 7.6. These illustrations use information from our cassette player scenario (unless explicit changes are mentioned).

Illustration 7.5

Assume one requires a profit of $400 to pursue selling of cassette players. How many cassette players must you sell before you achieve this profitability level? We use the equation-based analysis to answer this question (S equals sales):

$$\text{Sales} = (\text{Variable expense percent})(\text{Sales}) + \text{Fixed expenses} + \text{Profit}$$
$$S = 0.375\,S + \$150 + \$400$$
$$0.625\,S = \$550$$
$$S = \$880$$
$$\$880 \div \$8 = 110 \text{ units}$$

Illustration 7.6

The analysts' convention committee offers to provide you with a free booth if you agree to imprint the analysts' organization seal on the cassette player. You discuss this with the electronics company and they agree subject to the stipulation of an increase in cost from $3 to $4 per unit. What is the break-even point if you accept the convention committee's offer? To answer this, remember that their offer would reduce fixed expenses by $140 but increase variable expenses by $1 per unit. We can compute the break-even point in units sold (X) as follows:

$$\text{Sales} = \text{Variable expenses} + \text{Fixed expenses}$$
$$\$8X = \$4X + \$10$$
$$\$4X = \$10$$
$$X = 2.5 \text{ (or rounded up to 3)}$$

This offer involves a much lower break-even point and hence reduces your risk. However, it also lowers the contribution margin, which reduces profits at higher sales levels. Before you make a decision it is useful for you to compute the level of unit sales where the initial offer of $3 per unit variable expenses and $150 fixed expenses equals the committee's offer involving $4 per unit variable expenses and $10 fixed expenses. This is calculated as follows, where X is the number of units sold:

$$\$4X + \$10 = \$3X + \$150$$
$$\$1X = \$140$$
$$X = 140 \text{ units}$$

This result implies that if you sell *more* than 140 cassette players, the committee's offer involving the $3 variable expense is more profitable.

Limitations in Break-Even Analysis

The usefulness of break-even analysis depends on overcoming certain limitations. This section discusses those limitations and the assumptions underlying break-even analysis.

Identifying Fixed, Variable, and Semivariable Expenses

Our illustrations of break-even analysis clearly identified fixed variable expenses. Yet many expenses are not easily separable into fixed and variable components. They either do not remain constant over major changes in sales volume or do not respond in exact proportion to changes in sales. Expenses for food supermarkets are a typical case. Many of their fixed expenses do not vary within a wide range of sales including rent, depreciation, certain maintenance, utilities, and supervisory labor. Yet they can sometimes change independent of sales; for example, management can increase the grocery manager's salary. In addition, variable expenses like merchandise, trading stamps, supplies, and manual labor vary directly with sales. Nevertheless, there are expenses comprised of both fixed and variable components. Examples of these **semivariable expenses** are repairs, materials, indirect labor, fuel, and payroll taxes. Even utilities and rent can include variable components tied to sales activity. Break-even analysis requires the variable component of these expenses be separated from the fixed component. This is often difficult for our analysis without availability of internal data.

Assumptions in Break-Even Analysis

Break-even analysis typically includes several simplifying assumptions. While assumptions do not negate its results, our break-even analysis must be aware of assumptions and their potential effects. Important assumptions in break-even analysis include:

Assumptions about Expenses and Revenues:
- Expenses are separable into fixed and variable components.
- Variable expenses vary directly with sales volume.
- Fixed expenses are constant over the relevant range of analysis.
- Unit selling prices are constant over the relevant range of analysis.

Assumptions about Operating and Environmental Factors:

- Sales mix is unchanged over the analysis range.
- Operating efficiency remains constant.
- Prices of cost factors are constant.
- Volume is the only factor affecting expenses.
- Beginning and ending inventory levels remain essentially unchanged.
- General price levels are essentially constant.

This list of assumptions highlights the importance of *sensitivity tests* for break-even analysis. These tests examine how sensitive our conclusions are to changes in assumptions. For example, assuming the selling price does not change with volume is contrary to economic theory and experience—indeed, our sales line should be curved rather than straight. The degree of error in our analysis depends on the actual deviation of the sales line from our assumed straight line. We must also remember that not all assumptions are equally important or influential. We assume volume is the major factor affecting expenses, yet we know many factors like strikes, politics, legislation, and competition are influential. Our analysis must keep these assumptions in mind and be aware of factors or conclusions requiring adjustments.

Uses and Implications of Break-Even Analysis

Break-even analysis is a valuable analytical tool if we recognize its limitations and properly interpret its results. Its use extends beyond computing a break-even (zero profit) point. Break-even analysis is useful in examining revenue, expense, and profit projections under a wide range of future conditions (assumptions). Moreover, both internal (managerial) and external applications of break-even analysis are many. *For management,* it is useful in price determination, expense control, and profitability forecasts. It provides a basis for pricing decisions under differing levels of activity along with standard cost systems. It is a useful tool for expense control in conjunction with flexible budgets. It is also useful in providing break-even charts to measure the impact of specific managerial decisions like plant expansion and new product introduction, or even the impact of external influences on company profitability for various activity levels. *For external analysis,* the use of break-even analysis for profitability projections is useful in estimating the impact on profitability of various economic conditions and managerial strategies.

Application of Break-Even Analysis

This section shows how a reliably constructed break-even analysis is useful in forecasting profits, assessing operating risk, and evaluating profitability levels. We illustrate this through a break-even analysis of Cola-Company, a multiproduct business. We begin with a break-even chart for Cola-Company, shown in Exhibit 7.9 (numbers in thousands). This break-even chart is subject to the assumptions we described above including our ability to identify fixed and variable expense components. *At the break-even point,* Cola-Company's income statement appears as follows:

Sales		$1,387,000
Expenses:		
Variable	$887,000	
Fixed	500,000	1,387,000
Net income		$ –0–

The relevant break-even points are sales of $1,387,000; sales units of 1,156,000; and average selling price per unit of $1.20. The variable expense percent is $887/$1,387, or 64 percent. This implies that, on average, 64 cents of every sales dollar goes to cover variable expenses. The contribution margin ratio is 36 percent (100 minus the variable expense percent of 64). This indicates that each dollar of sales generates 36 cents toward covering fixed expenses and the earning of profit beyond break-even. Cola-Company's contribution margin earned on sales of $1,387,000 is exactly sufficient to cover $500,000 in fixed expenses. The lower are fixed costs, the less sales are necessary to cover them and the lower is the break-even point. If a business has only variable expenses (all costs vary directly with sales), there is no break-even point—this type of company makes a profit beginning with its first sale.

Cola-Company's break-even chart reflects revenues and expenses under its current product mix. Since each product has different revenue and expense patterns and profit margins, changes in product mix affect the break-even point and the relation between revenues, expenses, and profits. While Exhibit 7.9 shows the number of sales units on the horizontal axis,

Exhibit 7.9   Cola-Company's Break-Even Chart

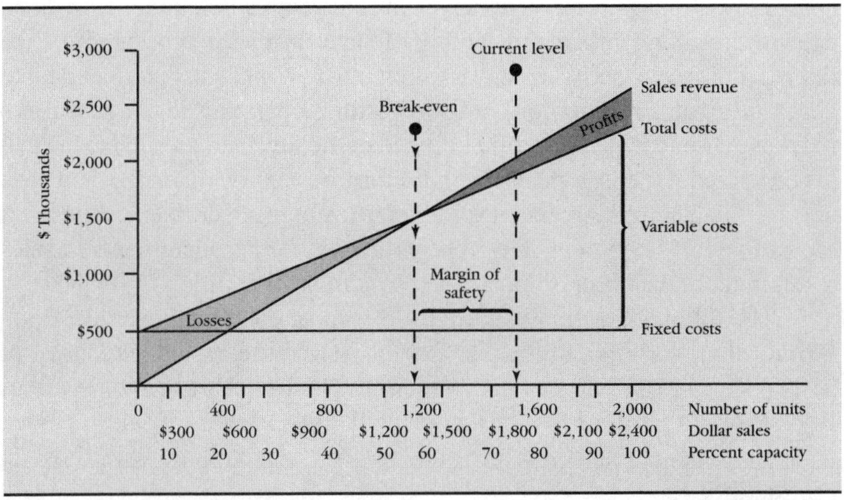

this number and the average selling price per unit are limited to the current product mix. The relevance of break-even analysis is confined to cases where the product mix is fairly stable, at least in the short term. It is also confined to cases where there are not dramatic and frequent fluctuations in selling prices or in costs of production like raw materials.

Exhibit 7.9 assumes fixed expenses of $500,000 will prevail up to a sales level of $2,400,000 (or 2,000 units). This is Cola-Company's point of nearly 100 percent capacity. The break-even point is near 60 percent of capacity, while current sales are near 75 percent of capacity. This implies that at 100 percent capacity, fixed expenses might require an upward revision. If Cola-Company is reluctant to expand capacity, and increase fixed expenses and its break-even point (assuming the variable expense rate does not change), it can consider alternatives including: (1) sacrificing sales growth, (2) increasing variable expenses (adding shift work), or (3) subcontracting work to outsiders and giving up some profit margin. The break-even chart also portrays Cola-Company's current position relative to its break-even. Its current sales of $1,800,000 are about $413,000 above break-even. This is referred to as the **safety margin.** Safety margin is the company's gap or buffer from the break-even point. We can use safety margin to indicate the point on the chart where a company earns a desired return on investment. It can also be used to indicate the point where common dividends are in jeopardy or where current earnings no longer cover preferred dividends.

Operating Leverage and Break-Even Analysis

Operating leverage refers to changes in sales with a certain level of fixed expenses resulting in larger than proportionate changes in profitability. Like financial leverage (see Chapter 5), which utilizes fixed interest financing to generate greater returns for equity investors, operating leverage utilizes fixed expenses for greater profitability. Specifically, increases in profits that exceed fixed expenses magnify the return on equity financing and vice versa. Until a company generates sales sufficient to cover fixed expenses, it incurs losses. Having covered fixed expenses, further increments in sales result in more than proportionate increases in profitability.

The following case illustrates the effects of operating leverage. Book World, Inc., has the following expense structure: fixed expenses of $100,000; and variable expense percent of 60. The chart below describes Book World's profit or loss at successively higher levels of sales activity. It also compares relative percent changes in sales volume with those in profitability.

| | | | | | Percent Increase over Prior Period | |
Year	Sales	Variable Expenses	Fixed Expenses	Profit (Loss)	Sales	Profit
1	$100,000	$ 60,000	$100,000	$(60,000)	—	—
2	200,000	120,000	100,000	(20,000)	100%	—
3	250,000	150,000	100,000	—	25	—
4	300,000	180,000	100,000	20,000	20	Infinite
5	360,000	216,000	100,000	44,000	20	120%
6	432,000	259,200	100,000	72,800	20	65

The effects of operating leverage are evident with Book World. Relative to the break-even period (Year 3), the 20 percent sales increase for Year 4 results in an infinite increase in profits because of zero profits for the prior year. Year 5's 20 percent increase in sales results in a 120 percent profit increase relative to Year 4, and Year 6's 20 percent sales increase results in a 65 percent profit increase relative to Year 5. Notice the effects of operating leverage diminish as sales progressively increase above the break-even level because the base on which increases in profits are compared gets progressively larger. Operating leverage also has downside risk. Notice that a drop in sales from $200,000 to $100,000 (Year 2 to Year 1), representing a 50 percent decrease, results in a tripling of the loss.

ANALYSIS   RESEARCH   INSIGHT   7.2

OPERATING LEVERAGE AND EQUITY RISK

Analysis research has examined the relation between accounting data and the risk associated with investing in a company's equity securities. In economic terms, *total risk* is related to the riskiness of the company's capital structure *(financial risk)* and its asset structure (operating risk). *Operating risk* is comprised of variability in sales and operating leverage.

Evidence indicates the existence of a positive association between operating leverage and total risk. There is also evidence of a negative relation between companies' financial leverage and operating leverage, especially for companies with a high degree of total risk. This implies that companies are strategically attempting to trade off financial risk and operating risk in their business activities.

Our analysis must be aware that companies performing near their break-even point have relatively larger percent changes in both profits and losses due to changes in sales. Consequently, *volatility in sales* increases a company's risk from operating leverage. On the upside, volatility is desirable. But on the downside, it can yield results much worse than those suggested by changes in sales alone. Our analysis must also be aware of operating potential, sometimes erroneously referred to as *leverage*. **Operating potential** refers to a case of high sales and very low profit margins. The potential rests with improvement in profit margins. Relatively minor changes in profit margins applied to a high sales level can produce dramatic changes in profits, both good and bad. We can make a similar analogy to sales volume per share and its link to earnings per share. That is, changes in profitability due to operating leverage or potential yield proportionately larger earnings per share changes.

Relevance of the Variable Expense Percent

Volatility of profits also depends on the variable expense percent. A company with a low variable expense percent achieves higher profits for a given increase in sales once break-even operations are reached relative to a company with a high variable expense percent. We show this in Illustration 7.7.

Illustration 7.7 shows that the break-even point is *not* the only criterion of risk assessment. Rather, our analysis must also pay attention to the variable expense percent.

Illustration 7.7

Company A has fixed expenses of $700,000 and variable expenses of 30 percent of sales. Company B has fixed expenses of $300,000 and variable expenses of 70 percent of sales. Both companies are operating at sales of $1,000,000 and are at break-even. Notice that a $100,000 increase in sales of both companies yields a profit of $70,000 for Company A but only $30,000 for Company B. Company A has greater operating leverage and can, as a result, incur greater risks in pursuing an extra $100,000 in sales than can Company B.

Relevance of the Fixed Expense Level

The higher are fixed costs, the higher is a company's break-even point when assuming no change in the variable expense percent. Provided other factors are constant, percent changes in fixed expenses yield equal percent changes in the break-even point. For example, Storytime, Inc.'s break-even income statement is:

Sales		$100,000
Variable expenses	$60,000	
Fixed expenses	40,000	100,000
Net income		$ –0–

If fixed expenses for Storytime increase by 20 percent for a total of $48,000, the break-even sales level must also increase by 20 percent to cover increases in both fixed and variable expenses as shown below:

Sales (increase of 20%)		$120,000
Variable expenses (60% of sales)	$72,000	
Fixed expenses ((40,000 × 120%)	48,000	120,000
Net income		$ –0–

An increase in the break-even point usually increases *operating risk.* This means that a company depends on higher sales to break even. Alternatively viewed, it means that a company is more vulnerable to economic downturns relative to having a lower break-even point. Airline companies often have high operating risk. Their large aircraft investment yields high break-even points. While large aircraft lower the variable expense per passenger, they depend on projected increases in passengers. When this fails to happen, airlines' profit margins deteriorate rapidly and losses are likely. There are other repercussions to high levels of fixed expenses. A higher break-even point often yields less freedom to accommodate other needs like labor demands. Higher fixed expenses make strikes more expensive and increase pressures to submit to higher wage demands. Increases in fixed expenses are common in areas of technological innovation to save variable costs like labor and to improve efficiency. These strategic actions can be very profitable in periods of at least reasonably good demand. Yet when demand declines, the higher fixed expenses are burdensome due to operating leverage that yields declining profits or increasing losses. High fixed expenses reduce a company's ability to maintain profits when sales decline.

We must recognize that investments in fixed assets, especially those requiring skilled operators, can yield increases in fixed expenses far exceeding the costs of maintaining and replacing these assets. The skills required to operate these assets can require high-cost personnel that a company is often reluctant to dismiss when operations decline for fear of not being able to replace them when operations improve. This situation transforms variable expenses into de facto fixed expenses.

While fixed expenses are often incurred to increase capacity or to decrease variable expenses, it is often more advisable to cut fixed expenses to reduce risks associated with a high break-even point. A company can reduce, for example, fixed expenses by switching from a salaried sales force to one paid by sales commissions. It can also avoid fixed expenses by extending work shifts, buying ready-made parts, subcontracting work, or discontinuing less profitable product lines. When we analyze past and potential profitability of a company, our analysis must remember the effects of fixed expenses on operating results. In forecasting profitability, our analysis must also remember that assuming constant fixed expenses is valid to the limits of practical capacity within a range of product mixes. Beyond this practical capacity, profitability forecasts must take into consideration increases in both fixed expenses and financing requirements to fund the expansion.

Importance of Contribution Margin

Our analysis must be alert to the absolute size of a company's contribution margin since operating leverage depends on it. We must also be aware of factors influencing contribution margin: changes in variable expenses and selling prices. While our discussion has focused on the individual factors affecting expenses, revenues, and profitability, changes often result from a combination of factors. Projected increases in sales will increase profits if fixed and variable expenses are controlled and kept within projected limits. Break-even analysis assumes efficiency remains constant. Experience indicates cost controls are more lax in prosperous times than in times of distress. Our analysis cannot blindly assume constant efficiency any more than we can assume constant product mix. Both are important variables demanding our attention. Questions of why a company achieved lower profits on higher sales are often explained, at least in part, by changes in product mix.

Break-even analysis, in spite of limitations, is an important analysis tool. Its value depends on our ability to separate expenses into fixed and variable components and use information available to estimate the necessary factors for analysis. Disclosure of cost components like materials, labor, and various overhead categories is especially helpful. The more detailed the expense breakdowns and other information, the more reliable is our break-even analysis.

GUIDANCE ANSWERS TO ANALYSIS VIEWPOINTS

YOU ARE THE SECURITIES LISTING DIRECTOR

Differences in users' information requests stem from their expertise and planned applications with financial data. Analysts' compensation depends on their ability to accurately assess and predict future risk and return characteristics of securities. Information that aids them in this task is welcome. Analysts typically possess the necessary expertise and training to effectively use this information. Unions, activists, and less sophisticated investors often do not possess the expertise, time, or motivation to seriously analyze financial statements. These users would prefer one number that captures a company's current financial position and future performance potential. Balancing these information needs (or analysis limitations) is delicate and demands consideration of both economic, political, *and social* factors. Social factors include public "access" to markets, fairness across users, costs to society, and other resource allocation implications. Establishing information listing requirements demands a broad perspective on fairness and is not unlike environmental or tax law.

YOU ARE THE BANKER

Additional segment information can cause you to reassess risk and return characteristics. The fact that a company's income is derived from 10 different segments generally lowers its riskiness. This is because a downturn in one segment has less of an impact on overall company profitability. In contrast, an economic downturn in the segment of the single industry company can have severe negative consequences. A comparative analysis of these two companies including segment information would favor the multisegment company. The segment information is especially important in this situation given the *marginal* status of both companies and the unlikelihood of accepting additional risk.

YOU ARE THE POLITICAL ACTIVIST

This information is extremely valuable to your candidate. While income for this company is similar to the industry norm, its executive compensation is substantially *higher* than the norm. Logging benefits appear to have substantially lowered this company's cost of sales, as indicated by its high gross margin, but excess profits are being paid to top executives of the company at a rate far exceeding the norm. This information is not only useful in your candidate's campaign, but hints at less than ethical practices.

Earnings-Based Analysis and Valuation

A LOOK BACK

The preceding two chapters dealt with analysis of company returns, both profitability and return on invested capital. Emphasis was on rate of return measures, disaggregation of returns, accounting analysis of earnings components, and break-even analysis. These return-based chapters complement earlier chapters that focused on risk, including liquidity and solvency.

A LOOK AT THIS CHAPTER

This chapter concludes returns analysis by emphasizing earnings-based analysis and valuation. Our earnings-based analysis focuses on assessing earnings quality, earnings persistence, and earning power. Attention is directed at techniques to aid us in measuring and applying these analysis concepts. Our discussion of earnings-based valuation focuses on issues in estimating company values and forecasting earnings.

A LOOK AHEAD

The Comprehensive Case applies many of the financial statement analysis tools and insights described in the book. These are illustrated using financial information from Campbell Soup Company. Explanation and interpretation accompany all analyses.

THIS CHAPTER WILL:

- Describe earnings quality, its measurement, and its importance to the analysis of company performance.
- Analyze earnings persistence, its determinants, and its relevance for earnings forecasting.
- Explain recasting and adjusting of earnings and earnings components for analysis.
- Describe earnings-based valuation and its relevance for financial analysis.
- Analyze earning power and its usefulness for forecasting and valuation.
- Explain earnings forecasting, its mechanics, and its effectiveness in assessing company performance.
- Analyze interim reports and consider their value in monitoring and revising earnings estimates.

PREVIEW OF CHAPTER 8

Earnings-based financial statement analysis is the focus of this chapter. The two previous chapters examine return and profitability analyses of financial statements. This chapter extends these analyses to consider earnings quality, persistence, valuation, and forecasting. *Earnings quality* refers to the relevance of earnings in measuring company performance. Its determinants include a company's business environment and its selection and application of accounting principles. *Earnings persistence* is broadly defined and includes the stability, predictability, variability, and trend in earnings. We also consider earnings management as a determinant of persistence. Our *valuation* analysis emphasizes earnings and other accounting measures for computing company value. *Earnings forecasting* considers earning power, estimation techniques, and monitoring mechanisms. This chapter describes several useful tools for earnings-based financial analysis. We describe recasting and adjustment of financial statements. We also distinguish between recurring and nonrecurring, operating and nonoperating, and extraordinary and nonextraordinary earnings components. Throughout the chapter we emphasize the application of earnings-based analysis with several illustrations. The content and organization of this chapter are as follows:

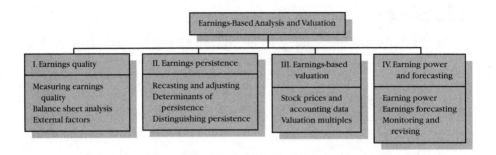

EARNINGS QUALITY

We know earnings (or income) measurement and recognition involve estimation and interpretation of business transactions and events. Our prior analysis of earnings emphasized that accounting earnings is not a unique amount but depends on the assumptions used and principles applied. Complicating earnings measurement are differences between accrual and cash accounting. Accrual accounting recognizes revenue when earned and expenses when incurred, while cash accounting recognizes inflows and outflows of cash irrespective of whether cash flows are earned or incurred. Despite limitations in cash flows, they are important to successful business operation and liquidity. For these reasons, we are interested in *both* cash and accrual measures of earnings.

The need for estimation and interpretation in accrual accounting has led some individuals to question the reliability of *all* accrual measures. This is an extreme and unwise reaction because of the considerable wealth of relevant information communicated in accrual measures. We know accrual accounting consists of adjusting cash flows to reflect universally accepted concepts: earned revenue and incurred expenses. What our analysis must focus on are the assumptions and principles applied, and the adjustments appropriate for our analysis objectives. We should use the information in accruals to our competitive advantage and to help us better understand current and future company performance. We must also be aware of both *accounting and audit risks* to rely on earnings. Improvements in both accounting and auditing have decreased the incidence of fraud and misrepresentation in financial statements. Nevertheless, management fraud and misrepresentation are far from eliminated, and audit failures do occur (e.g., Miniscribe, Phar-Mor, Leslie Fay, W. T. Grant, Equity Funding, Frigitemp, ESM Government Securities, Drysdale Securities, Crazy Eddie, Regina, and ZZZ Best). Our analysis must always evaluate accounting and audit risk, including the character and propensities of management, in assessing earnings.

Our evaluation of earnings persistence (trend and level) is linked with our evaluation of management. Similarly, evaluation of management cannot be separated from the earnings achieved. While other factors are relevant, earnings performance is the acid test of management's ability. Their ability is an extremely important (unqualifiable) factor in earnings forecasting. Our analysis must be alert to management changes and assess the company's dependence on management's ability, character, and risk taking.

Measuring Earnings Quality

Measuring earnings quality arose out of a need to compare earnings of different companies and a desire to recognize differences in quality for earnings-based valuation. There is not complete agreement on what earnings quality comprises. This section considers factors typically identified as comprising earnings quality and some examples of their assessment.

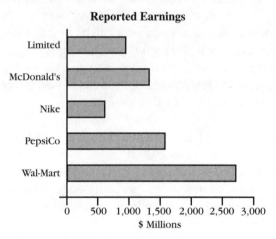

Reported Earnings

Source: Annual reports.

Determinants of Earnings Quality

Three factors are often identified as comprising earnings quality. We discuss them below.

Accounting Principles   One determinant of earnings quality is the discretion of management in *selecting accepted accounting principles*. This discretion can be liberal (optimistic) or conservative. The quality of conservatively determined earnings is perceived higher because they are less likely to overstate current and future performance expectations compared with those determined in a liberal manner. Conservatism reduces the likelihood of earnings overstatement and retrospective changes. Examples of conservative choices are LIFO inventory accounting in conjunction with rising prices and accelerated depreciation methods. However, excessive conservatism, while contributing temporarily to earnings quality, reduces the reliability and relevance of earnings in the long run. Examining the accounting principles selected can provide clues to management's propensities and attitudes.

Accounting Application   Another determinant of earnings quality is management's discretion in *applying* accepted accounting principles. Application of accounting relates to decisions such as whether adequate provision is made for asset reinvestment or for maintaining and increasing earning power. Management has discretion over the amount of earnings through their application of accounting principles determining revenues and expenses. Discretionary expenses like advertising, marketing, repairs, maintenance, research, and development can be *timed* to manage the level of reported earnings (or loss). Earnings reflecting timing elements unrelated to operating or business conditions can detract from earnings quality. Our analysis task is to identify the implications of management's accounting application and assess its motivations.

Business Risk   A third determinant of earnings quality is the relation between earnings and business risk. It includes the effect of cyclical and other business forces on earnings level, stability, sources, and variability. For example, earnings variability is generally undesirable and its increase harms earnings quality. Higher earnings quality is linked with companies more insulated from business risk. While business risk is not primarily a result of management's discretionary actions, this risk can be lowered by skillful management strategies.

Analyzing Discretionary Accounting Choices
Important determinants of earnings quality are management's selection and application of accounting principles. This section focuses on several important discretionary accounting expenditures to help us to assess earnings quality. *Discretionary expenditures* are outlays that management can

vary across periods to conserve resources and/or influence reported earnings. For this reason, they deserve special attention in our analysis. We assess their adequacy relative to current business conditions, prior periods' levels, and current and future expectations.

Maintenance and Repairs   As discussed in the prior chapter, management has considerable discretion in performing maintenance and some discretion with repairs. Our analysis can compare these costs to the level of activity that drives these expenditures. Two ratios are especially useful in comparing repairs and maintenance levels from year to year. The first ratio relates *repairs and maintenance costs to the level of operating activity:*

$$\frac{\text{Repairs and maintenance expenses}}{\text{Sales}}$$

In the absence of major inventory changes, sales are a good indicator of business activity. If year-to-year inventory levels change appreciably, an adjustment can be made. This adjustment is twofold: (1) estimate ending inventories at selling prices and add them to sales, and (2) estimate beginning inventories at selling prices and deduct them from sales.

The second ratio relates *repairs and maintenance costs to the level of investment* from which these costs are incurred:

$$\frac{\text{Repairs and maintenance expenses}}{\text{Property, plant, and equipment (excluding land) net of accumulated depreciation}}$$

Depending on the extent of information available to us, we can compute the ratio of repairs and maintenance costs to specified categories of assets. Evidence of substandard repairs and maintenance of assets can cause us to revise assumptions of useful lives for depreciation.

Trends in repairs and maintenance costs from year to year can be expressed in terms of index numbers and compared to related accounts. The purpose of this analysis and the two ratio measures is to determine whether repairs and maintenance are at normal and necessary levels or whether they are being "managed" in a way that affects earnings quality and its projection for valuation. Illustration 8.1 provides an example.

Advertising   A major portion of advertising outlays has effects beyond the current period. This yields a weak relation between advertising outlays and short-term performance. This also implies management can in certain cases cut advertising costs with no immediate effects on sales. However,

Illustration 8.1

Our analysis of maintenance and repairs expense for Campbell Soup Company using its annual report data in Supplement A reveals the following:

	Year 11	Year 10	Year 9
Maintenance and repairs ÷ net sales	2.8%	2.9%	3.1%
Maintenance and repairs ÷ property, plant and equipment—net*	12.2%	13.0%	13.1%

*Omitting land and construction in progress.

Evidence reveals a slight decline in these expenditures, requiring our further analysis.

long-run sales are likely to suffer. Our analysis must look at year-to-year variations in advertising expenses to assess their impact on future sales and earnings quality. Management's Discussion and Analysis for Adaptec in Supplement A reported that its 39 percent increase in sales and marketing expenses is primarily due to "advertising and promotional programs aimed at generating demand in the consumer and enterprise computer markets." There are several ways of assessing the trend in advertising outlays. One is to convert them into *trend percents* using a "normal" year as a base. We then compare these trend percents to the trend in sales, gross profits, and earnings. Another measure is the ratio of advertising outlays to sales:

$$\frac{\text{Advertising expenses}}{\text{Sales}}$$

We examine this ratio across periods to look for shifts in advertising expenditures. Analysis of advertising to sales over several years can reveal the degree of dependence for a company on a particular promotional strategy. See Illustration 8.2.

Illustration 8.2

Analyzing the ratio of advertising expense to sales for Campbell Soup reveals a decline from 3.5 percent in Year 10 to 3.1 percent in Year 11. Our analysis should pursue reasons for this decline because this ratio was as high as 4.1 percent in Year 6.

Another useful ratio compares advertising to total selling outlays:

$$\frac{\text{Advertising expenses}}{\text{Total selling costs}}$$

This ratio is often useful in identifying shifts to and from advertising to other methods of sales promotion. Comparison of both these ratios with those of competitors reveals the degree of market acceptance of a company's products *and* the relative promotional efforts needed for sales.

Research and Development Costs   Research and development costs are among the most difficult expenditures in financial statements to analyze and interpret. Yet they are important, not necessarily because of their amount but because of their effect on future performance. Interestingly, research and development costs have acquired an aura of productive potential in analysis exceeding that often warranted by experience. There exist numerous cases of successful research and development activities in areas like genetics, chemistry, electronics, photography, and biology. But for each successful project there are countless failures. These research failures represent vast sums expensed or written off without measurable benefits. There is also the question of what constitutes research and the potential for distortion. The research label has been used in reference to first-rate scientific inquiry and also for superficial or routine "testing" activities.

Our analysis must pay careful attention to research and development costs, and to their absence. They often represent substantial costs, many of them fixed, reflecting the key to future company performance. Our analysis must also distinguish between nonquantifiable (or qualitative) and quantifiable factors. *Qualitative factors* include research quality. *Research quality* involves the caliber of the staff and organization, reputation of its leaders, and its commercial applicability. This qualitative analysis must accompany other analyses. A distinction should also be drawn between external (including government) sponsored research and company-sponsored research. The latter is more likely to be identified with the company's objectives. It is clear that we cannot evaluate research on the basis of amounts spent alone. Research outlays represent an expense or an investment depending on how they are applied. Far from guaranteeing results, they represent highly speculative ventures depending on the application of extraordinary scientific as well as managerial skills for success.

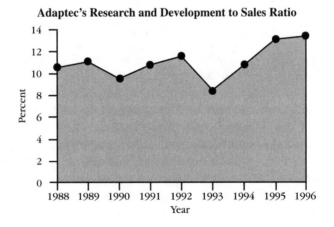

Adaptec's Research and Development to Sales Ratio

Quantifiable factors are also useful in our analysis of research and development outlays. Our intent is to determine the amount of current research and development costs having future benefits. These benefits are often measured by relating research and development outlays to:

- Sales growth.
- New products.
- Plant asset acquisitions (to exploit success).
- Profitability.

Another important measure of research and development outlays is their magnitude relative to a company's operating activities. While these outlays include fixed costs of research and development departments, most of these outlays are subject to the discretion of management, often with no immediate effects on sales. With regard to earnings quality, our analysis must evaluate year-to-year changes in research and development outlays. This is achieved through both trend percent analysis and ratio analysis. A useful ratio is:

$$\frac{\text{Research and development outlays}}{\text{Sales}}$$

Our careful comparison of this and similar ratios across periods reveals whether these research and development efforts are sustained or vary with operating activity. Transient research efforts usually lack the predictability or quality of a sustained long-term program.

Other Discretionary Future-Directed Costs   There are other future-directed outlays. Examples are costs of training, selling, and managerial development. While these human resource costs are usually expensed in the period incurred, they often have future utility. Our analysis should recognize this in assessing current earnings and future prospects.

Balance Sheet Analysis of Earnings Quality

Reported asset and liability values hold clues to our analysis of earnings quality. A **balance sheet analysis** is an important complement to our earnings-based analysis techniques. This section describes three variations of balance sheet analysis.

Conservatism in Reported Assets

The relevance of reported asset values is linked (with few exceptions like cash, held-to-maturity investments, and land) with their ultimate recognition as reported expenses. We can state this as a general proposition: When assets are *overstated,* cumulative earnings are *overstated.* This is because earnings are relieved of charges necessary to bring these assets down to realizable values. The converse is also true: When assets are *understated,* cumulative earnings are *understated.* At least two accounting practices qualify this proposition: conservatism and pooling accounting. Conservatism yields recognition of gains only when realized. While there is some movement away from strict interpretation of conservatism (e.g., trading securities), most assets are reported at cost even when their current or realizable values far exceed cost. Pooling of interests with business combinations allows an acquiring company to carry forward old book values of the assets of the acquired company even though such values can be far less than current market values or the consideration given for them. Pooling accounting allows the recording of profits when the values of understated assets are realized. This recording often represents recognition of previously understated assets. Since these profits are previously "purchased and paid for," they do not represent either earning power or the operating performance of management.

Conservatism in Reported Provisions and Liabilities

Our analysis must be alert to the proposition relating provisions and liability values to earnings: When provisions and liabilities are *understated,* cumulative earnings are *overstated.* This is because earnings are relieved of charges necessary to bring the provisions or liabilities up to their market values. Examples are understatements in provisions for taxes, product warranties, or pensions that yield overstatement in cumulative earnings. Conversely, an *overprovision* for current and future liabilities or losses yields an *understatement* of earnings (or overstatement of losses). Provisions for future costs and losses that are excessive shift the burden of costs and expenses from future income statements to the current period. Bearing in mind our propositions regarding the earnings effects from reported values of assets and liabilities, the critical analysis of these values represents an important factor in assessing earnings quality.

Risks in Reported Assets

There is another dimension to balance sheet analysis bearing on earnings quality. This dimension is based on exploiting the varying risks associated with future realizations of different assets. These risks span a spectrum of possibilities. Future realization of accounts receivable is typically higher than the realization of inventory costs. Similarly, future realization of inventory costs is typically higher than realization of goodwill or deferred start-up costs. Our analysis of assets by risk holds clues to earnings quality. If the reporting process yields deferrals of outlays with considerable risk of future realization, then earnings quality is lowered. To illustrate, we describe risk analysis on three specific assets to assess earnings quality.

Accounts Receivable   Sales quality depends on properly valuing accounts receivable. This valuation must recognize the risk of default and the time value of money. If receivables do not arise from transactions with customers or suppliers in the normal course of business with terms not exceeding a year, then, with minor exceptions, they are valued using the interest rate applicable to similar debt instruments. For example, if a receivable bears interest of 8 percent while similar receivables at the time bear interest of 12 percent, both the receivable and its corresponding sale are restated at the lower discounted amount. The level of accounts receivable and its relation to sales hold clues to earnings quality. If an increase in accounts receivable represents merely a shifting of inventory from the company to its distributor because of aggressive sales promotion or costly incentives, then these sales are nothing more than "borrowings" of future sales—reducing earnings quality.

Inventories   Overstated inventories yield overstated earnings. Overstatements can occur due to errors in quantities, costing, pricing, or valuation (of work in process). The more complex the inventory item or the more dependent is valuation on internally developed cost records, the more vulnerable are cost estimates to errors and misstatements. Overstatements are most likely when costs that companies should write off to expense are retained in inventory. Understatements of inventories derive from write-offs possessing future benefits that should be inventoried. An understatement of inventory results in understatement of current earnings and an overstatement of future earnings.

Deferred Charges   Deferred charges like deferred tooling, start-up, or preoperating costs must be scrutinized because their value depends vitally on estimates of future conditions. Experience shows these estimates are often overoptimistic or contain insufficient provisions for future contingencies. Risk of failure in achieving expectations with deferred charges is typically higher than with other assets.

External Factors and Earnings Quality

Earnings quality is affected by factors external to a company. These external factors make earnings more or less reliable. One factor is the quality of *foreign earnings*. Foreign earnings quality is affected by the difficulties and uncertainties in repatriation of funds, currency fluctuations, political and social conditions, and local customs and regulation. In certain countries companies lack flexibility in dismissing personnel which essentially converts labor into a fixed cost. Another factor affecting earnings quality is *regulation*. For example, the regulatory environment confronting a public utility affects its earnings quality. An unsympathetic or hostile regulatory environment can affect costs and selling prices and thereby diminish earnings quality due to increased uncertainty of future profits. Also, the stability and reliability of *earnings sources* affect earnings quality. Government defense-related revenues are dependable in times of high international tensions, but affected by political events in peacetime. *Changing price levels* affect earnings quality. When price levels are rising, "inventory profits" or understatements in expenses like depreciation lower earnings quality. Finally, because of uncertainties due to *complexities of operations,* earnings of certain conglomerates are considered of lower quality.

ANALYSIS VIEWPOINT

YOU ARE THE DIRECTOR

You are a new member of the board of directors of a toy merchandiser. You are preparing for your first meeting with the company's independent auditor. A stockholder writes you a letter raising concerns about earnings quality. What are some questions or issues that you can raise with the auditor to address these concerns and fulfill your fiduciary responsibilities to shareholders?

EARNINGS PERSISTENCE

A good analysis identifies components in earnings streams exhibiting stability and predictability, or *persistent* components. We separate these from random or nonrecurring components. This distinction aids us in producing reliable forecasts of earning power for valuation. Our analysis must be alert to earnings management or income smoothing. Earnings management or income smoothing can impart more stability and predictability than implied by the underlying characteristics. Company management often asserts that such activities remove distortions or peculiarities from operating results. Yet these activities can mask natural and cyclical irregularities that are part of a company's environment and experience. Identifying these influences is important for us in assessing a company's risk. This section considers elements bearing on our analysis of earnings persistence: earnings level, trend, and components.

Adaptec's Earnings per Share

Recasting and Adjusting Earnings for Analysis

Our objective in this part of our analysis is to recast earnings and earnings components so that stable, normal, and continuing elements comprising earnings are separated and distinguished from random, erratic, unusual, and nonrecurring elements. The latter elements require separate analytical treatment or investigation. Recasting also aims to identify elements included in current earnings that should more properly be included in the operating results of one or more prior periods.

Information on Earnings Persistence

The income statement and other financial disclosures represent the natural starting point for our earnings analysis. We prefer an income statement containing detailed component information and disclosure. The exact composition and treatment of earnings and earnings components depend on one's perspective. One position claims that gains or losses should be included or excluded from earnings on the basis of management's interpretation of "normal operations." This position is controversial and subject to various criticisms. Another position adopts an approach approximating the clean surplus relation. A clean surplus approach results in most gains and losses being reported in earnings in the period they occur. There is also the question of how to handle, if at all, restatement of prior periods' results. With few exceptions like corrections of errors, current practice discourages restatements.

Our analysis of operating results for the recasting and adjustment of earnings requires reliable and relevant information. The major sources of this information include:

- Income statement, including its subdivisions.

  Income from continuing operations.

  Income from discontinued operations.

  Extraordinary gains and losses.

  Cumulative effect of changes in accounting principles.
- Other financial statements and notes.
- Management commentary in financial statements.
- Management's Discussion and Analysis.

We often find "unusual" items separated within the income statement (typically on a pre-tax basis), but their disclosure is optional. Their disclosure does not always include sufficient information to assess significance or persistence. We access all available sources and management, if possible, to obtain this information. Relevant information includes that affecting earnings comparability and interpretation. Examples are product-mix changes, technological innovations, work stoppages, and raw material constraints.

Recasting Earnings and Earnings Components

Once we secure all available information, the income statements of several years (typically at least five) are recast and adjusted to assess earnings persistence. Recasting and adjusting earnings aids us in also determining the earning power of a company. We consider recasting in this section and adjusting in the next, although both can be performed in one statement.

Recasting aims at rearranging earnings components to provide a meaningful classification and relevant format for analysis. Components can be rearranged, subdivided, or tax effected, but the total must reconcile to net income of each period as reported. Analytical reclassification of components within a period helps in evaluating earnings level. Discretionary expenses should be segregated. The same applies to components like equity in income (loss) of unconsolidated subsidiaries or affiliates often reported net of tax. Components reported pre-tax must be removed along with their tax effects if reclassified apart from income from continuing operations.

Income tax disclosures enable us to separate factors that either reduce or increase taxes. This permits us to analyze the recurring nature of these factors. All permanent tax differences and credits are included. This analytical procedure involves computing taxes at the statutory rate (35 percent) and deducting tax benefits arising from various items including tax credits, capital gains rates, tax-free income, or lower foreign tax rates. We need also add factors like additional foreign taxes, nontax-deductible expenses, and state and local taxes (net of federal tax benefit). Immaterial items can be considered in a lump sum labeled *other.*

Analytically recast income statements contain as much detail as necessary for our analysis and are supplemented by notes. Exhibit 8.1 shows the analytically recast income statements for Campbell Soup. These statements are annotated with key numbers referencing Campbell's financial statements in Supplement A. Financial data preceding Year 10 are taken from company reports summarized in the Comprehensive Case chapter, which also contains a discussion and an integration of Exhibit 8.1.

Adjusting Earnings and Earnings Components

The adjusting stage uses data from recast income statements and other available information to assign earnings components to periods where they most properly belong. We must be especially careful with assigning extraordinary or unusual items (net of tax) to periods. Also, the income tax benefit of a carryforward of operating losses should normally be moved to the year of the loss occurrence. Costs or benefits from settlements of lawsuits can relate to one or more preceding periods. Similarly, gains or losses from disposal of discontinued operations usually relate to operating results of several years. For changes in accounting principles or estimates, all years under analysis should be adjusted to a comparable basis. If the new principle is the desirable one, prior years should be restated to this new method. This restatement redistributes the "cumulative effect of change in accounting principle" to the relevant prior years. Changes in estimates are accounted for prospectively in practice with few exceptions. Our ability to adjust all periods to a comparable basis depends on information availability.

Exhibit 8.1 Recast Income Statements

CAMPBELL SOUP COMPANY
Recast Income Statements For Years 6 to 11
($ millions)

Reference Item		Year 11	Year 10	Year 9	Year 8	Year 7	Year 6
13	Net sales	$6,204.1	$6,205.8	$5,672.1	$4,868.9	$4,490.4	$4,286.8
19	Interest income	26.0	17.6	38.3	33.2	29.5	27.4
	Total revenue	$6,230.1	$6,223.4	$5,710.4	$4,902.1	$4,519.9	$4,314.2
	Costs and expenses:						
	Cost of products sold (see Note 1 below)	$3,727.1	$3,893.5	$3,651.8	$3,077.8	$2,897.8	$2,820.5
145	Marketing and selling expenses (see Note 2 below)	760.8	760.1	605.9	514.2	422.7	363.0
144	Advertising (see Note 2 below)	195.4	220.4	212.9	219.1	203.5	181.4
16	Repairs and maintenance (see Note 1 below)	173.9	180.6	173.9	155.6	148.8	144.0
	Administrative expenses	306.7	290.7	252.1	232.6	213.9	195.9
17	Research and development expenses	56.3	53.7	47.7	46.9	44.8	42.2
102	Stock price–related incentive programs (see Note 3 below)	15.4	(0.1)	17.4	(2.7)	—	8.5
20	Foreign exchange adjustment	0.8	3.3	19.3	16.6	4.8	0.7
104	Other, net (see Note 3 below)	(3.3)	(2.0)	(1.4)	(4.7)	(0.4)	(9.0)
162A	Depreciation (see Note 1 below)	194.5	184.1	175.9	162.0	139.0	120.8
103	Amortization of intangible and other assets (see Note 3 below)	14.1	16.8	16.4	8.9	5.6	6.0
18	Interest expense	116.2	111.6	94.1	53.9	51.7	56.0
	Total costs and expenses	$5,557.9	$5,712.7	$5,266.0	$4,480.2	$4,132.2	$3,930.0
23	Earnings before equity in earnings of affiliates and minority interests	$ 672.2	$ 510.7	$ 444.4	$ 421.9	$ 387.7	$ 384.2
24	Equity in earnings of affiliates	2.4	13.5	10.4	6.3	15.1	4.3
25	Minority interests	(7.2)	(5.7)	(5.3)	(6.3)	(4.7)	(3.9)
26	Income before taxes	$ 667.4	$ 518.5	$ 449.5	$ 421.9	$ 398.1	$ 384.6
	Income taxes at statutory rate*	(226.9)	(176.3)	(152.8)	(143.5)	(179.1)	(176.9)
135	Income from continuing operations	$ 440.5	$ 342.2	$ 296.7	$ 278.4	$ 219.0	$ 207.7
	State taxes (net of federal tax benefit)	(20.0)	(6.6)	(3.8)	(11.8)	(8.6)	(8.0)
	Investment tax credit					4.4	11.6
137	Nondeductible amortization of intangibles	(4.0)	(1.6)	(1.2)	(2.6)	(1.4)	(1.4)
138	Foreign earnings not taxed or taxed at other than statutory federal rate	2.0	(2.2)	(0.2)	3.2	11.1	15.2
139	Other: Tax effects	(17.0)	(2.2)	(0.1)	(3.7)	7.5	(4.7)
	Alaska Native Corporation transaction					4.5	
22	Divestitures, restructuring, and unusual charges (Note 4)		(339.1)	(343.0)	(40.6)	(176.9)	
	Tax effect of divestitures, restructuring, and unusual charges in Year 7		13.9	64.7	13.9	9.7	
	Gain on sale of businesses in Year 8 and subsidiary in Year 7				3.1		
	Loss on sale of exercise equipment subsidiary, net of tax					(1.7)	
	LIFO liquidation gain (see Note 1 below)					2.8	1.4
	Income before cumulative effect of accounting change	$ 401.5	$ 4.4	$ 13.1	$ 241.6	$ 247.3	$ 223.2

Ref		Year 11	Year 10	Year 9	Year 8	Year 7	Year 6
153A	Cumulative effect of accounting change for income taxes				32.5		
28	Net income as reported	$ 401.5	$ 4.4	$ 13.1	$ 274.1	$ 247.3	$ 223.2
14	(Note 1) Cost of products sold	$4,095.5	$4,258.2	$4,001.6	$3,392.8	$3,180.5	$3,082.8
144	Less: Repair and maintenance expenses	(173.9)	(180.6)	(173.9)	(155.6)	(148.8)	(144.0)
162A	Less: Depreciation[a]	(194.5)	(184.1)	(175.9)	(162.0)	(139.0)	(120.0)
153A	Plus: LIFO liquidation gain[b]			2.6	2.6	5.1	2.6
		$3,727.1	$3,893.5	$3,651.8	$3,077.8	$2,897.8	$2,821.4
15	(Note 2) Marketing and selling expenses	$ 956.2	$ 980.5	$ 818.8	$ 733.3	$ 626.2	$ 544.4
145	Less: Advertising	(195.4)	(20.4)	(212.9)	(219.1)	(203.5)	(181.4)
		$ 760.8	$ 960.1	$ 605.9	$ 514.2	$ 422.7	$ 363.0
21	(Note 3) Other expenses (income)	$ 26.2	$ 14.7	$ 32.4	$ (3.2)	$ (9.5)	$ 5.5
102	Less: Stock price–related incentive programs	(15.4)	0.1	(17.4)	2.7	(5.6)	(8.5)
103	Less: Amortization of intangible and other assets	(14.1)	(16.8)	(16.4)	(8.9)		(6.0)
104	Less: Gain on sale of businesses (Year 8) and subsidiary (Year 7)				4.7	14.7	
	Other, net	$ (3.3)	$ (2.0)	$ (1.4)	$ (4.7)	$ (0.4)	$ (9.0)
136	(Note 4) Tax effect of divestitures, restructuring, and unusual charges at statutory rate		$ 115.3[c]	$ 116.6[d]			
	Nondeductible divestitures, restructuring, and unusual charges		(101.4)[e]	(51.9)[f]			
			$ 13.9	$ 64.7			

*The statutory federal tax rate was 34% in Year 8 through Year 11, 45% in Year 7, and 46% in Year 6.

†This amount was not disclosed for Year 6.

[a]We assume most depreciation is included in cost of products sold.

[b]LIFO liquidation gain before tax. For example, for Year 8 this is $2.58 million, computed as $1.7/(1 − 0.34).

[c]$339.1 [22] × 0.34 = $115.3.

[d]$343.0 [22] × 0.34 = $116.6.

[e]$179.4 [26] × 0.565 [136] = $101.4.

[f]$106.5 [26] × 0.487 [136] = $51.9.

Before we assess earnings persistence it is necessary to obtain the best earnings estimate possible with our adjustments. Exhibit 8.2 shows the adjusted income statements of Campbell Soup Company. All earnings components must be considered. If we decide a component should be excluded from the period it is reported, we can either (1) shift it (net of tax) to the operating results of one or more prior periods, or (2) spread (average) it over earnings for the period under analysis. We should only spread it over prior earnings if it cannot be identified with a specific period. While spreading (averaging) helps us in determining earning power, it is not helpful to us in determining earnings trend. We must also realize moving gains or losses to other periods does not remedy the misstatements of prior years' results. For example, a damage award for patent infringement in one period implies prior periods suffered from lost sales or other impairments. We return to discuss the details of Exhibit 8.2 in our Comprehensive Case.

Our analysis must also recognize certain characterizations of revenue or expense items as unusual, nonrecurring, infrequent, and extraordinary are attempts to reduce earnings volatility or minimize certain earnings components. These characterizations also extend to the inclusion in equity of certain transactions like gains or losses on available-for-sale securities or foreign currency translation adjustments. We often exclude equity effects from our adjustment process. Yet these items are part of a company's lifetime earnings. These items increase or decrease owners' equity and affect

Exhibit 8.2   Adjusted Income Statements

CAMPBELL SOUP COMPANY
Adjusted Income Statements For Year 6 through Year 11
($ millions)

	Year 11	Year 10	Year 9	Year 8	Year 7	Year 6	Total
Net income as reported	$401.5	$ 4.4	$ 13.1	$274.1	$247.3	$223.2	$1,163.6
Divestitures, restructuring & unusual charges		339.1	343.0	40.6			
Tax effect of divestitures, restructuring, etc.		(13.9)	(64.7)	(13.9)			
Gain on sale of businesses (Year 8) and sale of subsidiary (Year 7), net of tax				(3.1)	(9.7)		
Loss on sale of exercise equipment subsidiary					1.7		
Alaska Native Corporation transaction					(4.5)		
LIFO liquidation gain				(1.7)	(2.8)	(1.4)	
Cumulative effect of change in accounting for income taxes				(32.5)			
Adjusted net income	$401.5	$329.6	$291.4	$263.5	$232.0	$221.8	
Total net income for the period							$1,163.6
Average earnings for the period							$ 193.9

earning power. Accordingly, even if we omit these items from our adjustment process, they belong in our analysis of average earning power.

Determinants of Earnings Persistence

After recasting and adjusting earnings for forecasting and valuation purposes, our analysis next focuses on determining earnings persistence. Earnings variability, trend, management, and incentives are all potential determinants of earnings persistence. We should assess earnings persistence over both the business cycle and the long term.

Earnings Variability and Persistence

Earnings fluctuating up and down with the business cycle are less desirable than earnings with a large degree of stability. This is because earnings variability is associated with stock price fluctuations. We can use standard variability measures for this purpose. In evaluating earnings variability, our analysis must recognize the limitations of examining a limited period of earnings. Depending on our objectives, our analysis considers at least two alternatives to the limited information provided by earnings variability measures:

1. *Average earnings.* Computed typically using 5 to 10 years of data. Averaging smooths erratic, extraordinary, and cyclical factors, and can provide a more reliable measure of earning power.
2. *Minimum earnings.* Typically selected from the most recent business cycle. Use of minimum earnings can be helpful in analyses sensitive to high-risk factors. Minimum earnings reflect a worst-case scenario.

Earnings Trend and Persistence

Earnings reflecting steady growth trends are desirable. We can assess earnings trends by purely statistical means or with **trend statements.** Examples of trend statements for selected financial data of Campbell Soup are reported in Exhibits CC.8 and CC.9 in the Comprehensive Case chapter. Trend analysis uses earnings numbers from our recasting and adjusting procedures as exemplified in Exhibit 8.2. Earnings trends often contain important clues to a company's current and future performance (cyclical, growth, defensive) and bear on the quality of management. We must be alert to accounting distortions affecting trends. Especially important are changes in accounting principles and the effect of business combinations, particularly purchases. We must make adjustments for these changes.

Probably one major motivation of earnings management is to effect earnings trends. Earnings management practices assume earnings trends are important for valuation. They also reflect a belief that retroactive revisions of earnings previously reported have little effect on security prices. That is, once a company incurs and reports a loss, its existence is often as important as its magnitude for valuation purposes. These assumptions and the propensities of some managements to use accounting as a means of improving earnings trend has led to sophisticated earnings management techniques, including income smoothing.

Earnings Management and Persistence

There are several requirements for our specification of *earnings management*. These requirements are important as they distinguish earnings management from misrepresentations and distortions. Earnings management uses "acceptable" accounting principles for purposes of reporting specific results. It uses the available discretion in selecting and applying accounting principles to achieve these ends, and is arguably performed within the framework of accepted practice. It is a matter of form rather than of substance. It does not affect actual transactions (e.g., postponing expenses to later periods to shift earnings), but does affect a redistribution of credits or charges across periods. A major objective is to moderate earnings variability across periods by shifting earnings between good and bad years, between future and current years, or various combinations. Actual earnings management takes many forms. Some forms of earnings management that we should be especially alert to include:

- *Changes in accounting methods or assumptions.* Examples of companies who changed methods or assumptions include Chrysler, who revised upward the assumed rate of return on its pension portfolio and substantially increased earnings when sales were slumping, and Union Carbide, who switched to more liberal accounting methods and increased earnings.

- *Offsetting extraordinary/unusual gains and losses.* This practice removes unusual or sudden earnings effects that can adversely impact earnings trend.

- *Big baths.* This technique recognizes future periods' costs and losses in the current period, when the current period is unavoidably badly performing. This practice relieves future periods' earnings of these costs and losses.

- *Write-downs.* Write-downs of operating assets like plant and equipment or intangibles like goodwill when operating results are poor is another technique. Companies often justify write-downs by arguing that current economics do not support reported asset values. An example is CSX who wrote down $533 million of assets in a restructuring. Especially objectionable is writing down operating assets to a level meeting management's targeted return on invested capital.

- *Timing revenue and expense recognition.* This technique times revenue and expense recognition to manage earnings, including trend. Examples are the timing of revenues, asset sales, research expenditures, advertising, maintenance, and repairs. Unlike most earnings management techniques, these decisions can involve the timing of actual transactions. An example is Franklin Mint, who inflated earnings by premature recognition of sales.

- *Aggressive accounting applications.* Aggressive accounting applications, sometimes borderline misstatements, are used to redistribute earnings across periods. Examples include creating an excessive number or unusual categories of inventory pools to influence reported earnings. These practices occasionally are outside of accepted norms.

> McCormick Co. managed earnings by having its advertising agency delay mailing invoices until later periods.

Management Incentives and Persistence

We previously described the impact of management incentives for the accounting measurements in our analysis of financial statements. This is especially relevant in assessing earnings persistence and other analyses (investing and lending). Experience shows that certain managements, owners, or employees sometimes manipulate or distort reported earnings to serve personal objectives and interests. Companies in financial distress are particularly vulnerable to these pressures. These practices are too often justified by these individuals as a battle for survival. Prosperous companies also sometimes try to preserve hard-earned reputations as earnings growth companies through earnings management. Compensation plans and other accounting-based incentives or constraints provide motivation for

Second-level divisional executives at H. J. Heinz used *earnings manipulation* to meet earnings targets. This occurred without knowledge of top management. Divisional executives created *hidden reserves* by prepaying for services not yet received like advertising, and they improperly recognized sales.

To meet its profit goals, the syndication division of J. W. T. Grant falsified records. This division bought programming from independent producers and sold it to television stations in return for future commercial time. This created "commercial time banks" for sale to agency clients. It involved creating fictitious time banks, clients, and revenues over several years. The deception was so successful that top management invested additional capital in the division.

management to manage earnings. The impact of management incentives reveal themselves in the following cases:

Our analysis must recognize the incentives confronting management when reporting earnings. Earnings management is often initially achieved by understating reported earnings. This creates a "reserve" to call on in future low earnings periods. For example, Firestone Tire and Rubber Company concealed earnings in undisclosed accounts for purposes of drawing on these during lean years. Interestingly, some companies suggest earnings management can help users better assess their true earning power. While this point is arguable, this is not the purpose of financial reporting. We are better served by full disclosure of earnings components along with management's explanation. We can then average, smooth, or adjust reported earnings in accordance with our analysis objectives. A probable instance of earnings management is that of General Motors; see Illustration 8.3.

Today's accounting practices discourage earnings management. Yet given the incentives of management and the use of accounting numbers to control and monitor performance, our analysis must recognize the potential for earnings management and even misstatements. Our analysis must distinguish between companies' incentives to manage earnings, and especially scrutinize these companies' accounting practices to ensure the integrity of financial statements.

Illustration 8.3

GM reported a revision in useful lives of its plant and equipment. This reduced depreciation and amortization charges by $1.2 billion. GM's chairperson reported *"GM earned $3.6 billion for the year, up 21 percent . . . despite a 9 percent reduction in worldwide unit sales."* Yet without the $1.2 billion decline in depreciation and amortization, earnings would have decreased. This accounting change followed a year-before provision of $1.3 billion for plant closings and restructurings. Yet only $0.5 billion had been charged against this provision four years later, leaving the rest to absorb future years' costs. Four years after this provision there was a change in leadership at GM. This change is accompanied by another $2.1 billion charge to earnings to cover costs of closing several plants, including closings planned several years into the future. This sequence of events impairs confidence in both financial statements and management. Accordingly, we need to reliably estimate earning power using techniques like averaging, recasting, and adjusting of earnings.

Persistence of Extraordinary Items in Earnings

Recasting and adjusting earnings, including assessing earnings levels and trends, for valuation purposes relies on separating stable, persistent earnings components from random, transitory components. Persistence is important in determining earning power. Earnings forecasting also relies on persistence. A crucial step in our analysis is to assess the persistence of gains and losses. This section describes how we can determine the persistence of nonrecurring, unusual, or extraordinary items. We also discuss how they should be handled in evaluating earnings level, management performance, and earnings forecasting.

Reporting of Extraordinary Items

The value of financial reporting depends on its usefulness to those making decisions based on financial statements. The reporting of extraordinary items is affected by its importance to both management and users of financial statements. Management is concerned with both measuring and reporting operating results. This concern reflects a widespread belief that many users accept reported numbers and their accompanying explanations as true measures of performance. Accordingly, extraordinary items are often means to modify reported numbers and to explain performance. These explanations are usually subjective and designed to communicate management's view of events. Practice recognizes the role

Companies Reporting Extraordinary Items

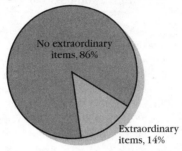

Source: *Accounting Trends & Techniques.*

of management's incentives in procedures governing the reporting of extraordinary items through explicit disclosure requirements and their inclusion in earnings.

Analyzing and interpreting Extraordinary Items

Our purpose in analyzing and interpreting extraordinary items is twofold:

1. Determine whether an item is extraordinary (less persistent) for our analysis. This involves assessing whether an item is unusual, nonoperating, or nonrecurring.
2. Determine adjustments necessary given our assessment of persistence. Special adjustments are sometimes necessary for both evaluating and forecasting earnings.

We describe both of these analyses in this section.

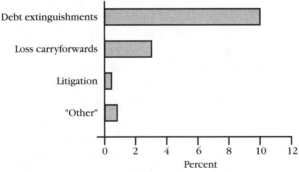

Source: *Accounting Trends & Techniques.*

Determining Persistence (Extraordinary Nature) of Items   Given
the incentives confronting management in reporting extraordinary items,
we must render our independent evaluation of whether a gain or loss is
extraordinary—including where it fits on the spectrum of highly persistent
to transitory earnings. We need also determine how to adjust for it. For this
purpose we can arrange items into three broad categories: nonrecurring
operating; recurring nonoperating; and nonrecurring nonoperating.

- *Nonrecurring operating gains or losses.* These gains or losses relate
to operating activities but recur infrequently or unpredictably. Operating
items relate to a company's *normal* business activities. The concept of normal operations is far less clear than many realize. A machine shop's operating revenues and expenses are those associated with the workings of the
shop. In contrast, proceeds from selling available-for-sale marketable
securities are nonoperating gains or losses. But a gain (or loss) on the sale
of a lathe, even if disposed of to make room for a more productive one, is
a nonoperating item. The other important concept, that of *recurrence,* is
one of frequency. There are no predetermined generally accepted bound-
aries separating a recurring event from a nonrecurring one. For example, a
regular event generating a gain or loss is classified as recurring. An unpredictable event, which occurs infrequently, is classified as nonrecurring. Yet
an event occurring infrequently but whose occurrence is predictable raises
questions as to its classification. An example is the relining of blast fur-
naces. They endure for many years and their replacement is infrequent, but
the need for it predictable. Some companies provide for these types of
replacements with a reserve.

Our analysis of nonrecurring operating gains and losses must recognize
their inherent infrequency and lack of recurring patterns. We treat them as
belonging to results of the reporting period. We must also address the
question of normal operations. It is a bakery's purpose to bake bread, rolls,
and cakes, but it is presumably outside normal activities to buy and sell
marketable securities for gain or loss, or even to sell baking machinery that
is replaced with more efficient machinery. This limited interpretation of
operating activities can be challenged. Some argue the objective is not
baking but for management to increase owners' equity, or common stock
valuation. This is accomplished through strategic application of financing,
investing, and operating activities. It is not limited to a narrow view of
normal operations. We can usefully evaluate a much wider range of gains
and losses as being derived from operating activities. This view results in

many nonrecurring operating gains and losses considered as part of operating activities in the year they occur.

Our analysis of nonrecurring operating items does not readily fit a mechanical rule. We must review the information and will doubtless find some items more likely to be recurring than others and some more operating than others. This affects our recasting, adjusting, and forecasting of earnings. We should also recognize the magnitude of an item as an important factor. Once we complete our analysis of recurring earnings, we often need to focus on *average earnings* experience over a few years rather than the result of a single year. A focus on average earnings is especially important for companies with fluctuating amounts of nonrecurring and other extraordinary items. A single year is too short and too arbitrary a period to evaluate the earning power of a company or for forecasting earnings. Illustration 8.4 sheds more light on this point.

Illustration 8.4

In the past few years we have seen several large charges to earnings for reorganization, redeployment, or regrouping. Companies taking substantial write-offs include ($ billions) AT&T $2.6, Occidental Petroleum $2, Continental Airlines $1.8, Digital Equipment $1, Columbia Gas System $.8, General Dynamics $.6, and Bethlehem Steel $.6. Information supplied with these events is often limited, but there is no denying these companies' enormous "revisions" of previously reported results. In one stroke, these write-offs *correct* prior year's overreporting of earnings. Our analysis must also be alert to aggressive write-offs to relieve future periods of charges properly attributable to them.

- *Recurring nonoperating gains or losses.* These include items of a nonoperating nature that recur with some frequency. An example is the recurring amortization of a bargain purchase credit. Other possible examples are interest income and rent received from employees renting company-owned houses. While these items can be classified as unusual in financial statements, the limited definition of *nonoperating* and their recurrent nature are reasons why we should consider their potential inclusion in current operating earnings. They typically result from management's planned activities, and their recurrence requires the inclusion of these gains or losses in forecasts of future results.

- *Nonrecurring nonoperating gains or losses.* These items are nonrepeating and unpredictable, and fall outside normal operations. Events driving these items are typically extraneous, unintended, and unplanned.

Yet they are rarely entirely unexpected. Business is subject to risks of adverse events and random shocks, be they natural or manmade. Business transactions are subject to the same. An example is damage to plant facilities due to the crash of an aircraft when your plant is not located near an airport. Other examples might include: (1) substantial uninsured casualty losses not within the usual risk of the company, (2) expropriation by a foreign government of assets owned by the company, or (3) seizure or destruction of property from war, insurrection, or civil disorders when not expected. These occurrences are typically nonrecurring but their relation to operating activities varies. All are occurrences in the regular course of business. Even assets destroyed by acts of nature are acquired for operating activities and are subject to all risks. The third example is close to meeting the criterion of extraordinary. But unique events are rare. What often appears unique is frequently symptomatic of new risks affecting earning power and future operations. Our analysis must consider this possibility. But barring evidence to the contrary, these items are regarded as extraordinary and omitted from operating results of a single year. They are, nevertheless, part of the long-term performance of a company.

Adjustments to Extraordinary Items Reflecting Persistence   Our second step in analyzing extraordinary, or transitory, items is to consider their effects on both the resources of the company and our evaluation of management.

- *Effects of extraordinary items on company resources.* Every extraordinary gain or loss has a dual effect. For example, when recording a gain, a company also records an increase in resources. Similarly, a loss results in a decrease in resources. Since return on invested capital measures the relation of net income to resources, extraordinary gains and losses affect this measure. The larger the extraordinary item, the larger its effect on return. If we use earnings and current events in forecasting, then extraordinary items convey more than past performance. If an extraordinary loss decreases capital for expected returns, then future returns are lost. Conversely, an extraordinary gain increases capital and future expected returns. In forecasting profitability and return on investment, our analysis must take account of the effects of recorded extraordinary items and the likelihood of future events causing extraordinary items.

- *Effect of extraordinary items on evaluation of management.* One implication frequently associated with extraordinary gains and losses is their lack of association with normal or planned business activities.

Because of this they are often not used when evaluating management performance. Our analysis should question their exclusion from management performance evaluation. What are the normal or planned activities that relate to management's decisions? Whether we consider securities transactions, plant asset transactions, or activities of divisions and subsidiaries, these all reflect actions taken by management with specific purposes. These actions typically require more consideration or deliberation than ordinary operating decisions because they are often unusual in nature and involve substantial amounts. All of these actions reflect on management's ability.

Standard Oil Co. reported an extraordinary charge of $1.15 billion in writing down its ill-fated investment in Kennecott. This loss implies prior years' earnings are overstated *and* questions about the ability of management.

Management should be aware of the risks of natural or manmade disasters or impediments. Business decisions are their responsibility. For example, a decision to pursue international activities is made with the knowledge of the special risks involved. A decision to insure or not is a normal operating decision. Essentially nothing is entirely unexpected or unforeseeable. Management does not engage, or is at least not expected to engage, in business activities unknowingly. Decision making is within the expected activities of a business. Every company is subject to inherent risks, and management should not blindly pursue activities.

In our assessment of operating results, distinguishing between normal and extraordinary items is sometimes meaningless. Management's beliefs about the quality of its decisions are nearly always related to the normalcy, or lack thereof, of business conditions. This is evident in the Management Discussion and Analysis. Yet the best management anticipates the unexpected. When failures or shortcomings occur, poor management typically takes time to "explain" these in a way to avoid responsibility. While success rarely requires explanation, failure evokes long explanations and blame to unusual or unforeseeable events. In a competitive economy, normal conditions rarely prevail for any length of time. Management is paid to anticipate and expect the unusual. Explanations are not a substitute for performance.

ANALYSIS VIEWPOINT

YOU ARE THE ANALYST/FORECASTER

You are analyzing a company's earnings persistence in preparing its earnings forecasts for publication in your company's online forecasting service. Its earnings and earnings components ("net income" and "income from continuing operations") are stable and exhibit a steady growth trend. However, you find "unusual gains" relating to litigation comprising 40 percent of current earnings. You also find "extraordinary losses" from environmental costs. How do these disclosures affect your earnings persistence estimate?

EARNINGS-BASED VALUATION

Company valuation is an important responsibility for many users of financial statements. Reliable estimates of value enable us to make buy/sell/hold decisions regarding securities, assess the value of a company for credit decisions, estimate prices for business combinations, determine prices for public offerings of a company's securities, and many other useful applications. This section introduces us to accounting-based equity valuation and incorporates it within our analysis of financial statements. Many of the elements comprising accounting-based valuation are described in this and prior chapters but are not explicitly assimilated in a valuation framework.

Traditional descriptions of company equity valuation rely on the *discounted cash flow (DCF) method*. Under the DCF method, the value of a company's equity is computed based on forecasts of cash flows available to equity investors. These forecasts are then discounted using the company's cost of equity capital.[1] it is important to emphasize that the accounting-based equity valuation model introduced earlier in this book and discussed in this section is theoretically consistent with the DCF method. If correctly applied, the accounting-based and DCF methods yield identical value estimates.

---

[1] A common alternative is to discount expected cash flows available to both debt and equity holders using the company's weighted-average cost of debt and equity capital. This yields an estimate of the total value of the company. The value of a company's equity is obtained by subtracting the value of its debt.

Relation between Stock Prices and Accounting Data

Recall the accounting-based equity valuation model introduced in Chapter 2 and expanded upon in Chapter 6:

$$V_t = BV_t + \frac{(ROCE_{t+1} - k) \times BV_t}{(1 + k)} + \frac{(ROCE_{t+2} - k) \times BV_{t+1}}{(1 + k)^2} + \ldots + \frac{(ROCE_{t+n} - k) \times BV_{t+n-1}}{(1 + k)^n} + \ldots$$

This model indicates a company's equity value (V_t) at time t equals its book value (BV_t) at time t plus the present value of future abnormal earnings. Abnormal earnings equal the difference between a company's return on common shareholders' equity ($ROCE_t$) and its cost of equity capital (k), multiplied by beginning period book value (BV_{t-1}).[2] The model directly shows the importance of future profitability in estimating company value—by using estimates of future ROCE and book values. Accurate estimates of these measures can be made only after consideration of the quality and persistence of a company's earnings and earning power.

A common criticism of accounting-based valuation methods is that earnings are subject to manipulation and distortion at the hands of management whose personal objectives and interests depend on reported accounting numbers. Indeed, a good portion of the book focuses on the need for our analysis to go "beyond the numbers." A reasonable question, therefore, is: Does the potential manipulation of accounting data influence the accuracy of accounting-based estimates, or forecasts, of company value? The answer is both yes *and* no.

We can demonstrate that accounting choices necessarily affect both earnings and book value (the "no" part of the answer). Aggressive (income increasing) accounting choices lead to higher earnings and book values. Yet this is only in the short run, as all costs must eventually flow through the income statement (assuming clean surplus accounting). Later periods' earnings for companies making aggressive accounting choices are lower than those employing conservative accounting choices. The "yes" part of the answer is based on the reality that analysis uses reported accounting data (and other information) as a basis for projecting future profitability. To the extent accounting choices mask the current true economic perfor-

---

[2]Abnormal earnings (NI_t^a) can also be computed as net income (NI_t) less the quantity of beginning period book value (BV_{t-1}) multiplied by the cost of equity capital (k).

mance of the company, a less experienced analyst can be misled regarding the company's current and future performance. Consequently, the analysis techniques described in this book are important to our analysis even though the accounting-based valuation model is mathematically free from accounting manipulations.

Fundamental Valuation Multiples

Two widely cited valuation measures are the price-to-book (PB) and price-to-earnings (PE) ratios. Users often base investment decisions on the observed values of these ratios. We describe how our analysis can arrive at "fundamental" PB and PE ratios without referring to the trading price of a company's shares. By comparing our fundamental ratios to those implicit in current stock prices, we can evaluate the investment merits of a publicly traded company. For those companies whose shares are not traded in active markets, the fundamental ratios serve as a means for estimating equity value.

Price-to-Book (PB) Ratio
The **price-to-book (PB) ratio** is expressed as:

$$\frac{\text{Market value of equity}}{\text{Book value of equity}}$$

By substituting the accounting-based expression for equity value in the numerator, the PB ratio can be expressed in terms of accounting data as follows:

$$\frac{V_t}{BV_t} = 1 + \left[\frac{(ROCE_{t+1} - k)}{(1 + k)}\right] + \left[\frac{(ROCE_{t+2} - k)}{(1 + k)^2} \times \frac{BV_{t+1}}{BV_t}\right] + \left[\frac{(ROCE_{t+3} - k)}{(1 + k)^3} \times \frac{BV_{t+2}}{BV_t}\right] + \dots$$

This expression yields several important insights. As future ROCE and growth in book value increase, the PB ratio increases. As the cost (risk) of equity capital, k, increases, the PB ratio decreases. Recognize that PB ratios deviate from 1.0 when the market expects abnormal earnings (both positive and negative) in the future. If the present value of future abnormal earnings is positive (negative), the PB ratio is greater (less) than 1.0.

Price-to-Earnings (PE) Ratio
The **price-to-earning (PE) ratio** is expressed as:

ANALYSIS RESEARCH INSIGHT 8.1

EARNINGS PERSISTENCE

Earnings persistence plays an important role in company valuation. Analysis research indicates nonrecurring earnings increase company value on a dollar-for-dollar basis, while the stock price reaction to persistent sources of earnings is higher and positively associated with the degree of persistence.

An analyst cannot rely solely on income statement classifications in assessing the persistence of a company's earnings. Research indicates many types of nonrecurring items can be included in income from continuing operations. Examples include gains/losses on asset disposals, changes in accounting estimates, asset writedowns, and provisions for future losses. Our analysis must carefully examine the financial statement notes, MD&A, and other disclosures for the existence of these items. Evidence also shows that extraordinary items and discontinued operations ("special items") may be partly predictable and can provide information regarding future profitability.

Recent analysis research indicates that companies currently reporting negative income along with special items are more likely to report special items in the following year. These subsequent years' special items are likely to be of the same sign, although profitable companies with discontinued operations are more likely to report higher earnings in subsequent years.

$$\frac{\text{Market value of equity}}{\text{Net income}}$$

By substituting the accounting-based expression for equity value in the numerator and simplifying, the PE ratio can be expressed in terms of accounting data as follows:

$$\frac{V_t}{NI_t} = \overline{PE} + \frac{\overline{PE}}{NI_t}\left[\frac{\Delta NI^a_{t+1}}{(1+k)} + \frac{\Delta NI^a_{t+2}}{(1+k)^2} + \cdots\right] - \frac{d_t}{NI_t}$$

where $\overline{PE}$ [equaling $(1+k)/k$] is a "normal" PE ratio, ΔNI^a_{t+1} is the expected change in abnormal earnings for year $t+1$ compared to the prior year (i.e., $NI^a_{t+1} - NI^a_t$), and d_t is dividends for year t.

This expression yields a number of key insights. As the cost of equity capital (k) increases, the PE ratio decreases. PE ratios deviate from a normal $\overline{PE}$ whenever investors expect abnormal earnings in the future. If future abnormal earnings are increasing (decreasing), the PE ratio is greater (less) than normal $\overline{PE}$. In the presence of future abnormal earnings, the extent to which PE deviates form normal $\overline{PE}$ depends on the current level of earnings. As the level of current earnings increases (decreases), the PE ratio decreases (increases).

Articulation of PB and PE Ratios

By studying actual PB and PE ratios jointly, our analysis gains insight into the market's expectations of future profitability.[3] As we showed, the PB ratio is a function of future profitability relative to book value and growth in book value, while the PE ratio is a function of future profitability relative to the current level of earnings. The following table summarizes the implications of various combinations of PB and PE ratios:

	Low PB	High PB
Low PE	Earnings expected to grow slowly or decline relative to current level, with low expected ROCE.	Earnings expected to grow slowly or decline relative to current level, but with high expected ROCE.
High PE	Earnings expected to grow quickly relative to current level, but with low expected ROCE.	Earnings expected to grow quickly relative to current level, with high expected ROCE.

---

[3]For more detail on this issue, see S. H. Penman, "the Articulation of Price-Earnings Ratios and Market-to-Book Ratios and the Evaluation of Growth," *Journal of Accounting Research,* Autumn 1996. For an excellent summary of the accounting-based equity valuation model, see M. P. Bauman, "A Summary of Fundamental Analysis Research in Accounting," *Journal of Accounting Literature,* 1996.

Illustration of Earnings-Based Valuation

We illustrate earnings-based valuation using financial information from Christine Company. The book value of equity for Christine Company at January 1, Year 1, is $50,000. The company has a 15 percent cost of equity capital (k). After careful study of the company and its prospects using analysis techniques described in this book, we obtain the following predictions of accounting data:

	Year 1	Year 2	Year 3	Year 4	Year 5
Sales	$100,000	$113,000	$127,690	$144,290	$144,290
Operating expenses	77,500	90,000	103,500	118,000	199,040
Depreciation	10,000	11,300	12,770	14,430	14,430
Net income	$ 12,500	$ 11,700	$ 11,420	$ 11,860	$ 10,820
Dividends	6,000	4,355	3,120	11,860	10,820

For Year 6 and beyond we predict both accounting data and dividends will approximate Year 5 levels. To apply the accounting-based valuation model we compute expected future book values and ROCEs using our accounting predictions above. Provided with these data, estimation of book value is straightforward. For example, book value at January 1, Year 2, is computed as $56,500 ($50,000 beginning book value + $12,500 net income − $6,000 dividends). Expected book values at January 1, Years 3 through 5, are $63,845, $72,145, and $72,145, respectively.

Recall that the accounting-based valuation model uses ROCEs computed using *beginning-of-period* book value. Therefore, expected ROCE for Year 1 is 25 percent ($12,500 ÷ $50,000). Expected ROCEs for Years 2 through 5 are 20.71 percent, 17,89 percent, 16.44 percent, and 15 percent, respectively.

The value of Christine Company's equity at January 1, Year 1, is computed using the valuation model on page 352 and equals:

$$\$58,594 = 50,000 + \frac{(0.25 - 0.15) \times 50,000}{1.15} + \frac{(0.2071 - 0.15) \times 56,500}{1.15^2}$$

$$+ \frac{(0.1789 - 0.15) \times 63,845}{1.15^3} + \frac{(0.1644 - 0.15) \times 72,145}{1.15^4}$$

$$+ \frac{(0.15 - 0.15) \times 72,145}{1.15^5} + 0 + \ldots$$

This accounting-based valuation implies that Christine's stock should sell at a PB ratio of 1.17 ($58,594 ÷ $50,000) at January 1, Year 1. To the extent expectations of stock market participants differ from those implied by the valuation model, the PB ratio using actual stock price will differ from 1.17. In this case, we must consider two possibilities: (1) estimates of future profitability are too optimistic or pessimistic, and/or (2) the company's stock is mispriced. This determination is a major part of fundamental analysis. Three additional observations regarding this illustration are important.

1. Expected ROCE equals 15 percent for Year 5 and beyond. This 15 percent return is equal to Christine Company's cost of capital for those years. Since ROCE equals the cost of capital for Year 5 and beyond, these years' results do not change the value of Christine Company (i.e., abnormal earnings equal zero for those years). Our assumption that ROCE gradually nears the cost of capital arises from basic economics. That is, if companies in an industry are able to earn ROCEs in excess of the cost of capital, other companies will enter the industry and drive abnormal earnings to zero.[4] The anticipated effects of competition are implicit in our estimates of future profitability. For example, net income as a percent of sales steadily decreases from 12.5 percent ($12,500 ÷ $100,000) in Year 1 to 7.5 percent ($10,820 ÷ $144,290) in Year 5 and beyond.

2. Since PE ratios are based on both *current* and *future* earnings, a PE ratio for Christine Company as of January 1, Year 1, cannot be calculated since prior years' data are unavailable. We can compute the PE ratio at January 1, Year 2. It is calculated as follows:

$$4.91 = \frac{1.15}{0.15} + \frac{\left(\frac{1.15}{0.15}\right)}{12{,}500}\left[\frac{3{,}225 - 5{,}000}{1.15} + \frac{1{,}844 - 3{,}226}{1.15^2} + \frac{1{,}039 - 1{,}845}{1.15^3} + \frac{0 - 1{,}039}{1.15^4}\right] - \frac{6{,}000}{12{,}500}$$

---

[4]We must be alert to the possibility that even when abnormal earnings are zero, conservatism in accounting principles can create the *appearance* of abnormal profitability. While this issue is not pursued here, our analysis must consider the effects of conservative accounting principles on future ROCEs. For example, due to mandated expensing of most research and development costs, firms in the pharmaceutical industry are characterized by relatively high ROCEs.

3.   Our valuation estimates assume dividend payments occur at the end
     of each year. A more realistic assumption is that, on average, these
     cash outflows occur midway through the year. To adjust valuation
     estimates for mid-year discounting, we multiply the present value of
     future abnormal earnings by $(1 + k/2)$. For Christine Company the
     adjusted valuation estimate equals $59,239. This is computed as
     $50,000 plus $(1 + [^{.15}\!/_2]) \times \$8,594$.

EARNING POWER AND FORECASTING FOR VALUATION

This section expands on the role of earning power and earnings forecasts
for valuation. We also discuss our use of interim reports to monitor and
revise these valuation inputs.

Earning Power

Earning power refers to the earnings level for a company that is expected
to persist into the foreseeable future. With few exceptions, earning power
is recognized as a primary factor in company valuation. Accounting-based
valuation models include the capitalization of earning power, where capitalization involves using a factor or multiplier reflecting the cost of capital
and future expected risks and returns. Most analyses of earnings and financial statements are also aimed at determining earning power.

Measuring Earning Power

Earning power is a concept derived from financial analysis, not accounting.
It focuses on the stability and persistence of earnings and earnings components. Financial statements are used in computing earning power. This
computation requires knowledge, judgment, experience, and perspective.
Many valuation models use future cash flows (although Chapter 2 showed
we can restate these models using earnings). Accrual earnings involve
adjustments to cash flows in recording revenue when earned and expenses
when incurred. Earnings are our most reliable and relevant measure for valuation purposes. While valuation is future oriented, we must recognize the
relevance of current and prior company performance for estimating future
performance. Recent periods' earnings extending over a business cycle represent actual operating performance and provide us a perspective on operating activities from which we can estimate future performance. We know

valuation is extremely important to many users (e.g., in investing, lending, tax planning, adjudication of valuation disputes). Accordingly, valuation estimates must be credible and defensible, and we must scrutinize departures from the norm. This is the reason courts and others are reluctant to replace past performance (earning power) with future estimates.

Time Horizon for Earning Power

A one-year period is often too short a period to reliably measure earnings. This is because of the long-term nature of many investing and financing activities, the effects of business cycles, and the existence of various nonrecurring factors. We can usually best measure a company's earning power by using average (or cumulative) earnings over several years. The preferred time horizon in measuring earning power varies across industries and other characteristics. A typical horizon is from 5 to 10 years in computing average earnings. This extended period is less subject to distortions, irregularities, and other transitory effects impairing the relevance of a single year's results. A five-year earnings computation often retains an emphasis on recent experience and avoids including less relevant performance results.

Our discussion of both earnings quality and persistence emphasizes the importance of several earnings attributes including trend. Earnings trend is an important factor in measuring earning power. If earnings exhibit a sustainable trend, we can adjust the averaging process to weigh recent earnings more heavily. As an example, in a five-year earnings computation, the most recent earnings is given a weight of 5/15, the next most recent earnings a weight of 4/15, and so on until earnings from five years ago receives a weight of 1/15. The more a company's recent experience is representative of future activities, the more relevant it is in the earnings computation. If recent performance is unlike a company's future plans, then less emphasis is placed on prior earnings and more on earnings forecasts.

Adjusting Earnings per Share

Earning power is measured using *all* earnings components. Every item of revenue and expense is part of a company's operating experience. The issue is to what year we assign these items when computing earning power. In certain cases our earnings analysis might be limited to a short time horizon. As described earlier in this chapter, we adjust short time series of earnings for items that better relate to other periods. If this is done on a per share basis, every item must be adjusted for its tax effect using the company's effective tax rate unless the applicable tax rate is specified. All items must also be divided by the number of shares used in computing earnings per share. An example of analytical adjustments for A. H. Robins Company appears below.

Example of Per Share Earnings Adjustment

Item	Year 2	Year 1
Effective tax rate change	+$0.02	
Settlement of litigation	+0.07	+$0.57
Change to straight-line depreciation	+0.02	
Reserves for losses on foreign assets	+0.02	−0.15
Loss on sale of divisions	−0.19	
Change to LIFO	−0.07	
Litigation settlements and expense	−0.09	−0.12
Foreign exchange translation	−0.03	−0.04
R&D expenditures exceeding prior levels	−0.11	
Higher percent allowance for doubtful accounts	−0.02	
±Per share earnings impact	−$0.38	+$0.26
Per share earnings as reported	$1.01	$1.71
Add back negative (−) impact to Year 2	0.38	
Subtract positive (+) impact from Year 1		(0.26)
Adjusted earnings per share	$1.39	$1.45

Earnings Forecasting

A major part of financial statement analysis and valuation is earnings forecasting. From our analytical perspective, evaluating earnings level is closely related to forecasting earnings. This is because a relevant forecast of earnings involves an analysis of earnings components and assessing their future levels. Accordingly, much of this chapter's previous discussion is applicable to earnings forecasting. Earnings forecasting follows our analysis of earnings components and estimates of their future levels. We should consider interactions among components and future business conditions. We should also consider persistence and stability of earnings components. This includes analysis of permanent (recurring) and transitory (nonrecurring) elements.

Mechanics of Earnings Forecasting

Chapter 4 considered certain mechanics of forecasting for short-term forecasting of cash flows. Forecasting requires us to effectively use all available information, including prior periods' earnings. Forecasting also benefits from disaggregation. Disaggregation involves using data by product lines or segments, and is especially useful when these segments differ by risk, profitability, or growth. Divisional earnings for TechCom, Inc., reveal how strikingly different divisional performance is masked by aggregate results:

	TechCom Earnings ($ millions)			
	1995	**1996**	**1997**	**1998**
Electronic products	$1,800	$1,700	$1,500	$1,200
Customer services	600	800	1,100	1,400
Total net income	$2,400	$2,500	$2,600	$2,600

We must also differentiate forecasting from extrapolation. *Extrapolation* typically assumes the continuation of a trend and mechanically projects that trend into the future. A *projection* also differs from a forecast in that it depends on certain assumptions that are not necessarily the most probable.

Analysis research reveals various statistical properties in earnings. Annual earnings growth often behaves in a random fashion. Some users interpret this as implying earnings growth cannot be forecasted. We must remember these studies reflect aggregate behavior and not individual company behavior. Furthermore, reliable earnings forecasting is *not* done by naïve extrapolation of past earnings growth or trends. It is done by analyzing earnings components and considering all available information, both quantitative and qualitative. It involves forecasting these components and speculating about future business conditions.

An often useful source of relevant information for earnings forecasting is Management's Discussion and Analysis. It contains information on management's views and attitudes about the future, along with a discussion of factors influencing company performance. While companies have been slow to respond to the market demand for forecasts, they are encouraged to report forward-looking information in this report.

Elements in Earnings Forecasting

While earnings forecasting depends on future prospects, the forecasting process must rely on current and past evidence. We forecast expected future conditions in light of this evidence. Our analysis must assess continuity and momentum of company performance, including its industry, but it should be put in perspective. We should not confuse a company's past with its future and the uncertainty of forecasting. We must also remember that earnings is total revenues less total costs, and that earnings forecasts reflect forecasts of these same components. Recognizing that earnings represents a relatively small portion of either component, we see how a relatively minor change in a component can cause a large change in earnings.

Another element in earnings forecasting is checking on a forecast's reasonableness. We often use return on invested capital for this purpose. If the earnings forecast yields returns substantially different from returns realized in the past or from industry returns, we should reassess our forecasts and the process. Differences in forecast returns must be explained, not necessarily to revise our forecast but to increase its reliability. We showed that return on invested capital depends on earnings—where earnings are a product of management quality and asset management.

- *Management quality.* It takes resourceful management to "breathe life" into assets by profitably and efficiently using them. Assuring stability of relations and trends implies there is no major change in the skill, depth, and continuity of management. It also implies no major changes in the type of business where management's skills are proven.

- *Asset management.* A second element of profitable operations is asset management and success in financing those assets. Companies require assets to expand operations. Continuity of success and forecasts of growth depend on financing sources and their effects on earnings.

A company's financial condition is another element to earnings forecasting. Lack of liquidity can constrain a successful management, and risky capital structure can limit management's actions. These and other economic, industry, and competitive factors are relevant to earnings forecasting. In forecasting earnings we must add expectations about the future to our knowledge of the past. We should also evaluate earnings trends with special emphasis on indicators of future performance like capital expenditures, order backlogs, and demand trends for products or services. It is important for us to realize that earnings forecasting is accompanied by considerable uncertainty. Forecasts may prove quite different from realizations because of unpredictable events or circumstances. We counter uncertainty by continual monitoring of performance relative to forecasts and revising forecasts as appropriate.

Reporting Earnings Forecasts

Recent years have witnessed increasing interest in disclosures of earnings forecasts by companies. Britain requires forecast disclosures under certain situations and there is a growing belief in practice that management forecasts would be useful additions to annual reports. We should recognize that management (insider) forecasting is different from forecasts made by financial analysts (outsiders). The reliability of forecasts depends on information access and assumptions made. Use of management or analyst forecasts in our analysis depends on our assessment of the assumptions underlying them. The SEC encourages forecasts made in *good faith* and that have a reasonable basis. It recommends they be reported in financial statement format and accompanied by information adequate for investors to assess reliability. To encourage forecast disclosures, the SEC has "safe harbor" rules protecting companies from lawsuits in case their predictions do not come true. These rules protect companies provided their forecasts are reasonably based and made in good faith. Because of practical legal considerations, few companies avail themselves of these safe harbor rules and publish forecasts.

The Company cautions that any forward-looking statements . . . involve risks and uncertainties, and are subject to change based on various important factors . . . changes in consumer spending patterns, consumer preferences and overall economic conditions, the impact of competition and pricing, changes in weather patterns, political stability, currency and exchange risks and changes in existing or potential duties, tariffs or quotas, postal rate increases and charges, paper and printing costs, availability of suitable store locations at appropriate terms, ability to develop new merchandise and ability to hire and train associates.

—The Limited, Inc.

Interim Reports for Monitoring and Revising Earnings Estimates

Assessing the earning power or earnings forecasts of a company relies on estimates of future conditions not amenable to verification. Our analysis must continually monitor company performance and compare it with our most recent forecasts and assumptions. We should regularly revise our forecasts incorporating current business conditions. Interim (less than one year) financial statements are a valuable source of information for monitoring performance. Interim statements are usually issued quarterly and are designed to meet users' needs. They are useful in revising our estimates of earning power and earnings forecasts. Yet we must recognize certain limitations in interim reporting related to difficulties in assigning earnings components to periods of under one year in length. The remainder of this chapter describes these limitations and their effects on interim reports.

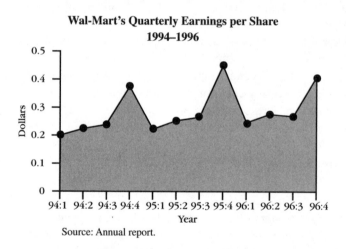

**Wal-Mart's Quarterly Earnings per Share
1994–1996**

Source: Annual report.

Period-End Accounting Adjustments

Determining operating results for a one-year period requires many adjustments including use of accrual accounting. These year-end adjustments are often complex, time-consuming, and costly. Examples include revenue recognition, determining inventory costs, allocating overhead, obtaining market values of securities, and estimating bad debts. These adjustments for interim periods are often less complete and use less reliable information than their year-end counterparts. This likely yields a less accurate earnings measure for interim periods.

Seasonality in Business Activities

Many companies experience seasonality in their business activities. Sales, production, and other operating activities are often unevenly distributed across interim periods. This can distort comparisons of interim earnings. It also creates problems in allocating certain discretionary costs like advertising, research, development, repairs, and maintenance. If these expenses vary with sales, they are usually accrued on the basis of expected sales for the entire year. Reporting problems also extend to allocating fixed costs across interim periods. See Illustration 8.5 for an example.

Illustration 8.5

Seasonality led to the following adjustments in the interim reports of Toronto Electech: "Because of seasonality in the production cycle, and in accordance with practices followed by the Company in reporting interim financial statements, $435,000 of unabsorbed factory overhead is deferred at June 30, 1998. Due to uncertainties in production and sales for the entire 1998 year, $487,000 of unabsorbed overhead is expensed during the first 6 months of the year."

Integral Reporting Method

Interim reports are generally reported in a manner consistent with annual reporting requirements. Adopting the view that quarterly reports are integral to the entire year rather than a discrete period, practice requires accrual of revenues and expenses across interim periods. This includes accruals for inventory shrinkages, quantity discounts, and uncollectible accounts. Also, losses are not usually deferred beyond the interim period in which they occur, and extraordinary items are reported in the interim period when they occur. But accrual of advertising costs is not acceptable on the basis that their benefits cannot be anticipated. Similarly, LIFO inventory liquidations are not considered for interim periods, and only permanent declines in inventory values are recorded for interim reports. Yet income taxes are accrued using the effective tax rate expected for the annual period.

SEC Interim Reporting Requirements

The SEC is keenly interested in interim reporting. It requires quarterly reports (Form 10-Q), reports on current developments (Form 8-K), disclosure of separate fourth-quarter results, and details of year-end adjustments.

There exist several reporting requirements for interim reports filed with the SEC. Principal requirements include:

- Comparative interim and year-to-date income statement data— can be labeled *unaudited* but must be included in annual reports (small companies are exempt).
- Comparative balance sheets.
- Year-to-date statement of cash flows.
- Pro forma information on business combinations accounted for as purchases.
- Conformity with accepted accounting principles, and disclosure of accounting changes including a letter from the auditor reporting whether the changes are preferable.
- Management's narrative analysis of operating results, with explanations of changes in revenues and expenses across interim periods.
- Disclosure as to whether a Form 8-K is filed during the period— reporting either unusual earnings adjustments or change of auditor.

These disclosures are believed to assist users in better understanding a company's business activities. They are also believed to assist users in estimating the trend in business activities across periods in a timely manner. We can see Adaptec's interim disclosure in note 11 of its annual report in Supplement A.

Analysis Implications of Interim Reports

Our analysis must be aware of estimation errors and the discretion inherent in interim reports. The limited involvement of auditors with interim data reduces their reliability relative to yearly audited financial statements. Exchange regulations offer some, albeit limited, assurance. Yet not all reporting requirements for interim reports are necessarily best for our analysis. For example, including extraordinary items in the interim period in which they occur requires adjustment for use in our analysis. Similarly, while accruing expenses across interim periods is reasonable, our analysis must remember there are no precise rules governing these accruals. Shifting expenses across periods is often easier than shifting revenues. Therefore, our analysis often emphasizes interim revenues as a measure of interim performance. We should also remember that common stock prices influence a company's earnings per share. Our analysis of per share results should separate price effects from operating performance. Certain seasonality problems with interim reports are overcome by computing *year-to-date cumulative numbers,* including the results of the most recent quarter. This is a very effective means to monitor a company's recent performance.

GUIDANCE ANSWERS TO ANALYSIS VIEWPOINTS

YOU ARE THE DIRECTOR

Your concern with earnings quality is to ensure earnings accurately reflect the company's return and risk characteristics. Low earnings quality implies *inflated earnings* (returns) and/or *deflated risk* not reflecting actual return or risk characteristics. Regarding inflated earnings (returns), you can ask the auditor for evidence of management's use of liberal accounting principles or applications, aggressive behavior in discretionary accruals, asset overstatements, and liability understatements. Regarding deflated risk, you can ask about earnings sources, stability, variability, and trend. Additional risk-related questions can focus on the character or propensities of management, the regulatory environment, and overall business risk.

YOU ARE THE ANALYST/FORECASTER

More persistent earnings reflect recurring, stable, predictable, and operating elements. Your estimate of earnings persistence should consider these elements. More persistent earnings comprise recurring operating elements. Finding 40% of earnings from unusual gains implies less persistence because its source is nonoperating. You can also question classification of litigation gains as "unusual"—they are sometimes better viewed as extraordinary. The extraordinary loss component also implies less persistence. In this case you need to assess whether environmental costs are truly extraordinary for this company's business. Together, these components suggest less persistence than suggested by the stable and steady growth trend in aggregate earnings. This lower persistence should be reflected in both the level and uncertainty of your earnings forecast.

Applying Financial Statement Analysis

A LOOK BACK

Part One of the book provided us a broad overview of financial statement analysis using Adaptec as a primary example. Part Two described key financial statement analysis tools and techniques.

A LOOK AT THIS CASE

This case is a comprehensive analysis of financial statements and related notes. We use Campbell Soup Company as our focus. We describe the steps in analyzing financial statements, the building blocks of analysis, and the essential attributes of an analysis report. We support our analysis using many of the tools and techniques described throughout the book. Explanation and interpretation accompany all of our analyses.

THIS CHAPTER WILL:

- Describe the steps in analyzing financial statements.
- Review the building blocks of financial statement analysis.
- Explain important attributes of reporting on financial statement analysis.
- Describe implications to financial statement analysis from evaluating companies in specialized industries or with unique characteristics.
- Analyze in a comprehensive manner the financial statements and notes of Campbell Soup Company.

PREVIEW OF COMPREHENSIVE CASE

Comprehensive case analysis of the financial statements and notes of Campbell Soup Company is our focus. The three major parts of the book have prepared us to tackle all facets of financial statement analysis. This comprehensive case analysis provides us the opportunity to illustrate and apply these analysis tools and techniques. This case also gives us the opportunity to show how we draw conclusions and inferences from detailed analysis. We review the basic steps of analysis, the building blocks, and key attributes of an expert analysis report. Throughout the case we emphasize applications and inferences associated with financial statement analysis. The content and organization of this chapter are as follows:

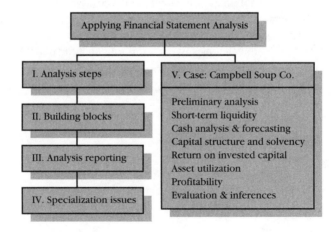

STEPS IN ANALYZING FINANCIAL STATEMENTS

Our task in analyzing financial statements can be usefully summarized for consistency and organizational efficiency. There are generalizations and guidelines that help us conduct financial statement analysis, although we must remember that analysis depends on our judgments and should be flexible. This flexibility is necessary because of the diversity of situations and circumstances in practice, and the need for us to aggressively apply ideas, experience, and knowledge.

Financial statement analysis is oriented toward achieving definite objectives. *Our first step is to explicitly define the analysis objectives.* (See Illustration CC.1a.) Our evaluation of the issues leading up to specification of objectives is an important part of analysis. This evaluation helps us develop an understanding of pertinent and relevant objectives. It also helps eliminate extraneous objectives and to avoid unnecessary analysis. Identifying objectives is important to our effective and efficient analysis. Effectiveness in analysis implies a focus on the important and relevant elements of financial statements. Efficiency in analysis implies economy of time and effort.

Illustration CC.1a

Assume you are a bank loan officer handling a request for a short-term loan to finance inventory. A reasonable objective is for you to *assess the intent and ability of the borrower to repay the loan in a timely manner.* Your analysis concentrates on what information is necessary to assess the borrower's intent and ability. You need not focus on extraneous issues like long-term industry conditions affecting the borrower's long-run performance.

Our second step in analysis is to formulate specific questions and criteria consistent with the analysis objectives (See Illustration CC.1b). Answers to these questions should be relevant in achieving the analysis objectives and reliable in making business decisions. Criteria for answers must be consistent with our risk and return requirements.

Addressing these questions and defining criteria depend on a variety of information sources, including those bearing on the borrower's character. Financial statement analysis can answer many of these questions, but not all. Tools other than financial statement analysis must be used to answer some important questions.

Illustration CC.1b

In your role as bank loan officer you need to specify relevant questions and criteria for making the above loan decision. Questions for the borrower include:

- Willingness to repay the short-term loan?
- Ability to repay the short-term loan (liquidity)?
- What are your future sources and uses of cash during the loan period?

Our third step in is identifying the most effective and efficient tools of analysis. These tools must be relevant in answering the questions posed and the criteria established, and appropriate for the business decision at hand. These tools include many of the procedures and techniques discussed throughout the book (See Illustration CC.1c).

Illustration CC.1c

Your role as loan officer requires decisions regarding what financial statement analysis tools to use for the above short-term loan request. You will probably choose one or more of the following tools:

- Short-term liquidity measures.
- Inventory turnover measures.
- Cash flow forecasts.
- Pro forma analysis.

Many of these analysis tools include estimates and projections of future conditions. This future orientation is a common thread of all analysis tools.

Our fourth step in analysis is interpreting the evidence. Interpretation of financial data and measures is the basis of our decision and subsequent action. This is a critical and difficult step in analysis, and requires us to apply our skills and knowledge of business and nonbusiness factors. It is a step demanding study and evaluation. It requires us to picture the business reality behind the numbers. There is no mechanical substitute for this step. Yet the quality of our interpretation depends on properly identifying the objectives of analysis, defining the questions and their criteria, and selecting efficient and effective analysis tools (See Illustration CC.1d).

This step is similar to requirements of many professions. For example, weather forecasting offers an abundance of analytical data demanding interpretation. Most of us exposed to weather information could not

---

Illustration CC.1d

Your loan decision requires you to integrate and evaluate the evidence, and then interpret it for purposes of reaching a decision on whether to make the loan or not. It can also include various loan parameters: amount, interest rate, term, payment pattern, and loan restrictions.

---

reliably interpret barometric pressure, relative humidity, or wind velocity. We only need to know the weather forecast resulting from the professional interpretation of weather data. Medicine, law, engineering, biology, and genetics provide similar examples.

Our analysis and interpretation of financial statements must remember that these data depict a richer reality. Analysis of financial data results in further levels of abstraction. As an example, no map or picture of the Rocky Mountains conveys their magnificence. One must visit these mountains to fully appreciate them because maps or pictures, like financial statements, are abstractions. This is why it is often advantageous for us to go beyond financial statements and "visit" companies—that is, use their products, buy services, visit stores, talk with customers, and immerse oneself in companies' business activities. The static reality portrayed by abstractions in financial statements is unnatural. Reality is dynamic and evolving. Recognizing the limitations of financial statements is necessary in analysis. This does not detract from their importance. Financial statements are the means by which a company's financial realities are reduced to a common denominator. This common denominator is quantifiable, can be statistically evaluated, and is amenable to prediction.

BUILDING BLOCKS OF FINANCIAL STATEMENT ANALYSIS

Financial statement analysis focuses on one or more elements of a company's financial condition or operating results. Our analysis emphasizes six areas of inquiry—with varying degrees of importance. We described these six areas of inquiry and illustrated them throughout the book. They are considered "building blocks" of financial statement analysis:

- **Short-term liquidity.** Ability to meet short-term obligations.
- **Cash flow and forecasting.** Future availability and disposition of cash.

- **Capital structure and solvency.** Ability to generate future revenues and meet long-term obligations.
- **Return on invested capital.** Ability to provide financial rewards sufficient to attract and retain financing.
- **Asset turnover.** Asset intensity in generating revenues to reach a sufficient profitability level.
- **Operating performance and profitability.** Success at maximizing revenues and minimizing expenses from operating activities over the long run.

Applying the building blocks to financial statement analysis involves determining:

1. Objectives of our analysis.
2. Relative emphasis among the building blocks.

For example, an equity investor when evaluating the investment merit of a common stock often emphasizes earnings- and returns-based analyses. This involves assessing operating performance and return on invested capital. A thorough analysis requires an equity investor to assess other building blocks although with perhaps lesser emphasis. Attention to these other areas is necessary to assess risk exposure. This usually involves some analysis of liquidity, solvency, and financing. Further analysis can reveal important risks that outweigh earning power, and lead to major changes in the financial statement analysis of a company.

We distinguish among these six building blocks to emphasize six distinct aspects of a company's financial condition or performance. Yet we must remember these areas of analysis are interrelated. For example, a company's operating performance is affected by availability of financing and short-term liquidity conditions. Similarly, a company's credit standing is not limited to satisfactory short-term liquidity, but depends also on its operating performance and asset turnover. Early in our analysis, we tentatively determine the relative emphasis of each building block and their order of analysis. Order of emphasis and analysis can subsequently change due to evidence collected.

REPORTING ON FINANCIAL STATEMENT ANALYSIS

The foundation of a reliable analysis is an understanding of the objectives. This understanding leads to efficiency of effort, effectiveness in application, and relevance in focus. Most analyses face constraints on availability of information. Decisions must be made using incomplete or inadequate information. One goal of financial statement analysis is reducing uncertainty through a rigorous and sound evaluation. A **financial statement analysis report** helps us on each of these points by addressing all the building blocks of analysis. It helps us identify weaknesses in inference by requiring explanation, and it forces us to organize our reasoning and to verify the flow and logic of analysis. The report serves as our communication device with readers. The writing process reinforces our judgments and vice versa, and it helps us refine inferences from evidence on key building blocks.

A good report separates interpretations and conclusions of analysis from the information underlying them. This separation enables readers to see our process and rationale of analysis. It also enables the reader to draw personal conclusions and make modifications as appropriate. A good analysis report typically contains at least six distinct sections devoted to:

1. **Analysis overview.** Background material on the company, its industry, and its economic environment.
2. **Evidential matter.** Financial statements and information used in the analysis. This includes ratios, trends, statistics, and all analytical measures assembled.
3. **Assumptions.** Identification of important assumptions regarding a company's industry and economic environment, and other important assumptions for estimates or forecasts.
4. **Crucial factors.** Listing of important favorable and unfavorable factors, both quantitative and qualitative, for company performance—usually listed by areas of analysis.
5. **Inferences.** Includes forecasts, estimates, interpretations, and conclusions drawing on all four prior sections of the report.

An analysis report should begin with an **Executive Summary** section. The executive summary is brief and focuses on important analysis results. We must remember that *importance* is defined by the user. The analysis report should also include a brief table of contents to help readers focus on those areas most relevant to their decisions. All irrelevant matter must be eliminated. For example, century-old details of the beginnings of a company and a detailing of the miscues of our analysis are irrelevant. Ambiguities and qualifications to avoid responsibility or hedge inferences should also be eliminated. Finally, writing is important. Mistakes in grammar and errors of fact compromise the credibility of our analysis.

SPECIALIZATION IN FINANCIAL STATEMENT ANALYSIS

Our analysis of financial statements is usually viewed from the perspective of a "typical" company. Yet we must recognize the existence of several distinct factors (e.g., unique accounting methods). These factors arise from several influences including special industry conditions, government regulations, social concerns, and political visibility. Our analysis of financial statements for these companies requires we understand their accounting peculiarities. We must prepare for this by learning the specialized areas of accounting relevant to the company under analysis. For example, analysis of an oil and gas company would require knowledge of accounting concepts peculiar to that industry, including determining cost centers, prediscovery costs, discovery costs, and disposing of capitalized costs. In addition, analysis of an oil and gas company would confront special problems in analyzing exploratory, development, and related expenditures, and in amortization and depletion practices. Another example is life insurance accounting. This analysis would require knowledge of the industry and its regulation. Challenges arise in understanding recognition of premium revenues, accounting for acquisition costs of new business, and determination of policy reserves. Another example is public utilities. Regulation results in specialized accounting concepts and problems for analysis. There are questions related to the adequacy of provisions for depreciation, and problems concerning the utility's "rate base" and the method used in determining it. Like any profession, specialized areas of inquiry require specialized knowledge. Financial statement analysis is no exception.

COMPREHENSIVE CASE: CAMPBELL SOUP COMPANY

We illustrate the major components of financial statement analysis using information and data from Campbell Soup Company.

Preliminary Financial Analysis

Campbell Soup Company is one of the world's largest food companies focusing on convenience foods for human consumption. The company's operations are organized within three divisions: Campbell North America, Campbell Biscuit and Bakery, and Campbell International. Within each division there are groups and business units. Major groups within the Campbell North America division are Soups, Convenience Meals, Grocery, Condiments, and Canadian operations.

The company's products are primarily for home use, but various items are also manufactured for restaurants, vending machines, and institutions. The company distributes its products through direct customer sales. These include chain stores, wholesalers, distributors (with central warehouses), institutional and industrial customers, convenience stores, club stores, and government agencies. In the United States, sales solicitation activities are conducted by subsidiaries, independent brokers, and contract distributors. No major part of Campbell's business depends on a single customer. Shipments are made promptly after receipt and acceptance of orders as reflected in no significant backlog of unfilled orders.

Sales Analysis by Source

Campbell's sales by division from Year 6 through Year 11 are shown in Exhibit CC.1. Its North American and International divisions are the largest contributors of sales, accounting for 68.7 percent and 19.7 percent, respectively, in Year 11.

Campbell's Sales by Divisions

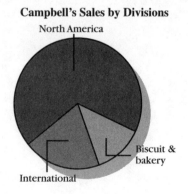

Source: Annual report.

Soup is the primary business of Campbell U.S., capturing about 60 percent of the entire soup market. This includes recent introductions of dry, ramen noodle, and microwavable soups. Other Campbell Soup brands include ready-to-serve soups: Home Cooking, Chunky, and Healthy Request. An integral part of the soup business is Swanson's canned chicken broth. Americans purchase more than 2.5 billion cans of Campbell's soups each year, and on average have nine cans in their pantry at any time during the year.

Fiscal Year 11 is a successful transition year for Campbell. It has completed major divestitures and accomplished significant restructuring and reorganization projects. Corporate goals concerning earnings, returns, and cash flows are being exceeded. The North American and International divisions produced exceptionally strong earnings results. The company enters Year 12 with a reconfigured product portfolio, positioned to support a continued strong financial performance. The solid margin growth gives

---

Exhibit CC.1

CAMPBELL SOUP COMPANY
Sales Contribution and Percent of Sales by Division
($ millions)

	Year 11	Year 10	Year 9	Year 8	Year 7	Year 6
Sales Contribution:						
Campbell North America:						
Campbell U.S.A	$3,911.8	$3,932.7	$3,666.9	$3,094.1	$2,881.4	$2,910.1
Campbell Canada	352.0	384.0	313.4	313.1	312.8	255.1
	$4,263.8	$4,316.7	$3,980.3	$3,407.2	$3,194.2	$3,165.2
Campbell Biscuit and Bakery:						
Pepperidge Farm	$ 569.0	$ 582.0	$ 548.4	$ 495.0	$ 458.5	$ 420.1
International Biscuit	219.4	195.3	178.0	—	—	—
	$ 788.4	$ 777.3	$ 726.4	$ 495.0	$ 458.5	$ 420.1
Campbell International	$1,222.9	$1,189.8	$1,030.3	$1,036.5	$ 897.8	$ 766.2
Interdivision	(71.0)	(78.0)	(64.9)	(69.8)	(60.1)	(64.7)
Total sales	$6,204.1	$6,205.8	$5,672.1	$4,868.9	$4,490.4	$4,286.8
Percent of Sales:						
Campbell North America:						
Campbell U.S.A.	63.0%	63.4%	64.7%	63.6%	64.2%	67.9%
Campbell Canada	5.7	6.2	5.5	6.4	6.9	5.9
	68.7	69.6	70.2	70.0	71.1	73.8
Campbell Biscuit and Bakery:						
Pepperidge Farm	9.2	9.4	9.7	10.2	10.2	9.8
International Biscuit	3.5	3.1	3.1	—	—	—
	12.7	12.5	12.8	10.2	10.2	9.8
Campbell International	19.7	19.2	18.2	21.3	20.0	17.9
Interdivision	(1.1)	(1.3)	(1.2)	(1.4)	(1.3)	(1.5)
Total sales	100.0%	100.0%	100.0%	100.0%	100.0%	100.0%

Campbell an opportunity to increase consumer advertising and to further the introduction of new product lines and continue support for flagship products.

Comparative Financial Statements

Complete financial statements and related information for Campbell Soup are in Supplement A. These reports include information from SEC Form 10-K. Comparative financial statements for Campbell for Years 6 through 11 are presented in Exhibits CC.2, CC.3, and CC.4. The auditor's opinions on their financial statements for the past six years are unqualified.

Exhibit CC.2

CAMPBELL SOUP COMPANY
Income Statements ($ millions)
For Years 6 through 11

	Year 11	Year 10	Year 9	Year 8	Year 7	Year 6
Net sales	$6,204.1	$6,205.8	$5,672.1	$4,868.9	$4,490.4	$4,286.8
Costs and expenses:						
Cost of products sold	$4,095.5	$4,258.2	$4,001.6	$3,392.8	$3,180.5	$3,082.7
Marketing and selling expenses	956.2	980.5	818.8	733.3	626.2	544.4
Administrative expenses	306.7	290.7	252.1	232.6	213.9	195.9
Research and development expenses	56.3	53.7	47.7	46.9	44.8	42.2
Interest expense	116.2	111.6	94.1	53.9	51.7	56.0
Interest income	(26.0)	(17.6)	(38.3)	(33.2)	(29.5)	(27.4)
Foreign exchange losses, net	0.8	3.3	19.3	16.6	4.8	0.7
Other expense (income)	26.2	14.7	32.4	(3.2)	(9.5)	5.5
Divestitures, restructuring, and unusual charges	0.0	339.1	343.0	40.6	0.0	0.0
Total costs and expenses	$5,531.9	$6,034.2	$5,570.7	$4,480.3	$4,082.9	$3,900.0
Earnings before equity in earnings of affiliates and minority interests	$ 672.2	$ 171.6	$ 101.4	$ 388.6	$ 407.5	$ 386.8
Equity in earnings of affiliates	2.4	13.5	10.4	6.3	15.1	4.3
Minority interests	(7.2)	(5.7)	(5.3)	(6.3)	(4.7)	(3.9)
Earnings before taxes	$ 667.4	$ 179.4	$ 106.5	$ 388.6	$ 417.9	$ 387.2
Taxes on earnings	265.9	175.0	93.4	147.0	170.6	164.0
Earnings before cumulative effect of accounting change	$ 401.5	$ 4.4	$ 13.1	$ 241.6	$ 247.3	$ 223.2
Cumulative effect of change in accounting for income taxes	0	0	0	32.5	0	0
Net earnings	$ 401.5	$ 4.4	$ 13.1	$ 274.1	$ 247.3	$ 223.2
Earnings per share	$ 3.16	$ 0.03	$ 0.10	$ 2.12*	$ 1.90	$ 1.72
Weighted-average shares outstanding	127.00	126.60	129.30	$ 129.30	$ 129.90	129.50

*Including $0.25 per share cumulative effect of change in accounting for income taxes.

Exhibit CC.3

CAMPBELL SOUP COMPANY
Balance Sheets
For Years 6 to 11 ($ millions)

	Year 11	Year 10	Year 9	Year 8	Year 7	Year 6
Assets						
Current assets:						
Cash and cash equivalents	$ 178.90	$ 80.70	$ 120.90	$ 85.80	$ 145.00	$ 155.10
Other temporary investments	12.80	22.50	26.20	35.00	280.30	238.70
Accounts receivable	527.40	624.50	538.00	486.90	338.90	299.00
Inventories	706.70	819.80	816.00	664.70	623.60	610.50
Prepaid expenses	92.70	118.00	100.40	90.50	50.10	31.50
Total current assets	$1,518.50	$1,665.50	$1,601.50	$1,362.90	$1,437.90	$1,334.80
Plant assets, net of depreciation	$1,790.40	$1,717.70	$1,540.60	$1,508.90	$1,349.00	$1,168.10
Intangible assets, net of amortization	435.50	383.40	466.90	496.60	—	—
Other assets	404.60	349.00	323.10	241.20	310.50	259.90
Total assets	$4,149.00	$4,115.60	$3,932.10	$3,609.60	$3,097.40	$2,762.80
Liabilities and Shareowners' Equity						
Current liabilities:						
Notes payable	$ 282.20	$ 202.30	$ 271.50	$ 138.00	$ 93.50	$ 88.90
Payable to suppliers and others	482.40	525.20	508.20	446.70	374.80	321.70
Accrued liabilities	408.70	491.90	392.60	236.90	182.10	165.90
Dividend payable	37.00	32.30	29.70	—	—	—
Accrued income taxes	67.70	46.40	30.10	41.70	43.40	49.60
Total current liabilities	$1,278.00	$1,298.10	$1,232.10	$ 863.30	$ 693.80	$ 626.10
Long-term debt	$ 772.60	$ 805.80	$ 629.20	$ 525.80	$ 380.20	$ 362.30
Other liabilities, mainly deferred income tax	305.00	319.90	292.50	325.50	287.30	235.50

Shareowner's equity:						
Preferred stock; authorized 40,000,000 sh.; none issued	—	—	—	—	—	—
Capital stock, $0.15 par value; authorized 140,000,000 sh.; issued 135,622,676 sh.	20.30	20.30	20.30	20.30	20.30	20.30
Capital surplus	107.30	61.90	50.80	42.30	41.10	38.10
Earnings retained in the business	1,912.60	1,653.30	1,775.80	1,879.10	1,709.60	1,554.00
Capital stock in treasury, at cost	(270.40)	(107.20)	(70.70)	(75.20)	(46.80)	(48.40)
Cumulative translation adjustments	23.60	63.50	2.10	28.50	11.90	(25.10)
Total shareowner's equity	$1,793.40	$1,691.80	$1,778.30	$1,895.00	$1,736.10	$1,538.90
Total liabilities and shareowners' equity	$4,149.00	$4,115.60	$3,932.10	$3,609.60	$3,097.40	$2,762.80

CC13

Exhibit CC.4

CAMPBELL SOUP COMPANY
Statements of Cash Flows
For Years 6 to 11 ($ millions)

	Year 11	Year 10	Year 9	Year 8	Year 7	Year 6	Total
Cash flows from operating activities:							
Net earnings	$ 401.5	$ 4.4	$ 13.1	$ 274.1	$ 247.3	$ 223.2	$ 1,163.6
To reconcile net earnings to net cash provided by operating activities:							
Depreciation and amortization	208.6	200.9	192.3	170.9	144.6	126.8	1,044.1
Divestitures and restructuring provisions	—	339.1	343.0	17.6	—	—	699.7
Deferred taxes	35.5	3.9	(67.8)	13.4	45.7	29.0	59.7
Other, net	63.2	18.6	37.3	43.0	28.0	16.6	206.7
Cumulative effect of accounting change	—	—	—	(32.5)	—	—	(32.5)
(Increase) decrease in accounts receivable	17.1	(60.4)	(46.8)	(104.3)	(36.3)	(3.6)	(234.3)
(Increase) decrease in inventories	48.7	10.7	(113.2)	54.2	(3.9)	23.1	19.6
Net change in other current assets and liabilities	30.6	(68.8)	(0.6)	30.2	42.9	48.7	83.0
Net cash provided by operating activities	$ 805.2	$ 448.4	$ 357.3	$ 466.6	$ 468.3	$ 463.8	$ 3,009.6
Cash flows from investing activities:							
Purchases of plant assets	$(361.1)	$(387.6)	$(284.1)	$(245.3)	$(303.7)	$(235.3)	$(1,817.1)
Sale of plant assets	43.2	34.9	39.8	22.6	—	29.8	170.3
Businesses acquired	(180.1)	(41.6)	(135.8)	(471.9)	(7.3)	(20.0)	(856.7)
Sale of businesses	67.4	21.7	4.9	23.5	20.8	—	138.3
Increase in other assets	(57.8)	(18.6)	(107.0)	(40.3)	(50.1)	(18.0)	(291.8)
Net change in other temporary investments	9.7	3.7	9.0	249.2	(60.7)	(144.1)	66.8
Net cash used in investing activities	$(478.7)	$(387.5)	$(473.2)	$(462.2)	$(401.0)	$(387.6)	$(2,590.2)

Cash flows from financing activities:							
Long-term borrowings	$ 402.8	$ 12.6	$ 126.5	$ 103.0	$ 4.8	$ 203.9	$ 853.6
Repayments of long-term borrowings	(129.9)	(22.5)	(53.6)	(22.9)	(23.9)	(164.7)	(417.5)
Increase (decrease) in short-term borrowings*	(137.9)	(2.7)	108.2	8.4	(20.7)	4.6	(40.1)
Other short-term borrowings	117.3	153.7	227.1	77.0	89.3	72.9	737.3
Repayments of other short-term borrowings	(206.4)	(89.8)	(192.3)	(87.6)	(66.3)	(88.5)	(730.9)
Dividends paid	(137.5)	(124.3)	(86.7)	(104.6)	(91.7)	(104.6)	(649.4)
Treasury stock purchases	(175.6)	(41.1)	(8.1)	(29.3)	—	—	(254.1)
Treasury stock issued	47.7	12.4	18.5	0.9	1.6	4.0†	85.1
Other, net	(0.1)	(0.1)	23.5	2.3	18.6	17.9	62.1
Net cash provided (used in) financing activities	$(219.6)	$(101.8)	$ 163.1	$ (52.8)	$ (88.3)	$ (54.5)	$ (353.9)
Effect of exchange rate change on cash	$ (8.7)	$ 0.7	$ (12.1)	$ (10.8)	$ (7.1)	$ (3.7)	$ (41.7)
Net increase (decrease) in cash and cash equivalents	98.2	(40.2)	35.1	(59.2)	(28.1)	18.0	23.8
Cash and cash equivalents at the beginning of year	80.7	120.9	85.8	145.0	173.1	155.1	760.6
Cash and cash equivalents at end of year	$ 178.9	$ 80.7	$ 120.9	$ 85.8	$ 145.0	$ 173.1	$ 784.4

*With less than three month maturities.
†2.8 issued for a pooling of interest.

Further Analysis of Financial Statements

Growth rates for important financial measures, annually compounded, are reported in Exhibit CC.5. These rates are computed using four different periods and are based on per share data (see Exhibit CC.9). Most impressive is the growth in net income per share over the past five years (12.93%). Growth in sales per share over the same recent five-year period is at a rate less than that of net income. Equity per share growth in the recent 5-year period declined compared to the 10-year period. This finding, including the two negative growth rates in the exhibit, is due to divestitures and restructurings in Years 9 and 10. We also compute common-size income statements and balance sheets in Exhibits CC.6 and CC.7. Exhibit CC.8 presents the trend indexes of selected accounts for Campbell Soup. Exhibit CC.9 presents Campbell Soup's per share results.

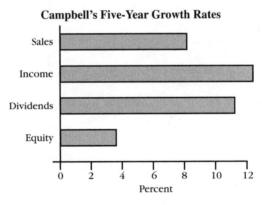

Campbell's Five-Year Growth Rates

Source: Annual report.

Alternative Perspectives on Analysis

We analyze the financial statements of Campbell Soup Company from the perspective of three alternative points of view. These alternative perspectives yield different objectives and emphases in our final analysis. The three perspectives are:

- **Extending bank credit line.** The company requests our bank to make available a line of credit (for short-term operating purposes) of up to $60 million.

Exhibit CC.5

CAMPBELL SOUP COMPANY
Five-Year Growth Rates*
(annually compounded)

Per Share	Years 6 to 11	$\begin{bmatrix} \text{Average for} \\ \text{Years 6 to 8} \end{bmatrix}$ to $\begin{bmatrix} \text{Average for} \\ \text{Years 9 to 11} \end{bmatrix}$
Sales	8.09%	5.95 %
Net income	12.93	−10.53
Dividends	11.50	6.69
Equity	3.55	0.53

Ten-Year Growth Rates*
(annually compounded)

Per Share	Years 1 to 11	$\begin{bmatrix} \text{Average for} \\ \text{Years 1 to 3} \end{bmatrix}$ to $\begin{bmatrix} \text{Average for} \\ \text{Years 9 to 11} \end{bmatrix}$
Sales	8.51%	7.22%
Net income	12.19	−0.44
Dividends	8.18	6.62
Equity	6.22	5.13

*Growth rates (annually compounded) are computed using the compound interest method (where n = Compounding period, and r = Rate of growth):

$$\text{Future value } (FV) = \text{Present value } (PV) \times \left(1 + \frac{r}{100}\right)^n$$

For example, net sales per share during Years 6 to 11 grew at a rate of:

$$FV = PV\left(1 + \frac{r}{100}\right)^n \Longleftrightarrow \$48.85 = \$33.10\left(1 + \frac{r}{100}\right)^5$$

$$r = 8.09\%$$

- **Private purchase of debt.** The company wishes to privately place $50 million of 25-year bonds with our insurance company.
- **Equity investment.** As an equity investor we consider a substantial investment in the company's common stock.

These diverse perspectives have commonalities in requiring us to analyze all major aspects of the company's financial condition and operating results. We also draw on industry composite figures for comparative purposes. These figures are drawn primarily from *Dun & Bradstreet Industry Norms and Key Business Ratios,* and are based on Year 11 financial statements of companies in SIC classification 2033. We will return to these perspectives at the end of our analysis.

Exhibit CC.6

CAMPBELL SOUP COMPANY
Common-Size Income Statements
For Years 6 to 11

	Year 11	Year 10	Year 9	Year 8	Year 7	Year 6
Net sales	100.00%	100.00%	100.00%	100.00%	100.00%	100.00%
Costs and expenses:						
Cost of products sold	66.01%	68.62%	70.55%	69.68%	70.83%	71.91%
Marketing and selling expenses	15.41	15.80	14.44	15.06	13.95	12.70
Administrative expenses	4.94	4.68	4.44	4.78	4.76	4.57
Research and development expenses	0.91	0.87	0.84	0.96	1.00	0.98
Interest expense	1.87	1.80	1.66	1.11	1.15	1.31
Interest income	(0.42)	(0.28)	(0.68)	(0.68)	(0.66)	(0.64)
Foreign exchange losses, net	0.01	0.05	0.34	0.34	0.11	0.02
Other expense (income)	0.42	0.24	0.57	(0.07)	(0.21)	0.13
Divestitures, restructuring, and unusual charges	—	5.46	6.05	0.83	—	—
Total costs and expenses	89.17%	97.23%	98.21%	92.02%	90.93%	90.98%
Earnings before equity in earnings of affiliates and minority interests	10.83%	2.77%	1.79%	7.98%	9.07%	9.02%
Equity in earnings of affiliates	0.04	0.22	0.18	0.13	0.34	0.10
Minority interests	(0.12)	(0.09)	(0.09)	(0.13)	(0.10)	(0.09)
Earnings before taxes	10.76%	2.89%	1.88%	7.98%	9.31%	9.03%
Taxes on earnings	4.29	2.82	1.65	3.02	3.80	3.83
Earnings before cumulative effect of accounting change	6.47%	0.07%	0.23%	4.96%	5.51%	5.21%
Cumulative effect of change in accounting for income taxes	—	—	—	0.67	—	—
Net earnings	6.47%	0.07%	0.23%	5.63%	5.51%	5.21%

Short-Term Liquidity

Important measures of short-term liquidity for the most recent six years are reported in Exhibit CC.10. This exhibit also reports industry composite data for Year 11. The current ratio in Year 11 is at its lowest level for the past six years. Its value of 1.19 is measurably lower than the industry composite of 1.86. This is due in part to growth in current liabilities over recent years. Current liabilities are double what they were in Year 6, while current assets in Year 11 are but 114 percent of their Year 6 level. A substantial amount of notes payable are reclassified as long-term debt in Year 10. This helps improve the current ratio. Exhibit CC.11 reveals that cash and cash equivalents in Year 11 represent a larger proportion of current assets (11.78%) compared with the industry (5.60%).

Campbell's acid-test ratio for the past three years (0.56) is slightly below the Year 11 industry composite (0.61). The assets and liabilities comprising the acid-test ratio can be compared against the industry composite using Exhibit CC.7. This exhibit along with Exhibit CC.11 reveals that inventories comprise a lower proportion of total assets (17%) and total current assets (47%) than they do for the industry (39% and 64%, respectively). Also, inventory turnover for Campbell in Year 11 is 5.37 versus 2.53 for the industry. These measures indicate Campbell has less funds invested in inventory relative to the industry. This conclusion is supported with evidence from Exhibit CC.8 where inventory growth is less than sales growth (116% versus 145%). These improvements in inventory management are concurrent with Campbell's launching of its just-in-time

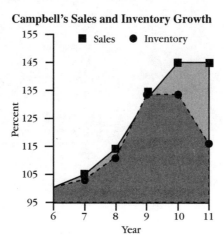

Campbell's Sales and Inventory Growth

Exhibit CC.7

CAMPBELL SOUP COMPANY
Common-Size Balance Sheets
For Years 6 to 11

	Year 11	Year 10	Year 9	Year 8	Year 7	Year 6	Year 11 Industry Composite
Current assets:							
Cash and cash equivalents	4.31%	1.96%	3.07%	2.38%	4.69%	5.61%	3.4%
Other temporary investments	0.31	0.55	0.67	0.97	9.05	8.64	
Accounts receivable	12.71	15.17	13.68	13.49	10.94	10.82	16.5
Inventories	17.03	19.92	20.75	18.41	20.13	22.10	38.6
Prepaid expenses	2.23	2.87	2.55	2.51	1.62	1.14	2.2
Total current assets	36.60%	40.47%	40.73%	37.76%	46.43%	48.31%	60.70%
Plant assets, net of depreciation	43.15%	41.74%	39.18%	41.80%	43.55%	42.28%	21.0%
Intangible assets, net of amortization	10.50	9.32	11.87	13.76	—	—	
Other assets	9.75	8.48	8.22	6.68	10.02	9.41	18.3
Total assets	100.00%	100.00%	100.00%	100.00%	100.00%	100.00%	100.00%
Current liabilities:							
Notes payable	6.80%	4.92%	6.90%	3.82%	3.02%	3.22%	6.7%
Payable to suppliers and others	11.63	12.76	12.92	12.38	12.10	11.64	10.2
Accrued liabilities	9.85	11.95	9.98	6.56	5.88	6.00	15.8
Dividend payable	0.89	0.78	0.76	—	—	—	
Accrued income taxes	1.63	1.13	0.77	1.16	1.40	1.80	
Total current liabilities	30.80%	31.54%	31.33%	23.92%	22.40%	22.66%	32.70%
Long-term debt	18.62%	19.58%	16.00%	14.57%	12.27%	13.11%	19.7%
Other liabilities, mainly deferred taxes	7.35	7.77	7.44	9.02	9.28	8.52	1.5

Shareowner's equity:							
Preferred stock; authorized 40,000,000 sh.; none issued	—	—	—	—	—	—	—
Capital stock, $0.15 par value; authorized 140,000,000 sh.; issued 135,622,676 sh.	0.49	0.49	0.52	0.56	0.66	0.73	
Capital surplus	2.59	1.50	1.29	1.17	1.33	1.38	
Earnings retained in the business	46.10	40.17	45.16	52.06	55.19	56.25	
Capital stock in treasury, at cost	−6.52	−2.60	−1.80	−2.08	−1.51	−1.75	
Cumulative translation adjustments	0.57	1.54	0.05	0.79	0.38	−0.91	
Total shareowner's equity	43.22%	41.11%	45.22%	52.50%	56.05%	55.70%	46.10%
Total liabilities and equity	100.00%	100.00%	100.00%	100.00%	100.00%	100.00%	100.00%

Exhibit CC.8

CAMPBELL SOUP COMPANY
Trend Index of Selected Accounts
(Year 6 = 100)

	Year 11	Year 10	Year 9	Year 8	Year 7	Year 6
Cash and cash equivalents	115%	52%	78%	55%	93%	$ 155.1
Accounts receivable	176	209	180	163	113	299.0
Temporary investments	5	9	11	15	117	238.7
Inventory	116	134	134	109	102.	610.5
Total current assets	114	125	120	102	108	1,334.8
Total current liabilities	204	207	197	138	111	626.1
Working capital	34	52	52	70	105	708.7
Plant assets, net	153	147	132	129	115	1,168.1
Other assets	156	134	124	93	119	259.9
Long-term debt	213	222	174	145	105	362.3
Total liabilities	192	198	176	140	111	1,223.9
Shareowners' equity	117	110	116	123	113	1,538.9
Net sales	145	145	132	114	105	4,268.8
Cost of products sold	133	138	130	110	103	3,082.7
Admin. and research expenses	157	148	129	119	109	195.9
Marketing and sales expenses	176	180	150	135	115	544.4
Interest expense	199	191	161	104	101	58.5
Total costs and expenses	142	155	143	115	105	3,900.0
Earnings before taxes	172	46	28	100	108	387.2
Net income	180	2*	6*	123	111	223.2

*Excluding the net effect of divestitures, restructuring, and unusual charges will change these amounts to:
Year 10–$137 and Year 9–$123.

Exhibit CC.9

CAMPBELL SOUP COMPANY
Per Share Results

	Year 11	Year 10	Year 9	Year 8	Year 7	Year 6
Sales	$48.85	$47.88	$43.87	$37.63	$34.57	$33.10
Net income	3.16	0.03	0.10	2.12	1.90	1.72
Dividends	1.12	0.98	0.90	0.81	0.71	0.65
Book value	14.12	13.09	13.76	14.69	13.35	11.86
Average shares outstanding (mil.)	127.0 sh.	129.6 sh.	129.3 sh.	129.4 sh.	129.9 sh.	129.5 sh.

inventory system. This improvement is especially evident with raw materials. Exhibit CC.12 reports inventory data showing a decline in the proportion of raw materials to total inventories consistent with our inference.

The LIFO inventory method is used in accounting for approximately 70 percent of inventories in Year 11 and 64 percent in Year 10 (see annual report note 14 in Supplement A). Exhibit CC.13 compares income and cost of goods sold using the LIFO and FIFO inventory methods. When prices are rising, LIFO income is typically lower than FIFO. In Campbell's case LIFO yielded income less than FIFO in Years 7, 9, and 11. During other years the reverse occurs. This might be due to declining costs or inventory liquidation.

Campbell's accounts receivable turnover has been declining over the past six years, but it is still above the industry level in Year 11 (see Exhibit CC.10). We also see from Exhibit CC.8 that accounts receivable are growing faster than sales, reaching a peak in Year 10 (209) with a decline in Year 11 (176). This is suggestive of a more aggressive credit policy. The collection period for accounts receivable (see Exhibit CC.10) worsened between Years 6 and 10, but improved slightly in Year 11. Similar behavior is evidenced with the inventory conversion period, with a general worsening from Years 6 through 10. Yet the conversion period in Year 11 returns to 92.7 days versus the 96.4 days for Year 6. This is primarily due to an improved inventory turnover, and helps Campbell in comparison to industry norms.

Campbell's success in managing current liabilities is varied. While the period in paying accounts payable increased from Year 6 through Year 8, the recent three years' payment period has leveled off (see Exhibit CC.10). Similarly, its average net trade cycle fluctuates over the past six years. But by Year 11 (47 days) it is below the Year 6 level of 57 days. This finding is consistent with the company's improving liquidity.

Cash Flow Analysis and Forecasting

Our cash flow analysis of Campbell Soup has two primary objectives:

- Analyze the statement of cash flows to assess long-term cash flows (solvency) and investigate cash flow patterns.
- Extend our analysis of static measures of short-term liquidity to include cash forecasting.

Exhibit CC.10

CAMPBELL SOUP COMPANY
Short-Term Liquidity Analysis

Units	Measure	Year 11	Year 10	Year 9	Year 8	Year 7	Year 6	Year 11 Industry Composite
1. Ratio	Current ratio	1.19	1.28	1.30	1.58	2.07	2.13	1.86
2. Ratio	Acid-test ratio	0.56	0.56	0.56	0.70	1.10	1.11	0.61
3. Times	Accounts receivable turnover	10.77	10.68	11.07	11.79	14.08	15.13	8.37
4. Times	Inventory turnover	5.37	5.21	5.41	5.27	5.15	5.14	2.53
5. Days	Days' sales in receivables	30.60	36.23	34.15	36.00	27.17	25.11	43.01
6. Days	Days' sales in inventory	62.12	69.31	73.41	70.53	70.59	71.29	142.03
7. Days	Approximate conversion period	92.72	105.54	107.56	106.53	97.76	96.40	185.32
8. Percent	Cash to current assets	11.78%	4.84%	7.55%	6.30%	10.14%	11.62%	5.60%
9. Percent	Cash to current liabilities	14.00%	6.22%	9.81%	9.94%	20.90%	24.77%	10.40%
10. Days	Liquidity index	59.87	72.62	72.55	71.46	52.29	52.07	130.62
11. M$'s	Working capital	240.50	367.40	369.40	499.60	744.10	708.70	54.33
12. Days	Days' purchases in accounts payable	46.03	46.56	46.20	49.30	44.25	39.33	
13. Days	Average net trade cycle	46.69	58.98	61.36	57.23	53.51	57.07	
14. Percent	Cash provided by operations to average current liabilities	62.51%	35.44%	34.10%	60.22%	71.36%	77.34%	

Notes:

For Year 11 (in millions):

(3) $\dfrac{\text{Net sales } \boxed{13}}{\text{Average accounts receivable } \boxed{33}} = \dfrac{6,204.1}{(527.4 + 624.5)/2} = 10.77$

(4) $\dfrac{\text{Cost of products sold } \boxed{14}}{\text{Average inventory } \boxed{34}} = \dfrac{4,095.5}{(706.7 + 819.8)/2} = 5.37$

(5) $\dfrac{\text{Ending accounts receivable } \boxed{33}}{\text{Sales } \boxed{13}/360} = \dfrac{527.4}{6{,}204.1/360} = 30.6$

(6) $\dfrac{\text{Ending inventory } \boxed{34}}{\text{Cost of products sold } \boxed{14}/360} = \dfrac{706.7}{4{,}095.5/360} = 62.12$

(7) Approximate conversion period = (5) Days' sales in receivables + (6) Days' sales in inventory

(10) *Financial item*

		Days Removed from Cash	Product
Cash and temporary investments $\boxed{31} + \boxed{32}$	191.7 ×	0 =	0
Accounts receivable $\boxed{33}$	527.4 ×	30.6 =	16138
Inventories $\boxed{34}$	706.7 ×	92.7 =	65511
Prepaid expenses $\boxed{35}$	92.7 ×	100* =	9270
	1,518.5		90919

Liquidity index $= \dfrac{90919}{1518.5} = 59.87$ days

*Assumed number.

(12) $\dfrac{\text{Accounts payable } \boxed{41}}{\text{Purchases per day}^\dagger} = \dfrac{482.4}{10.48} = 46.03$

†From Exhibit CC.12.

(13) Number of days' sales in:

Accounts receivable	30.60
Inventories	62.12
	92.72
Less: accounts payable	46.03
	46.69

(14) $\dfrac{\text{Cash from operations } \boxed{64}}{\text{Beginning + Ending current liabilities } \boxed{45} \div 2} = \dfrac{805.2}{1{,}288} = 62.51$

CC25

Exhibit CC.11

CAMPBELL SOUP COMPANY
Common-Size Analysis of
Current Assets and Current Liabilities

	Year 11	Year 10	Year 9	Year 8	Year 7	Year 6	Year 11 Industry Composite
Current assets:							
Cash and cash equivalents	11.78%	4.85%	7.55%	6.30%	10.09%	11.62%	5.60%
Other temporary investments	0.84	1.35	1.64	2.57	19.49	17.88	—
Accounts receivable	34.73	37.50	33.59	35.72	23.57	22.40	27.18
Inventories	46.54	49.22	50.95	48.77	43.37	45.74	63.60
Prepaid expenses	6.11	7.08	6.27	6.64	3.48	2.36	3.62
Total current assets	100.00%	100.00%	100.00%	100.00%	100.00%	100.00%	100.00%
Current liabilities:							
Notes payable	22.08%	15.58%	22.04%	15.99%	13.48%	14.20%	20.49%
Payable to suppliers and others	37.75	40.46	41.25	51.74	54.02	51.38	31.19
Accrued liabilities	31.98	37.89	31.86	27.44	26.25	26.50	48.32
Dividend payable	2.89	2.49	2.41	—	—	—	
Accrued income taxes	5.30	3.58	2.44	4.83	6.25	7.92	
Total current liabilities	100.00%	100.00%	100.00%	100.00%	100.00%	100.00%	100.00%

Exhibit CC.12

CAMPBELL SOUP COMPANY
Inventory Data
($ millions)

	Year 11	Year 10	Year 9	Year 8	Year 7	Year 6
1. Beginning inventory	$ 819.8	$ 816.0	$ 664.7	$ 623.6	$ 610.5	$ 623.1
2. Plus: production inputs	3,982.4	4,262.0	4,152.9	3,433.9	3,193.6	3,070.1
3. Goods available for sale	$4,802.2	$5,078.0	$4,187.6	$4,057.5	$3,804.1	$3,693.2
4. Less: Ending inventory	706.7	819.8	816.0	664.7	623.6	610.5
5. Cost of products sold	$4,095.5	$4,258.2	$4,001.6	$3,392.8	$3,180.5	$3,082.7
6. Depreciation	$ 208.6	$ 200.9	$ 192.3	$ 170.9	$ 144.6	$ 126.8
7. (2) − (6) = Purchases	3,773.8	4,061.1	3,960.6	3,263.0	3,049.0	2,943.3
8. (7)/360 = Purchases per day	$ 10.48	$ 11.28	$ 11.00	$ 9.06	$ 8.47	$ 8.18
Ending inventories:						
Raw materials, containers, and supplies	$ 342.3	$ 384.4	$ 385.0	$ 333.4	$ 333.6	$ 340.4
Finished products	454.0	520.0	519.0	412.5	372.4	348.1
	$ 796.3	$ 904.4	$ 904.0	$ 745.9	$ 706.0	$ 688.5
Less: Adjustment of inventories to LIFO	89.6	84.6	88.0	81.2	82.4	78.5
Total ending inventories	$ 706.7	$ 819.8	$ 816.0	$ 664.7	$ 623.6	$ 610.5
Raw materials, containers, and supplies	43.0%	42.5%	42.6%	44.7%	47.3%	49.4%
Finished products	57.0	57.5	57.4	55.3	52.7	50.6
	100.0%	100.0%	100.0%	100.0%	100.0%	100.0%

Exhibit CC.13

CAMPBELL SOUP COMPANY
Inventory Data Using FIFO versus LIFO
($ millions)

	Year 11	Year 10	Year 9	Year 8	Year 7	Year 6
Beginning inventory	$ 904.4	$ 904.0	$ 745.9	$ 706.0	$ 688.5	$ 707.0
Production inputs (same as LIFO)	3,982.4	4,262.0	4,152.9	3,433.9	3,193.6	3,070.1
Goods available for sale	$4,886.8	$5,166.0	$4,898.8	$4,139.9	$3,882.1	$3,777.1
Less: Ending inventory	796.3	904.4	904.0	745.9	706.0	688.5
Cost of products sold (FIFO)	$4,090.5	$4,261.6	$3,994.8	$3,394.0	$3,176.1	$3,088.6
Cost of products sold (LIFO)	$4,095.5	$4,258.2	$4,001.6	$3,392.8	$3,180.5	$3,082.7
Effect of restatement to FIFO increases (decreases) cost of products sold by:	$ (5.0)	$ 3.4	$ (6.8)	$ 1.2	$ (4.4)	$ 5.9
Net of tax* effect of restatement to FIFO decreases (increases) net income by:	$ (3.3)	$ 2.2	$ (4.5)	$ — 0.8	$ (2.4)	$ 3.2

*Tax rate is 34% for Years 8 through 11, 45% for Year 7, and 46% for Year 6.

We begin by analyzing cash flows from operations. Campbell reports cash flows from operations using the indirect method and we recast these to the more relevant inflow-outflow format (direct method). Results of our recasting are shown in Exhibit CC.14. This analysis reveals operating cash flows are a steady and growing source of cash, with a substantial increase in Year 11 ($805 million). The slight cash downturn in Year 9 is due primarily to an increase in inventories ($113 million) and a decrease in (negative) deferred taxes ($68 million). The increase in inventories is tied to management's desire to improve customer service, and the decrease in deferred taxes relates to restructuring and unusual charges that are not tax deductible, resulting in $78 million of credits to tax expense but higher current tax liabilities. We also note that the declines in net income for Years 9 and 10 are not reflected in operating cash flows. This is because these declines are from restructuring and divestiture charges having no immediate cash flow effects.

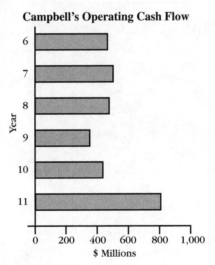

Campbell's Operating Cash Flow

Source: Annual report.

Our analysis of cash outflows reveals an increasing trend through Year 10. In Year 11, outflows decline mainly due to a $215 million decrease in cost of products sold. There is also evidence in Year 11 of improvements in cash flows due to a decrease of $38 million in inventory. These factors are partially offset by $91 million in higher taxes. Yet Campbell has successfully translated growing sales and increasingly larger margins into a steady growth in operating cash flows.

Exhibit CC.14

CAMPBELL SOUP COMPANY
Analysis of Cash from Operations: Direct Method
($ millions)

	Year 11	Year 10	Year 9	Year 8	Year 7	Year 6
Inflows:						
Net sales	$6,204.1	$6,205.8	$5,672.1	$4,868.9	$4,490.4	$4,286.8
(Increase) decrease in accounts receivable	17.1	(60.4)	(46.8)	(104.3)	(36.3)	(3.6)
Cash collections on sales	$6,221.2	$6,145.4	$5,625.3	$4,764.6	$4,454.1	$4,283.2
Interest income	26.0	17.6	38.3	33.2	29.5	27.4
Total cash collections from operations	$6,247.2	$6,163.0	$5,663.6	$4,797.8	$4,483.6	$4,310.6
Outflows:						
Cost of products sold*	3,823.7	4,038.7	3,772.0	3,178.9	3,007.9	2,939.3
Marketing and sales expenses	956.2	980.5	818.8	733.3	626.2	544.4
Administrative expenses	306.7	290.7	252.1	232.6	213.9	195.9
Foreign exchange losses	0.8	3.3	19.3	16.6	4.8	0.7
Interest expense	116.2	111.6	94.1	53.9	51.7	56.0
(Increase) decrease in deferred taxes	(35.5)	(3.9)	67.8	(13.4)	(45.7)	(29.0)
Research and development expenses	56.3	53.7	47.7	46.9	44.8	42.2
Other expenses (income)	26.2	14.7	32.4	19.8	(9.5)	5.5
Increase (decrease) in inventories	(48.7)	(10.7)	113.2	(54.2)	3.9	(23.1)
Net change in other current assets and liabilities	(30.6)	68.8	0.6	(30.2)	(42.9)	(48.7)
Income tax expense	265.9	175.0	93.4	147.0	170.6	164.0
Net effect of equity in earnings of affiliates and minority interests†	4.8	(7.8)	(5.1)	0.0	(10.4)	(0.4)
Total cash outflows for operations	$5,442.0	$5,714.6	$5,306.3	$4,331.2	$4,015.3	$3,846.8
Cash from operations	$ 805.2	$ 448.4	$ 357.3	$ 466.6	$ 468.3	$ 463.8

* Adjusted by items not effecting cash. For Year 11 the computation is:

Cost of products sold as per income statement (item [14]) $4,095.5
Less: Depreciation and amortization as per statement of cash flows (item [57]) 208.6
Less: Other, net as per statement of cash flows (item [60]) 63.2
$3,823.7

† This is aggregated for convenience. It is also appropriate to include dividend receipts under cash inflows.

Campbell's common-size statements of cash flows for the six years ending with Year 11 are shown in Exhibit CC.15. This exhibit reveals several patterns in the company's cash flows over these six years. Transitory fluctuations in cash like those due to the high usage of cash for investing activities in Year 7 (62%) are put in perspective by including aggregate figures for the six years in a total column. Total operating cash flows constitute more than one-half of all cash inflows. This finding along with evidence that financing activities (using 7% of cash inflows) are mostly refinancing is indicative of Campbell's financial strength and financing practices. The total column reveals that cash used for acquiring assets and businesses consumes nearly 50 percent of cash inflows, and about 12 percent of cash inflows are used for dividends. Overall, cash inflows from operations (56%) are used for both financing (7%) and investing (48%) activities. Campbell's net cash position over these six years is stable, never deviating more than 7 percent from the prior year. Its growth for the entire six-year period is less than 1 percent.

It is often useful for us to construct a summary of cash inflows and outflows by major categories of activity. Using Exhibit CC.4, we prepare the following chart of cash inflows and outflows ($ millions):

	Year 11	Year 10	Year 9	Year 8	Year 7	Year 6	Total
Operating activities	$805.2	$448.4	$357.3	$466.6	$468.3	$463.8	$3,009.6
Investing activities	(478.7)	(387.5)	(473.2)	(462.2)	(401.0)	(387.6)	(2,590.2)
Financing activities	(219.6)	(101.8)	(163.1)	(52.8)	(88.3)	(54.5)	(353.9)
Increase (decrease) in cash	98.2	(40.2)	35.1	(59.2)	(28.1)	18.0	23.8

The picture emerging from this summary is that Campbell has major outlays for (1) investing—$2,590.2 million, and (2) financing (including dividends)—$353.9 million. Through this, Campbell experienced a slight cumulative increase of $23.8 million in cash. Notably, these activities are funded by Campbell's net operating cash inflows of $3,009.6 million. Notice that in Years 7, 8, and 10 the cash balances are drawn down to fund investing and financing activities. Yet operating cash flows for this six-year period are sufficient to fund all of Campbell's investing and financing needs and still leave excess cash of $23.8 million.

Our next stage of analysis is forecasting short-term cash flows. This forecasting analysis supplements the above static measures of short-term

Exhibit CC.15

CAMPBELL SOUP COMPANY
Common-Size Statements of Cash Flows*
For Years 6 to 11

	Year 11	Year 10	Year 9	Year 8	Year 7	Year 6	Total
Cash flows from operating activities:							
Net earnings	26.89%	0.54%	1.15%	25.14%	38.42%	27.88%	21.54%
To reconcile net earnings to net cash provided by operating activities:							
Depreciation and amortization	13.97	24.58	16.82	15.67	22.47	15.84	19.33
Divestitures and restructuring provisions	—	41.49	30.00	1.61	—	—	12.95
Deferred taxes	2.38	0.48	(5.93)	1.23	7.10	3.62	1.11
Other, net	4.23	2.28	3.26	3.94	4.35	2.07	3.83
Cumulative effect of accounting change	—	—	—	(2.98)	—	—	(0.60)
(Increase) decrease in accounts receivable	1.15	(7.39)	(4.09)	(9.57)	(5.64)	(0.45)	(4.34)
(Increase) decrease in inventories	3.26	1.31	(9.90)	4.97	(0.61)	2.89	0.36
Net change in other current assets and liabilities	2.05	(8.42)	(0.05)	2.77	6.67	6.08	1.54
Net cash provided by operating activities	53.92%	54.86%	31.25%	42.80%	72.76%	57.94%	55.72%
Cash flows from investing activities:							
Purchase of plant assets	(24.18)%	(47.42)%	(24.85)%	(22.50)%	(47.19)%	(29.39)%	(33.64)%
Sale of plant assets	2.89	4.27	3.48	2.07	—	3.72	3.15
Businesses acquired	(12.06)	(5.09)	(11.88)	(43.28)	(1.13)	(2.50)	(15.86)
Sale of businesses	4.51	2.66	0.43	2.16	3.23	—	2.56
Increase in other assets	(3.87)	(2.28)	(9.36)	(3.70)	(7.78)	(2.25)	(5.40)
Net change in other temporary investments	0.65	0.45	0.79	22.86	(9.43)	(18.00)	1.24
Net cash used in investing activities	(32.06)%	(47.41)%	(41.39)%	(42.39)%	(62.31)%	(48.42)%	(47.95)%

Cash flows from financing activities:							
Long-term borrowings	26.97%	1.54%	11.07%	9.45%	0.75%	25.47%	15.80%
Repayments of long-term borrowings	(8.70)	(2.75)	(4.69)	(2.10)	(3.71)	(20.57)	(7.73)
Increase (decrease) in short-term borrowings	(9.23)	(0.33)	9.46	0.77	(3.22)	0.57	(0.74)
Other short-term borrowings	7.86	18.81	19.87	7.06	13.88	9.11	13.65
Repayments of other short-term borrowings	(13.82)	(10.99)	(16.82)	(8.03)	(10.30)	(11.06)	(13.53)
Dividends paid	(9.21)	(15.21)	(7.58)	(9.59)	(14.25)	(13.07)	(12.02)
Treasury stock purchases	(11.76)	(5.03)	(0.71)	(2.69)	—	—	(4.70)
Treasury stock issued	3.19	1.52	1.62	0.08	0.25	0.50	1.58
Other, net	(0.01)	(0.01)	2.06	0.21	2.89	2.24	1.15
Net cash provided (used in) financing activities	(14.71)%	(12.46)%	14.27%	(4.84)%	(13.72)%	(6.81)%	(6.55)%
Effect of exchange rate change on cash	(0.58)%	0.09%	1.06%	(0.99)%	(1.10)%	(0.46)%	(0.77)%
Net increase (decrease) in cash and cash equivalents	6.58	(4.92)	3.07	(5.43)	(4.37)	2.25	0.44

*Common-size percentages are based on total cash inflows = 100%. For Year 11 the 100 percent is composed of: CFO (53 92) + Sale of plant assets (2.89) + Sale of bus. (4.51) + Decrease in temp. invest. (0.65) + LT borrowings (26.97) + ST borrowings (7.86) + Treas. stock issued (3.19).

liquidity. A first step in forecasting operating cash flows is predicting earnings. We prepare forecasts for Campbell's statement of earnings for Year 12 (see Exhibit CC.16 and its footnotes for assumptions). We begin with a forecast of net sales—predicted to be 2.35 percent higher than the prior year. We forecast net earnings in Year 12 at $480 million, about 20 percent higher than the previous year (this reflects Campbell's five-year earnings growth of 13% plus an increment for predictably good business strategy). This earnings increase reflects more a predicted increase in operating margin than in sales. The increase in operating margin is primarily due to decreases in overall manufacturing costs. While labor costs are slightly higher, the costs of metal food containers are considerably lower due to increased competition and production in the aluminum industry. We also expect financing costs to decline from a drop in short-term interest rates. Because of their restructuring we expect Campbell to benefit from favorable operating leverage. Details behind these forecasts are reported in the notes to Exhibit CC.16.

Forecasts for the statement of cash flows for Years 12 and 13 appear in Exhibit 4.7. These forecasts use the assumptions above plus a few additional ones. The forecasted statements of cash flows expect Campbell to finance investing activities primarily from operating cash flows and redeem some of its high coupon long-term debt. If these forecasts are realized, Campbell will have enough cash for dividends and other uses.

Two additional measures of Campbell's cash flows are reported in Exhibit CC.17. The cash flow adequacy ratio provides us insight into whether Campbell generates sufficient cash from operations to cover capital expenditures, investments in inventories, and cash dividends. Campbell's cash flow adequacy ratio for the six-year period is 0.875, implying that funds generated from operations are insufficient to cover these items (see denominator) and that there is a need for external financing. We must remember this is an aggregate (six-year sum) ratio. When we look at individual years, including Year 11, the cash flow adequacy ratio suggests sufficient cash resources. The exceptions are Years 7 and 9. A second measure, the cash reinvestment ratio, provides us insight into the amount of cash retained and reinvested into the company for both asset replacement and growth. Campbell's cash reinvestment ratio is 11.8 percent for the six-year period. This reinvestment rate is satisfactory for the industry. The Year 11 reinvestment ratio is much higher (18.7%) than normal. Years 9 and 10 show a lower ratio due to decreases in operating cash flows.

Exhibit CC.16

CAMPBELL SOUP COMPANY
Forecasted Statement of Earnings
For Year Ended Year 12
($ millions)

	Forecast	Percent
Net sales*	$6,350.0	100.00%
Costs and expenses†		
Cost of products sold	4,095.8	64.50
Marketing and selling expenses	990.6	15.60
Administrative expenses	308.0	4.85
Research and development expenses	57.2	0.90
Interest expense	114.3	1.80
Interest income	(31.8)	−0.50
Other expense (income), including foreign exchange losses	88.9	1.40
Total costs and expenses	$5,623.0	88.55%
Earnings before taxes‡	$ 727.0	11.45%
Taxes on earnings§	(247.0)	−3.89
Net earnings	$ 480.0	7.56%

*Projected at 2.35 percent higher than Year 11 sales of $6,204.1 (consistent with analysts' forecasts from the Value Line Investment Survey, Feb. 21, Year 12).

†Forecasts for costs and expenses are based on the following expectations:

(1) Cost of products sold is expected to be 64.5 percent of Year 12 sales. This is consistent with the Year 9 through Year 11 average and recognizes the increase in gross margin in recent years.

(2) Marketing and selling expenses are expected to approximate the Year 9 through Year 11 average with a slight increase due to an increase in advertising.

(3) Administrative expenses are expected to increase slightly from the average for Year 9 through Year 11.

(4) All other items are expected to approximate the same level as their average for Year 9 through Year 11.

‡Effects of equity in earnings of affiliates and minority interests are considered immaterial.

§At the expected federal statutory rate of 34 percent.

Capital Structure and Solvency

We next analyze Campbell's capital structure and solvency (the analysis above related to cash forecasting is relevant to solvency). Changes in the company's capital structure are measured using various analyses and comparisons. Campbell's capital structure for the six years ending in Year 11 is depicted in Exhibit CC.18. For analytical purposes, one-half of deferred taxes is considered a long-term liability and the other half as equity. Exhibit CC.19 shows a common-size analysis of capital structure. For Year 11, liabilities constitute 53 percent and equity 47 percent of Campbell's financing.

Campbell's Financing Sources

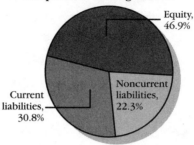

Source: Annual reports

Exhibit CC.17

CAMPBELL SOUP COMPANY
Analysis of Cash Flow Ratios
($ millions)

(1) Cash flow adequacy ratio* = $\dfrac{\text{6-year sum of sources of cash from operations}}{\begin{array}{c}\text{6-year sum of capital expenditures, inventory additions,}\\ \text{and cash dividends}\end{array}}$

$= \dfrac{3,009.6}{(1,817.1 + 856.7) + (113.2 + 3.9) + 649.4}$

$= 0.875$

(2) Cash reinvestment ratio† = $\dfrac{\text{Cash provided by operations} - \text{Dividends}}{\text{Gross PPE} + \text{Investments} + \text{Other assets} + \text{Working capital}}$

Year 6 to Year 11 average =	$\dfrac{3,009.6 - 649.4}{15,183.7 + 1,888.3 + 2,929.7}$	= 11.8%
Year 11 =	$\dfrac{805.2 - 137.5}{2,921.9 + 404.6 + 240.5}$	= 18.7%
Year 10 =	$\dfrac{448.4 - 124.3}{2,734.9 + 349.0 + 367.4}$	= 9.4%
Year 9 =	$\dfrac{357.3 - 86.7}{2,543.0 + 323.1 + 369.4}$	= 8.4%
Year 8 =	$\dfrac{466.6 - 104.6}{2,539.7 + 241.2 + 499.6}$	= 11.0%
Year 7 =	$\dfrac{468.3 - 91.7}{2,355.1 + 310.5 + 744.1}$	= 11.0%
Year 6 =	$\dfrac{463.8 - 104.6}{2,089.1 + 259.9 + 708.7}$	= 11.7%

*All amounts are from the statement of cash flows.
†Numerator amounts are from the statement of cash flows and denominator amounts are from the balance sheet.

Selected capital structure and long-term solvency ratios are reported in Exhibit CC.20. The total debt to equity ratio increases markedly in the past three years, yet remains at or below the industry norm (1.17). The source of this increase is attributed to long-term debt (see Exhibit CC.8). In particular, Exhibit CC.8 shows the trend index of long-term debt (213) exceeds that for current liabilities (204), total liabilities (192), and share-owners' equity (117). This is also evident in Campbell's long-term debt to equity ratio, where in Year 11 the ratio for Campbell (48%) exceeds the industry composite of 43 percent. We also compute the analytically adjusted long-term debt to equity ratio. For Campbell this ratio does not differ markedly from its unadjusted counterpart. These measures suggest that Campbell is moving away from its historically conservative capital structure toward a more aggressive one. This is corroborated by a lower level of fixed charge coverage ratios using both earnings and operating cash flow compared with Years 6–8. Consistent with our analysis,

Exhibit CC.18

CAMPBELL SOUP COMPANY
Analysis of Capital Structure
(millions)

	Year 11	Year 10	Year 9	Year 8	Year 7	Year 6
Long-term liabilities:						
Notes payable	$ 757.8	$ 792.9	$ 610.3	$ 507.1	$ 358.8	$ 346.7
Capital lease obligation	14.8	12.9	18.9	18.7	21.4	15.6
Total long-term debt	$ 772.6	$ 805.8	$ 629.2	$ 525.8	$ 380.2	$ 362.3
Deferred income taxes*	129.3	117.6	109.0	140.3	124.0	99.6
Other long-term liabilities	23.0	28.5	19.6	15.6	15.8	16.3
Total long-term liabilities	$ 924.9	$ 951.9	$ 757.8	$ 681.7	$ 520.0	$ 478.2
Current liabilities†	1,278.0	1,298.1	1,232.1	863.3	693.8	626.1
Total liabilities	$2,202.9	$2,250.0	$1,989.9	$1,545.0	$1,213.8	$1,104.3
Equity capital:						
Common shareholders' equity	$1,793.4	$1,691.8	$1,778.3	$1,895.0	$1,736.1	$1,538.9
Minority interests	23.5	56.3	54.9	29.3	23.5	20.1
Deferred income taxes*	129.2	117.5	109.0	140.3	124.0	99.5
Total equity capital	$1,946.1	$1,865.6	$1,942.2	$2,064.6	$1,883.6	$1,658.5
Total liabilities and equity	$4,149.0	$4,115.6	$3,932.1	$3,609.6	$2,097.4	$2,762.8

*For analytical purposes 50 percent of deferred income taxes are considered debt and the remainder equity.
†Including notes payable—current.

Exhibit CC.19

CAMPBELL SOUP COMPANY
Common-Size Analysis of Capital Structure

	Year 11	Year 10	Year 9	Year 8	Year 7	Year 6
Long-term liabilities:						
Notes payable	18.26%	19.27%	15.52%	14.05%	11.59%	12.55%
Capital lease obligation	0.36	0.31	0.48	0.52	0.69	0.56
Total long-term debt	18.62%	19.58%	16.00%	14.57%	12.28%	13.11%
Deferred income taxes*	3.12	2.86	2.77	3.88	4.00	3.61
Other long-term liabilities	0.55	0.69	0.50	0.43	0.51	0.59
Total long-term liabilities	22.29%	23.13%	19.27%	18.88%	16.79%	17.31%
Current liabilities†	30.80	31.54	31.34	23.92	22.40	22.66
Total liabilities	53.09%	54.67%	50.61%	42.80%	39.19%	39.97%
Equity capital:						
Common shareholders' equity	43.22%	41.11%	45.22%	52.50%	56.05%	55.70%
Minority interests	0.57	1.37	1.40	0.81	0.76	0.73
Deferred income taxes*	3.12	2.85	2.77	3.89	4.00	3.60
Total equity capital	46.91%	45.33%	49.39%	57.20%	60.81%	60.03%
Total liabilities and equity	100.00%	100.00%	100.00%	100.00%	100.00%	100.00%

*For analytical purposes 50 percent of deferred income taxes are considered debt and the remainder equity.
†Including notes payable—current.

Campbell's long-term debt is rated AA by the major rating agencies—down from the AAA rating the company enjoyed previously, but still an excellent rating. The company's creditors enjoy sound asset protection and superior earning power.

Return on Invested Capital

Return on invested capital ratios for Campbell are reported in Exhibit CC.21. These ratios reveal several insights. The return on assets is stable during Years 6 through 8, declines sharply for Years 9 and 10, and then rebounds strongly to 11.75 percent in Year 11. Analysis of Years 9 and 10 shows these years' low returns are due to divestitures and restructuring charges. Yet we must keep in mind the marked increase in return for Year 11 is probably due in part to the two prior years' write-offs.

Further analysis of return on assets for Year 11 shows it is comprised of a 7.83 percent profit margin (not shown in Exhibit CC.21) and an asset

Exhibit CC.20

CAMPBELL SOUP COMPANY
Capital Structure and Solvency Ratios

	Year 11	Year 10	Year 9	Year 8	Year 7	Year 6	Year 11 Industry Composite
1. Total debt to equity	1.13	1.21	1.02	0.75	0.64	0.67	1.17
2. Total debt ratio	0.53	0.55	0.51	0.43	0.39	0.40	0.54
3. Long-term debt to equity	0.48	0.51	0.39	0.33	0.28	0.29	0.43
4. Adjusted long-term debt to equity	0.49	0.50	0.38	0.33	0.27	0.28	—
5. Equity to total debt	0.88	0.83	0.98	1.34	1.56	1.50	0.86
6. Fixed assets to equity	0.92	0.92	0.79	0.73	0.72	0.70	0.46
7. Current liabilities to total liabilities	0.58	0.58	0.62	0.56	0.58	0.57	0.61
8. Earnings to fixed charges	5.16	2.14	1.84	6.06	6.41	6.28	—
9. Cash flow to fixed charges	7.47	5.27	5.38	8.94	8.69	9.26	—

Computations for Year 11:

(1) $\dfrac{\text{Total debt}^*}{\text{Equity capital}^*} = \dfrac{2,202.9}{1,946.1} = 1.13$

(2) $\dfrac{\text{Total debt}^*}{\text{Total debt and equity } \boxed{55}} = \dfrac{2,202.9}{4,149.0} = 0.53$

(3) $\dfrac{\text{Long-term debt}^*}{\text{Equity capital}^*} = \dfrac{924.9}{1,946.1} = 0.48$

(4) $\dfrac{\text{Long-term debt}^* + \text{Estimated present value of operating lease obligations } \boxed{143}}{\text{Equity capital}^* + \text{Excess of FIFO over LIFO inventory } \boxed{153}} = \dfrac{924.9 + 64.1^{\ddagger}}{1,946.1 + 89.6} = 0.49$

(5) $\dfrac{\text{Equity capital}^*}{\text{Total debt}^*} = \dfrac{1,946.1}{2,202.9} = 0.88$

(6) $\dfrac{\text{Plant assets } \boxed{37}}{\text{Equity capital}^*} = \dfrac{1,790.4}{1,946.1} = 0.92$

(7) $\dfrac{\text{Current liabilities } \boxed{45}}{\text{Total liabilities}^*} = \dfrac{1,278.0}{2,202.9} = 0.58$

(8) $\dfrac{\text{Pre-tax income } \boxed{26} + \text{Interest expense } \boxed{18} + \text{Interest portion of rent expense}^{\dagger} - \text{Undistributed equity in earnings in affiliates } \boxed{24},\ \boxed{169A}}{\text{Interest incurred } \boxed{98} + \text{Interest portion of rent expense}^{\dagger}\ \boxed{143}} = \dfrac{667.4 + 116.2 + 20 - (2.4 - 8.2)}{136.9 + 20} = 5.16$

(9) $\dfrac{\text{Cash flows from operations } \boxed{64} + \text{Current tax expense } \boxed{124A} + \text{Interest expense } \boxed{18} + \text{Interest portion of rent expense}^{\dagger}\ \boxed{143}}{\text{Interest incurred } \boxed{98} + \text{Interest portion of rent expense}^{\dagger}\ \boxed{143}} = \dfrac{805.2 + 230.4 + 116.2 + 20}{136.9 + 20} = 7.47$

* From Exhibit CC.18.
† One-third of rent expense under operating leases. For Year 11: 1/3 of $59.7 $\boxed{143}$.
‡ Computed as $71.9/1.1$^{1.204}$ (see Appendix 5C for explanation).

turnover of 1.50. Both these components show improvement over their values from Year 8 (comparisons with Year 10 and Year 9 ratios are less relevant due to accounting charges). They also compare favorably with industry norms. Campbell's management hopes these improvements for Year 11 are reflective of their major restructuring, closings, and business reorganizations during Years 9 and 10. Because of those restructuring programs and cost-cutting efforts, profit margins are widening. Prior years' returns are depressed by several poorly performing or ill-fitting businesses. Those businesses are now divested and Campbell has streamlined and modernized its manufacturing.

Exhibit CC.21

CAMPBELL SOUP COMPANY
Return on Invested Capital Ratios

	Year 11	Year 10*	Year 9*	Year 8	Year 7	Year 6	Year 11 Industry Composite
1. Return on assets (ROA)	11.75%	2.08%	2.13%	9.42%	9.57%	9.90%	9.20%
2. Return on common equity (ROCE)*	21.52%	0.24%	0.67%	14.07%	14.14%	14.40%	19.80%
3. Return on long-term debt and equity	17.07%	3.04%	2.96%	12.27%	12.35%	12.90%	13.50%
4. Financial leverage index (ROCE ÷ ROA)	1.83	0.12	0.31	1.49	1.48	1.46	2.15
5. Equity growth rate	13.85%	−6.30%	−3.67%	8.59%	8.79%	8.96%	—
6. Disaggregation of return on common equity*							
Adjusted profit margin	6.47%	0.07%	0.23%	5.63%	5.51%	5.10%	6.60%
	×	×	×	×	×	×	×
Asset turnover	1.50	1.54	1.50	1.45	1.53	1.68	1.38
	×	×	×	×	×	×	×
Financial leverage ratio	2.22	2.18	1.92	1.72	1.68	1.68	2.17
	21.52%	0.24%	0.67%	14.07%	14.14%	14.40%	19.80%

Computations for Year 11:

$$(1)\ \text{ROA} = \frac{\text{Net income} + \text{Interest expense } (1 - \text{Tax rate}) + \text{Minority interest (MI)}}{\text{Average total assets}} = \frac{401.5 + 116.2\ (1 - 0.34) + 7.2}{(4,149.0 + 4,115.6)/2} = 11.75\%$$

$$\text{ROA disaggregated} = \frac{\text{Net income} + \text{Interest expense } (1 - \text{Tax rate}) + \text{Minority interest}}{\text{Sales}} \times \frac{\text{Sales}}{\text{Average total assets}}$$

$$= \left[\frac{401.5 + 116.2\ (1 - 0.34) + 7.2}{6,204.1} = 7.83\%\right] \times \left[\frac{6,204.1}{(4,149.0 + 4,115.6)/2} = 1.5\right] = 11.75\%$$

$$\text{Industry ROA composite} = \qquad 6.6\% \qquad\qquad \times \qquad 1.4 \qquad\qquad = 9.24\%$$

$$(2)\ \text{ROCE} = \frac{\text{Net income} - \text{Preferred dividend}}{\text{Average common equity}^\dagger} = \frac{401.5}{[(1,946.1 - 23.5) + (1,865.6 - 56.3)]/2} = 21.52\%$$

$$\text{ROCE disaggregated} = \frac{\text{Adjusted profit}}{\text{margin}} \times \text{Asset turnover} \times \frac{\text{Financial}}{\text{leverage ratio}} = \frac{401.5}{6,204.1} \times \frac{6,204.1}{(4,149.0 + 4,115.6)/2} \times \frac{(4,149.0 + 4,115.6)/2}{1,865.95^\dagger}$$

$$= 6.47\% \times \qquad 1.50 \qquad \times \qquad 2.22 \qquad = 21.52\%$$

$$(3)\ \text{Return on LTD and equity} = \frac{\text{Net income} + \text{Interest expense } (1 - \text{Tax rate}) + \text{MI}}{\text{Average long-term liabilities}^\dagger + \text{Average equity}^\dagger} = \frac{401.5 + 116.2\ (1 - 0.34) + 7.2}{(924.9 + 951.9)/2 + (1,946.1 + 1,865.6)/2} = 17.07\%$$

$$(4)\ \text{Financial leverage index} = \frac{\text{Return on common equity}}{\text{Return on assets}} = \frac{21.52\%}{11.75\%} = 1.83$$

$$(5)\ \text{Equity growth rate} = \frac{\text{Net income} - \text{Dividends paid}}{\text{Average common equity}^\dagger} = \frac{401.5 - 137.5}{(1,946.1 + 1,865.6)/2} = 13.85\%$$

* Excluding the effect of divestitures, restructuring, and unusual charges, net of tax, of $301.6 million in Year 10, and $260.8 million in Year 9, drastically changes these ratios. For example, ROA, for Year 10 and Year 9 becomes 9.57 percent and 9.03 percent, respectively.

† Including 50 percent of deferred taxes assumed as equity, and excluding minority interests (MI). See Exhibit CC.18.

‡ Including 50 percent of deferred taxes. See Exhibit CC.18.

Campbell's return on common equity (21.52%) exceeds both the industry norm and its most recent performance. The source of improvement is due to a solid net income margin and leverage ratio. Like the profit component in return on assets, the improved net income margin likely benefits from write-offs in Years 10 and 9. Disaggregation of Campbell's return on equity (item 6 in Exhibit CC.21) shows that changes in the net income margin are primarily responsible for fluctuations in return on equity during recent years. Net income margin is as low as 0.07 percent in Year 10 from the divestitures and restructurings, and is as high as 6.47

percent in Year 11 partly due to the rebound from prior years' changes and potential cost overprovisions. The other two components are reasonably stable. Asset turnover declined slightly in Year 7 from Year 6, but remained relatively level through other years, while the leverage ratio increases gradually during the six-year period because of Campbell's increasingly leveraged capital structure.

Comparison of these dissaggregated components with industry norms reveals a favorable asset turnover ratio (1.50 versus 1.38), a typical leverage ratio (2.22 versus 2.17), and a normal or slightly unfavorable net income margin (6.57 versus 6.60). This implies Campbell's higher asset turnover (1.50) and higher leverage ratio (2.22) are primarily responsible for the favorable return on equity (21.52%) compared to the industry norm (19.8%). Recall that Campbell's increased leverage ratio yielded costs in the form of a lower credit rating.

The leverage ratio for Year 11 implies that Campbell is borrowing $1.22 on each dollar of equity. This inference is based on considering 50 percent of deferred taxes as interest-free debt. The total $2.22 in funds is then able to generate $3.33 in sales because assets are turning over at a rate of 1.50 times. This $3.33 in sales earns 6.47 percent in net income, yielding a return on equity of 21.52 percent.

Campbell's return on long-term debt and equity displays a pattern similar to return on equity over the past six years. For Year 11, return on long-term liabilities and equity is 17.07 percent. This compares favorably with the industry composite of 13.50 percent. Campbell's financial leverage index (1.83) is positive and reasonably stable, the exception being Years 9 and 10 for reasons discussed earlier. In Year 11, it rebounds strongly and improves from earlier years. This ratio confirms what we already know from our other evidence—Campbell utilizes its debt profitably.

Notice that Campbell's Year 11 equity growth rate (13.85%) markedly improved relative to prior years. Even if we exclude Years 9 and 10, this rate is nearly double the level for Years 6 through 8. The negative ratios for Years 9 and 10 are because Campbell maintained its dividend payout with its divestitures and restructuring. The strong rebound in this ratio for Year 11 bodes well for future growth in sales and earnings. A higher level of reinvestment frees Campbell from reliance on outside financing sources to fund its growth. The Year 11 net income of $401.5 million and dividends of $142.2 million leave sufficient funds for reinvestment and internally financed growth.

Campbell's Financial Leverage

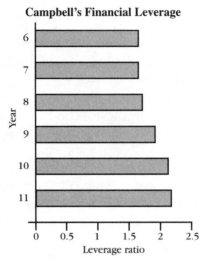

Source: Annual report.

Analysis of Asset Utilization

Campbell's asset utilization measures are reported in Exhibit CC.22. Campbell's asset turnover (1.5 for Year 11) is stable over the past six years. Yet this stability in asset turnover masks significant changes in turnover for individual asset components. Cash and cash equivalents evidence the most significant variability during this period. Variability in cash and cash equivalents is also evidenced in both the sales to working capital turnover ratio and in the common-size balance sheet in Exhibit CC.7. Exhibit CC.7 reveals a gradual disposal of temporary investments. The sizeable $98.2 million increase in Year 11 cash and cash equivalents is primarily due to improvements in operating performance (see Exhibit CC.4).

Campbell's accounts receivable turnover shows a slight improvement in Years 8 through 11 relative to earlier years. The continued improvement in Year 11 is helped by this year's decrease of $97.1 million in receivables. Regarding inventory turnover, Campbell's expressed desire to decrease inventories at every stage of its manufacturing process is revealing itself through an improved turnover ratio (8.8). It is important to see that Campbell's asset and asset component turnover ratios often compare favorably to industry norms. In several key areas like receivables (11.8 versus 8.4), inventories (8.8 versus 3.6), and working capital (25.8 versus 4.9), its turnover ratio is better than the industry composite.

Exhibit CC.22

CAMPBELL SOUP COMPANY
Asset Utilization Ratios

	Year 11	Year 10	Year 9	Year 8	Year 7	Year 6	Year 11 Industry Composite
1. Sales to cash and equivalents	34.7	76.9	46.9	56.8	31.0	27.6	40.6
2. Sales to receivables	11.8	9.9	10.5	10.0	13.2	14.3	8.4
3. Sales to inventories	8.8	7.6	7.0	7.3	7.2	7.0	3.6
4. Sales to working capital	25.8	16.9	15.4	9.8	6.0	6.1	4.9
5. Sales to fixed assets	3.5	3.6	3.7	3.2	3.3	3.7	6.6
6. Sales to other assets*	7.4	8.5	7.2	6.6	14.5	16.5	7.5
7. Sales to total assets	1.5	1.5	1.4	1.4	1.5	1.6	1.4
8. Sales to short-term liabilities	4.9	4.8	4.6	5.6	6.5	6.9	4.2

*Including intangible assets.

Analysis of Operating Performance and Profitability

Selected profit margin measures for Campbell are reported in Exhibit CC.23. We see that Campbell's gross profit margin for Year 11 is better than the industry norm (34.0% versus 29.3%). However its net profit margin is at or slightly below the industry level (6.47% versus 6.60%). After the divestitures and restructuring of Years 9 and 10, Campbell's net profit margin is better than it was in Years 6 through 8. These moves included eliminating administrative personnel and unsuccessful divisions. Results in Year 11 already show indications of tighter control over several areas of operating expenses. Continued cost control should allow Campbell to further improve its profitability and exceed industry norms.

We link these profitability measures with evidence in earlier analyses. Improvement evidenced in the gross profit margin confirms earlier results in Exhibit CC.6 showing a gradual decline in cost of products sold (66.01% in Year 11 versus 71.91% in Year 6).While continued improvement in gross profit margin is possible, it will be difficult to achieve. The key for a profit ratio to benefit from improved gross profit margin is continued control over administrative and marketing expenses. This analysis is corroborated by our earlier trend index analysis. Exhibit CC.8 shows sales in Year 11 are 145 percent higher than for Year 6. Yet cost of products sold is only 133 percent greater, and the total of costs and expenses is 142 percent greater. This combination yields a net income that is 180 percent larger than the Year 6 level. The general inference from these trend indexes

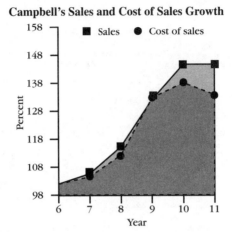

is that sales, gross margin, and net income are growing at a relatively faster rate than costs and expenses.

Exhibit CC.8 reveals that interest expense grew throughout the six-year period but at a relatively lower rate than did total liabilities, except for Year 11. This reflects a lower cost of borrowing resulting primarily from lower interest rates. We also note that Campbell is probably a more risky borrower compared to three to five years earlier as reflected in its increasing debt to equity ratio.

The Supplemental Schedule of Sales and Earnings in Campbell's annual report (item $\boxed{1}$) shows the contributions of international operations to Year 11. International earnings total $92.3 million, including $35.3 million from Campbell Canada, $17.6 million from International Biscuit, and $39.4 million from Campbell International. International earnings represents about 11.6 percent of total operating earnings. In Years 10 and 9, international operations contribute negatively to total earnings. This is due to the restructuring in those years, reducing total operating earnings by $134.1 million in Year 10 and by $82.3 million in Year 9. These negative contributions are in addition to losses from foreign currency translation of $3.8 million and $20.0 million in Years 10 and 9, respectively. Foreign currency translation is not significant in Year 11. Nevertheless, international operations for the past six years comprise nearly 20 percent of total sales (see Exhibit CC.1). International operations are expected to continue to exert a significant impact on Campbell's profitability.

Campbell's effective tax rate (note 9) is 39.8 percent in Year 11, 97.5 percent in Year 10, and 87.7 percent in Year 9. The extraordinarily high

Exhibit CC.23

CAMPBELL SOUP COMPANY
Analysis of Profit Margin Ratios

Profit margins	Year 11	Year 10	Year 9	Year 8	Year 7	Year 6	Year 11 Industry Composite
1. Gross profit margin	34.00%	31.38%	29.45%	30.32%	29.17%	28.09%	29.30%
2. Operating profit margin	12.63%	4.69%	3.54%	9.09%	10.46%	10.34%	—
3. Net profit margin	6.47%	0.07%	0.23%	5.63%	5.51%	5.21%	6.60%

Computations for Year 11:

(1) Gross profit margin $= \dfrac{\text{Net sales} - \text{Cost of products sold}}{\text{Net sales}} = \dfrac{6{,}204.1 - 4{,}095.5}{6{,}204.1} = 34\%$

(2) Operating profit margin $= \dfrac{\text{Income before taxes and interest expense}}{\text{Net sales}} = \dfrac{667.4 + 116.2}{6{,}204.1} = 12.63\%$

rates for the latter two years are due mainly to the large amounts of non-deductible divestiture, restructuring, and unusual charges, representing 56.5 and 48.7 percent of earnings before taxes, respectively (note 9). If we exclude these divestitures, the effective tax rate declines to about 40 percent. Campbell is also taking advantage of tax loss carryforward benefits from international subsidiaries. At the end of Year 11 the company has $77.4 million remaining in unused tax loss carryforward benefits. About one-half of these expire by Year 16 and the remainder are available indefinitely. Most deferred taxes result from pensions, depreciation timing differences, divestiture, restructuring, and unusual charges. Deferred taxes due to depreciation differences are relatively large through Year 10, then decline to a low of $ 5.9 million in Year 11.

Analysis of depreciation data for Campbell is reported in Exhibit CC.24. This evidence shows that accumulated depreciation as a percent of gross plant assets remains stable (44.6% in Year 11). Stability in depreciation expense, as a percent of either plant assets or sales, is also evident in Exhibit CC.24. Accordingly, there is no evidence that earnings quality is affected due to changes in depreciation.

Analysis of discretionary expenditures in Exhibit CC.25 shows spending in all major categories during Year 11 declines compared to most prior years. This potentially results from more controlled spending and enhanced efficiencies. Recall our common-size analysis of factors affecting net earnings in Exhibit CC.6. This analysis is corroborative of some of the factors evidenced in Exhibit CC.25. For example, gross margin is increasing while (on a relative basis) increases in marketing, selling,

Exhibit CC.24

CAMPBELL SOUP COMPANY
Analysis of Depreciation

	Year 11	Year 10	Year 9	Year 8	Year 7	Year 6
1. Accumulated depreciation as a percent of gross plant assets*	44.6%	42.3%	43.1%	43.7%	46.6%	48.6%
2. Annual depreciation expenses as a percent of gross plant	7.7%	7.7%	7.6%	6.9%	6.4%	6.4%
3. Annual depreciation expenses as a percent of sales	3.1%	3.0%	3.1%	3.3%	3.1%	2.8%

Computations for Year 11:

(1) $\dfrac{1,131.5 \; \boxed{162}}{758.7 \; \boxed{159} + 1,779.3 \; \boxed{160}} = 44.6\%$

(2) $\dfrac{194.5 \; \boxed{162A}}{758.7 \; \boxed{159} + 1,779.3 \; \boxed{160}} = 7.7\%$

(3) $\dfrac{194.5 \; \boxed{162A}}{6,204.1 \; \boxed{13}} = 3.1\%$

* Exclusive of land and projects in progress.

interest, and "other" expenses outpace increases in sales. Administrative expenses and research and development expenses are not increasing with sales. Statutory tax rates decline over this period, thereby holding down growth in tax expenses. Profitability increases because the growth in gross margin is not offset with increases in expenses.

Recast income statements of Campbell for the most recent six years were reported in Exhibit 8.1. These recast statements support many of the observations recognized in this section. Campbell's adjusted income statements for this same period are shown in Exhibit 8.2. The adjusted statements reveal an increasing trend in net income from Year 9 to Year 10—this contrasts with reported income. The average earning power calculation for the six-year period includes all charges and is $193.9 million.

Summary Evaluation and Inferences

Our comprehensive case analysis considered all facets of Campbell Soup Company's operating results and financial position. We also forecasted accrual and cash flow figures. This type of analysis, modified for our analysis perspective, is valuable for informed business decisions. While these data and information from our analysis are indispensable, they are not sufficient in arriving at a final decision. This is because other qualitative and quantitative factors should be brought to bear on our decision. For

Exhibit CC.25

CAMPBELL SOUP COMPANY
Analysis of Discretionary Expenditures
($ millions)

	Year 11	Year 10	Year 9	Year 8	Year 7	Year 6
Net sales	$6,204.1	$6,205.8	$5,672.1	$4,868.9	$4,490.4	$4,286.8
Plant assets (net)*	1,406.5	1,386.9	1,322.6	1,329.1	1,152.0	974.1
Maintenance and repairs	173.9	180.6	173.9	155.6	148.8	144.0
Advertising	195.4	220.4	212.9	219.1	203.5	181.4
Research & development (R&D)	56.3	53.7	47.7	46.9	44.8	42.2
Maintenance and repairs ÷ sales	2.8%	2.9%	3.1%	3.2%	3.3%	3.4%
Maintenance and repairs ÷ plant	12.4	13.0	13.1	11.7	12.9	14.8
Advertising ÷ sales	3.1	3.6	3.8	4.5	4.5	4.2
R&D ÷ sales	0.9	0.9	0.8	1.0	1.0	1.0

*Exclusive of land and projects in process.

example, our earlier banker's decision on whether to extend short-term credit must take into consideration the character of management, prior loan experience, and the bank's relationship with the loan applicant. If this involved a long-term loan decision, our banker would also want to assess collateral arrangements, event risk, solvency of the applicant, and possible loan restrictions. An equity investor would be interested in earning power and other earnings-based analyses before making an investment decision. Financial analysis gives us information on what earnings are and are likely to be. It also gives us insight into price-to-book and price-to-earnings ratios. An equity investor would also want information on a company's business risk, earnings volatility, and the breadth and quality of the market for its securities. These additional factors determine whether an investment fits with one's portfolio and investment objectives.

Since our lending, investing, or other business analysis decisions require more information than provided in financial analysis, we often summarize our analysis and its inferences in a financial analysis report. This report (see the discussion earlier in this chapter) lists the most relevant and salient findings from our analysis, which depend on our analysis perspective. The remainder of this section provides a brief listing of the main findings of our analysis of Campbell Soup Company.

Short-Term Liquidity

Our assessment of Campbell's short-term liquidity is a mixed one. Both current and acid-test ratios do not compare favorably with industry norms. Yet Campbell's cash position compares favorably with its industry, and its accounts receivable and inventory turnover ratios are better than industry norms. Moreover, Campbell's conversion period is better (less) than that of the industry, and its cash position is strong, allowing for cash to be used for nonoperating activities like acquisitions and retirement of debt.

Cash Flows and Forecasts

Campbell has substantial and increasing operating cash flows; the only exception is Year 9 due to inventory increases. Its operating cash flows comprise over half of all cash inflows. Purchases and acquisitions of plant assets represent outflows totaling nearly 50 percent of the cash inflows. Another 12 percent of cash inflows are used for dividends.

Cash forecasts for Years 12 and 13, using various assumptions, suggest that Campbell will likely finance expected investments in plant assets from its growing operating cash flows. We predict little to no additions to liabilities. Campbell's cash flow adequacy ratio confirms these inferences and implies that operating cash flows are sufficient to cover most capital expenditures, investment in inventories, and cash dividends. Campbell's average cash reinvestment ratio is at a solid 16.5 percent for the past six years.

Capital Structure and Solvency

Campbell has aggressively transformed its capital structure in recent years to a less conservative one. This inference is drawn from absolute and industry comparative measures. Total liabilities comprise about 53 percent of total financing, and long-term liabilities alone equal about one-half of equity. On the positive side, both earnings to fixed charges and cash flow to fixed charges ratios are strong, the exception being earnings coverage ratios for Years 9 and 10 (due to restructuring). These strong ratios imply solid protection for Campbell's creditors. The company also has the strength to take on additional debt, and the market continues to assign Campbell a superior credit rating (AA).

Return on Invested Capital

Campbell's return on assets varies. In Years 6 through 8 it is stable at around 9.5 percent, but in Years 9 and 10 it declines to a low of around 2 percent due primarily to divestiture, restructuring, and unusual charges. In Year 11, return on assets rebounds to a strong 11.75 percent, comprised of a 6.47 percent profit margin and an asset turnover of 1.50. Campbell's return on assets for Year 11 compares favorably to the industry average of 9.2 percent. Campbell's return on common equity is 21.52 percent for Year 11 and exceeds the industry average of 19.8 percent. This return also evidences setbacks in Years 9 and 10 for the same reasons as the return on assets. An important factor affecting return on common equity (beyond the same components comprising return on assets) is financial leverage. The leverage ratio equals 2.22 in Year 11 and is higher than in prior years mainly due to a more risky capital structure. Another favorable finding is Campbell's increased equity growth rate for Year 11, due in large part to strong earnings and a higher rate of earnings retention.

Asset Turnover (Utilization)

Campbell's asset turnover is relatively stable. While its turnover of cash and cash equivalents fluctuates from year to year, Campbell's accounts receivable and inventory turnovers are improving and exceed industry norms. These improvements are due mainly to Campbell's efforts to reduce working capital through, among other activities, less receivables and inventories. Nevertheless, asset turnover compares favorably to the industry despite the relatively low cash turnover and fixed assets turnover.

Operating Performance and Profitability

Campbell's gross profit margin is steadily improving and above the industry average. Yet its net profit margin is not as solid. This is due primarily to increased operating expenses, and the limitations with Campbell's management in controlling these expenses. Recent activities suggest that Campbell is attempting to gain greater control over these expenses.

Financial Market Measures

Selected financial market measures for Campbell are shown in Exhibit CC.26. The first four measures reflect the market's valuation of Campbell's equity securities, while the fifth (dividend payout) reflects more management discretion. Earnings per share figures for Years 9 and 10 are adjusted to exclude the effect of divestitures, restructuring, and unusual charges. Without these adjustments, the market measures are less relevant for our analysis. While earnings per share increases from $1.72 in Year 6 to $3.16 in Year 11, the earnings yield declines over the same period because of steadily increasing price-to-earnings and price-to-book ratios. This is mainly due to strong equity markets. Similarly, while dividends per share increase from $0.65 in Year 6 to $1.12 in Year 11 the dividend yield declines from 2.5 percent to 1.74 percent over the same period. Declines in earnings yield and dividend yield are attributable mainly to steady increases in price-to-earnings and price-to-book ratios. Both ratios reflect the market's appreciation and confidence in Campbell's prior and expected performance. Our analysis shows Campbell's operating performance is strong despite temporary declines in Years 9 and 10.

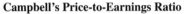

Campbell's Price-to-Earnings Ratio

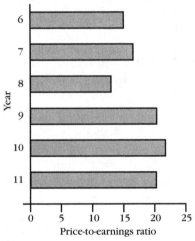

Source: Exhibit CC.26.

Higher price-to-earnings and price-to-book ratios benefit a company in several ways. These include the ability to raise a given amount of equity capital by issuing fewer shares and the ability to use common stock as a means of payment for acquisitions. Yet increasing stock valuations expose existing and particularly new common shareholders to increasing risks, including the risk of stagnating or reversing stock valuations. This occurs because, unlike in early stages of a bull market, prices can potentially deviate from company fundamentals in reflecting upward price momentum. When stock valuations reflect this price momentum, experience shows it is promptly erased once information on the fundamentals fails to support it. Assessing price momentum, as important and crucial as it is for

Exhibit CC.26

CAMPBELL SOUP COMPANY
Market Measures

	Year 11	Year 10*	Year 9*	Year 8	Year 7	Year 6
1. Price-to-earning (range)	27–14	26–18	29–12	16–11	19–14	20–10
2. Price-to-book (range)	6.0–3.1	4.7–3.2	4.5–1.8	2.3–1.6	2.7–2.0	2.9–1.5
3. Earnings yield	4.91%	4.53%	4.91%	7.45%	6.20%	6.61%
4. Dividend yield	1.74%	1.88%	2.08%	2.85%	2.32%	2.50%
5. Dividend payout ratio	35.44%	41.53%	42.45%	38.21%	37.37%	37.79%

Computations for Year 11:

(1) High and Low for the year: High—84.88/3.16 = 27; Low—43.75/3.16 = 14 [see item 184].

(2) High and Low for the year: High—84.88/14.12 = 6.0; Low—43.75/14.12 = 3.1 [see item 185].

(3) Earnings per share/Average market price = 3.16/[(84.88 + 43.75)/2] = 4.91%.

(4) Dividend per share/Average market price = 1.12/64.32 = 1.74%.

(5) Dividend per share/Earnings per share = 1.12/3.16 = 35.44%.

*Year 10 and Year 9 results are shown for EPS *before* effects of divestitures, restructuring, and unusual charges of $2.33 and $2.02 per share, respectively.

equity investing, cannot be gauged by means of the analysis tools here. They involve our study of market expectations and cycles. The difference between Campbell's return on its invested capital and an equity investor's return on investment is discussed in Chapter 6.

Using Financial Statement Analysis

Our comprehensive analysis of the financial statements of Campbell Soup Company consisted of two major parts: (1) detailed analysis, and (2) summary and inferences. In our *analysis report,* the summary and inferences (executive summary) often precedes detailed analysis. The detailed analysis section is usually directed at a specific user. For example, our bank loan officer who must decide on a short-term loan application typically directs attention to short-term liquidity and cash flow analysis and forecasting. A secondary objective of the loan officer is to assess capital structure and operating performance. Regarding the investment committee of our insurance company scenario, it would take a more long-term perspective. This implies primary attention directed at capital structure and long-term solvency. Its secondary focus is on operating performance, return on invested capital, asset utilization, and short-term liquidity (in order of emphasis). Finally, the potential investor in Campbell shares has varying interest in all aspects of our analysis. The emphasis across areas is different, and the likely order of priority is operating performance, return on invested capital, capital structure, long-term solvency, and short-term liquidity. A competent financial statement analysis contains sufficient detailed evaluation along with enough information and inferences to permit its use by different users with varying perspectives.

Financial Statements

Supplement A contains Annual Report and/or Form 10-K disclosures for two companies: Adaptec, Inc., and Campbell Soup Company.

ADAPTEC, INC. A2–A31

Annual Report

CAMPBELL SOUP COMPANY A32–A52

Annual Report*

Form 10-K selections

*For ease in referencing, selected items are identified by key numbers $\boxed{1}$ – $\boxed{187}$.

AB C&D

All About
Being Connected
to Data

ADAPTEC 1996 ANNUAL REPORT

Dear Shareholders,

Adaptec had an outstanding year in fiscal 1996. We are pleased to report that we achieved our 47th consecutive profitable quarter and again posted record revenues and profits. Our financial results reflect our strengths in providing several important market segments with the high-performance I/O, connectivity, and network products they require. The results also underscore our ability to expand opportunities and increase the number of solutions we offer. We are proud of Adaptec's leading role as a provider of foundation technology to the burgeoning global information infrastructure.

For the year, revenues were $659 million, a 41 percent increase over the prior year's $466 million. After a one-time charge for acquired in-process technology, net income was $103 million, an 11 percent increase over last year's $93 million. Earnings per share for the fiscal year were $1.89, an 8 percent increase over fiscal year 1995. Excluding this one-time charge of $0.73 per share, earnings grew 50 percent over fiscal 1995, to $2.62 per share. Adaptec's cash and investments at the end of the fiscal year were $295 million, compared to $247 million in the previous fiscal year.

Demand for our products during the fiscal year was very strong. All our major business areas grew substantially, including host adapter solutions for both high-performance desktop systems and network servers and embedded controller chips for peripherals. We also achieved our first revenues from our entry into the market for ATM network interface cards.

Our OEM customer list now includes all major PC system manufacturers such as Compaq, Dell, Digital, Gateway, Hewlett-Packard, IBM, Intel, Siemens, as well as other well-known brands. As these companies continued to supply the high-end market, we experienced growth in the number of servers and desktops using our products. PCI-based products also became dominant in the PC and server markets, and our introduction of UltraSCSI products saw immediate strong market acceptance. And, with our continued focus on high-performance solutions, we also achieved new design wins with RISC systems manufacturers.

The explosive growth of Internet and Intranet applications is driving new demands for bandwidth — demand that is being met by Adaptec's range of host adapters. The rapid acceptance of PCI-based servers and our introduction of Fast SCSI and Ultra Wide SCSI host adapters are enabling Web sites to move more data from storage to the Internet. In fact, server performance can be more restricted by the I/O bandwidth than by the CPU performance, which is why there is such a growing market for the expandability and speed offered by Adaptec's products.

Developments in our international business were also positive. Throughout the year we saw good growth in Europe. Growth in Japan was extremely strong as the entire country upgrades its computing infrastructure, including corporate networks.

Our mass storage electronics business achieved strong sales, particularly in Asia and Japan where we have achieved strategic supplier status with several important customers. Subsequent to the fiscal year end, our leadership position in this market was further under-scored by the acquisition of Western Digital's Connectivity Solutions Group business unit, which has been consolidated with our business. We are particularly pleased by the growth in backlog of design wins and the penetration we are achieving in new markets. We anticipate further growth with the market acceptance of new peripherals such as recordable CD and popular removable storage devices.

Throughout the year we took advantage of healthy cash flows from operations to make strategic investments. This included acquiring complementary companies and technologies, selected for their potential to help us gain market share, expand our business reach, leverage our core competencies, and enable us to add value on a long-term basis.

In our second fiscal quarter we acquired Trillium Research, Inc., a developer and manufacturer of RAID software solutions for the Apple market. In the same quarter we acquired Future Domain Corporation, which added a complementary set of desktop I/O products to our portfolio and has added to our processor-independent solutions for the RISC-based systems market.

Also in the second quarter we acquired Incat Systems Software USA, Inc., which develops and markets application and I/O management software for recordable CD peripherals. And in the third quarter we acquired Power I/O Corporation, a developer of high-speed I/O and networking technologies that will enhance our offering in the client-server computing environment.

Assuring a high-quality, uninterrupted source of semiconductors for our products was a critical success factor for the year. We supported this goal through an agreement with Taiwan Semiconductor Manufacturing Company Ltd. to guarantee silicon supply into the next century for both current and future technologies. We also signed a significant agreement with AT&T Microelectronics, which expands our technology base as well as assures silicon supply. And, as part of our Western Digital transaction, we obtained capacity with SGS-Thomson Microelectronics, a world-class supplier of foundry services.

Looking forward, we expect the percentage of systems using SCSI to continue to grow and for SCSI to retain its position as the dominant high-functionality, high-performance I/O interface. We also continue to prepare for new market opportunities in the longer term through ongoing development of products based on serial interfaces such as 1394 and Fibre Channel.

In the last year, we achieved a significant share of the ATM market for network interface cards. As we move ahead, we anticipate bringing our proven core competencies to other high-performance networking areas with products based on technologies other than ATM.

Since our inception, Adaptec's technologies and products have grown and evolved in breadth and sophistication, until they have become a keystone to high-performance computing. Yet the shorthand term we use to refer to our business — bandwidth management — often conceals its enormous value.

The ability to achieve high-performance connectivity and to move digital data quickly and reliably is critical to a growing information infrastructure that is global in scale. Whether it takes place between the desktop PC and its high-capacity peripherals, between a mobile computer and a remote server, or between enterprise clients and servers on a network, the ability to manage and transfer data streams at ever faster speeds represents a fundamental contribution to productivity. This foundation technology is as important to computing performance as are multitasking operating systems or the latest generation of central processing unit.

With the adoption of exciting applications and tools like distributed storage, data warehousing, and RAID, the need for reliable, high-performance connectivity is expanding rapidly.

Businesses today are built around the availability of computers and data. The value of the data to the business can be incalculable, yet the cost of the devices storing and using it is really very small. This is where Adaptec's core competencies of performance, compatibility, reliability, and ease of use, add sustainable value to our customers. We enable our customers to exploit the full value of their data by reliably, easily, and speedily moving it to wherever users need it.

Despite our many products, our expertise in silicon design, and our broad software competencies, Adaptec's business is elegantly simple: we provide technology to manage the bandwidth our customers need to use information more quickly and more easily. As in past years, our annual report's thematic section is designed to communicate our business and its value in a memorable, straightforward way. Together with the information in our financial section, we hope it tells a compelling story of Adaptec's value. As always, we thank our employees, shareholders, partners, suppliers and customers for their support. We look forward to sharing our future with you.

Results of Operations

The following table sets forth the items in the consolidated statements of operations as a percentage of net revenues:

Year Ended March 31	1996	1995	1994
Net revenues	100%	100%	100%
Cost of revenues	42	44	51
Gross margin	58	56	49
Operating expenses			
Research and development	13	13	11
Sales and marketing	13	13	12
General and administrative	5	5	5
Write-off of acquired in-process technology	8	—	—
	39	31	28
Income from operations	19	25	21
Shareholder settlement	—	—	(1)
Interest income, net	2	2	1
Income before income taxes	21	27	21
Provision for income taxes	5	7	5
Net income	16%	20%	16%

Management's Discussion and Analysis

OF FINANCIAL CONDITION AND RESULTS OF OPERATIONS

Fiscal 1996 Compared to Fiscal 1995

The Company experienced growth worldwide as net revenues increased 41% to $659 million in fiscal 1996 from $466 million in fiscal 1995. The Company's continued increase in net revenues was driven by growth of client-server networking environments, complex microcomputer based applications requiring high-performance I/O, and the expanded adoption of various peripheral devices. This growth combined with the Company's market leadership in SCSI solutions resulted in increased net revenues from the Company's host adapters. During the year, the Company also began shipping products incorporating newer technologies such as RAID, ATM and CD-Recordable (CD-R) software. Fiscal 1996 net revenue from sales of mass storage integrated circuits (ICs) also increased from the prior year as the Company benefitted from next-generation design wins for higher capacity disk drives that are required for advanced applications.

Gross margin of 58% in fiscal 1996 increased from 56% in fiscal 1995. Gross margin was favorably affected by the increased revenues from the Company's higher margin products. The Company's focus on design for manufacturability allowed it to continue to experience efficiencies in the manufacturing process and accelerate time to customer volume.

Research and development expenditures in fiscal 1996 were $88 million, an increase of 44% over fiscal 1995. As a percentage of net revenues, research and development expenses were 13% for both fiscal 1996 and fiscal 1995. The Company's research and development efforts continue to be focused on solutions which enhance performance in single-user desktop, enterprise-wide computing, and networked environments. This commitment included investing in its current core SCSI business as well as several emerging technologies encompassing RAID, CD-R, ATM, and serial architectures such as 1394 and Fibre Channel. The Company believes these expenditures, consisting primarily of increased staffing levels, have allowed the Company to maintain its position in technical leadership and product innovation. The Company believes it is essential to continue this significant level of investment in research and development and anticipates actual spending in fiscal 1997 will increase.

Sales and marketing expenses increased to $82 million in fiscal 1996, an increase of 39% over fiscal 1995. As a percentage of net revenues, fiscal 1996 sales and marketing expenses were 13% in both fiscal 1996 and fiscal 1995. The increase in actual spending was a result of advertising and promotional programs aimed at generating demand in the consumer and enterprise computer markets and increased staffing levels to support the continued growth of the Company. The Company's promotional and advertising programs have allowed it to leverage its brand image around the globe. The Company believes that sales and marketing expenditures will increase in fiscal 1997 primarily to support its existing products as well as products resulting from newer technologies.

General and administrative expenses as a percentage of net revenues were consistent at

5% for both fiscal 1996 and fiscal 1995. Actual spending increased from fiscal 1995, primarily due to increased staffing to support the continued growth of the Company. The Company anticipates general and administrative expenditures will increase in fiscal 1997 to support its growth.

During the year, the Company acquired Trillium Research, Inc. (Trillium), Future Domain Corporation (Future Domain), Incat Systems Software USA, Inc. (Incat), and Power I/O, Inc. (Power I/O). These acquisitions were accounted for using the purchase method of accounting. Among the assets acquired was in-process technology, resulting in write-offs totaling $52 million. Excluding these write-offs, the Company's results of operations for fiscal 1996 were not materially affected by these acquisitions.

Interest income, net of interest expense, was $12 million in fiscal 1996, an increase of $5 million over fiscal 1995. The increase was primarily due to the increase in cash and cash equivalents and marketable securities partially offset by lower interest expense.

The Company's effective tax rate for fiscal 1996 was 25%, the same as fiscal 1995. During fiscal 1996, the Company concluded negotiations with the Singapore government extending the tax holiday for the Company's manufacturing subsidiary. The terms of the tax holiday provide that profits derived from certain products will be exempt from tax for a period of 10 years, subject to certain conditions. In addition, profits derived from the Company's remaining products will be taxed at a rate of 15%, which is lower than the statutory rate of 27%, through fiscal 1998.

While the Company has experienced significant growth in revenues and profitability, various factors could adversely affect its results of operations in the future including its reliance on the high-performance microcomputer and server markets, changes in product mix, competitive pricing pressures, fluctuations in manufacturing yields, changes in technological standards, availability of components, changes in product costs, timing of new product introductions and market demand for these products, capacity for wafer fabrication, the accounting effect of acquisitions of other companies or businesses that the Company may make from time to time, or general economic downturns.

Fiscal 1995 Compared to Fiscal 1994

Net revenues increased 25% to $466 million in fiscal 1995 from $372 million in fiscal 1994. The continued adoption of SCSI in personal computers (PCs) resulted in increased sales of the Company's SCSI host adapter products across all performance ranges. Additionally, demand for the Company's host adapters was driven by the growing use of file servers where SCSI usage approaches 100%. During fiscal 1995, the Company introduced several new IOware* solutions ranging from connectivity products for the single-user and small-office markets, to high-performance products for enterprise-wide computing and networked environments. The market acceptance of the Company's high-performance host adapters for the PCI local bus market resulted in the fastest product ramp in the Company's history. The Company's fiscal 1995 revenue from mass storage ICs was comparable to the prior year. The Company believes this was due to the timing of design win cycles at original equipment manufacturers (OEMs) coupled with significant fluctuations in demand experienced in the disk drive market. During fiscal 1995 the Company won key designs for next-generation products at major OEMs in the Pacific Rim.

Gross margin of 56% in fiscal 1995 increased from 49% in fiscal 1994. Gross margin was favorably affected by the increased revenues from the Company's higher margin SCSI host adapters. The Company also continued to experience component cost reductions and manufacturing efficiencies, including the move of the IC production test facility to Singapore where costs are lower. This also allowed the Company to shorten the manufacturing cycle time and better serve its customers.

Research and development expenditures in fiscal 1995 were $61 million, an increase of 52% over fiscal 1994. As a percentage of net revenues, research and development expenses increased to 13% in fiscal 1995 compared to 11% in fiscal 1994. This was primarily due to increased staffing levels. The Company continued to invest in its SCSI products, where it has captured a leadership position by improving system performance as the computer industry has become more I/O intensive with more powerful CPUs, multitasking operating systems, and a new generation of intelligent peripherals. While SCSI solutions remained the core of the Company's business, fiscal 1995 saw the Company broaden its portfolio of solutions to include ATM, RAID, serial I/O and infrared technology.

Sales and marketing expenses increased to $59 million in fiscal 1995, an increase of 27% over fiscal 1994. As a percentage of net revenues, fiscal 1995 sales and marketing expenses were 13% compared to 12% in fiscal 1994. The increase in actual spending was a result of increased staffing levels to support the continued growth of the Company, including expansion of the Company's international sales and marketing infrastructure. Additionally, increases in advertising and promotional expenses were aimed at strategies to further accelerate and expand SCSI acceptance in the marketplace and drive demand for the Company's products.

General and administrative expenses as a percentage of net revenues in fiscal 1995 were consistent with fiscal 1994 at 5%. Actual spending increased from fiscal 1994, primarily due to increased staffing to support the continued growth of the Company.

Interest income, net of interest expense, was $7 million in fiscal 1995, an increase of $3 million over fiscal 1994. The increase was primarily due to the increase in cash and cash equivalents and marketable securities coupled with slightly higher average yields on cash and investment balances.

The Company's effective tax rate for fiscal 1995 was 25%, the same as fiscal 1994.

Liquidity and Capital Resources
Operating Activities Net cash generated from operating activities during fiscal 1996 was $103 million compared to $118 million in fiscal 1995. This aggregate decrease was a result of the

increase in the Company's current assets to support its overall growth. During fiscal 1996, the majority of funds generated from operations resulted from $103 million of net income adjusted by non-cash items including a non-recurring write-off of acquired in-process technology (net of taxes) of $40 million and depreciation and amortization of $18 million. Additionally contributing to favorable operating cash flows was an increase in accrued liabilities of $22 million reflecting the overall growth of the Company. Offsetting these were increases in current assets, excluding cash and investments, of $60 million. This increase in assets primarily resulted from the Company's continued overall growth.

During fiscal 1996, the Company signed an agreement with Taiwan Semiconductor Manufacturing Co., Ltd. (TSMC) that will ensure availability of a portion of the Company's wafer capacity for both current and future technologies. The agreement, which runs through 2001, provides the Company with a guarantee of increased capacity for wafer fabrication in return for advance payments. The Company made advance payments of $20 million during fiscal 1996 relating to this agreement. This agreement is in addition to an existing contract with TSMC for guaranteed supply and technology.

During fiscal 1995, the majority of funds generated from operations resulted from $93 million of net income adjusted by non-cash items including depreciation and amortization of $16 million. Also contributing to favorable cash flows was a decrease in net inventories of $7 million and

increases in accrued liabilities and accounts payable of $7 million. During fiscal 1995, the Company paid an additional advance payment on a deposit and supply agreement to support its silicon wafer requirements.

During fiscal 1994, the Company's net cash generated from operating activities primarily resulted from $59 million of net income adjusted by non-cash items including depreciation and amortization of $11 million. An increase in accrued liabilities of $9 million also contributed to positive cash flows. These items were mainly offset by increases in accounts receivable and other assets totaling $24 million.

Investing Activities The Company made payments of $31 million in connection with the acquisitions of Trillium, Future Domain, and Power I/O during the year. Additionally, the Company acquired Incat through the issuance of 385,000 shares of common stock with a fair market value of $17 million. Also in fiscal 1996, the Company continued to invest in equipment for product development and manufacturing to support increased demand for its products and future business requirements. Additionally, to provide for future growth the Company purchased land for $12 million.

During fiscal years 1996, 1995, and 1994, the Company continued to invest significant amounts of funds in marketable securities consisting mostly of highly rated municipal instruments.

During the 1997 fiscal year, the Company anticipates it will invest approximately $75 million in equipment for future product innovation and development as well as land and facilities to support its growth. Also, during fiscal 1996, the Company signed an agreement with AT&T Corporation (AT&T), acting through its Microelectronics business division, that will ensure availability of a portion of the Company's wafer capacity for both current and future technologies. This contract, which runs through 2001, provides the Company with a guaranteed supply of wafers in return for an investment in fabrication equipment of up to $25 million for AT&T's fabrication facility located in Madrid, Spain. The sources for capital expenditures are expected to be funds generated from operations and available sources of financing as well as working capital presently on hand.

Subsequent to year end, the Company acquired certain assets and the ongoing business of Western Digital's Connectivity Solutions Group (CSG) which primarily designs, manufactures and markets controller ICs for high-capacity disk drives. In connection with the acquisition, the Company was assigned capacity for wafer fabrication. The Company paid $33 million cash for CSG and will pay future consideration based on certain performance criteria. The Company will account for this acquisition using the purchase method of accounting and will evaluate the allocation of the purchase price to assets acquired, which includes in-process technology that will be written off. The results of operations for CSG were immaterial relative to the Company's financial statements.

Financing Activities During fiscal 1996, the Company continued to receive proceeds from the issuance of common stock under its Employee Stock Option and Employee Stock Purchase Plans totaling $27 million. Also, the Company repurchased 260,000 shares of its common stock through open market transactions totaling $8 million. In fiscal 1995, two million shares totaling $37 million were repurchased. In connection with the TSMC agreement, the Company also issued a $46 million note payable due in June 1996.

Subsequent to year end, the Company acquired all of the outstanding capital stock of Cogent Data Technologies, Inc. (Cogent) in a $68 million stock transaction. Cogent provides high-performance Fast Ethernet products for the networking market. The Company will record this acquisition using the pooling method of accounting and will record acquired assets and assumed liabilities at their book values as of the acquisition date. The results of operations for Cogent for the three year period ended March 31, 1996 were immaterial relative to the Company's financial statements.

The Company has an unsecured $17 million revolving line of credit under which there were no outstanding borrowings as of March 31, 1996. The Company's liquidity is affected by various factors, some based on its continuing operations of the business and others related to the industry and global economies. Although the Company's cash situation will fluctuate based on the timing of these factors, the Company believes that existing working capital combined with expected cash generated from operations and available sources of bank and equipment financing will be sufficient to meet its cash requirements throughout fiscal 1997.

Consolidated Statements of Operations

IN THOUSANDS, EXCEPT PER SHARE AMOUNTS

Year Ended March 31	1996	1995	1994
Net revenues	$659,347	$466,194	$372,245
Cost of revenues	275,939	205,596	189,526
Gross profit	383,408	260,598	182,719
Operating expenses			
Research and development	87,628	60,848	39,993
Sales and marketing	81,548	58,737	46,192
General and administrative	35,784	23,229	19,399
Write-off of acquired in-process technology	52,313	—	—
	257,273	142,814	105,584
Income from operations	126,135	117,784	77,135
Shareholder settlement	—	—	(2,409)
Interest income	12,694	7,932	5,183
Interest expense	(840)	(1,179)	(1,306)
	11,854	6,753	1,468
Income before income taxes	137,989	124,537	78,603
Provision for income taxes	34,614	31,135	19,653
Net income	$103,375	$ 93,402	$ 58,950
Net income per share	$ 1.89	$ 1.75	$ 1.10
Weighted average number of common and common equivalent shares outstanding	54,569	53,357	53,602

See accompanying notes.

Consolidated Balance Sheets

IN THOUSANDS

As of March 31	1996	1995
Assets		
Current assets		
Cash and cash equivalents	$ 91,211	$ 66,835
Marketable securities	204,283	179,911
Accounts receivable, net of allowance for doubtful accounts of $4,220 in 1996 and $4,431 in 1995	89,487	56,495
Inventories	55,028	31,712
Prepaid expenses and other	25,271	15,519
Total current assets	465,280	350,472
Property and equipment, net	92,778	67,863
Other assets	88,428	17,373
	$646,486	$435,708
Liabilities and Shareholders' Equity		
Current liabilities		
Current portion of long-term debt	$ 3,400	$ 3,400
Note payable	46,200	—
Accounts payable	23,974	22,008
Accrued liabilities	56,717	31,006
Total current liabilities	130,291	56,414
Long-term debt, net of current portion	4,250	7,650
Commitments (Note 7)		
Shareholders' equity		
Preferred stock		
Authorized shares, 1,000		
Outstanding shares, none	—	—
Common stock		
Authorized shares, 200,000		
Outstanding shares, 53,020 in 1996 and 51,677 in 1995	182,932	140,191
Retained earnings	329,013	231,453
Total shareholders' equity	511,945	371,644
	$646,486	$435,708

See accompanying notes.

Consolidated Statements of Cash Flows

IN THOUSANDS

Year Ended March 31	1996	1995	1994
Cash Flows From Operating Activities:			
Net income	$103,375	$ 93,402	$ 58,950
Adjustments to reconcile net income to net cash provided by operating activities:			
Write-off of acquired in-process technology, net of taxes	39,686	—	—
Depreciation and amortization	17,593	15,662	11,489
Provision for doubtful accounts	250	150	2,069
Changes in assets and liabilities:			
Accounts receivable	(30,727)	(1,311)	(13,020)
Inventories	(20,516)	7,228	(5,563)
Prepaid expenses	(8,973)	460	(5,470)
Other assets	(19,111)	(4,107)	(11,478)
Accounts payable	(167)	2,354	(2,781)
Accrued liabilities	21,969	4,251	8,867
Net Cash Provided by Operating Activities	103,379	118,089	43,063
Cash Flows From Investing Activities:			
Purchase of Trillium, Future Domain and Power I/O, net of cash acquired	(31,177)	—	—
Investments in property and equipment	(39,748)	(31,576)	(17,314)
Investments in marketable securities, net	(24,372)	(32,291)	(20,250)
Net Cash Used for Investing Activities	(95,297)	(63,867)	(37,564)
Cash Flows From Financing Activities:			
Proceeds from issuance of common stock	27,459	17,174	13,511
Repurchase of common stock	(7,765)	(36,548)	—
Principal payments on debt	(3,400)	(3,400)	(2,968)
Net Cash Provided by (Used for) Financing Activities	16,294	(22,774)	10,543
Net Increase in Cash and Cash Equivalents	24,376	31,448	16,042
Cash and Cash Equivalents at Beginning of Year	66,835	35,387	19,345
Cash and Cash Equivalents at End of Year	$ 91,211	$ 66,835	$ 35,387

See accompanying notes.

Consolidated Statements of Shareholders' Equity

IN THOUSANDS

	Common Stock		Retained	
	Shares	Amount	Earnings	Total
Balance, March 31, 1993	50,714	$124,806	$100,349	$225,155
Sale of common stock under employee purchase and option plans	1,577	7,728	—	7,728
Income tax benefit of employees' stock transactions	—	5,783	—	5,783
Net income	—	—	58,950	58,950
Balance, March 31, 1994	52,291	138,317	159,299	297,616
Sale of common stock under employee purchase and option plans	1,426	11,245	—	11,245
Income tax benefit of employees' stock transactions	—	5,929	—	5,929
Repurchases of common stock	(2,040)	(15,300)	(21,248)	(36,548)
Net income	—	—	93,402	93,402
Balance, March 31, 1995	51,677	140,191	231,453	371,644
Sale of common stock under employee purchase and option plans	1,218	16,512	—	16,512
Issuance of common stock in connection with acquisition	385	17,232	—	17,232
Income tax benefit of employees' stock transactions	—	10,947	—	10,947
Repurchases of common stock	(260)	(1,950)	(5,815)	(7,765)
Net income	—	—	103,375	103,375
Balance, March 31, 1996	53,020	$182,932	$329,013	$511,945

See accompanying notes.

Notes to Consolidated Financial Statements

NOTE ONE: SUMMARY OF SIGNIFICANT
ACCOUNTING POLICIES

Basis of Presentation The consolidated financial statements include the accounts of the Company and its wholly-owned subsidiaries after elimination of intercompany transactions and balances. Foreign currency transaction gains and losses are included in income as they occur. The preparation of financial statements in conformity with generally accepted accounting principles requires management to make estimates and assumptions that affect the reported amounts of assets and liabilities and disclosure of contingent assets and liabilities at the date of the financial statements and the reported amounts of revenues and expenses during the reporting period. Actual results could differ from those estimates.

Revenue Recognition The Company recognizes revenue generally at the time of shipment or upon satisfaction of contractual obligations. The Company records provisions for estimated returns at the time of sale.

Fair Value of Financial Instruments The Company measures its financial assets and liabilities in accordance with generally accepted accounting principles. For certain of the Company's financial instruments, including cash and cash equivalents, marketable securities, accounts receivable, accounts payable and accrued expenses, the carrying amounts approximate fair value due to their short maturities. The amounts shown for long-term debt also approximate fair value because current interest rates offered to the Company for debt of similar maturities are substantially the same.

Marketable Securities At March 31, 1996, the Company's marketable securities are classified as available for sale and are reported at fair market value which approximates cost. Marketable securities with maturities after one through three years totaled $153,996,000 with all remaining securities maturing less than one year. Realized gains and losses are based on the book value of the specific securities sold and were immaterial during fiscal 1996, 1995 and 1994.

Concentration of Credit Risk Financial instruments that potentially subject the Company to significant concentrations of credit risk consist principally of cash and cash equivalents, marketable securities and trade accounts receivable. The Company places its marketable securities primarily in municipal securities. The Company, by policy, limits the amount of credit exposure through diversification and investment in highly rated securities. Sales to customers are primarily denominated in U.S. dollars. As a result, the Company believes its foreign currency risk is minimal.

The Company sells its products to original equipment manufacturers and distributors throughout the world. The Company performs ongoing credit evaluations of its customers' financial condition and, generally, requires no collateral from its customers. The Company maintains an allowance for uncollectible accounts receivable based upon the expected collectibility of all accounts receivable. There were no significant amounts charged to this allowance during the current year.

Inventories Inventories are stated at the lower of cost (first-in, first-out) or market.

Property and Equipment Property and equipment are stated at cost and depreciated or amortized using the straight-line method over the estimated useful lives of the assets. During 1995, the Financial Accounting Standards Board issued Statement of Financial Accounting Standards No. 121 "Accounting for the Impairment of Long-Lived Assets and for Long-Lived Assets to be Disposed Of" (SFAS 121) which will be effective for the Company in fiscal 1997. The Company does not expect that adoption of SFAS 121 to have a material impact on its financial position or results of operations.

Income Taxes The Company accounts for income taxes under the asset and liability method. Under this method, deferred tax assets and liabilities are recognized for the future tax consequences attributable to temporary differences between the financial statement carrying amounts and the tax basis of existing assets and liabilities measured using enacted tax rates expected to apply to taxable income in the years in which the temporary differences are expected to be recovered or settled.

Net Income Per Share Net income per share is computed under the treasury stock method using the weighted average number of common and common equivalent shares from dilutive options outstanding during the respective periods.

Cash and Cash Equivalents Cash and cash equivalents consist of funds in checking accounts, money market funds and marketable securities with original maturities of three months or less.

NOTE TWO: SUPPLEMENTAL FINANCIAL INFORMATION

Marketable Securities

IN THOUSANDS	1996	1995
Municipal securities	$203,305	$169,972
U.S. Government securities and other	978	9,939
	$204,283	$179,911

Inventories

IN THOUSANDS	1996	1995
Raw materials	$23,415	$12,230
Work-in-process	12,865	5,839
Finished goods	18,748	13,643
	$55,028	$31,712

Property and Equipment

IN THOUSANDS	Life	1996	1995
Land	—	$ 25,154	$ 13,240
Buildings and improvements	5–40 years	20,328	18,088
Machinery and equipment	3–5 years	59,290	42,810
Furniture and fixtures	3–8 years	22,944	17,005
Leasehold improvements	Life of lease	5,245	3,968
		132,961	95,111
Accumulated depreciation and amortization		(40,183)	(27,248)
		$ 92,778	$ 67,863

Accrued Liabilities

IN THOUSANDS	1996	1995
Accrued compensation and related taxes	$22,440	$15,740
Sales and marketing related	7,443	4,877
Tax related	16,218	5,746
Other	10,616	4,643
	$56,717	$31,006

Supplemental Disclosures of Cash Flows

IN THOUSANDS	1996	1995	1994
Interest paid	$ 764	$ 1,125	$ 1,300
Income taxes paid	$32,869	$29,411	$14,927

NOTE THREE: LINE OF CREDIT

The Company has available an unsecured $17 million revolving line of credit which expires on December 31, 1997. Of the total line of credit available, $7 million has been issued as an irrevocable standby letter of credit to guarantee component purchases from a supplier (see Note 7) at a fee of ¾% per annum. As of March 31, 1996, no borrowings were outstanding under this line of credit. The Company may select its own method of interest payment on borrowings based upon the bank's CD rate plus one percent, Eurodollar rate plus one percent or prime lending rate. A commitment fee of ¼% per annum is payable on the unused line of credit. In addition, the arrangement requires the Company to comply with certain financial covenants. The Company was in compliance with all such covenants as of March 31, 1996.

NOTE FOUR: LONG-TERM DEBT

The Company entered into a $17 million term loan agreement in June 1992 bearing interest at 7.65%, with principal and interest payable in quarterly installments of $850,000. All outstanding principal and accrued but unpaid interest is due and payable in June 1998. The arrangement requires the Company to comply with certain financial covenants. The Company was in compliance with all such covenants as of March 31, 1996.

NOTE FIVE: ACQUISITIONS

During fiscal 1996, the Company acquired all of the outstanding capital stock of Future Domain, Power I/O, Trillium, and Incat for $25 million, $7 million, $3 million, and 385,000 shares of the Company's common stock with a fair market value of $17 million, respectively. Also in connection with the Incat acquisition, the Company will pay consideration, contingent upon certain future performance criteria. These companies design and develop high-performance I/O products, networking technologies and software for recordable CD peripherals for both the consumer and enterprise computing markets.

The Company accounted for these acquisitions using the purchase method of accounting, and excluding the aggregate $52 million write-off of purchased in-process technology from these companies, the aggregate impact on the Company's results of operations from the acquisition date was not material.

The allocation of the Company's aggregate purchase price to the tangible and identifiable intangible assets acquired and liabilities assumed was based on independent appraisals and is summarized as follows:

IN THOUSANDS

Tangible assets	$ 8,108
In-process technology	52,313
Goodwill	8,200
Assets acquired	68,621
Accounts payable and accrued liabilities	3,125
Deferred tax liability	12,627
Liabilities assumed	15,752
Net assets acquired	$52,869

Subsequent to year end, the Company acquired certain assets and the ongoing business of Western Digital's Connectivity Solutions Group (CSG), which primarily designs, manufactures and markets controller ICs for high-capacity disk drives. In connection with the acquisition, the Company was assigned capacity for wafer fabrication. The Company paid $33 million cash for CSG and will pay future consideration based on certain performance criteria. The Company will account for this acquisition using the purchase method of accounting and will evaluate the allocation of the purchase price to assets acquired, which includes in-process technology that will be written off. The results of operations for CSG were immaterial relative to the Company's financial statements.

Also subsequent to year end, the Company acquired all of the outstanding capital stock of Cogent Data Technologies, Inc. (Cogent) in a $68 million stock transaction. Cogent provides high-performance Fast Ethernet products for the networking market. The Company will record this acquisition using the pooling method of accounting and will record acquired assets and assumed liabilities at their book values as of the acquisition date. The results of operations for Cogent for the three year period ended March 31, 1996 were immaterial relative to the Company's financial statements.

NOTE SIX: STOCK PLANS

1986 Employee Stock Purchase Plan The Company has authorized 2,800,000 shares of common stock for issuance under the 1986 Employee Stock Purchase Plan (1986 Plan). Qualified employees may elect to have a certain percentage (not to exceed 10%) of their salary withheld pursuant to the 1986 Plan. The salary withheld is then used to purchase shares of the Company's common stock at a price equal to 85% of the market value of the stock at the beginning or ending of a three-month offering period, whichever is lower. Under this Plan, 139,275 shares were issued during fiscal 1996, representing approximately $4,578,000 in employee contributions.

1990 Stock Plan The Company's 1990 Stock Plan allows the Board of Directors to grant to employees, officers and consultants options to purchase common stock or other stock rights at exercise prices not less than 50% of the fair market value on the date of grant. The expiration of options or other stock rights is not to exceed ten years after the date of grant. To date, the Company has issued substantially all incentive and non-statutory stock options under this Plan at exercise prices of 100% of fair market value on the respective dates of grant. Generally, options vest and become exercisable over a four year period.

Option activity under the 1990 Stock Plan is as follows:

	Options Available	Options Outstanding Shares	Options Outstanding Price
Balance, March 31, 1993	2,280,412	3,751,052	$ 2.47 to $13.88
Authorized	2,000,000	—	—
Granted	(1,837,500)	1,837,500	$11.31 to $21.38
Exercised	—	(859,513)	$ 2.47 to $15.44
Terminated	330,662	(330,662)	$ 2.85 to $16.50
Balance, March 31, 1994	2,773,574	4,398,377	$ 2.47 to $21.38
Authorized	2,500,000	—	—
Granted	(1,914,500)	1,914,500	$15.63 to $35.88
Exercised	—	(930,574)	$ 2.47 to $21.38
Terminated	599,053	(599,053)	$ 2.84 to $27.63
Balance, March 31, 1995	3,958,127	4,783,250	$ 2.47 to $35.88
Authorized	2,193,900	—	—
Granted	(2,294,750)	2,294,750	$22.88 to $56.00
Exercised	—	(1,017,131)	$ 2.47 to $44.75
Terminated	241,038	(241,038)	$ 3.06 to $45.75
Balance, March 31, 1996	4,098,315	5,819,831	$ 2.47 to $56.00

At March 31, 1996, there were 1,956,767 exercisable options under this Plan at prices ranging from $2.47 to $45.88 per share.

1990 Directors' Option Plan The 1990 Directors' Option Plan provides for the automatic grant to non-employee directors of non-statutory stock options to purchase common stock at the fair market value on the date of grant, which is generally the last day of each fiscal year except for the first grant to any newly elected director. Each current director receives an option at the end of each fiscal year for 10,000 shares, which vests and becomes exercisable over a four year period. Each newly elected director receives an initial option on the date of his or her appointment or election for 40,000 shares, which also vests and becomes exercisable over a four year period. The options expire five years after the date of grant.

Option activity under the 1990 Directors' Option Plan is as follows:

	Options Available	Options Outstanding Shares	Options Outstanding Price
Balance, March 31, 1993	40,000	157,500	$ 2.91 to $13.88
Authorized	500,000	—	—
Granted	(50,000)	50,000	$18.38
Exercised	—	(5,000)	$ 2.91
Balance, March 31, 1994	490,000	202,500	$ 2.91 to $18.38
Granted	(50,000)	50,000	$33.00
Exercised	—	(21,250)	$ 2.91 to $13.88
Balance, March 31, 1995	440,000	231,250	$ 2.91 to $33.00
Granted	(150,000)	150,000	$44.50 to $48.25
Exercised	—	(55,000)	$ 2.91 to $18.38
Balance, March 31, 1996	290,000	326,250	$ 7.69 to $48.25

At March 31, 1996 there were 93,750 exercisable options under this Plan at prices ranging from $7.69 to $33.00 per share.

Rights Plan The Company has reserved 120,000,000 shares of common stock for issuance under the Rights Plan which was amended and restated as of June 30, 1992. Under this plan, shareholders will receive one Common Share Purchase Right ("Right") for each outstanding share of the Company's common stock. Each Right will entitle shareholders to buy one share of common stock at an exercise price of $50.00 per share. The Rights will trade automatically with shares of the Company's common stock. The Rights are not exercisable until ten days after a person or group announces acquisition of 20% or more of the Company's outstanding common stock or the commencement of a tender offer which would result in ownership by a person or group of 20% or more of the then outstanding common stock.

The Company is entitled to redeem the Rights at $.005 per Right anytime on or before the tenth day following such an acquisition or tender offer. This redemption period may be extended by the Company in some cases. If, prior to such redemption, the Company is acquired in a merger or other business combination, a party acquires 20% or more of the Company's common stock, a 20% shareholder engages in certain self-dealing transactions, or the Company sells 50% or more of its assets, each right will entitle the holder to purchase from the surviving corporation, for $50.00 per share, common stock having a then current market value of $100.00 per share.

At March 31, 1996, the Company has reserved the following shares of authorized but unissued common stock:

1986 Employee Stock Purchase Plan	869,187
1990 Stock Plan	9,918,146
1990 Directors' Option Plan	616,250
Rights Plan	120,000,000
	131,403,583

NOTE SEVEN: COMMITMENTS

The Company leases certain office facilities, vehicles and certain equipment under operating lease agreements that expire at various dates through fiscal 2001. As of March 31, 1996, the minimum future payments on existing leases totaled $7,290,000. Rent expense was approximately $3,715,000, $2,377,000 and $1,640,000 during fiscal 1996, 1995 and 1994, respectively.

During fiscal 1996, the Company signed an agreement with TSMC totaling $66 million that ensures availability of a portion of the Company's wafer capacity for both current and future technologies. The agreement runs through 2001 providing the Company with a guarantee of increased capacity for wafer fabrication in return for advance payments. As of March 31, 1996, the Company made advance payments to TSMC totaling $20 million and has signed a $46 million promissory note payable which becomes due June 30, 1996. The majority of these amounts are included in other assets in the fiscal 1996 consolidated balance sheets.

In addition to this agreement, the Company has an existing deposit and supply agreement with TSMC to secure supply of silicon wafers. Under the deposit and supply agreement, the Company has made deposits aggregating $14,650,000 which are classified as other assets in the accompanying consolidated balance sheets. These advances are repayable at the expiration of the agreement in June 1997. The supplier has provided an irrevocable standby letter of credit to the Company in an equal amount to guarantee the repayment of deposits made by the Company. Under the agreement, the Company is committed to minimum purchases of $19,800,000 and $4,950,000 in fiscal 1997 and 1998, respectively.

During fiscal 1996, the Company signed an agreement with AT&T, acting through its Microelectronics business division, that will ensure availability of a portion of the Company's wafer capacity for both current and future technologies. This contract, which runs through 2001, provides the Company with a guaranteed supply of wafers at a specified level in return for an investment in fabrication equipment of up to $25 million for AT&T's fabrication facility located in Madrid, Spain. As of March 31, 1996 the Company has not made any payments in connection with this agreement.

NOTE EIGHT: INCOME TAXES

The components of income before income taxes for the years ended March 31 are as follows:

IN THOUSANDS	1996	1995	1994
Domestic	$ 57,882	$ 74,397	$54,972
Foreign	80,107	50,140	23,631
Income before income taxes	$137,989	$124,537	$78,603

The split of domestic and foreign income was impacted mainly by the acquisition related write-offs of in-process technology, which reduced domestic income by $52,313,000.

The components of the provision for income taxes for the years ended March 31 are as follows:

IN THOUSANDS	1996	1995	1994
Federal			
Current	$22,066	$26,455	$13,899
Deferred	(4,263)	(311)	2,658
	17,803	26,144	16,557
Foreign			
Current	15,074	1,106	317
Deferred	(1,491)	—	—
	13,583	1,106	317
State			
Current	3,611	3,177	3,474
Deferred	(383)	708	(695)
	3,228	3,885	2,779
Provision for income taxes	$34,614	$31,135	$19,653

Significant components of the Company's deferred tax assets, included in prepaid expenses in the accompanying consolidated balance sheets as of March 31 are as follows:

IN THOUSANDS	1996	1995
Inventory reserves	$ 3,426	$ 1,048
State taxes	1,323	990
Bad debt reserve	1,901	1,829
Compensatory accruals	5,091	4,355
Various expense accruals	5,581	3,725
Other, net	764	2
Net deferred tax assets	$18,086	$11,949

The provision for income taxes differs from the amount computed by applying the federal statutory tax rate to income before income taxes for the years ended March 31 as follows:

	1996	1995	1994
Federal statutory rate	35.0%	35.0%	35.0%
State taxes, net of federal benefit	2.7	2.2	2.9
Foreign subsidiary income at other than the U.S. tax rate	(11.8)	(9.9)	(10.5)
Tax-exempt interest income, net	(2.1)	(1.7)	(1.6)
Other	1.3	(.6)	(.8)
Effective income tax rate	25.1%	25.0%	25.0%

The Company's effective tax rate for fiscal 1996 was 25%, the same as fiscal 1995 and 1994. During fiscal 1996, the Company concluded negotiations with the Singapore government extending the tax holiday for the Company's manufacturing subsidiary. The terms of the tax holiday provide that profits derived from certain products will be exempt from tax for a period of 10 years, subject to certain conditions. In addition, profits derived from the Company's remaining products will be taxed at a rate of 15%, which is lower than the statutory rate of 27%, through fiscal 1998. As of March 31, 1996, the Company had not accrued income taxes on $186,100,000 of accumulated undistributed earnings of its Singapore subsidiary, as these earnings will be reinvested indefinitely.

NOTE NINE: SEGMENT INFORMATION

Adaptec operates in the microcomputer input/output industry and is a leading supplier of high-performance intelligent subsystems and associated software and very large-scale integrated circuits used to control the flow of data between a microcomputer's CPU and its peripherals. The Company focuses its worldwide marketing efforts on major OEM customers through its direct sales force located in the United States, Europe and Far East and also sells through distributors and sales representatives in each of these geographic areas.

Income from operations consists of net revenues less cost of revenues and operating expenses incurred in supporting the revenues of each geographic area. The Company's write-offs of acquired in-process technology are included in the corporate income from operations. All of the Company's identifiable assets are used to support the operations in each geographic area. Corporate assets include cash and cash equivalents, marketable securities, deferred tax assets and certain other assets. Intercompany sales are made at arms-length prices, and revenues for the European subsidiaries consist mainly of commissions earned in connection with obtaining foreign orders.

NOTE NINE: SEGMENT INFORMATION CONTINUED

IN THOUSANDS	United States	Singapore, Far East, Other	Europe	Corporate	Adjustments and Eliminations	Consolidated Total
Fiscal 1996						
Revenues						
Sales to customers	$609,060	$ 49,211	$1,076	$ —	$ —	$659,347
Intercompany sales between geographic areas	7,205	399,036	6,175	—	(412,416)	—
Net revenues	$616,265	$448,247	$7,251	$ —	$(412,416)	$659,347
Income from operations	100,838	76,942	668	(52,313)	—	126,135
Identifiable assets	201,128	259,179	2,644	322,910	(139,375)	646,486
Fiscal 1995						
Revenues						
Sales to customers	$464,707	$ 1,487	$ —	$ —	$ —	$466,194
Intercompany sales between geographic areas	10,401	191,360	3,905	—	(205,666)	—
Net revenues	$475,108	$192,847	$3,905	$ —	$(205,666)	$466,194
Income from operations	68,594	48,847	343	—	—	117,784
Identifiable assets	122,097	123,044	1,070	262,383	(72,886)	435,708
Fiscal 1994						
Revenues						
Sales to customers	$371,863	$ 382	$ —	$ —	$ —	$372,245
Intercompany sales between geographic areas	10,344	119,305	2,375	—	(132,024)	—
Net revenues	$382,207	$119,687	$2,375	$ —	$(132,024)	$372,245
Income from operations	53,945	23,074	116	—	—	77,135
Identifiable assets	153,340	74,512	347	207,591	(77,315)	358,475

Export Revenues The following table represents export revenues by geographic region as a percentage of total revenues:

	1996	1995	1994
Singapore, Far East, Other	32%	37%	38%
Europe	24	25	20
	56%	62%	58%

Major Customers In fiscal 1996, sales to one distributor represented 10% of net revenues. In fiscal 1995 and 1994, no customer accounted for more than 10% of net revenues.

NOTE TEN: LEGAL MATTERS

A class action lawsuit alleging federal securities law violations and negligent misrepresentation was filed against the Company, its directors, and certain of its officers on February 21, 1991. That action was settled by letter agreement on July 29, 1993. The Company has made all payments required under the terms of the letter agreement. Final settlement of the class action lawsuit was made on May 15, 1995 pursuant to the Court's final judgment and order of dismissal.

NOTE ELEVEN: COMPARATIVE QUARTERLY FINANCIAL DATA UNAUDITED

Summarized quarterly financial data is as follows:

IN THOUSANDS, EXCEPT PER SHARE AMOUNTS	First	Second	Third	Fourth	Year
Fiscal 1996					
Net revenues	$138,025	$149,110	$176,187	$196,025	$659,347
Gross profit	81,359	86,451	101,986	113,612	383,408
Net income*	31,163	557	30,587	41,068	103,375
Net income per share*	$ .58	$ .01	$ .56	$ .75	$ 1.89
Weighted average shares outstanding	53,942	54,461	54,792	55,061	54,569

*The second and third quarters of fiscal 1996 include write-offs of acquired in-process technology, net of taxes, totaling $33 million and $7 million, respectively.

	First	Second	Third	Fourth	Year
Fiscal 1995					
Net revenues	$106,061	$106,574	$123,367	$130,192	$466,194
Gross profit	54,888	57,413	71,563	76,734	260,598
Net income	17,592	18,458	27,403	29,949	93,402
Net income per share	$ .33	$ .35	$ .52	$ .56	$ 1.75
Weighted average shares outstanding	53,944	53,182	52,958	53,802	53,357

Report of Management

Management is responsible for the preparation and integrity of the consolidated financial statements and other financial information presented in the annual report. The accompanying financial statements were prepared in conformity with generally accepted accounting principles and as such include some amounts based on management's best judgments and estimates. Financial information in the annual report is consistent with that in the financial statements.

Management is responsible for maintaining a system of internal business controls and procedures to provide reasonable assurance that assets are safeguarded and that transactions are authorized, recorded and reported properly. The internal control system is continuously monitored by management review, written policies and guidelines, and careful selection and training of qualified people who are provided with and expected to adhere to the Company's standards of business conduct. Management believes the Company's internal controls provide reasonable assurance that assets are safeguarded against material loss from unauthorized use or disposition and the financial records are reliable for preparing financial statements and other data and maintaining accountability for assets.

The Audit Committee of the Board of Directors meets periodically with the independent accountants and management to discuss internal business controls, auditing and financial reporting matters. The Committee also reviews with the independent accountants the scope and results of the audit effort.

The independent accountants, Price Waterhouse LLP, are engaged to examine the consolidated financial statements of the Company and conduct such tests and related procedures as they deem necessary in accordance with generally accepted auditing standards. The opinion of the independent accountants, based upon their audit of the consolidated financial statements, is contained in this annual report.

F. Grant Saviers
President and Chief Executive Officer

Paul G. Hansen
Vice President, Finance and
Chief Financial Officer

Christopher G. O'Meara
Vice President and Treasurer

Andrew J. Brown
Corporate Controller and
Principal Accounting Officer

Report of Independent Accountants

To the Board of Directors and
Shareholders of Adaptec, Inc.:

In our opinion, the accompanying consolidated balance sheets and the related consolidated statements of operations, of cash flows and of shareholders' equity present fairly, in all material respects, the financial position of Adaptec, Inc. and its subsidiaries at March 31, 1996 and 1995, and the results of their operations and their cash flows for the years then ended in conformity with generally accepted accounting principles. These financial statements are the responsibility of the Company's management; our responsibility is to express an opinion on these financial statements based on our audits. We conducted our audits of these statements in accordance with generally accepted auditing standards which require that we plan and perform the audit to obtain reasonable assurance about whether the financial statements are free of material misstatement. An audit includes examining, on a test basis, evidence supporting the amounts and disclosures in the financial statements, assessing the accounting principles used and significant estimates made by management, and evaluating the overall financial statement presentation. We believe that our audits provide a reasonable basis for the opinion expressed above. The financial statements of Adaptec, Inc. as of and for the year ended March 31, 1994 were audited by other independent accountants whose report dated April 25, 1994 expressed an unqualified opinion on those statements.

Price Waterhouse LLP

San Jose, California
April 22, 1996

Selected Financial Data

IN THOUSANDS, EXCEPT PER SHARE AMOUNTS

	1996	1995	1994	1993	1992
Statement of Operations Data					
Year Ended March 31					
Net revenues	$659,347	$466,194	$372,245	$311,339	$150,315
Cost of revenues	275,939	205,596	189,526	174,179	84,549
Gross profit	383,408	260,598	182,719	137,160	65,766
Operating expenses					
Research and development	87,628	60,848	39,993	26,324	17,514
Sales and marketing	81,548	58,737	46,192	32,525	21,338
General and administrative	35,784	23,229	19,399	15,568	10,517
Write-off of acquired in-process technology	52,313	—	—	—	—
	257,273	142,814	105,584	74,417	49,369
Net income	$103,375	$ 93,402	$ 58,950	$ 49,390	$ 14,614
Net Income Per Share					
Net income per share	$ 1.89	$ 1.75	$ 1.10	$ .96	$ .35
Weighted average shares outstanding	54,569	53,357	53,602	51,652	41,664
Balance Sheet Data as of March 31					
Working capital	$334,989	$294,058	$243,451	$191,693	$105,671
Total assets	646,486	435,708	358,475	282,896	138,615
Long-term debt, net of current portion	4,250	7,650	11,050	14,450	423
Shareholders' equity	511,945	371,644	297,616	225,155	117,742

Common Stock Prices and Dividends The Company's common stock is traded in the over-the-counter market under the NASDAQ symbol ADPT. The following table sets forth the range of the high and low prices by quarter as reported by the NASDAQ National Market System.

	1996		1995	
	High	Low	High	Low
First quarter	$39⅞	$29¼	$19½	$14
Second quarter	47¼	34½	21¼	16¼
Third quarter	48⅜	35⅝	24¾	17¼
Fourth quarter	56⅜	35⅛	37	21¾

In March 1992 and January 1994, the Company's Board of Directors approved a two-for-one-split of its common stock. The above net income per share information has been adjusted to reflect the stock splits.

At March 31, 1996, there were 724 holders of record of the Company's common stock. The Company has not paid cash dividends on its common stock and does not currently plan to pay cash dividends to its shareholders in the near future.

Adaptec in the Community

PROVIDING OPPORTUNITIES

Wally and Molly are the information users of tomorrow. But they are the children of today, and often children need our help. Adaptec believes in the importance of giving back to the communities where Wally and Molly are growing and learning. In fiscal 1996 we helped the groups and agencies below in their efforts to make our world more livable for children.

Through our commitment to children, Adaptec in fiscal 1997 is making a special $150,000 donation to support literacy and reading programs to help children get a head start on their futures.

The Children's Health Council

Make-A-Wish Foundation

United Way

The Tech Museum of Innovation

Leavey School of Business, Santa Clara University

Reading Research Center, Mission San Jose Elementary School

Junior Achievement

Second Harvest Food Bank

Ronald McDonald House

Leukemia Society of America

Adaptec Scholarship

Indian Peaks Elementary School

Milpitas High School

San Jose State University

Bellarmine College Preparatory

Girl Scouts of Santa Clara County

Los Altos Educational Foundation

Keys School

SUPPLEMENTAL SCHEDULE OF SALES AND EARNINGS

Campbell Soup Company
Annual Report Year 11

(million dollars)

	Year 11		Year 10		Year 9	
	Sales	Earnings	Sales	Earnings	Sales	Earnings
1 CONTRIBUTIONS BY DIVISION:						
Campbell North America						
Campbell U.S.A.	$3,911.8	$632.7	$3,932.7	$370.8	$3,666.9	$242.3
Campbell Canada	352.0	35.3	384.0	25.6	313.4	23.8
	4,263.8	668.0	4,316.7	396.4	3,980.3	266.1
Campbell Biscuit and Bakery						
Pepperidge Farm	569.0	73.6	582.0	57.0	548.4	53.6
International Biscuit	219.4	17.6	195.3	8.9	178.0	11.7
	788.4	91.2	777.3	65.9	726.4	65.3
Campbell International	1,222.9	39.4	1,189.8	(168.6)	1,030.3	(117.8)
Interdivision	(71.0)		(78.0)		(64.9)	
TOTAL SALES	$6,204.1		$6,205.8		$5,672.1	
TOTAL OPERATING EARNINGS		798.6		293.7		213.6
Unallocated corporate expenses		(41.1)		(16.5)		(31.3)
Interest, net		(90.2)		(94.0)		(55.8)
Foreign currency translation adjustments		.1		(3.8)		(20.0)
Taxes on earnings		(265.9)		(175.0)		(93.4)
NET EARNINGS		$401.5		$4.4		$13.1
NET EARNINGS PER SHARE		$3.16		$.03		$.10

Contributions by division in Year 10 include the effects of divestitures, restructuring and unusual charges of $339.1 million as follows: Campbell U.S.A. $121.8 million, Campbell Canada $6.6 million, Pepperidge Farm $11.0 million, International Biscuit $14.3 million, and Campbell International $185.4 million. Contributions by division in Year 9 include the effects of restructuring and unusual charges of $343.0 million as follows: Campbell U.S.A. $183.1 million, Campbell Canada $6.0 million, Pepperidge Farm $7.1 million, International Biscuit $9.5 million, and Campbell International $137.3 million.

MANAGEMENT'S DISCUSSION AND ANALYSIS OF RESULTS OF OPERATIONS AND FINANCIAL CONDITION

2 **RESULTS OF OPERATIONS**

Overview

Campbell had record net earnings in Year 11 of $401.5 million, or $3.16 per share, compared to net earnings of $4.4 million, or 3 cents per share, in Year 10. Excluding Year 10's divestiture and restructuring charges, earnings per share increased 34% in Year 11. In Year 11, the Company sold five non-strategic businesses, sold or closed several manufacturing plants, and discontinued certain unprofitable product lines. Net sales of $6.2 billion in Year 11 were even with Year 10. Sales were up 4% excluding businesses that were divested and product lines that were discontinued in Year 11.

In Year 10 the Company incurred charges for divestitures and restructuring of $2.33 per share, reducing net earnings to 3 cents per share. In Year 9 restructuring charges of $2.02 per share reduced earnings to 10 cents per share. Excluding these charges from both years, earnings per share rose 11% in Year 10. Sales increased 9%. In Year 10 the company's domestic divisions had strong earnings performances, excluding the divestiture and restructuring charges, but the International Division's performance was disappointing principally due to the poor performance of United Kingdom frozen food and Italian biscuit operations. The Italian biscuit operations were divested in Year 11.

The divestiture and restructuring programs were designed to strengthen the Company's core businesses and improve long-term profitability. The Year 10 divestiture program involved the sale of several low-return or nonstrategic businesses. The Year 10 restructuring charges provided for the elimination of underperforming assets and unnecessary facilities and included a write-off of goodwill. The restructuring charges in Year 9 involved plant consolidations, work force reductions, and goodwill write-offs.

Year 11 Compared to Year 10

3 RESULTS BY DIVISION

CAMPBELL NORTH AMERICA—Operating earnings of Campbell North America, the Company's largest division, were $668.0 million in Year 11 compared to $396.4 million in Year 10 after restructuring charges of $128.4 million. Operating earnings increased 27% in Year 11 over Year 10, excluding the restructuring charges from Year 10. All of the division's core businesses had very strong earnings growth. Continued benefits of restructuring drove significant improvements in operating margins.

Sales were $4.26 billion in Year 11. Excluding divested businesses and discontinued product lines, sales increased 2% with overall volume down 2%. Soup volume was off 1.5% as a result of reduced year-end trade promotional activities. Significant volume increases were achieved in the cooking soup, ramen noodle and family-size soup categories and "Healthy Request" soup. Exceptionally strong volume performances were turned in by "Swanson" frozen dinners, "Franco-American" gravies and "Prego" spaghetti sauces with positive volume results for "LeMenu Healthy" entrees, Food Service frozen soups and entrees, and Casera Foods in Puerto Rico.

CAMPBELL BISCUIT AND BAKERY—Operating earnings of the Biscuit and Bakery division, which includes Pepperidge Farm in the United States, Delacre in Europe and an equity interest in Arnotts Limited in Australia, were $91.2 million in Year 11 compared with $65.9 million in Year 10 after restructuring charges of $25.3 million. Operating earnings were flat in Year 11 excluding the restructuring charges from Year 10. Sales increased 1%, however, volume declined 3%.

Pepperidge Farm operating earnings in Year 11 increased despite a drop in sales, which reflects the adverse effect of the recession on premium cookies. Several new varieties of "Hearty Slices" bread performed well. Delacre, benefiting from new management and integration into the worldwide biscuit and bakery organization, turned in significant improvement in Year 11 sales and operating earnings. Arnotts' performance in Year 11 was disappointing and included restructuring charges. Its restructuring program should have a positive impact on fiscal Year 12 results. The Year 11 comparison with Year 10 was also adversely impacted by gains of $4.0 million realized in Year 10 on the sales of businesses by Arnotts.

CAMPBELL INTERNATIONAL—Operating earnings of the International division were $39.4 million in Year 11 compared to an operating loss of $168.6 million in Year 10 after restructuring charges of $185.4 million.

In Year 11, Campbell International achieved a significant turnaround. Operating earnings for the year more than doubled above the pre-restructuring results of the prior year. There were margin improvements throughout the system. Europe led the division's positive results. A key component was the United Kingdom's move from a loss position to profitability, driven by the benefits of restructuring and product line reconfiguration.

European Food and Confectionery units turned in another year of solid earnings growth. Mexican operations, strengthened by a new management team, also turned around from a loss to a profit position. Sales were $1.22 billion in Year 11, an increase of 6%, excluding divested businesses and discontinued product lines, and the effects of foreign currency rates. Volume was approximately the same as in Year 10.

4 STATEMENTS OF EARNINGS

Sales in Year 11 were even with Year 10. Excluding divested businesses and unprofitable product lines discontinued during Year 11, sales increased 4% while volume declined approximately 2%. The decline in volume was caused by reduced year-end trade promotional activities and the adverse effect of the recession on certain premium products.

Gross margins improved 2.6 percentage points to 34.0% in Year 11 from 31.4% in Year 10. All divisions improved due to the significant benefits from restructuring and the divestitures and product-pruning activities. Productivity improvements worldwide and declining commodity prices also contributed to the higher margins.

Marketing and selling expenses, as a percentage of net sales, were 15.4% in Year 11 compared to 15.8% in Year 10. The decrease in Year 11 is due to more focused marketing efforts and controlled new product introductions. For each of the prior 10 fiscal years, these expenses had increased significantly. Advertising was down 11% in Year 11. Management expects advertising expenditures to increase in Year 12 in order to drive volume growth of core products and to support the introduction of new products.

Administrative expenses, as a percentage of net sales, were 4.9% in Year 11 compared to 4.7% in Year 10. The increase in Year 11 results principally from annual executive incentive plan accruals due to outstanding financial performance and foreign currency rates.

Interest expense increased in Year 11 due to timing of fourth quarter borrowings in order to obtain favorable long-term interest rates. Interest income was also higher in Year 11 as the proceeds from these borrowings were invested temporarily until needed. Interest expense, net of interest income, decreased from $94.0 million in Year 10 to $90.2 million in Year 11 as the increased cash flow from operations exceeded cash used for share repurchases and acquisitions.

Foreign exchange losses declined principally due to reduced effects of currency devaluations in Argentina.

Other expense was $26.2 million in Year 11 compared to $14.7 million in Year 10. The increase results principally from accruals for long-term incentive compensation plans reflecting changes in Campbell's stock price.

As discussed in the "Overview" section above, Year 10 results include divestiture, restructuring, and unusual charges of $339.1 million ($301.6 million or $2.33 per share after taxes).

Equity in earnings of affiliates declined in Year 11 principally due to the disappointing performance at Arnotts and to a $4.0 million gain on sales of businesses realized by Arnotts in Year 10.

Year 10 Compared to Year 9

5 RESULTS BY DIVISION

CAMPBELL NORTH AMERICA—In Year 10, Campbell North America had operating earnings of $396.4 million after restructuring charges of $128.4 million. In Year 9 the division had operating earnings of $266.1 million, after restructuring charges of $189.1 million. Excluding restructuring charges from both Year 10 and Year 9 operating earnings increased 15% in Year 10, led by strong performances by the soup, grocery, "Mrs. Paul's" frozen seafood, and Canadian sectors. The olives business performed poorly in Year 10.

Sales increased 8% in Year 10 to $4.32 billion on a 3% increase in volume. There were solid volume increases in ready-to-serve soups, "Great Starts" frozen breakfasts, and "Prego" spaghetti sauces. Overall soup volume was up 1%. "Mrs. Paul's" regained the number one share position in frozen prepared seafood.

CAMPBELL BISCUIT AND BAKERY—In Year 10, Campbell Biscuit and Bakery had operating earnings of $65.9 million after restructuring charges of $25.3 million. In Year 9, the division's operating earnings were $65.3 million after restructuring charges of $16.6 million. Excluding restructuring charges from both Year 10 and Year 9, operating earnings of the division increased 11% in Year 10. The increase in operating earnings was driven by Pepperidge Farm's biscuit and bakery units along with Arnott's gain on sales of businesses. Pepperidge Farm's frozen unit and Delacre performed poorly. Sales increased 7% to $777.3 million. Volume increased 1%, with Pepperidge Farm's biscuit, bakery and food service units and Delacre the main contributors to the growth.

**MANAGEMENT'S DISCUSSION AND ANALYSIS OF
RESULTS OF OPERATIONS AND FINANCIAL CONDITION**
· ·

CAMPBELL INTERNATIONAL—In Year 10, Campbell International had an operating loss of $168.6 million after restructuring charges of $185.4 million. In Year 9, the division sustained an operating loss of $117.8 million after restructuring charges of $137.3 million. Excluding restructuring charges from both Year 10 and Year 9, operating earnings declined 14% in Year 10, as strong performances in the European Food and Confectionery and Argentine operations were more than offset by poor performances in the United Kingdom frozen food and Italian biscuit operations. Sales in Year 10 were $1.19 billion, an increase of 15%. Volume was up 14% of which 11% came from acquisitions.

6 STATEMENTS OF EARNINGS

In Year 10 sales increased 9% on a 5% increase in volume, about half of which came from established businesses.

Gross margins improved by 1.9 percentage points to 31.4% in Year 10 from 29.5% in Year 9. All divisions had improved margins in Year 10, with Campbell North America operations posting substantial improvements.

Marketing and selling expenses, as a percentage of net sales, were 15.8% in Year 10 compared to 14.4% in Year 9. The Year 10 increase was due to heavy marketing expenditures by Campbell U.S.A. at both the national and regional levels.

Administrative expenses, as a percentage of net sales, were 4.7% in Year 10 compared to 4.4% in Year 9. The increase in Year 10 was driven by some unusual one-time expenditures, employee benefits, the weakening dollar and acquisitions.

Interest expense increased in Year 10 due to higher debt levels resulting from funding of acquisitions, higher inventory levels during the year, purchases of Campbell's stock for the treasury and restructuring program expenditures. Interest income declined in Year 10 because of a shift from local currency to lower-yielding dollar denominated temporary investments in Latin America to minimize foreign exchange losses.

Foreign exchange losses resulted principally from currency devaluations in Argentina. There was a large devaluation in Argentina in Year 9. Also, Year 10 losses were lower due to the shift in temporary investments described in the previous paragraph.

Other expense was $14.7 million in Year 10 compared to $32.4 million in Year 9. This decline results principally from reduced accruals for long-term incentive compensation plans reflecting changes in Campbell's stock price.

As discussed in the "Overview" section above, results include divestiture, restructuring and unusual charges of $339.1 million ($301.6 million or $2.33 per share after taxes) in Year 10 and 343.0 million ($260.8 million or $2.02 per share after taxes) in Year 9.

Equity in earnings of affiliates increased in Year 10 principally due to a $4.0 million gain on sales of businesses realized by Arnotts in Year 10.

7 **Income Taxes**

The effective income tax rate was 39.8% in Year 11, 97.5% in Year 10 an 87.7% in Year 9. The principal reason for the high tax rates in Year 10 and Year 9 is that certain of the divestiture, restructuring and unusual charges are not tax deductible. Excluding the effect of these charges, the rate would be 41.0% in Year 10 and 38.9% in Year 9. The variances in all years are principally due to the level of certain foreign losses for which no tax benefit is currently available.

8 **Inflation**

The Company attempts to mitigate the effects of inflation on sales and earnings by appropriately increasing selling prices and aggressively pursuing an ongoing cost improvement effort which includes capital investments in more efficient plants and equipment. Also, the divestiture and restructuring programs enacted in Year 9 and Year 10 have made the Company a more cost-effective producer, as previously discussed with reference to cost of products sold.

9 **Recent Developments**

In December Year 10, the Financial Accounting Standards Board issued Statement of Financial Accounting Standards No. 106, "Employer's Accounting for Post-retirement Benefits Other Than Pensions," which requires employers to account for retiree health obligations on an accrual basis beginning with the Company's Year 14 fiscal year. For a discussion of its impact on the Company, see Note 8 to the Consolidated Financial Statements.

10 **LIQUIDITY AND CAPITAL RESOURCES**

The Consolidated Statements of Cash Flows and Balance Sheets demonstrate the Company's continued superior financial strength.

11 Statements of Cash Flows

OPERATING ACTIVITIES—Cash provided by operations was $805.2 million in Year 11, an 80% increase from $448.4 million in Year 10. This increased cash flow was driven by the Company's record earnings level and reduced working capital resulting from improved asset management and the restructuring program.

INVESTING ACTIVITIES—The majority of the Company's investing activities involve the purchase of new plant assets to maintain modern manufacturing processes and increase productivity. Capital expenditures for plant assets amounted to $371.1 million in Year 11, including $10.0 million of capital lease activity, down slightly from Year 10. The Company expects capital expenditures in Year 12 to be about $400 million.

Another key investing activity of the Company is acquisitions. The total cost of acquisitions in Year 11 was $180.1 million, most of which was spent to acquire the publicly held shares of the Company's 71% owned subsidiary, Campbell Soup Company Ltd. in Canada. This will allow Campbell North America to more efficiently integrate its U.S. and Canadian operations to provide Campbell with competitive advantage in North America.

One of the Company's strategies has been to prune low-return assets and businesses from its portfolio. In Year 11 the Company realized over $100 million in cash from these activities, with $67.4 million coming from sales of businesses and $43.2 million realized from asset sales.

Also, during Year 11 the Company made contributions to its pension plans substantially in excess of the amounts expensed. This was the principal reason for the increase in other assets.

FINANCING ACTIVITIES—During Year 11, the Company issued debt in the public markets for a total of $400 million: $100 million of 9% Notes due Year 18. $100 million of Medium-Term Notes due Year 21 at interest rates from 8.58% to 8.75%, and $200 million of 8.875%. Debentures due Year 41. The proceeds were used to reduce short-term debt by $227 million, pay off long-term debt maturing in Year 11 of $129.9 million, and to fund the purchase of the minority interest of Campbell Canada.

During Year 11, the Company repurchased approximately 3.4 million shares of its capital stock at a cost of $175.6 million. Cash received from the issuance of approximately 1.1 million treasury shares pursuant to the stock option and long-term incentive plans amounted to $47.7 million in Year 11.

Dividends of $137.5 million represent the dividends paid in Year 11. Dividends declared in Year 11 were $142.2 million or $1.12 per share, an increase of 14% over Year 10.

12 Balance Sheets

Total borrowings at the end of fiscal Year 11 were $1.055 billion compared to $1.008 billion at the end of Year 10. Even after the effects of the borrowing and treasury stock activity previously discussed, total debt as a percentage of total capitalization was 33.7%—the same as a year ago. The Company has ample sources of funds. It has access to the commercial paper markets with the highest rating. The Company's long-term debt is rated double A by the major rating agencies. It has filed a shelf registration with the Securities and Exchange Commission for the issuance from time to time of up to $100 million of debt securities. Also, the Company has unused lines of credit of approximately $635 million.

Debt-related activity is discussed in the Statements of Cash Flows section above. In addition to that, the debt balances on the Balance Sheets were affected by current maturities of long-term debt and by the classification of commercial paper to be refinanced as long-term debt in Year 10.

Aggressive management of working capital and the effect of divested businesses are evidenced by a $235.5 million decrease in current assets exclusive of changes in cash and temporary investments. Receivables are down $97.1 million and inventories declined $113.1 million from Year 10. Accounts payable are down $42.8 million because of the reduced inventory levels and divestitures. Accrued liabilities and accrued income taxes declined $61.9 million as increases due to higher earnings levels and the timing of certain payments were offset by payments and charges resulting from the divestitures and restructuring programs.

Plant assets increased $72.7 million due to capital expenditures of $371.1 million offset by the annual provision for depreciation of $194.5 million, asset sales and divestitures. Intangible assets increased $52.1 million as the acquisitions resulted in $132.3 million of additional goodwill. Amortization and divestitures accounted for the remainder of the change. Other assets increased principally as the result of the pension contribution.

Other liabilities decreased $14.9 million as the reduction of minority interest resulting from the purchase of the publicly-held shares of Campbell Canada and changes in foreign currency rates of other liabilities offset the annual deferred tax provision.

CONSOLIDATED STATEMENTS OF EARNINGS   Campbell Soup Company

(millions)

		Year 11	Year 10	Year 9
13	**NET SALES**	$6,204.1	$6,205.8	$5,672.1
	Costs and expenses			
14	Cost of products sold	4,095.5	4,258.2	4,001.6
15	Marketing and selling expenses	956.2	980.5	818.8
16	Administrative expenses	306.7	290.7	252.1
17	Research and development expenses	56.3	53.7	47.7
18	Interest expense (Note 3)	116.2	111.6	94.1
19	Interest income	(26.0)	(17.6)	(38.3)
20	Foreign exchange losses, net (Note 4)	.8	3.3	19.3
21	Other expense (Note 5)	26.2	14.7	32.4
22	Divestitures, restructuring and unusual charges (Note 6)	—	339.1	343.0
22A	Total costs and expenses	5,531.9	6,034.2	5,570.7
23	Earnings before equity in earnings of affiliates and minority interests	672.2	171.6	101.4
24	Equity in earnings of affiliates	2.4	13.5	10.4
25	Minority interests	(7.2)	(5.7)	(5.3)
26	Earnings before taxes	667.4	179.4	106.5
27	Taxes on earnings (Note 9)	265.9	175.0	93.4
28	**NET EARNINGS**	$401.5	$4.4	$13.1
29	**NET EARNINGS PER SHARE (NOTE 22)**	$3.16	$.03	$.10
30	Weighted average shares outstanding	127.0	129.6	129.3

The accompanying Summary of Significant Accounting Policies and Notes are an integral part of the financial statements.

CONSOLIDATED BALANCE SHEETS
Campbell Soup Company

(million dollars)

	July 28, Year 11	July 29, Year 10
CURRENT ASSETS		
31 Cash and cash equivalents (Note 12)	$178.9	$80.7
32 Other temporary investments, at cost which approximates market	12.8	22.5
33 Accounts receivable (Note 13)	527.4	624.5
34 Inventories (Note 14)	706.7	819.8
35 Prepaid expenses (Note 15)	92.7	118.0
36 Total current assets	1,518.5	1,665.5
37 **PLANT ASSETS, NET OF DEPRECIATION (NOTE 16)**	1,790.4	1,717.7
38 **INTANGIBLE ASSETS, NET OF AMORTIZATION (NOTE 17)**	435.5	383.4
39 **OTHER ASSETS (NOTE 18)**	404.6	349.0
Total Assets	$4,149.0	$4,115.6
CURRENT LIABILITIES		
40 Notes payable (Note 19)	$282.2	$202.3
41 Payable to suppliers and others	482.4	525.2
42 Accrued liabilities (Note 20)	408.7	491.9
43 Dividend payable	37.0	32.3
44 Accrued income taxes	67.7	46.4
45 Total current liabilities	1,278.0	1,298.1
46 **LONG-TERM DEBT (NOTE 19)**	772.6	805.8
47 **OTHER LIABILITIES, PRINCIPALLY DEFERRED INCOME TAXES (NOTE 21)**	305.0	319.9
SHAREOWNERS' EQUITY (NOTE 22)		
48 Preferred stock; authorized 40,000,000 shares; none issued	—	—
49 Capital stock, $.15 par value; authorized 140,000,000 shares; issued 135,622,676 shares	20.3	20.3
50 Capital surplus	107.3	61.9
51 Earnings retained in the business	1,912.6	1,653.3
52 Capital stock in treasury, 8,618,911 shares in Year 11 and 6,353,697 shares in Year 10, at cost	(270.4)	(107.2)
53 Cumulative translation adjustments (Note 4)	23.6	63.5
54 Total shareowners' equity	1,793.4	1,691.8
55 Total liabilities and shareowners' equity	$4,149.0	$4,115.6

The accompanying Summary of Significant Accounting Policies and Notes are an integral part of the financial statements.

CONSOLIDATED STATEMENTS OF CASH FLOWS   Campbell Soup Company

(million dollars)

		Year 11	Year 10	Year 9
	CASH FLOWS FROM OPERATING ACTIVITIES:			
56	Net earnings	$401.5	$4.4	$13.1
	To reconcile net earnings to net cash provided by operating activities:			
57	Depreciation and amortization	208.6	200.9	192.3
58	Divestitures and restructuring provisions		339.1	343.0
59	Deferred taxes	35.5	3.9	(67.8)
60	Other, net	63.2	18.6	37.3
61	(Increase) decrease in accounts receivable	17.1	(60.4)	(46.8)
62	(Increase) decrease in inventories	48.7	10.7	(113.2)
63	Net change in other current assets and liabilities	30.6	(68.8)	(.6)
64	Net cash provided by operating activities	805.2	448.4	357.3
	CASH FLOWS FROM INVESTING ACTIVITIES:			
65	Purchases of plant assets	(361.1)	(387.6)	(284.1)
66	Sales of plant assets	43.2	34.9	39.8
67	Businesses acquired	(180.1)	(41.6)	(135.8)
68	Sales of businesses	67.4	21.7	4.9
69	Increase in other assets	(57.8)	(18.6)	(107.0)
70	Net change in other temporary investments	9.7	3.7	9.0
71	Net cash used in investing activities	(478.7)	(387.5)	(473.2)
	CASH FLOWS FROM FINANCING ACTIVITIES:			
72	Long-term borrowings	402.8	12.6	126.5
73	Repayments of long-term borrowings	(129.9)	(22.5)	(53.6)
74	Increase (decrease) in borrowings with less than three month maturities	(137.9)	(2.7)	108.2
75	Other short-term borrowings	117.3	153.7	227.1
76	Repayments of other short-term borrowings	(206.4)	(89.8)	(192.3)
77	Dividends paid	(137.5)	(124.3)	(86.7)
78	Treasury stock purchases	(175.6)	(41.1)	(8.1)
79	Treasury stock issued	47.7	12.4	18.5
80	Other, net	(.1)	(.1)	23.5
81	Net cash provided by (used in) financing activities	(219.6)	(101.8)	163.1
82	Effect of exchange rate changes on cash	(8.7)	.7	(12.1)
83	**NET INCREASE (DECREASE) IN CASH AND CASH EQUIVALENTS**	98.2	(40.2)	35.1
84	Cash and cash equivalents at beginning of year	80.7	120.9	85.8
85	**CASH AND CASH EQUIVALENTS AT END OF YEAR**	$178.9	$80.7	$120.9

The accompanying Summary of Significant Accounting Policies and Notes are an integral part of the financial statements.
Prior years have been reclassified to conform to the Year 11 presentation.

CONSOLIDATED STATEMENTS OF SHAREOWNERS' EQUITY   Campbell Soup Company

(million dollars)

	Preferred stock	Capital stock	Capital surplus	Earnings retained in the business	Capital stock in treasury	Cumulative translation adjustments	Total Shareowners' Equity
86 Balance at July 31, Year 8	—	$20.3	$42.3	$1,879.1	$(75.2)	$28.5	$1,895.0
Net earnings				13.1			13.1
Cash dividends							
($.90 per share)				(116.4)			(116.4)
Treasury stock purchased					(8.1)		(8.1)
Treasury stock issued under							
Management incentive and							
Stock option plans			8.5		12.6		21.1
Translation adjustments						(26.4)	(26.4)
87 Balance at July 30, Year 9	—	20.3	50.8	1,775.8	(70.7)	2.1	1,778.3
Net earnings				4.4			4.4
Cash dividends							
($.98 per share)				(126.9)			(126.9)
Treasury stock purchased					(41.1)		(41.1)
Treasury stock issued under							
Management incentive and							
Stock option plans			11.1		4.6		15.7
Translation adjustments						61.4	61.4
Balance at July 29, Year 10	—	20.3	61.9	1,653.3	(107.2)	63.5	1,691.8
88 Net earnings				401.5			401.5
89 Cash dividends							
($1.12 per share)				(142.2)			(142.2)
90 Treasury stock purchased					(175.6)		(175.6)
91 Treasury stock issued under							
Management incentive and							
Stock option plans			45.4		12.4		57.8
92 Translation adjustments						(29.9)	(29.9)
93 Sale of foreign operations						(10.0)	(10.0)
94 Balance at July 28, Year 11	—	$20.3	$107.3	$1,912.6	$(270.4)	$23.6	$1,793.4

95 **CHANGES IN NUMBER OF SHARES**

(thousands of shares)

	Issued	Out- standing	In Treasury
Balance at July 31, Year 8	135,622.7	129,038.6	6,584.1
Treasury stock purchased		(250.6)	250.6
Treasury stock issued under Management incentive and Stock option plans		790.6	(790.6)
Balance at July 30, Year 9	135,622.7	129,578.6	6,044.1
Treasury stock purchased		(833.0)	833.0
Treasury stock issued under Management incentive and Stock option plans		523.4	(523.4)
Balance at July 29, Year 10	135,622.7	129,269.0	6,353.7
Treasury stock purchased		(3,395.4)	3,395.4
Treasury stock issued under Management incentive and Stock option plans		1,130.2	(1,130.2)
Balance at July 28, Year 11	135,622.7	127,003.8	8,618.9

The accompanying Summary of Significant Accounting Policies and Notes are an integral part of the financial statements.

NOTES TO CONSOLIDATED FINANCIAL STATEMENTS

(million dollars)

[96] **❶ SUMMARY OF SIGNIFICANT ACCOUNTING POLICIES**

CONSOLIDATION—The consolidated financial statements include the accounts of the Company and its majority-owned subsidiaries. Significant intercompany transactions are eliminated in consolidation. Investments in affiliated owned 20% or more are accounted for by the equity method.

INVENTORIES—Substantially all domestic inventories are priced at the lower of cost or market, with cost determined by the last-in, first-out (LIFO) method. Other inventories are priced at the lower of average cost or market.

INTANGIBLES—The excess of cost of investments over net assets of purchased companies is amortized on a straight-line basis over periods not exceeding forty years.

PLANT ASSETS—Alterations and major overhauls which substantially extend the lives of properties or materially increase their capacity are capitalized. The amounts for property disposals are removed from plant asset and accumulated depreciation accounts and any resultant gain or loss is included in earnings. Ordinary repairs and maintenance are charged to operating costs.

DEPRECIATION—Depreciation provided in costs and expenses is on the straight-line method. The United States, Canadian and certain other foreign companies use accelerated methods of depreciation for income tax purposes.

PENSION PLANS—Pension costs are accrued over employees' careers based on plan benefit formulas.

CASH AND CASH EQUIVALENTS—All highly liquid debt instruments purchased with a maturity of three months or less are classified as Cash Equivalents.

FINANCIAL INSTRUMENTS—In managing interest rate exposure, the Company at times enters into interest rate swap agreements. When interest rates change, the difference to be paid or received is accrued and recognized as interest expense over the life of the agreement. In order to hedge foreign currency exposures on firm commitments, the Company at times enters into forward foreign exchange contracts. Gains and losses resulting from these instruments are recognized in the same period as the underlying hedged transaction. The Company also at times enters into foreign currency swap agreements which are effective as hedges of net investments in foreign subsidiaries. Realized and unrealized gains and losses on these currency swaps are recognized in the Cumulative Translation Adjustments account in Shareowners' Equity.

[97] **❷ GEOGRAPHIC AREA INFORMATION**

The Company is predominantly engaged in the prepared convenience foods industry. The following presents information about operations in different geographic areas:

	Year 11	Year 10	Year 9
Net sales			
United States	**$4,495.6**	$4,527.2	$4,233.4
Europe	**1,149.1**	1,101.4	983.7
Other foreign countries	**656.0**	673.6	542.9
Adjustment and elimination	**(96.6)**	(96.4)	(87.9)
Consolidated	**$6,204.1**	$6,205.8	$5,672.1
Earnings (loss) before taxes			
United States	**$694.8**	$427.8	$294.5
Europe	**48.8**	(178.7)	(21.3)
Other foreign countries	**55.0**	44.6	(59.6)
	798.6	293.7	213.6
Unallocated corporate expenses	**(41.1)**	(16.5)	(31.3)
Interest, net	**(90.2)**	(94.0)	(55.8)
Foreign currency translation adjustment	**.1**	(3.8)	(20.0)
Consolidated	**$667.4**	$179.4	$106.5
Identifiable assets			
United States	**$2,693.4**	$2,535.0	$2,460.5
Europe	**711.3**	942.2	886.9
Other foreign countries	**744.3**	638.4	584.7
Consolidated	**$4,149.0**	$4,115.6	$3,932.1

Transfers between geographic areas are recorded at cost plus markup or at market. Identifiable assets are all assets identified with operations in each geographic area.

❸ INTEREST EXPENSE

	Year 11	Year 10	Year 9
[98] Interest expense	**$136.9**	$121.9	$97.6
[99] Less interest expense capitalized	**20.7**	10.3	3.5
[100]	**$116.2**	$111.6	$94.1

Campbell Soup Company

(million dollars)

101 ❹ FOREIGN CURRENCY TRANSLATION

Fluctuations in foreign exchange rates resulted in decreases in net earnings of $.3 in Year 11, $3.2 in Year 10 and $19.1 in Year 9.

The balances in the Cumulative translation adjustments account are the following:

	Year 11	Year 10	Year 9
Europe	$ 5.6	$43.2	$(3.5)
Canada	3.8	3.6	(2.5)
Australia	13.4	16.1	7.3
Other	.8	.6	.8
	$23.6	$63.5	$ 2.1

102 ❺ OTHER EXPENSE

Included in other expense are the following:

	Year 11	Year 10	Year 9
102 Stock price related incentive programs	$15.4	$ (.1)	$17.4
103 Amortization of intangible and other assets	14.1	16.8	16.4
104 Other, net	(3.3)	(2.0)	(1.4)
	$26.2	$14.7	$32.4

104 ❻ DIVESTITURES, RESTRUCTURING AND UNUSUAL CHARGES

In Year 10, charges for divestiture and restructuring programs, designed to strengthen the Company's core businesses and improve long-term profitability, reduced operating earnings by $339.1; $301.6 after taxes, or $2.33 per share. The divestiture program involves the sale of several low-return or non-strategic businesses. The restructuring charges provide for the elimination of underperforming assets and unnecessary facilities and include a charge of $113 to write off goodwill in the United Kingdom.

In Year 9, charges for a worldwide restructuring program reduced operating earnings by $343.0; $260.8 after taxes, or $2.02 per share. The restructuring program involved plant consolidations, work force reductions, and goodwill write-offs.

106 ❼ ACQUISITIONS

Prior to July Year 11, the Company owned approximately 71% of the capital stock of Campbell Soup Company Ltd. ("Campbell Canada"), which processes, packages and distributes a wide range of prepared foods exclusively in Canada under many of the Company's brand names. The financial position and results of operations of Campbell Canada are consolidated with those of the Company. In July Year 11, the Company acquired the remaining shares (29%) of Campbell Canada which it did not already own at a cost of $159.7. In addition, the Company made one other acquisition at a cost of $20.4. The total cost of Year 11 acquisitions of $180.1 was allocated as follows:

107	
Working capital	$ 5.1
Fixed assets	4.7
Intangibles, principally goodwill	132.3
Other assets	1.5
Elimination of minority interest	36.5
	$180.1

During Year 10 the Company made several small acquisitions at a cost of $43.1 which was allocated as follows:

108	
Working capital	$ 7.8
Fixed assets	24.7
Intangibles, principally goodwill	18.5
Long-term liabilities and other	(7.9)
	$43.1

During Year 9, the Company made several acquisitions at a cost of $137.9, including a soup and pickle manufacturing business in Canada. The cost of the acquisitions was allocated as follows:

109	
Working capital	$ 39.9
Fixed assets	34.6
Intangibles, principally goodwill	65.5
Long-term liabilities and other	(2.1)
	$137.9

These acquisition were accounted for as purchase transactions, and operations of the acquired companies are included in the financial statements from the dates the acquisitions were recorded. Proforma results

NOTES TO CONSOLIDATED FINANCIAL STATEMENTS
. . . .

(million dollars)

of operations have not been presented as they would not vary materially from the reported amounts and would not be indicative of results anticipated following acquisition due to significant changes made to acquired companies' operations.

. . . .

110 ⑧ PENSION PLANS AND RETIREMENT BENEFITS

PENSION PLANS—Substantially all of the employees of the Company and its domestic and Canadian subsidiaries are covered by noncontributory defined benefit pension plans. Plan benefits are generally based on years of service and employees' compensation during the last years of employment. Benefits are paid from funds previously provided to trustees and insurance companies or are paid directly by the Company or its subsidiaries. Actuarial assumptions and plan provisions are reviewed regularly by the Company and its independent actuaries to ensure that plan assets will be adequate to provide pension and survivor benefits. Plan assets consist primarily of shares of or units in common stock, fixed income, real estate and money market funds.

Pension expense included the following:

For Domestic and Canadian trusteed plans:	Year 11	Year 10	Year 9
111 Service cost-benefits earned during the year	$ 22.1	$ 19.3	$ 17.2
112 Interest cost on projected benefit obligation	69.0	63.3	58.8
113 Actual return on plan assets	(73.4)	(27.1)	(113.8)
114 Net amortization and deferral	6.3	(38.2)	57.8
	24.0	17.3	20.0
115 Other pension expense	7.4	6.4	6.8
116 Consolidated pension expense	$ 31.4	$ 23.7	$ 26.8

Principal actuarial assumptions used in the United States were:

Measurements of projected benefit obligation—			
117 Discount rate	8.75%	9.00%	9.00%
118 Long-term rate of compensation increase	5.75%	5.50%	5.00%
119 Long-term rate of return on plan assets	9.00%	9.00%	9.00%

The funded status of the plans was as follows:

120	July 28, Year 11	July 29, Year 10
Actuarial present value of benefit obligations:		
Vested	$(679.6)	$(624.4)
Non-vested	(34.8)	(35.0)
Accumulated benefit obligation	(714.4)	(659.4)
Effect of projected future salary increases	(113.3)	(101.0)
Projected benefit obligation	(827.7)	(760.4)
Plan assets at market value	857.7	773.9
Plan assets in excess of projected benefit obligation	30.0	13.5
Unrecognized net loss	122.9	86.3
Unrecognized prior service cost	54.9	55.9
Unrecognized net assets at transition	(35.3)	(39.5)
Prepaid pension expense	$ 172.5	$ 116.2

Pension coverage for employees of the Company's foreign subsidiaries, other than Canada, and other supplemental pension benefits of the Company are provided to the extent determined appropriate through their respective plans. Obligations under such plans are systematically provided for by depositing funds with trusts or under insurance contracts. The assets and obligations of these plans are not material.

SAVINGS PLANS—The Company sponsors employee savings plans which cover substantially all domestic employees. After one year of continuous service the Company matches 50% of employee contributions up to five percent of compensation within certain limits. In fiscal Year 12, the Company will increase its contribution by up to 20% if certain earnings' goals are achieved. Amounts charged to costs and expenses were $10.0 in Year 11, $10.6 in Year 10, and $10.7 in Year 9.

(million dollars)

RETIREE BENEFITS—The Company and its domestic subsidiaries provide certain health care and life insurance benefits to substantially all retired employees and their dependents. The cost of these retiree health and life insurance benefits are expensed as claims are paid and amounted to $15.3 in Year 11, $12.6 in Year 10, and $11.0 in Year 9. Substantially all retirees of foreign subsidiaries are provided health care benefits by government sponsored plans. The cost of life insurance provided to retirees of certain foreign subsidiaries is not significant.

In December Year 10, the Financial Accounting Standards Board issued Statement of Financial Accounting Standards No. 106, "Employer's Accounting for Post-retirement Benefits Other Than Pensions," which will require the Company to account for retiree health obligations on an accrual basis beginning with the Year 14 fiscal year. The Company is in the process of studying the effects of this complex new accounting standard. The standard permits an employer to recognize the effect of the initial liability either immediately or to amortize it over a period of up to 20 years. The Company has not yet decided which option to select. Management expects that the adoption of this standard will increase annual expense, but the amount has not yet been determined.

. . . .

121 🙂 **TAXES ON EARNINGS**

The provision for income taxes consists of the following:

		Year 11	Year 10	Year 9
	Currently payable			
122	Federal	**$185.8**	$132.4	$118.8
123	State	**23.4**	20.8	20.9
124	Foreign	**21.2**	17.9	21.5
124A		**230.4**	171.1	161.2
	Deferred			
125	Federal	**21.9**	1.2	(49.3)
126	State	**7.5**	2.6	(8.0)
127	Foreign	**6.1**	.1	(10.5)
127A		**35.5**	3.9	(67.8)
127B		**$265.9**	$175.0	$ 93.4

The deferred income taxes result from temporary differences between financial statement earnings and taxable earnings as follows:

		Year 11	Year 10	Year 9
128	Depreciation	**$ 5.9**	$ 18.6	$ 11.9
129	Pensions	**13.6**	11.7	8.3
130	Prefunded employee benefits	**(3.3)**	(4.8)	(3.4)
131	Accruals not currently deductible for tax purposes	**(11.4)**	(5.8)	(5.3)
132	Divestitures, restructuring and unusual charges	**29.3**	(11.1)	(78.2)
133	Other	**1.4**	(4.7)	(1.1)
		$35.5	$ 3.9	$(67.8)

The following is a reconciliation of effective income tax rates with the statutory Federal income tax rate:

		Year 11	Year 10	Year 9
134	Statutory Federal income tax rate	**34.0%**	34.0%	34.0%
135	State income taxes (net of Federal tax benefit)	**3.0**	3.7	3.6
136	Nondeductible divestitures, restructuring and unusual charges		56.5	48.7
137	Nondeductible amortization of intangibles	**.6**	.9	1.1
138	Foreign earnings not taxed or taxed at other than statutory Federal rate	**(.3)**	1.2	.2
139	Other	**2.5**	1.2	.1
140	Effective income tax rate	**39.8%**	97.5%	87.7%

The provision for income taxes was reduced by $3.2 in Year 11, $5.2 in Year 10 and $3.5 in Year 9 due to the utilization of loss carryforwards by certain foreign subsidiaries.

Certain foreign subsidiaries of the Company have tax loss carryforwards of approximately $103.4 ($77.4 for financial purposes), of which $10.5 relate to periods prior to acquisition of the subsidiaries by the Company. Of these carryforwards, $54.8 expire through Year 16 and $48.6 may be carried forward indefinitely. The current statutory tax rates in these foreign countries range from 20% to 51%.

NOTES TO CONSOLIDATED FINANCIAL STATEMENTS

(million dollars)

Income taxes have not been accrued on undistributed earnings of foreign subsidiaries of $219.7 which are invested in operating assets and are not expected to be remitted. If remitted, tax credits are available to substantially reduce any resultant additional taxes.

The following are earnings before taxes of United States and foreign companies.

	Year 11	Year 10	Year 9
141 United States	$570.9	$277.0	$201.5
142 Foreign	96.5	(97.6)	(95.0)
	$667.4	$179.4	$106.5

143 ⑩ LEASES

Rent expense was $59.7 in Year 11, $62.4 in Year 10 and $60.2 in Year 9 and generally relates to leases of machinery and equipment. Future minimum lease payments under operating leases are $71.9.

⑪ SUPPLEMENTARY STATEMENTS OF EARNINGS INFORMATION

	Year 11	Year 10	Year 9
144 Maintenance and repairs	$173.9	$180.6	$173.9
145 Advertising	$195.4	$220.4	$212.9

146 ⑫ CASH AND CASH EQUIVALENTS

Cash and Cash Equivalents includes cash equivalents of $140.7 at July 28, Year 11, and $44.1 at July 29, Year 10.

⑬ ACCOUNTS RECEIVABLE

	Year 11	Year 10
147 Customers	$478.0	$554.0
148 Allowances for cash discounts and bad debts	(16.3)	(19.9)
	461.7	534.1
148A Other	65.7	90.4
150	$527.4	$624.5

⑭ INVENTORIES

	Year 11	Year 10
151 Raw materials, containers and supplies	$342.3	$384.4
152 Finished products	454.0	520.0
	796.3	904.4
153 Less—adjustments of inventories to LIFO basis	89.6	84.6
	$706.7	$819.8

Liquidation of LIFO inventory quantities had no significant effect on net earnings in Year 11, Year 10, or Year 9. Inventories for which the LIFO method of determining cost is used represented approximately 70% of consolidated inventories in Year 11 and 64% in Year 10.

⑮ PREPAID EXPENSES

	Year 11	Year 10
154 Pensions	$19.8	$ 22.3
155 Deferred taxes	36.6	37.7
156 Prefunded employee benefits	1.2	13.9
157 Other	35.1	44.1
	$92.7	$118.0

⑯ PLANT ASSETS

	Year 11	Year 10
158 Land	$ 56.3	$ 63.8
159 Buildings	758.7	746.5
160 Machinery and equipment	1,779.3	1,657.6
161 Projects in progress	327.6	267.0
161A	2,921.9	2,734.9
162 Accumulated depreciation	(1,131.5)	(1,017.2)
	$1,790.4	$1,717.7

Depreciation provided in costs and expenses was $194.5 in Year 11, $184.1 in Year 10 and $175.9 in Year 9. Approximately $158.2 of capital expenditures is required to complete projects in progress at July 28, Year 11.

(million dollars)

17 INTANGIBLE ASSETS

	Year 11	Year 10
163 Cost of investments in excess of net assets of purchased companies (goodwill)	$347.8	$281.1
164 Other intangibles	129.8	134.0
	477.6	415.1
165 Accumulated amortization	(42.1)	(31.7)
	$435.5	$383.4

18 OTHER ASSETS

	Year 11	Year 10
166 Investment in affiliates	$155.8	$169.4
167 Noncurrent prepaid pension expense	152.7	93.9
168 Other noncurrent investments	44.2	52.0
169 Other	51.9	33.7
169A	$404.6	$349.0

Investment in affiliates consists principally of the Company's ownership of 33% of the outstanding capital stock of Arnotts Limited, an Australian biscuit manufacturer. This investment is being accounted for by the equity method. Included in this investment is goodwill of $28.3 which is being amortized over 40 years. At July 28, Year 11, the market value of the investment based on quoted market prices was $213.8. The Company's equity in the earnings of Arnotts Limited was $1.5 in Year 11, $13.0 in Year 10 and $8.7 in Year 9. The Year 10 amount includes a $4.0 gain realized by Arnotts on the sales of businesses. Dividends received were $8.2 in Year 11, $7.4 in Year 10 and $6.6 in Year 9. The Company's equity in the undistributed earnings of Arnotts was $15.4 at July 28, Year 11 and $22.1 at July 29, Year 10.

170 19 NOTES PAYABLE AND LONG-TERM DEBT

Notes payable consists of the following:

	Year 11	Year 10
Commercial paper	$ 24.7	$191.8
8.25% Notes due Year 11		100.3
13.99% Notes due Year 12	182.0*	
Banks	23.6	91.1
Other	51.9	69.4
Amounts reclassified to long-term debt		(250.3)
	$282.2	$202.3

*Present value of $200.0 zero coupon notes, net of unamortized discount of $18.0.

At July 29, Year 10, $150 of outstanding commercial paper and $100.3 of currently maturing notes were reclassified to long-term debt and were refinanced in Year 11.

Information on notes payable follows:

171	Year 11	Year 10	Year 9
Maximum amount payable at end of any monthly accounting period during the year	$603.3	$518.7	$347.1
Approximate average amount outstanding during the year	$332.5	$429.7	$273.5
Weighted average interest rate at year-end	10.1%	10.7%	12.1%
Approximate weighted average interest rate during the year	9.8%	10.8%	10.6%

The amount of unused lines of credit at July 28, Year 11 approximates $635. The lines of credit are unconditional and generally cover loans for a period of a year at prime commercial interest rates.

NOTES TO CONSOLIDATED FINANCIAL STATEMENTS
. . . .

(million dollars)

Long-term debt consists of the following:

172 Fiscal year maturities	Year 11	Year 10
13.99% Notes due Year 12	$	$159.7***
9.125% Notes due Year 14	100.6	100.9
10.5% Notes due Year 16*	100.0	100.0
7.5% Notes due Year 18*	99.6	99.5
9.0% Notes due Year 18	99.8	
8.58%–8.75% Medium-Term Notes due Year 21**	100.0	
8.875% Debentures due Year 41	199.6	
Other Notes due Year 12–24 (interest 4.7%–14.4%)	58.2	82.5
Notes payable, reclassified		250.3
Capital lease obligations	14.8	12.9
	$772.6	$805.8

Redeemable in Year 13.
**$50 redeemable in Year 18.*
***Present value of $200.0 zero coupon notes, net of unamortized discount of $40.3.*

173 Future minimum lease payments under capital leases are $28.0 and the present value of such payments, after deducting implicit interest of $6.5, is $21.5 of which $6.7 is included in current liabilities.

Principle amounts of long-term debt mature as follows: Year 12-$227.7 (in current liabilities); Year 13-$118.9; Year 14-$17.8; Year 15-$15.9; Year 16-$108.3 and beyond-$511.7.

The Company has filed a shelf registration statement with the Securities and Exchange Commission for the issuance from time to time of up to $300 of debt securities, of which $100 remains unissued.

Information on financial instruments follows:

At July 28, Year 11, the Company had an interest rate swap agreement with financial institutions having a notional principal amount of $100, which is intended to reduce the impact of changes in interest rates on floating rate commercial paper. In addition, at July 28, Year 11, the Company had two swap agreements with financial institutions which covered both interest rates and foreign currencies. These agreements have a total notional principal amount of $103, and are intended to reduce exposure to higher foreign interest rates and to hedge the Company's net investments in the United Kingdom and Australia. The Company is exposed to credit loss in the event of nonperformance by the other parties to the interest rate swap agreements; however, the Company does not anticipate nonperformance by the counterparties.

At July 28, Year 11, the Company had contracts to purchase approximately $109 in foreign currency. The contracts are mostly for European currencies and have maturities through Year 12.

. . . .

20 ACCRUED LIABILITIES

	Year 11	Year 10
174 Divestiture and restructuring charges	$ 88.4	$238.8
175 Other	320.3	253.1
	$408.7	$491.9

. . . .

21 OTHER LIABILITIES

	Year 11	Year 10
176 Deferred income taxes	$258.5	$235.1
177 Other liabilities	23.0	28.5
178 Minority interests	23.5	56.3
	$305.0	$319.9

Campbell Soup Company

(million dollars)

[179] 22 SHAREOWNERS' EQUITY

The Company has authorized 140 million shares of Capital Stock of $.15 par value and 40 million shares of Preferred Stock issuable in one or more classes, with or without par as may be authorized by the Board of Directors. No Preferred Stock has been issued.

The following summarizes the activity in option shares under the Company's employee stock option plans:

(thousands of shares)	Year 11	Year 10	Year 9
Beginning of year	4,301.1	3,767.9	3,257.0
Granted under the Year 4 long-term incentive plan at average price of $63.64 in Year 11; $47.27 in Year 10; $30.37 in Year 9	2,136.3	1,196.0	1,495.5
Exercised at average price of $29.82 in Year 11; $24.78 in Year 10; $20.65 in Year 9 in form of:			
Stock appreciation rights	(14.9)	(110.2)	(137.3)
Shares	(1,063.7)	(367.2)	(615.1)
Terminated	(216.9)	(185.4)	(232.2)
End of year	5,141.9	4,301.1	3,767.9
Exercisable at end of year	2,897.0	2,654.4	2,104.1
Shares under option-price per share:			
Range of prices: Low	$14.68	$ 6.98	$ 6.98
High	$83.31	$57.61	$34.31
Average	$46.73	$33.63	$28.21

In addition to options granted under the Year 4 long-term incentive plan, 233,200 restricted shares of capital stock were granted to certain key management employees in Year 11; 168,850 in Year 10; and 162,000 in Year 9.

There are 4,229,111 shares available for grant under the long-term incentive plan.

Net earnings per share are based on the weighted average shares outstanding during the applicable periods. The potential dilution from the exercise of stock options is not material.

23 STATEMENTS OF CASH FLOWS

	Year 11	Year 10	Year 9
[180] Interest paid, net of amounts capitalized	$101.3	$116.3	$ 88.9
[181] Interest received	$ 27.9	$ 17.1	$ 35.5
[182] Income taxes paid	$199.3	$152.8	$168.6
[183] Capital lease obligations incurred	$ 10.0	$ 9.7	$ 18.0

[184] 24 QUARTERLY DATA (unaudited)

	Year 11			
	First	Second	Third	Fourth
Net sales	$1,594.3	$1,770.9	$1,490.8	$1,348.1
Cost of products sold	1,082.7	1,152.6	981.6	878.6
Net earnings	105.1	135.3	76.4	84.7
Per share				
Net earnings	.82	1.07	.60	.67
Dividends	.25	.29	.29	.29
Market price				
High	54.00	60.38	87.13	84.88
Low	43.75	48.50	58.75	72.38

	Year 10			
	First	Second	Third	Fourth
Net sales	$1,523.5	$1,722.5	$1,519.6	$1,440.2
Cost of products sold	1,057.2	1,173.0	1,049.3	978.7
Net earnings (loss)	83.0	105.2	54.6	(238.4)
Per share				
Net earnings (loss)	.64	.81	.42	(1.84)
Dividends	.23	.25	.25	.25
Market price				
High	58.50	59.63	54.13	62.00
Low	42.13	42.50	45.00	50.13

The fourth quarter of Year 10 includes divestitures, restructuring and unusual charges of $301.6 after taxes, or $2.33 per share.

ELEVEN YEAR REVIEW—CONSOLIDATED

(millions except per share amounts)

Fiscal Year	Year 11	Year 10 (a)	Year 9 (b)
185 SUMMARY OF OPERATIONS			
Net sales	$6,204.1	$6,205.8	$5,672.1
Earnings before taxes	667.4	179.4	106.5
Earnings before cumulative effect of accounting change	401.5	4.4	13.1
Net earnings	401.5	4.4	13.1
Percent of sales	6.5%	.1%	.2%
Return on average shareowners' equity	23.0%	.3%	.7%

FINANCIAL POSITION			
Working capital	$ 240.5	$ 367.4	$ 369.4
Plant assets–net	1,790.4	1,717.7	1,540.6
Total assets	4,149.0	4,115.6	3,932.1
Long-term debt	772.6	805.8	629.2
Shareowners' equity	1,793.4	1,691.8	1,778.3

PER SHARE DATA			
Earnings before cumulative effect of accounting change	$ 3.16	$ .03	$ .10
Net earnings	3.16	.03	.10
Dividends declared	1.12	.98	.90
Shareowners' equity	14.12	13.09	13.76

OTHER STATISTICS			
Salaries, wages, pensions, etc.	$1,401.0	$1,422.5	$1,333.9
Capital expenditures	371.1	397.3	302.0
Number of shareowners (in thousands)	37.7	43.0	43.7
Weighted average shares outstanding	127.0	129.6	129.3

(a) Year 10 includes pre-tax divestiture and restructuring charges of $339.1 million; 301.6 million or $2.33 per share after taxes.
(b) Year 9 includes pre-tax restructuring charges of $343.0 million; $260.8 million or $2.02 per share after taxes.
(c) Year 8 includes pre-tax restructuring charges of $49.3 million; $29.4 million or 23 cents per share after taxes. Year 8 also includes cumulative effect of change in accounting for income taxes of $32.5 million or 25 cents per share.
(d) Includes employees under the Employee Stock Ownership Plan terminated in Year 7.

Campbell Soup Company

Year 8	Year 7	Year 6	Year 5	Year 4	Year 3	Year 2	Year 1
(c)							
$4,868.9	$4,490.4	$4,286.8	$3,916.6	$3,636.9	$3,292.4	$2,955.6	$2,797.7
388.6	417.9	387.2	333.7	332.4	306.0	276.9	244.4
241.6	247.3	223.2	197.8	191.2	165.0	149.6	129.7
274.1	247.3	223.2	197.8	191.2	165.0	149.6	129.7
5.6%	5.5%	5.2%	5.1%	5.3%	5.0%	5.1%	4.6%
15.1%	15.1%	15.3%	15.0%	15.9%	15.0%	14.6%	13.2%
$ 499.6	$ 744.1	$ 708.7	$ 579.4	$ 541.5	$ 478.9	$ 434.6	$ 368.2
1,508.9	1,349.0	1,168.1	1,027.5	970.9	889.1	815.4	755.1
3,609.6	3,097.4	2,762.8	2,437.5	2,210.1	1,991.5	1,865.5	1,722.9
525.8	380.2	362.3	297.1	283.0	267.5	236.2	150.6
1,895.0	1,736.1	1,538.9	1,382.5	1,259.9	1,149.4	1,055.8	1,000.5
$ 1.87	$ 1.90	$ 1.72	$ 1.53	$ 1.48	$ 1.28	$ 1.16	$ 1.00
2.12	1.90	1.72	1.53	1.48	1.28	1.16	1.00
.81	.71	.65	.61	.57	.54	.53	.51
14.69	13.35	11.86	10.69	9.76	8.92	8.19	7.72
$1,222.9	$1,137.3	$1,061.0	$ 950.1	$ 889.5	$ 755.1	$ 700.9	$ 680.9
261.9	328.0	251.3	212.9	183.1	154.1	147.6	135.4
43.0	41.0	50.9(d)	49.5(d)	49.4(d)	40.1	39.7	41.6
129.4	129.9	129.5	129.1	129.0	129.0	129.0	129.6

186

Form 10-K

Schedule V
CAMPBELL SOUP COMPANY AND CONSOLIDATED SUBSIDIARIES
Property, Plant, and Equipment at Cost
(million dollars)

	Land	Buildings	Machinery and equipment	Projects in progress	Total
Balance at July 31, Year 8	$53.2	$735.5	$1,624.4	$126.6	$2,539.7
Additions	2.8	47.6	216.4	35.2	302.0
Acquired assets*	4.8	13.6	22.6	—	41.0
Retirements and sales	(4.5)	(88.4)	(238.3)	—	(331.2)
Translation adjustments	(.5)	(2.5)	(5.9)	.4	(8.5)
Balance at July 30, Year 9	55.8	705.8	1,619.2	162.2	2,543.0
Additions	3.2	69.2	219.6	105.3	397.3
Acquired assets*	3.8	14.1	6.8	—	24.7
Retirements and sales	(2.8)	(64.0)	(222.9)	(1.1)	(290.8)
Translation adjustments	3.8	21.4	34.9	.6	60.7
Balance at July 29, Year 10	63.8	746.5	1,657.6	267.0	2,734.9
Additions	1.5	70.2	239.5	59.9	371.1
Acquired assets*	.5	3.3	.9	—	4.7
Retirements and sales	(7.5)	(49.3)	(99.9)	—	(156.7)
Rate variance	(2.0)	(12.0)	(18.8)	.7	(32.1)
Balance at July 28, Year 11	$56.3	$758.7	$1,779.3	$327.6	$2,921.9

*See "Acquisitions" in Notes to Consolidated Financial Statements.

187

Form 10-K

Schedule VI
CAMPBELL SOUP COMPANY AND CONSOLIDATED SUBSIDIARIES
Accumulated Depreciation and Amortization of Property, Plant and Equipment
(million dollars)

	Buildings	Machinery and Equipment	Total
Balance at July 31, Year 8	$285.4	$745.4	$1,030.8
Additions charged to income	31.5	144.4	175.9
Retirements and sales	(57.8)	(143.5)	(201.3)
Translations adjustments	(.8)	(2.2)	(3.0)
Balance at July 30, Year 9	258.3	744.1	1,002.4
Additions charged to income	34.2	149.9	184.1
Retirements and sales	(32.5)	(154.7)	(187.2)
Translations adjustments	5.2	12.7	17.9
Balance at July 29, Year 10	265.2	752.0	1,017.2
Additions charged to income	35.3	159.2	194.5
Retirements and sales	(17.4)	(52.1)	(69.5)
Translations adjustments	(2.8)	(7.9)	(10.7)
Balance at July 28, Year 11	$280.3	$851.2	$1,131.5

Interest Tables

TABLE 1: Future Value of 1, $f = (1 + i)^n$

Periods	2%	2½%	3%	4%	5%	6%	7%	8%	9%	10%
1	1.02000	1.02500	1.03000	1.04000	1.05000	1.06000	1.07000	1.08000	1.09000	1.10000
2	1.04040	1.05063	1.06090	1.08160	1.10250	1.12360	1.14490	1.16640	1.18810	1.21000
3	1.06121	1.07689	1.09273	1.12486	1.15763	1.19102	1.22504	1.25971	1.29503	1.33100
4	1.08243	1.10381	1.12551	1.16986	1.21551	1.26248	1.31080	1.36049	1.41158	1.46410
5	1.10408	1.13141	1.15927	1.21665	1.27628	1.33823	1.40255	1.46933	1.53862	1.61051
6	1.12616	1.15969	1.19405	1.26532	1.34010	1.41852	1.50073	1.58687	1.67710	1.77156
7	1.14869	1.18869	1.22987	1.31593	1.40710	1.50363	1.60578	1.71382	1.82804	1.94872
8	1.17166	1.21840	1.26677	1.36857	1.47746	1.59385	1.71819	1.85093	1.99256	2.14359
9	1.19509	1.24886	1.30477	1.42331	1.55133	1.68948	1.83846	1.99900	2.17189	2.35795
10	1.21899	1.28008	1.34392	1.48024	1.62889	1.79085	1.96715	2.15892	2.36736	2.59374
11	1.24337	1.31209	1.38423	1.53945	1.71034	1.89830	2.10485	2.33164	2.58043	2.85312
12	1.26824	1.34489	1.42576	1.60103	1.79586	2.01220	2.25219	2.51817	2.81266	3.13843
13	1.29361	1.37851	1.46853	1.66507	1.88565	2.13293	2.40985	2.71962	3.06580	3.45227
14	1.31948	1.41297	1.51259	1.73168	1.97993	2.26090	2.57853	2.93719	3.34173	3.79750
15	1.34587	1.44830	1.55797	1.80094	2.07893	2.39656	2.75903	3.17217	3.64248	4.17725
16	1.37279	1.48451	1.60471	1.87298	2.18287	2.54035	2.95216	3.42594	3.97031	4.59497
17	1.40024	1.52162	1.65285	1.94790	2.29202	2.69277	3.15882	3.70002	4.32763	5.05447
18	1.42825	1.55966	1.70243	2.02582	2.40662	2.85434	3.37993	3.99602	4.71712	5.55992
19	1.45681	1.59865	1.75351	2.10685	2.52695	3.02560	3.61653	4.31570	5.14166	6.11591
20	1.48595	1.63862	1.80611	2.19112	2.65330	3.20714	3.86968	4.66096	5.60441	6.72750
21	1.51567	1.67958	1.86029	2.27877	2.78596	3.39956	4.14056	5.03383	6.10881	7.40025
22	1.54598	1.72157	1.91610	2.36992	2.92526	3.60354	4.43040	5.43654	6.65860	8.14027
23	1.57690	1.76461	1.97359	2.46472	3.07152	3.81975	4.74053	5.87146	7.25787	8.95430
24	1.60844	1.80873	2.03279	2.56330	3.22510	4.04893	5.07237	6.34118	7.91108	9.84973
25	1.64061	1.85394	2.09378	2.66584	3.38635	4.29187	5.42743	6.84848	8.62308	10.83471

TABLE 1 *concluded*

Periods	11%	12%	14%	15%	16%	18%	20%	22%	24%	25%
1	1.11000	1.12000	1.14000	1.15000	1.16000	1.18000	1.20000	1.22000	1.24000	1.25000
2	1.23210	1.25440	1.29960	1.32250	1.34560	1.39240	1.44000	1.48840	1.53760	1.56250
3	1.36763	1.40493	1.48154	1.52088	1.56090	1.64303	1.72800	1.81585	1.90662	1.95313
4	1.51807	1.57352	1.68896	1.74901	1.81064	1.93878	2.07360	2.21533	2.36421	2.44141
5	1.68506	1.76234	1.92541	2.01136	2.10034	2.28776	2.48832	2.70271	2.93163	3.05176
6	1.87041	1.97382	2.19497	2.31306	2.43640	2.69955	2.98598	3.29730	3.63522	3.81470
7	2.07616	2.21068	2.50227	2.66002	2.82622	3.18547	3.58318	4.02271	4.50767	4.76837
8	2.30454	2.47596	2.85259	3.05902	3.27841	3.75886	4.29982	4.90771	5.58951	5.96046
9	2.55804	2.77308	3.25195	3.51788	3.80296	4.43545	5.15978	5.98740	6.93099	7.45058
10	2.83942	3.10585	3.70722	4.04556	4.41144	5.23384	6.19174	7.30463	8.59443	9.31323
11	3.15176	3.47855	4.22623	4.65239	5.11726	6.17593	7.43008	8.91165	10.65709	11.64153
12	3.49845	3.89598	4.81790	5.35025	5.93603	7.28759	8.91610	10.87221	13.21479	14.55192
13	3.88328	4.36349	5.49241	6.15279	6.88579	8.59936	10.69932	13.26410	16.38634	18.18989
14	4.31044	4.88711	6.26135	7.07571	7.98752	10.14724	12.83918	16.18220	20.31906	22.73737
15	4.78459	5.47357	7.13794	8.13706	9.26552	11.97375	15.40702	19.74229	25.19563	28.42171
16	5.31089	6.13039	8.13725	9.35762	10.74800	14.12902	18.48843	24.08559	31.24259	35.52714
17	5.89509	6.86604	9.27646	10.76126	12.46768	16.67225	22.18611	29.38442	38.74081	44.40892
18	6.54355	7.68997	10.57517	12.37545	14.46251	19.67325	26.62333	35.84899	48.03860	55.51115
19	7.26334	8.61276	12.05569	14.23177	16.77652	23.21444	31.94800	43.73577	59.56786	69.38894
20	8.06231	9.64629	13.74349	16.36654	19.46076	27.39303	38.33760	53.35764	73.86415	86.73617
21	8.94917	10.80385	15.66758	18.82152	22.57448	32.32378	46.00512	65.09632	91.59155	108.42022
22	9.93357	12.10031	17.86104	21.64475	26.18640	38.14206	55.20614	79.41751	113.57352	135.52527
23	11.02627	13.55235	20.36158	24.89146	30.37622	45.00763	66.24737	96.88936	140.83116	169.40659
24	12.23916	15.17863	23.21221	28.62518	35.23642	53.10901	79.49685	118.20502	174.63064	211.75824
25	13.58546	17.00006	26.46192	32.91895	40.87424	62.66863	95.39622	144.21013	216.54199	264.69780

TABLE 2: Present Value of 1, $p = \dfrac{1}{(1 \times i)^n}$

Periods	2%	2½%	3%	4%	5%	6%	7%	8%	9%	10%
1	.98039	.97561	.97087	.96154	.95238	.94340	.93458	.92593	.91743	.90909
2	.96177	.95181	.94260	.92456	.90703	.89000	.87344	.85734	.84168	.82645
3	.94232	.92860	.91514	.88900	.86384	.83962	.81630	.79383	.77218	.75131
4	.92385	.90595	.88849	.85480	.82270	.79209	.76290	.73503	.70843	.68301
5	.90573	.88385	.86261	.82193	.78353	.74726	.71299	.68058	.64993	.62092
6	.88797	.86230	.83748	.79031	.74622	.70496	.66634	.63017	.59627	.56447
7	.87056	.84127	.81309	.75992	.71068	.66506	.62275	.58349	.54703	.51316
8	.85349	.82075	.78941	.73069	.67684	.62741	.58201	.54027	.50187	.46651
9	.83676	.80073	.76642	.70259	.64461	.59190	.54393	.50025	.46043	.42410
10	.82035	.78120	.74409	.67556	.61391	.55839	.50835	.46319	.42241	.38554
11	.80426	.76214	.72242	.64958	.58468	.52679	.47509	.42888	.38753	.35049
12	.78849	.74356	.70138	.62460	.55684	.49697	.44401	.39711	.35553	.31863
13	.77303	.72542	.68095	.60057	.53032	.46884	.41496	.36770	.32618	.28966
14	.75788	.70773	.66112	.57748	.50507	.44230	.38782	.34046	.29925	.26333
15	.74301	.69047	.64186	.55526	.48102	.41727	.36245	.31524	.27454	.23939
16	.72845	.67362	.62317	.53391	.45811	.39365	.33873	.29189	.25187	.21763
17	.71416	.65720	.60502	.51337	.43630	.37136	.31657	.27027	.23107	.19784
18	.70016	.64117	.58739	.49363	.41552	.35034	.29586	.25025	.21199	.17986
19	.68643	.62553	.57029	.47464	.39573	.33051	.27651	.23171	.19449	.16351
20	.67297	.61027	.55368	.45639	.37689	.31180	.25842	.21455	.17843	.14864
21	.65978	.59539	.53755	.43883	.35894	.29416	.24151	.19866	.16370	.13513
22	.64684	.58086	.52189	.42196	.34185	.27751	.22571	.18394	.15018	.12285
23	.63416	.56670	.50669	.40573	.32557	.26180	.21095	.17032	.13778	.11168
24	.62172	.55288	.49193	.39012	.31007	.24698	.19715	.15770	.12640	.10153
25	.60953	.53939	.47761	.37512	.29530	.23300	.18425	.14602	.11597	.09230

TABLE 2   *concluded*

Periods	11%	12%	14%	15%	16%	18%	20%	22%	24%	25%
1	.90090	.89286	.87719	.86957	.86207	.84746	.83333	.81967	.80645	.80000
2	.81162	.79719	.76947	.75614	.74316	.71818	.69444	.67186	.65036	.64000
3	.73119	.71178	.67497	.65752	.64066	.60863	.57870	.55071	.52449	.51200
4	.65873	.63552	.59208	.57175	.55229	.51579	.48225	.45140	.42297	.40960
5	.59345	.56743	.51937	.49718	.47611	.43711	.40188	.37000	.34111	.32768
6	.53464	.50663	.45559	.43233	.41044	.37043	.33490	.30328	.27509	.26214
7	.48166	.45235	.39964	.37594	.35383	.31393	.27908	.24859	.22184	.20972
8	.43393	.40388	.35056	.32690	.30503	.26604	.23257	.20376	.17891	.16777
9	.39092	.36061	.30751	.28426	.26295	.22546	.19381	.16702	.14428	.13422
10	.35218	.32197	.26974	.24718	.22668	.19106	.16151	.13690	.11635	.10737
11	.31728	.28748	.23662	.21494	.19542	.16192	.13459	.11221	.09383	.08590
12	.28584	.25668	.20756	.18691	.16846	.13722	.11216	.09198	.07567	.06872
13	.25751	.22917	.18207	.16253	.14523	.11629	.09346	.07539	.06103	.05498
14	.23199	.20462	.15971	.14133	.12520	.09855	.07789	.06180	.04921	.04398
15	.20900	.18270	.14010	.12289	.10793	.08352	.06491	.05065	.03969	.03518
16	.18829	.16312	.12289	.10686	.09304	.07078	.05409	.04152	.03201	.02815
17	.16963	.14564	.10780	.09293	.08021	.05998	.04507	.03403	.02581	.02252
18	.15282	.13004	.09456	.08081	.06914	.05083	.03756	.02789	.02082	.01801
19	.13768	.11611	.08295	.07027	.05961	.04308	.03130	.02286	.01679	.01441
20	.12403	.10367	.07276	.06110	.05139	.03651	.02608	.01874	.01354	.01153
21	.11174	.09256	.06383	.05313	.04430	.03094	.02174	.01536	.01092	.00922
22	.10067	.08264	.05599	.04620	.03819	.02622	.01811	.01259	.00880	.00738
23	.09069	.07379	.04911	.04017	.03292	.02222	.01509	.01032	.00710	.00590
24	.08170	.06588	.04308	.03493	.02838	.01883	.01258	.00846	.00573	.00472
25	.07361	.05882	.03779	.03038	.02447	.01596	.01048	.00693	.00462	.00378

TABLE 3: Future Value of an Ordinary Annuity of n Payments of 1 Each, $F_0 = \dfrac{(1+i)^n - 1}{i}$

Periods (n)	2%	2½%	3%	4%	5%	6%	7%	8%	9%	10%
1	1.00000	1.00000	1.00000	1.00000	1.00000	1.00000	1.00000	1.00000	1.00000	1.00000
2	2.02000	2.02500	2.03000	2.04000	2.05000	2.06000	2.07000	2.08000	2.09000	2.10000
3	3.06040	3.07563	3.09090	3.12160	3.15250	3.18360	3.21490	3.24640	3.27810	3.31000
4	4.12161	4.15252	4.18363	4.24646	4.31013	4.37462	4.43994	4.50611	4.57313	4.64100
5	5.20404	5.25633	5.30914	5.41632	5.52563	5.63709	5.75074	5.86660	5.98471	6.10510
6	6.30812	6.38774	6.46841	6.63298	6.80191	6.97532	7.15329	7.33593	7.52333	7.71561
7	7.43428	7.54753	7.66246	7.89829	8.14201	8.39384	8.65402	8.92280	9.20043	9.48717
8	8.58297	8.73612	8.89234	9.21423	9.54911	9.89747	10.25980	10.63663	11.02847	11.43589
9	9.75463	9.95452	10.15911	10.58280	11.02656	11.49132	11.97799	12.48756	13.02104	13.57948
10	10.94972	11.20338	11.46388	12.00611	12.57789	13.18079	13.81645	14.48656	15.19293	15.93742
11	12.16872	12.48347	12.80780	13.48635	14.20679	14.97164	15.78360	16.64549	17.56029	18.53117
12	13.41209	13.79555	14.19203	15.02581	15.91713	16.86994	17.88845	18.97713	20.14072	21.38428
13	14.68033	15.14044	15.61779	16.62684	17.71298	18.88214	20.14064	21.49530	22.95338	24.52271
14	15.97394	16.51895	17.08632	18.29191	19.59863	21.01507	22.55049	24.21492	26.01919	27.97498
15	17.29342	17.93193	18.59891	20.02359	21.57856	23.27597	25.12902	27.15211	29.36092	31.77248
16	18.63929	19.38022	20.15688	21.82453	23.65749	25.67253	27.88805	30.32428	33.00340	35.94973
17	20.01207	20.86473	21.76159	23.69751	25.84037	28.21288	30.84022	33.75023	36.97370	40.54470
18	21.41231	22.38635	23.41444	25.64541	28.13238	30.90565	33.99903	37.45024	41.30134	45.59917
19	22.84056	23.94601	25.11687	27.67123	30.53900	33.75999	37.37896	41.44626	46.01846	51.15909
20	24.29737	25.54466	26.87037	29.77808	33.06595	36.78559	40.99549	45.76196	51.16012	57.27500
21	25.78332	27.18327	28.67649	31.96920	35.71925	39.99273	44.86518	50.42292	56.76453	64.00250
22	27.29898	28.86286	30.53678	34.24797	38.50521	43.39229	49.00574	55.45676	62.87334	71.40275
23	28.84496	30.58443	32.45288	36.61789	41.43048	46.99583	53.43614	60.89330	69.53194	79.54302
24	30.42186	32.34904	34.42647	39.08260	44.50200	50.81558	58.17667	66.76476	76.78981	88.49733
25	32.03030	34.15776	36.45926	41.64591	47.72710	54.86451	63.24904	73.10594	84.70090	98.34706

TABLE 3 *concluded*

Periods (n)	11%	12%	14%	15%	16%	18%	20%	22%	24%	25%
1	1.00000	1.00000	1.00000	1.00000	1.00000	1.00000	1.00000	1.00000	1.00000	1.00000
2	2.11000	2.12000	2.14000	2.15000	2.16000	2.18000	2.20000	2.22000	2.24000	2.25000
3	3.34210	3.37440	3.43960	3.47250	3.50560	3.57240	3.64000	3.70840	3.77760	3.81250
4	4.70973	4.77933	4.92114	4.99338	5.06650	5.21543	5.36800	5.52425	5.68422	5.76563
5	6.22780	6.35285	6.61010	6.74238	6.87714	7.15421	7.44160	7.73958	8.04844	8.20703
6	7.91286	8.11519	8.53552	8.75374	8.97748	9.44197	9.92992	10.44229	10.98006	11.25879
7	9.78327	10.08901	10.73049	11.06680	11.41387	12.14152	12.91590	13.73959	14.61528	15.07349
8	11.85943	12.29969	13.23276	13.72682	14.24009	15.32700	16.49908	17.76231	19.12294	19.84186
9	14.16397	14.77566	16.08535	16.78584	17.51851	19.08585	20.79890	22.67001	24.71245	25.80232
10	16.72201	17.54874	19.33730	20.30372	21.32147	23.52131	25.95868	28.65742	31.64344	33.25290
11	19.56143	20.65458	23.04452	24.34928	25.73290	28.75514	32.15042	35.96205	40.23787	42.56613
12	22.71319	24.13313	27.27075	29.00167	30.85017	34.93107	39.58050	44.87370	50.89495	54.20766
13	26.21164	28.02911	32.08865	34.35192	36.78620	42.21866	48.49660	55.74591	64.10974	68.75958
14	30.09492	32.39260	37.58107	40.50471	43.67199	50.81802	59.19592	69.01001	80.49608	86.94947
15	34.40536	37.27971	43.84241	47.58041	51.65951	60.96527	72.03511	85.19221	100.81514	109.68684
16	39.18995	42.75328	50.98035	55.71747	60.92503	72.93901	87.44213	104.93450	126.01077	138.10855
17	44.50084	48.88367	59.11760	65.07509	71.67303	87.06804	105.93056	129.02009	157.25336	173.63568
18	50.39594	55.74971	68.39407	75.83636	84.14072	103.74028	128.11667	158.40451	195.99416	218.04460
19	56.93949	63.43968	78.96923	88.21181	98.60323	123.41353	154.74000	194.25350	244.03276	273.55576
20	64.20283	72.05244	91.02493	102.44358	115.37975	146.62797	186.68800	237.98927	303.60062	342.94470
21	72.26514	81.69874	104.76842	118.81012	134.84051	174.02100	225.02560	291.34691	377.46477	429.68087
22	81.21431	92.50258	120.43600	137.63164	157.41499	206.34479	271.03072	356.44323	469.05632	538.10109
23	91.14788	104.60289	138.29704	159.27638	183.60138	244.48685	326.23686	435.86075	582.62984	673.62636
24	102.17415	118.15524	158.65862	184.16784	213.97761	289.49448	392.48424	532.75011	723.46100	843.03295
25	114.41331	133.33387	181.87083	212.79302	249.21402	342.60349	471.98108	650.95513	898.09164	1054.79118

TABLE 4: Present Value of an Ordinary Annuity of n Payments of 1 Each, $\bar{P}_0 = \dfrac{1 - \dfrac{1}{(1+i)^n}}{i}$

Periods (n)	2%	2½%	3%	4%	5%	6%	7%	8%	9%	10%
1	.98039	.97561	.97087	.96154	.95238	.94340	.93458	.92593	.91743	.90909
2	1.94156	1.92742	1.91347	1.88609	1.85941	1.83339	1.80802	1.78326	1.75911	1.73554
3	2.88388	2.85602	2.82861	2.77509	2.72325	2.67301	2.62432	2.57710	2.53129	2.48685
4	3.80773	3.76197	3.71710	3.62990	3.54595	3.46511	3.38721	3.31213	3.23972	3.16987
5	4.71346	4.64583	4.57971	4.45182	4.32948	4.21236	4.10020	3.99271	3.88965	3.79079
6	5.60143	5.50813	5.41719	5.24214	5.07569	4.91732	4.76654	4.62288	4.48592	4.35526
7	6.47199	6.34939	6.23028	6.00205	5.78637	5.58238	5.38929	5.20637	5.03295	4.86842
8	7.32548	7.17014	7.01969	6.73274	6.46321	6.20979	5.97130	5.74664	5.53482	5.33493
9	8.16224	7.97087	7.78611	7.43533	7.10782	6.80169	6.51523	6.24689	5.99525	5.75902
10	8.98259	8.75206	8.53020	8.11090	7.72173	7.36009	7.02358	6.71008	6.41766	6.14457
11	9.78685	9.51421	9.25262	8.76048	8.30641	7.88687	7.49867	7.13896	6.80519	6.49506
12	10.57534	10.25776	9.95400	9.38507	8.86325	8.38384	7.94269	7.53608	7.16073	6.81369
13	11.34837	10.98318	10.63496	9.98565	9.39357	8.85268	8.35765	7.90378	7.48690	7.10336
14	12.10625	11.60901	11.29607	10.56312	9.89864	9.29498	8.74547	8.24424	7.78615	7.36669
15	12.84926	12.38138	11.93794	11.11839	10.37966	9.71225	9.10791	8.55948	8.06069	7.60608
16	13.57771	13.05500	12.56110	11.65230	10.83777	10.10590	9.44665	8.85137	8.31256	7.82371
17	14.29187	13.71220	13.16612	12.16567	11.27407	10.47726	9.76322	9.12164	8.54363	8.01255
18	14.99203	14.35336	13.75351	12.65930	11.68959	10.82760	10.05909	9.37189	8.75563	8.20141
19	15.67846	14.97889	14.32380	13.13394	12.08532	11.15812	10.33560	9.60360	8.95011	8.36492
20	16.35143	15.58916	14.87747	13.59033	12.46221	11.46992	10.59401	9.81815	9.12855	8.51356
21	17.01121	16.18455	15.41502	14.02916	12.82115	11.76408	10.83553	10.01680	9.29224	8.64869
22	17.65805	16.76541	15.93692	14.45112	13.16300	12.04158	11.06124	10.20074	9.44243	8.77154
23	18.29220	17.33211	16.44361	14.85684	13.48857	12.30338	11.27219	10.37106	9.58021	8.88322
24	18.91393	17.88499	16.93554	15.24696	13.79864	12.55036	11.46933	10.52876	9.70661	8.98474
25	19.52346	18.42438	17.41315	15.62208	14.09394	12.78336	11.65358	10.67478	9.82258	9.07704

TABLE 4 *concluded*

Periods (n)	11%	12%	14%	15%	16%	18%	20%	22%	24%	25%
1	.90090	.89286	.87719	.86957	.86207	.84746	.83333	.81967	.80645	.80000
2	1.71252	1.69005	1.64666	1.62571	1.60523	1.56564	1.52778	1.49153	1.45682	1.44000
3	2.44371	2.40183	2.32163	2.28323	2.24589	2.17427	2.10648	2.04224	1.98130	1.95200
4	3.10245	3.03735	2.91371	2.85498	2.79818	2.69006	2.58873	2.49364	2.40428	2.36160
5	3.69590	3.60478	3.43308	3.35216	3.27429	3.12717	2.99061	2.86364	2.74538	2.68928
6	4.23054	4.11141	3.88867	3.78448	3.68474	3.49760	3.32551	3.16692	3.02047	2.95142
7	4.71220	4.56376	4.28830	4.16042	4.03857	3.81153	3.60459	3.41551	3.24232	3.16114
8	5.14612	4.96764	4.63886	4.48732	4.34359	4.07757	3.83716	3.61927	3.42122	3.32891
9	5.53705	5.32825	4.94647	4.77158	4.60654	4.30302	4.03097	3.78628	3.56550	3.46313
10	5.88923	5.65022	5.21612	5.01877	4.83323	4.49409	4.19247	3.92318	3.68186	3.57050
11	6.20652	5.93770	5.45273	5.23371	5.02864	4.65601	4.32706	4.03540	3.77569	3.65640
12	6.49236	6.19437	5.66029	5.42062	5.19711	4.79322	4.43922	4.12737	3.85136	3.72512
13	6.74987	6.42355	5.84236	5.58315	5.34233	4.90951	4.53268	4.20277	3.91239	3.78010
14	6.98187	6.62817	6.00207	5.72448	5.46753	5.00806	4.61057	4.26456	3.96160	3.82408
15	7.19087	6.81086	6.14217	5.84737	5.57546	5.09158	4.67547	4.31522	4.00129	3.85926
16	7.37916	6.97399	6.26506	5.95423	5.66850	5.16235	4.72956	4.35673	4.03330	3.88741
17	7.54879	7.11963	6.37286	6.04716	5.74870	5.22233	4.77463	4.39077	4.05911	3.90993
18	7.70162	7.24967	6.46742	6.12797	5.81785	5.27316	4.81219	4.41866	4.07993	3.92794
19	7.83929	7.36578	6.55037	6.19823	5.87746	5.31624	4.84350	4.44152	4.09672	3.94235
20	7.96333	7.46944	6.62313	6.25933	5.92884	5.35275	4.86958	4.46027	4.11026	3.95388
21	8.07507	7.56200	6.68696	6.31246	5.97314	5.38368	4.89132	4.47563	4.12117	3.96311
22	8.17574	7.64465	6.74294	6.35866	6.01133	5.40990	4.90943	4.48822	4.12998	3.97049
23	8.26643	7.71843	6.79206	6.39884	6.04425	5.43212	4.92453	4.49854	4.13708	3.97639
24	8.34814	7.78432	6.83514	6.43377	6.07263	5.45095	4.93710	4.50700	4.14281	3.98111
25	8.42174	7.84314	6.87293	6.46415	6.09709	5.46691	4.94759	4.51393	4.14742	3.98489

INDEX

ABI/Inform, 107
Abnormal earnings, 65
Accounting, 70
Accounting-based equity valuation model, 65, 67
Accounting equation, 18
Accounting information, 69–73
  limitations, 74–79
  qualitative characteristics, 94–100
  relevance, 71–73
  stock price and, 24, 352–353
Accounting principles, 90–94, 325–326
Accounting Principles Board (APB), 91
Accounting reconstruction, 80–82
Accounting Research Bulletins (ARBs), 91
Accounting risk, 54, 55, 79, 324
Accounting standards, 85–88, 90–94
Accounts payable, days' purchases in, 141–142
Accounts payable turnover, 142n
Accounts receivable, 44, 115, 121, 130–135, 254, 285, 333
Accounts receivable collection period, 42, 43, 131–133
Accounts receivable turnover, 130–131
Accrual basis of accounting, 19–20, 97, 324
Accumulated depreciation adjustment, 240–241
Acid-test ratio, 42, 43, 144
Adaptec, Inc., 6–30, A2–A48
Adjusted profit margin, 258–259
Adverse opinion, 27
Advertising, 327–339
Aging schedule, 133–134
Allocation, 97
Almanac of Business and Industrial Financial Ratios, 105
Altman, E., 229n, 230n
Altman's Z-score, 229–230
American Accounting Association (AAA), 90, 93
American Institute of Certified Public Accountants (AICPA), 91, 94
Amortization:
  of discount, in calculating fixed charges, 208

of premium, in calculating fixed charges, 208
  of special costs, 296
Analysis reporting, CC6–CC8
Analysis steps, CC3–CC5
Analysts Handbook, 105
Analytical use of standards/assumptions, 85–88
Annual registration statements, 29
Annual Statement Studies, 105
Annuities, I6–I9
Applying financial statement analysis:
  analysis reporting, CC6–CC8
  analysis steps, CC3–CC5
  building blocks, 31, CC5–CC6, CC7
  illustration (*see* Comprehensive case)
  specialization issues, CC8
Asset composition analysis, 203–204
Asset coverage, 204–205
Asset protection, 225–226
Asset turnover, 247–256
Asset utilization, 31, 42, 44, CC42–CC43
Assets, 18, 98, 193–195
  (*See also specific types of assets*)
Auditing risk, 324
Auditor opinions, 27
Auditors, 9, 27, 67–68
Auditor's report, 27, 28
Average effective interest rate, 297

Bad debts expense, 294
Balance sheet, 18–19, 24, 38–39, 331–333
Ball, B., 268n
Bankruptcy prediction models, 229–230
Bauman, M. P., 355n
Begley, M., 229n
Benefits versus costs, 95–97
Beta, 53, 54–55
Beta coefficient theory, 53, 54–55
Beta theorists, 54–55
Board of directors, 9, 68
Bond credit ratings, 134, 223–228
Bonds:
  convertible, 60, 192

Bonds (*cont.*)
  corporate, 225–226
  general obligation, 227
  housing, 227
  junk, 221
  municipal, 227
  rating of, 134, 223–228
  revenue, 227
  special tax, 227
  valuation, 63–64
Book values, adjustments to, 189–195
Break-even analysis, 305–320
  analytical uses/application, 313–320
  assumptions, 312–313
  contribution margin analysis, 309–310
  equation-based, 307–309
  fixed expense level, 318–319
  graphic-based, 309
  limitations, 312–313
  operating leverage and, 316–317
Buffett, Warren, 47
Building blocks of analysis, 31, CC5–CC6, CC7
Business activities, 9–17
  financial statements and, 16–17
  financing, 11–14
  investing, 14–15
  operating, 15–16
  planning, 9–11, 237–238
  reconstructing, 80–82
Business plan, 9–11
Business risk, 54, 326

Campbell Soup, 82, 164, 167–174, 260–263,
  305, 306, 337–342
  comprehensive case, CC8–CC52
  financial statements, A32–A52
Capital asset pricing model (CAPM), 55–56
Capital market efficiency, 45–48
Capital structure:
  accounting implications, 188–195
  composition of, and solvency, 195–203,
    CC35–CC38
  defined, 177, 178
  importance of, 179–186
  and long-term solvency ratios, 31, 42, 43,
    198–203
  (*See also* Solvency analysis)
  risk and return, 221–222
Capitalized interest, 208–209

Case study (*see* Comprehensive case)
Cash, 44, 115, 121, 254
Cash accounting, 324
Cash conversions, 153
Cash equivalents, 115, 121, 254
Cash flow adequacy ratio, 172–173
Cash flow patterns, 153–154
Cash flow ratio, 145
Cash flow to fixed charges ratio, 216–218
Cash ratio, 129
Cash reinvestment ratio, 173–174
Cash to current liabilities ratio, 129–130
Certainty of evidence, 64
Clean surplus accounting, 64–65
Collection period, 42, 43, 131–133
Committee on Accounting Procedure (CAP), 91
Common leverage, 258n
Common monetary unit, 72
Common shareholders' equity growth rate,
  263–264
Common-size analysis, 37–39, 124, 197,
  277, 291
Common stock valuation, 63–65, 67
Compact Disclosure, 107
Comparability, 83–85, 95
Comparative financial statement analysis,
  32–37, 124
Composition analysis, 197
Composition of current assets, 142
Comprehensive case (Campbell Soup):
  asset utilization, CC42–CC43
  capital structure/solvency, CC35–CC38
  cash analysis/forecasting, 164, 167–174,
    CC23–CC35
  evaluation/inferences, CC46–CC52
  operating performance, 337–342, CC43–CC46
  preliminary analysis, CC8–CC18
  return on invested capital, 260–263,
    CC38–CC42
  short-term liquidity, CC19–CC23
Comprehensive income, 98
Compustat, 107
Computerized databases, 107
Conceptual framework, 94–100, 100–101
Conservatism, 79, 326, 331–332
Consistency, 95
Contingent liabilities, 192
Contract, 13
Contrast analysis, 82–83
Contribution margin, 309–310, 319–320

Contribution margin analysis, 309–310
Contribution margin ratio, 310
Conversion period, 139
Convertible bonds, 60, 192
Corporate bonds, 225–226
*Corporate Information Research Reports
(CIRR)*, 107
Cost of capital, 181–182
Cost of sales/services, 287–291
Counterbalancing effects of transactions, 70, 71
Credit grantors, 59–61
Credit rating, 134, 223–228
Creditor financing, 12–13
Creditors, 8, 11, 50, 59–61
Current assets, 18, 115–116
Current assets composition, 142
Current liabilities, 18, 117–118, 140–142, 255
Current ratio:
  as analytical tool, 122–128
  defined, 42, 43, 119
  denominator, 122
  limitations, 120–121
  numerator, 121–122
  relevance, 119–120
  rule of thumb, 126
Customers, 9, 69

Days' purchases in accounts payable ratio,
  141–142
Days' sales in accounts receivable, 132–133
Days' sales in inventory, 137
Days to sell inventory ratio, 43, 136–137
DCF method, 351
Debt capital, 181–188
Debt covenants, 50
Debt-to-capital ratio, 42
Debt to equity ratio, 42, 43, 200, 203, 231–232
Debt valuation, 63–64
Deferral, 97
Deferred charges, 333
Deferred income, 190
Deferred income taxes, 189–190
Depreciation expense, 295
Directors, 9, 68
Disaggregation, 361
Disclaimer of opinion, 27
Discount, amortization of, 208
Discount factor, 65
Discounted cash flow (DCF) method, 351

Discretionary expenditures, 326–331
Distress models, 229–230
Distributions to owners, 98
Diversified companies, 276–282
Dividend payout ratio, 12, 44, 88
Dividend yield, 44, 88
Dividends on preferred stock, 207, 209–210,
  218–219
Double-entry accounting, 70
Du Pont method, 240–241
Dun & Bradstreet, Inc., 104

Earning power, 178–179, 205–214, 358–360
Earnings-based analysis, 322–367
  earning power, 358–360
  earnings-based valuation, 350–358
  earnings forecasting, 360–363
  earnings persistence, 334–351
  earnings quality, 324–334
  interim reports, 364–367
  monitoring/revising earnings estimates,
    364–367
Earnings-based valuation, 350–358
Earnings coverage analysis, 205–214, 218–221
Earnings coverage of preferred dividends,
  218–219
Earnings distribution, 11–12
Earnings forecasting, 237, 323, 360–363
Earnings leverage, 258n
Earnings management, 342–344
Earnings persistence, 220, 323, 334–351, 354
  earnings management, 342–344
  earnings variability, 341
  extraordinary items, 344–350
  management incentives, 343–344
  recasting/adjusting earnings, 335–341
  trend analysis, 341–342
Earnings quality, 323, 324–334
  accounting applications, 326
  accounting principles, 325–326
  advertising, 329
  balance sheet analysis, 331–333
  business risk, 54, 326
  changing price levels, 334
  complexities of operations, 334
  earnings sources, 334
  external factors, 334
  foreign earnings, 334
  maintenance and repairs, 327

Earnings quality (*cont.*)
  regulation, 334
  research and development costs, 329–331
Earnings reinvestment, 12
Earnings to fixed charges, 205–214
Earnings variability, 220, 341
Earnings yield, 44, 88
Economic risk, 54
Economists, 69
Effective tax rate, 298–300
Efficient market hypothesis (EMH), 45–48
Employees, 9, 69
Equation-based break-even analysis, 307–309
Equity, 98
Equity capital, 181, 241
Equity capital to total debt ratio, 199
Equity financing, 12, 13
Equity growth, 12
Equity growth rate, 263–264
Equity investors, 8, 11, 62–65
Estimates, 76–77
Event risk, 203
Evidence, 82–83
Expenses, 99, 299–305
Explanatory notes, 27–28
External auditor, 27
External users, 8
Extraordinary items, 206, 344–350
Extrapolation, 361

Feasibility tests, 159–162
Federal government:
  as regulator, 9, 69 (*See also* Securities and
    Exchange Commission)
  as source of information, 106
Feedback value, 95
Financial Accounting Foundation, 92
Financial Accounting Standards Board (FASB),
  91–92, 93
Financial flexibility, 145–146
Financial intermediaries, 9, 69
Financial leverage, 181–188, 264–266
Financial leverage index, 186
Financial leverage ratio, 187–188
Financial resources, 226
Financial risk, 54, 317
Financial statements, 6, 16–25
  accompanying information, 26–30
  balance sheet, 18–19

  elements of, 98–99
  examples, A1–A52
  income statement, 19–20, 21, 23–24
  links between statements, 22–24, 25
  statement of cash flows, 21–22, 23
  statement of shareholders' equity, 20–21,
    22–23
Financing activities, 11–14
Financing expenses, 297
Financing leases, 212
Fixed assets, 44, 255
Fixed assets to equity capital ratio, 205
Fixed charges:
  cash flow to, 216–218
  earnings to, 205–214
Fixed expenses, 312, 318–319
Forecast horizon, 155
Forecasting and pro forma analysis, 151–175
  analysis of prior cash flows, 163–166
  cash flow adequacy ratio, 172–173
  cash flow patterns, 153–154
  cash reinvestment ratio, 173–174
  earnings forecasting, 237, 323, 360–363
  long-term cash forecasting, 152–154, 162–174
  pro forma financial statements, 155–162
  short-term cash forecasting, 154–162
  statement of cash flows, 167–171
  what-if forecasting of cash flows, 171–172
Foreign earnings, 334
Form 8-K report, 29, 365–366
Form 10-K report, 28–29
Form 10-Q report, 29, 365–366
Formation of accounting principles, 90–94
Fundamental betas, 55
Funds flow, 31
Future-directed marketing expenses, 294–295
Future earnings power, 226
Future liquidity, 152
  (*See also* Forecasting and pro forma analysis)
Future value, I2–I3
Future value of annuity, I6–I7

Gains, 99
General and administrative expenses, 296
General obligation bonds, 227
Generally accepted accounting principles
  (GAAP), 90–94
Graphic-based break-even analysis, 309
Gross margin, 288–291

Gross profit, 288–291
Gross profit ratio, 44

Hickman, H. B., 219n
Hierarchy of accounting qualities, 95, 96
Historical cost, 77
Horizontal analysis, 32
Housing authority bonds, 227

Income, defined, 273–275
Income statement, 19–20, 21, 23–24, 38–39
Income tax disclosures, 300–305
Income tax expenses, 207, 298–305
Index-number trend series analysis, 33–37,
    291–292
Industry associations, 106–107
Industry comparability analysis, 83–85
Industry Surveys, 105
Information, sources of, 104–107
Information mosaic, 46
Information set, 73, 75
Intangible asset adjustment, 195, 240
Interest burden, 262
Interest incurred, 208
Interest tables, I1–I9
Interim reports, 29, 76–77, 364–367
Intermediaries, 9, 69
Internal users, 8
Inventories, 44, 115–116, 122, 135–140, 194,
    254–255, 286, 333
Inventory turnover ratio, 135–136
Investing activities, 14–15
Investment theory, 52–56
Investments by owners, 98

Junk bonds, 221

Labor unions, 69
Lawyers, 69
Leases:
    financing, 212
    interest implicit in, 209
    operating, 190, 212
Leverage:
    common, 258n
    earnings, 258n

financial, 181–188, 264–266
operating, 316–317
Leveraged buyout, 221
Liabilities, 18, 98, 140–142, 189–193
    (*See also specific types of liabilities*)
LIFO method of inventory valuation, 139, 194
LIFO reserve, 194
Liquidity analysis, 111–150
    accounts receivable measures, 130–135
    acid-test (quick) ratio, 144
    cash-based measures, 129–130
    cash flow measures, 145
    current assets composition, 142
    current liabilities, 140–142
    current ratio measure, 118–122
    financial flexibility, 145–146
    inventory turnover measures, 135–140
    liabilities liquidity, 140–142
    liquidity, defined, 112, 113
    liquidity index, 143–144
    MD&A, 146
    short-term, 42, 43
    what-if analysis, 146–147
    working capital measure, 118
Liquidity index, 143–144
Loan covenants/pledges, 179
Long-term capitalization, 241
Long-term cash forecasting, 152–154, 162–174
Long-term debt to equity capital ratio, 42, 43,
    200, 203, 231–232
Losses, 99
Lotus OneSource, 107

Maintenance and repairs, 295–296, 327
Management, 66–67, 237, 343–344
Management report, 26–27
Management's discussion and analysis
    (MD&A):
    liquidity, 146
    overview, 26
    persistence of revenues, 283–284
Market efficiency, 45–48
Market measures, 44, 88
Market value of equity, 201–202
Market value of invested capital, 241–242
Marketable securities, 115, 121, 194–195
Materiality, 95–97
MD&A (*see* Management's discussion and
    analysis)

Measurement and reporting function, 70
Merger and acquisition analysts, 8–9, 68
Ming, J., 229n
Minority interest, 192, 207
Modigliani-Miller hypothesis, 182
Monte Carlo trials, 103
Moody's Investor Service, 105
Municipal bonds, 227

Nelson's Directory of Investment Research, 105
Net income, 19
Net income to sales, 44
Net tangible assets to long-term debt ratio, 205
Net trade cycle, 127–128
Neutrality, 95
New York Stock Exchange, 93–94
Nondiversification, 53–54
Nontrade creditors, 59

Objectives of financial statement analysis,
    59–69
Objectives of financial statements, 94, 100–101
Off-balance-sheet financing, 191, 212
Operating activities, 15–16
Operating cycle, 139
Operating leases, 190, 212
Operating leverage, 316–317
Operating performance ratios, 31, 42, 43, 44,
    337–342, CC43–CC46
Operating potential, 317
Operating profit to sales, 44
Operating ratio analysis, 292
Operating risk, 317
Organized securities exchanges, 93

Payment in kind (PIK) securities, 221
PB ratio, 44, 353, 355
PE ratio, 44, 88, 353–355
Penman, S. H., 355n
Pension Benefit Guaranty Corporation, 191
Pensions, 191
Persistence of revenues, 283–284
Pervasive constraints, 95–97
Pie chart, 277
Planning activities, 9–11, 237–238
Portfolio theory, 52–53

Postretirement benefits, 191
Pre-tax income, 304
Prediction models of financial distress, 229–230
Predictive value, 95
Preferred stock, 60, 193
    dividends on, 207, 209–210, 218–219
Premium, amortization of, 208
Prepaid expenses, 116, 122
Present value, I4–I5
Present value of annuity, I8–I9
Present value theory, 63
Pretax profit to sales, 44
Price-to-book (PB) ratio, 44, 353, 355
Price-to-earnings (PE) ratio, 44, 88, 353–355
Principal, repayment of, 210–211
Principle of double-entry, 70
Pro forma analysis, 155–162, 214–215
Pro forma financial statements, 155–162
Profit margin, 248–253, 258–259
Profitability analysis, 237, 270–321
    amortization of special costs, 296
    break-even analysis, 305–320
    cost of sales, 287–291
    depreciation expense, 295
    expenses, 292–305
    financing/other expenses, 296–298
    general/administrative expenses, 296
    gross profit, 288–291
    importance, 271
    income, defined, 273–275
    income tax expenses, 298–305
    key revenue relations, 285–286
    maintenance/repairs expenses, 295–296
    persistence of revenues, 283–284
    revenue recognition/measurement, 286
    revenue sources, 276–282
    selling expenses, 292–294
    two-phase analysis of income, 275
    variation analysis, 305
Projection, 361
Proxy, 29–30
Proxy statement, 29–30

Qualified opinion, 27
Quality of current liabilities, 140–141
Quality of earnings, 323, 324–334
Quality of inventory, 138
Quality of sales forecast, 155

Quarterly registration statements, 29
Quick ratio, 42, 43, 144

Random walk hypothesis, 45
Rating of debt obligations:
  bond credit ratings, 134, 223–228
  industrial bond issues, 225–226
  municipal bonds, 227
Ratio analysis, 40–45
Rational investors, 52–53
Realization, 97
Recasting, 336–337
Receivables collection period, 42, 43, 131–133
Recognition, 99, 193–194, 286
Reconstruction of business transactions, 80–82
Recording function, 70
Regulators, 9, 69
Relevance, 95
Reliability, 95
Repairs and maintenance expenses, 295–296, 327
Representational faithfulness, 95
Research and development expenses, 329–331
Residual interests, 62
Restatement of financial statements, 84–85
Retained Earnings balance, 20–21, 24
Return, 11
Return on assets (ROA), 247–256
Return on common shareholders' equity
  (ROCE), 42, 43, 247, 256–264, 352
Return on invested capital, 234–269
  adjustments, 239–241, 244
  Campbell Soup case, 260–263, CC38–CC42
  computations, 244–247
  defined, 235, 236
  formula, 238
  importance, 236–238
  income, defined, 243–244
  invested capital, defined, 238–243
  return on assets (ROA), 247–256
  return on common shareholders' equity
    (ROCE), 42, 43, 247, 256–264, 352
Return on investment (ROI), 31, 42, 43, 236
  (*See also* Return on invested capital)
Return on long-term debt plus equity capital,
  245–247
Return on shareholders investment (ROSI),
  267–268

Return on total assets, 42, 43, 239, 244–245
Revenue bonds, 227
Revenues, 98–99
  accounts receivable and, 285
  inventories and, 286
  persistence, 283–284
  selling expenses and, 292–294
  sources, 276–282
Risk, 53–55
  accounting, 54, 55, 79, 324
  business, 54, 326
  economic, 54
  event, 203
  financial, 54, 317
  operating, 317
  systematic, 53
  total, 317
  unsystematic, 53–55
ROA (return on assets), 247–256
Robert Morris Associates, 105
ROCE (return on common shareholders'
  equity), 42, 43, 247, 256–264, 352
ROSI, 267–268

Safety margin, 315
Sales forecast, 155
Sales to accounts receivable, 44, 254
Sales to cash, 44, 254
Sales to current liabilities, 255
Sales to fixed assets, 44, 255
Sales to inventories, 44, 254–255
Sales to other assets, 255
Sales to total assets, 44
Sales to working capital, 44
Sales trend analysis, 128
Screening devices, 202–203
Seasonality, 365
SEC (*see* Securities and Exchange Commission)
Securities Act of 1933, 92
Securities and Exchange Commission (SEC),
  90, 92–93, 93
  interim reporting requirements, 29, 365–367
  MD&A, 26, 146, 283–284
  supplemental information and, 28–29
  web site, 29
Securities Exchange Act of 1934, 92
Security provisions, 61
Segment reports, 278–282

Segmented earnings contribution matrix, 278
Selling expenses, 292–294
Semistrong form EMH, 45
Semivariable expenses, 312
Sensitivity analysis, 103
Shareholder multiple measure, 268
Shareholders' equity, 18
Short term, defined, 113
Short-term cash forecasting, 154–162
Short-term debt to total debt, 201
Short-term liquidity, 31, 111–150, CC19–CC23
  (*See also* Liquidity analysis)
Short-term liquidity ratios, 42, 43
Sinking fund provision, 196
Social responsibility reports, 29, 30
Solvency analysis, 176–222
  adjustments to book values of assets, 193–195
  adjustments to book values of liabilities,
    189–193
  asset-based measures, 203–205
  capital structure measures, 31, 42, 43,
    198–203
  capital structure risk and return, 221–222
  common-size statements, 197
  debt and equity capital, 181–186
  earnings coverage measures, 205–214,
    218–221
  financial leverage, 181–188
  key elements, 178–179
  long-term projections, 196
  prediction models of financial distress,
    229–230
  rating debt obligations, 223–228
  solvency, defined, 177
*Source Book: Statistics of Income: Corporation
  Income Tax Returns*, 106
Special cash flow ratios, 172–174
Special-purpose tools, 45
Special tax bonds, 227
Specialization issues, CC8
Standard & Poor's Corporation, 105
Standards, accounting, 85–88, 90–94
Statement of cash flows, 21–22, 23, 167–171
Statement of Financial Accounting Standards
  (SFAS), 91–92
  No. 1, 94–95
  No. 2, 95
  No. 3, 97
  No. 5, 99–100

Statement of retained earnings, 22–23
Statement of shareholders' equity, 20–21, 22–23
Statement of variations in income and income
  components, 305, 306
Statements of Financial Accounting Concepts
  (SFACs), 94–100
*Statistics of Income: Corporation Income Tax
  Returns*, 106
Stock valuation, 63–65, 67
Strong form EMH, 45
Subsidiaries, unconsolidated, 191–192
Supplemental schedules, 28–29
Suppliers, 9, 69
Sustainable equity growth rate, 264
Systematic risk, 53

T-account, 81
Tax anticipation notes, 227
Tax deductibility of interest, 182, 185
Tax ratio, 298–300
Technology-based tools, 102–104
Timeliness, 95
Times interest earned ratio, 42, 43, 214
Total debt ratio, 198
Total debt to equity capital ratio, 43, 198–199
Total debt to total capital ratio, 43, 198
Total equity capital to total debt ratio, 199
Total liabilities to total net tangible assets, 205
Total risk, 317
Trade creditors, 59
Trading on the equity, 182–185
Trend analysis, 32, 124, 128, 341–342
Trend percent analysis, 283, 329
Trend statements, 341–342

Unconsolidated subsidiaries, 191–192
Unproductive asset adjustment, 240
Unqualified opinion, 27
Unsystematic risk, 53–55
Users of financial statements, 8–9, 59–69

Value Line Investment Survey, 106
Variable expense percent, 317
Variable expenses, 312
Variation analysis, 305
Verifiability, 95

Vertical analysis, 37–39
Volatility in sales, 317

Watts, S., 229n
Weak form EMH, 45
What-if analysis, 146–147
What-if forecasting of cash flows, 171–172
Window dressing, 124–125
Working capital, 18, 44, 114–118

Year-to-year change analysis, 32–33
Yield:
  dividend, 44, 88
  earnings, 44, 88

Z-score, 229–230